The WILEY *advantage*

Dear Valued Customer,

We realize you're a busy pro........ ...u. deadlines to hit. Whether your goal is to learn a new technology or solve a critical problem, we want to be there to lend you a hand. Our primary objective is to provide you with the insight and knowledge you need to stay atop the highly competitive and ever-changing technology industry.

Wiley Publishing, Inc., offers books on a wide variety of technical categories, including security, data warehousing, software development tools, and networking — everything you need to reach your peak. Regardless of your level of expertise, the Wiley family of books has you covered.

- For Dummies – The *fun* and *easy* way to learn
- The Weekend Crash Course –The *fastest* way to learn a new tool or technology
- Visual – For those who prefer to learn a new topic *visually*
- The Bible – The *100% comprehensive* tutorial and reference
- The Wiley Professional list – *Practical* and *reliable* resources for IT professionals

The book you hold now, *Perl Database Programming*, is the quintessential guide to building data-driven Web applications with Perl. Whether you have never created a data-driven application or are a Perl expert, *Perl Database Programming* is everything you need to build dynamic Web applications quickly and easily. Beginning with database fundamentals, *Dr. Dobb's Journal Online* Perl expert Brent Michalski guides you through generating reports with data, working with binary data, session management, database transactions, tied hashes, and even Web services. Not just another Perl book, *Perl Database Programming* is everything you need to take your Perl programming to the next level.

Our commitment to you does not end at the last page of this book. We'd want to open a dialog with you to see what other solutions we can provide. Please be sure to visit us at www.wiley.com/compbooks to review our complete title list and explore the other resources we offer. If you have a comment, suggestion, or any other inquiry, please locate the "contact us" link at www.wiley.com.

Sincerely,

Richard K. Swadley
Vice President & Executive Group Publisher
Wiley Technology Publishing

15 HOUR WEEKEND CRASH COURSE

V Visual

Bible

DUMMIES

WILEY
Independent Thinkers

more information on related titles

Perl Database
Programming

Perl Database Programming

Brent Michalski

Wiley Publishing, Inc.

Perl Database Programming

Published by
Wiley Publishing, Inc.
10475 Crosspoint Boulevard
Indianapolis, IN 46256
www.wiley.com

ISBN: 0-7645-4956-1

Manufactured in the United States of America

10 9 8 7 6 5 4 3 2 1

1O/RY/RQ/QS/IN

For general information on our other products and services or to obtain technical support, please contact our Customer Care Department within the U.S. at (800) 762-2974, outside the U.S. at (317) 572-3993 or fax (317) 572-4002.

Wiley also publishes its books in a variety of electronic formats. Some content that appears in print may not be available in electronic books.

Library of Congress Control Number: 2002107900

About the Author

Brent Michalski discovered Perl around 1994 while he was in the Air Force. There was no turning back from there, he became an avid "Perl freak" and has been using it ever since. Brent mainly develops CGI applications because he really enjoys the Web. Brent has written articles for *Web Review*, *Dr. Dobb's Journal* online, O'Reilly, and others. Brent also enjoys teaching others about Perl. In his spare time, he loves playing ice hockey, where he plays the one-and-only "real" position, goalie.

Credits

Executive Editor
Chris Webb

Acquisitions Editor
Grace Buechlein

Project Editor
Neil Romanosky

Technical Editor
Sean Burke

Copy Editor
C. M. Jones

Editorial Manager
Mary Beth Wakefield

**Vice President & Executive
Group Publisher**
Richard Swadley

**Vice President and
Executive Publisher**
Bob Ipsen

Executive Editorial Director
Mary Bednarek

Project Coordinator
Nancee Reeves

Graphics and Production Specialists
Beth Brooks, Melanie DesJardins,
Joyce Haughey, Barry Offringa,
Kathie Schutte

Quality Control Technicians
Laura Albert, John Greenough,
Andy Hollandbeck

Proofreading and Indexing
TECHBOOKS Production Services

For my wife and kids — my world.

Preface

Computers today store vast amounts of information. But simply having the information doesn't do you any good — you need to be able to search it, access it, and update it, and quickly. That's what databases are for, and that's what this book is about — using Perl to search, access, and update information in databases, whether it's a record of users accessing your system, an index of the thirty thousand products your company sells, or maybe just a catalog of your family snapshots.

Originating well before the World Wide Web was a reality, Perl has been around for over 12 years. Perl was not created for Web/CGI, even though it is very good at that particular task. Perl was created to process and manipulate text effectively.

Perl is an excellent choice for working with databases. Perl is extremely good at working with text, and most databases are simply a collection of text.

Another reason for using Perl is that a vast collection of modules is already written that assists with database access. To see what modules are available, go to `http://search.cpan.org`. CPAN is the Comprehensive Perl Archive Network. Over 1,000 modules are available on CPAN.

Perl runs on a multitude of platforms. In fact, Perl runs on more platforms than Java, which is supposed to be platform independent.

Who Should Read This Book

This book is for both the novice and the expert. A novice Perl programmer can learn a lot from this book. Each bit of code in this book is carefully explained so that the reader can see exactly how every part of the programs work. However, this book is not a comprehensive guide to Perl programming. At least a basic understanding of Perl is required before you can fully utilize this book. For the experts, this book is a valuable resource for picking up Perl database programming, since there are so many examples to learn from.

My goal for this book is to create a Perl guide that can help any Perl programmer who needs to learn how to use Perl with databases. In some cases, you may have an important database project on which your job depends. This book should enable you to get a very good start and give you a nice foundation to build your knowledge upon.

How This Book Is Organized

The following is a brief description of the topics covered in this book.

Part I: Perl and Database Fundamentals

In this section you will learn the basics about using Perl to work with databases. When you finish this section, you should have a good, basic understanding of what modules to use and how to use Perl to manipulate databases.

Part II: Advanced Database Programming

This part takes you one step further. We'll introduce database programming for the Web, more advanced data access methods, and more tricks and techniques to make your programs more powerful.

Part III: Perl and Web Services

This part introduces you to some basic Web Services techniques. You will create a SOAP client and a SOAP server that can be accessed with any SOAP client, using any programming language.

Part IV: Perl and General Web Programming

This part is designed to solidify your knowledge. In it, we cover more advanced, real-world database applications so that you can hone your newfound skills.

Databases Used in This Book

We have examples for several databases. We cover MySQL, PostgreSQL, Oracle, and CSV databases. The database we concentrate on is MySQL. Why? Several reasons exist. MySQL is very easy to install and to make operational. It is widely used, fast, and works on many platforms.

Database Concepts Simplified

The following are some of the key terms and concepts used in this book.

Database

A database is simply a collection of data. When we create a database in MySQL, we are creating a collection of data related to a similar topic. We cannot add data directly to a database; instead, we have to work with tables.

Tables

Tables are where data is stored. A database may have many tables, and tables may be dependent on one another.

Record

A record is an item in a table. If you have a database named books and a table named library, a record is the row of data that makes up the entry for a single book.

Field

A field is an item in a record. If you have a table named library, a record would be an individual item in that record, such as "book title".

Primary key

A primary key is a field that is unique to a table, and it cannot be NULL. Primary keys are used to ensure that records are unique in a database. Also, primary keys are used in the normalization of databases.

Normalization

Database normalization is a large topic when it comes to database design. The goal behind database normalization is to create links between database tables to minimize, or eliminate, the need for redundant data.

Relational database

A relational database arranges data into tables. These tables can then have relations among them to minimize redundant data being stored in the database. Consider that you have a database for ice hockey, with teams, players, stats, etc. A player can only be on one team at a time, so you could have a separate table for the team, that just contained the team's data, and another table for the players. Inside of that player data, you could create a "relation" to the team that they are on. This relation eliminates the need to have to type the team data over and over again for each player on the team. Instead, each player just has a relation to the team.

Database interfaces

Several database interfaces are available for Perl. We use the DBI module throughout this book. This is also the interface you are most likely to come across. The DBI module has many database drivers (DBDs) for the multitude of databases that exist. We use the DBD::mysql the most, but we also touch on the DBD::Oracle, DBD::Pg for Oracle, and PostgreSQL, respectively. There is also DBD::CSV for working with comma separated text files.

Conventions Used in This Book

This book may be formatted, and written differently than any other computer book you have. Throughout the book, you will find many different program examples, with little talk in between them. Instead, each line of the programs is described in detail, so that you can get a complete understanding of why the code is there, and how it works.

If you find that the line-by-line descriptions make it hard to get a complete picture of what the program is doing, we have provided the complete, uninterrupted code listings at the end of each chapter.

Throughout the book, code appears in `monospace` type, both within regular text and longer code listings.

 Icons are used throughout the book to draw your attention to important points.

Companion Web Site

The companion Web site for this book contains all of the program listings, the database table definitions, and any errata from the printed book. You can find the Web site at `www.wiley.com/compbooks/Michalski`.

Acknowledgments

Writing this book was a huge undertaking, and I could not have done it without the support of many others. First off, I want to thank Jesus Christ, my savior, for giving me the knowledge and persistence to see that this book is finally a reality. My wife, Chris, and my kids, Luc, Rae, and Logan also had to give up a lot (of my time) for me to get this done. I can't thank them enough!

My tech editor Sean Burke also helped out tremendously. Sean is a very knowledgeable Perl programmer and author who wasn't afraid to let me know how he really felt.

Finally, the people of #perl on IRC were also a great help. People like kane, who helped me acquire the needed software to write this book, thanks kane! Then there is kudra, merlyn, Pudge, lucs, waltman, DrForr, DrMath, Spoon, acme, aevil, boojum, Screwtape, beeer, amagosa, shit, cwest, cogent, crab, dngor, freeside, geoffeg, mendel, darkuncle, Masque, ology, obra, pdcawley, petdance, Roderick, sheriff, Schuyler, sky, sungo, uri, rootbeer, chip, Zenham, {KM}. Yes, their names all sound strange, and I am sure that I have missed some (sorry if I did), but #perl was my 24-hour resource for answers when I needed them.

Contents at a Glance

Contents

$\bullet \bullet$

Perl and Database Fundamentals

Database Basics

In this chapter, you receive an overview of databases: the concepts and jargon, their purposes, what you can do with them. In addition, you learn about database design, which involves how to structure your data so it is easy to use.

If you have used databases before, you can move to the next chapter and find out how to start using a database from Perl.

The Benefits of Databases

Before databases were developed, when programs shared data files any change to the data structure required by one program meant that all the programs had to be changed. Database Management Systems (DBMS) provide several services that alleviate some common database headaches:

✦ They store data securely and reliably, so that only the people and programs allowed to see and modify the data are able to do so. The DBMS should be able to withstand a computer crash without losing data.

✦ They make it easy to extract useful information from the data.

✦ They manage shared access to data: the DBMS locks data when it is updated to prevent multiple programs from corrupting it by updating it at the same time.

✦ They enforce consistency of both values and data structure: for example, no invoice record is without an address record; the state in an address must be valid.

✦ Most important, a DBMS isolates programs (and programmers!) from the details of data storage. Changes to the data structure do not automatically require changes to all programs.

Relational Databases

There are several types of databases. The most common nowadays is the relational database. The *relational* part comes from mathematics. *Relations* are what we call tables.

Tables in relational databases

In a relational database, a table is a collection of data, laid out like a spreadsheet. Each table has a name that must be unique in the database. Each column in a table holds the same sort of data: a name, a date of birth, an ISBN, and a phone number. Each column has a name that must be unique in the table. Each row in a table holds information about one thing (a person, a book, a CD — whatever the table has been created to store information about).

Figure 1-1 shows a simple address table with `name`, `phone_type`, `phone_number`, and `address` columns.

name	phone_type	phone_number	address
Chris	work	615-6355	25 Queens Road
Andy	mobile	722 5732-7685	12 High St
Andy	work	743-4576	12 High St
Andy	home	232-2123	12 High St
Brigitte	mobile	722 5332-8673	402 Sunnydale Lane
Chris	home	554-9992	25 Queens Road

Figure 1-1: A table of names, addresses, and phone numbers

Different DBMS have different rules for table and column names. Some are case-sensitive. Some allow spaces in names; some don't. A good policy is to assume the worst: use underscores to separate words. Use either uppercase or lowercase for all names. Make table names unique in a database, and make columns unique in a table.

Some people like to have column names unique in the database by prefixing an abbreviated table name: `pers_name`, `pers_address` and so on. I prefer not to use prefixes, but this means that queries using more than one table can have ambiguous column names.

Anywhere a column name can be used, you can prefix it with the full table name: `person.name`, `person.address`.

Values in tables

Each piece of information in the table (each cell in the spreadsheet) is atomic, or, in Perl-speak, a scalar value. The details of the types of data vary slightly among DBMS but include strings, numbers (separate types for integers, floating point, and currency), and dates. Common column types include:

✦ `INTEGER` columns store whole numbers. They can be signed or unsigned. DBMS usually provide different sizes of integer — `BIGINT`, `SMALLINT` — but all DBMS support `INTEGER`.

✦ `FLOAT`, `DOUBLE`. These are both floating-point numbers, but `DOUBLE` holds more significant digits (and takes up more space in memory and on disk).

✦ `DECIMAL` columns store numbers in a way that doesn't have the rounding problems of floating-point numbers. This is the data type to use for storing currency. You must tell the DBMS the maximum size and number of decimal places to store.

✦ `CHAR` and `VARCHAR` columns store fixed and variable-length strings. CHAR columns always take up the size you specify; `VARCHAR` columns take up only as much space as they need. Unlike Perl strings, these types have a limited size, often just 255 characters. Values longer than the column width are truncated.

✦ `BLOB` — The Binary Large OBject type. This is what you use for your long documents, images, soundtracks, and videos!

✦ `DATE`, `TIME`, `DATETIME`, `TIMESTAMP` columns provide different ways of storing the date and/or time. Most DBMS require the date/time values to be in a specific format.

The NULL value

Columns can hold one other value: `NULL`. `NULL` is different from all legal values. The `NULL` value enables you to distinguish a value that has never been set, from zero or an empty string.

Database Operations

The remaining chapters in this book show what you can do with databases. There are two main categories of operations. Chapter 3 shows you how to use the data-definition operators. These affect the structure of the database itself; they enable you to:

✦ Create new tables

✦ Delete tables and their contents

✦ Change the structure of (add and remove columns from) a table

✦ Add and remove indexes

These are important functions, but once the database is set up they will be infrequently used.

The data-manipulation operators are more interesting. Some of these modify an existing table by:

✦ Inserting new rows

✦ Updating existing rows

✦ Deleting rows

Other data manipulation operators work on tables and return collections of data. Think of them as virtual tables that you can apply other operators to or use in your programs. Logically, there are four of these operators:

✦ RESTRICT specifies the rows to be returned.

✦ PROJECT specifies the columns.

✦ JOIN tells the DBMS how tables are joined by specifying the relationships among columns of the various tables.

✦ UNION combines two or more tables that have the same structure.

In SQL (the Structured Query Language, used by all DBMS), these operations are combined in the SELECT statement. To start, however, look at each operation separately.

RESTRICT rows

RESTRICT lets you choose the *rows* you are interested in. It returns a virtual table, containing only the chosen rows. In Figure 1-2, the rows are specified where the name is "Andy."

name	phone_type	phone_number	address
Andy	mobile	722 5732-7685	12 High St
Andy	work	743-4576	12 High St
Andy	home	232-2123	12 High St

Figure 1-2: RESTRICT returns a subset of the rows.

The following is the SQL code for Figure 1-2:

```
SELECT * FROM person WHERE name = 'Andy'
```

PROJECT columns

The PROJECT operation specifies the *columns* you want. From the rows returned in Figure 1-2, the phone_type and phone_number columns are chosen, as shown in Figure 1-3.

phone_type	phone_number
mobile	722 5732-7685
work	743-4576
home	232-2123

Figure 1-3: PROJECT returns a subset of the columns.

You can treat the result of RESTRICT and PROJECT as another table — with fewer rows and columns — that you can print or process in your program, either a row at a time or all at once.

The following is the SQL code for Figure 1-3:

```
SELECT phone_type, phone_number FROM person WHERE name = 'Andy'
```

JOIN tables

A database with just one table is not very interesting. Most databases have more tables, and we often want to get related data from several tables. The JOIN operation creates a new virtual table by joining the tables on columns with the same value.

The top portion of Figure 1-4 shows a more realistic table structure, where the addresses and phone numbers have been split into separate tables. We can get our original table back by combining rows that have the same value in the name column of both tables, as shown in the bottom portion of Figure 1-4.

name	phone_type	phone_number
Chris	work	615-6355
Andy	mobile	722 5732-7685
Andy	work	743-4576
Andy	home	232-2123
Brigitte	mobile	722 5332-8673
Chris	home	554-9992

name	address
Andy	12 High St
Brigitte	402 Sunnydale Lane
Chris	25 Queens Road

name	phone_type	phone_number	address
Chris	work	615-6355	25 Queens Road
Andy	mobile	722 5732-7685	12 High St
Andy	work	743-4576	12 High St
Andy	home	232-2123	12 High St
Brigitte	mobile	722 5332-8673	402 Sunnydale Lane
Chris	home	554-9992	25 Queens Road

Figure 1-4: JOIN returns a table made by combining the source tables.

The following is the SQL code for Figure 1-4:

```
SELECT phone.name, phone_type, phone_number, address
FROM phone, address
WHERE phone.name = address.name
```

Note   If you don't tell the DBMS which columns to join, you will get a natural join: every possible combination of rows from each table.

Being able to join tables by any columns with common values is what makes relational databases so powerful and useful. Sometimes joining tables does not provide the result you want. If there is an address with no matching phone number, the address is not selected. If what you want is "all the addresses with any phone numbers that exist," you need an OUTER JOIN. If an OUTER JOIN can't find a matching row in a table, it returns a row with NULL values in the missing fields, as shown in Figure 1-5.

name	phone_type	phone_number
Chris	work	615-6355
Andy	mobile	722 5732-7685
Andy	work	743-4576
Andy	home	232-2123
Chris	home	554-9992

name	address
Andy	12 High St
Brigitte	402 Sunnydale Lane
Chris	25 Queens Road

name	phone_type	phone_number	address
Chris	work	615-6355	25 Queens Road
Andy	mobile	722 5732-7685	12 High St
Andy	work	743-4576	12 High St
Andy	home	232-2123	12 High St
Brigitte	NULL	NULL	402 Sunnydale Lane
Chris	home	554-9992	25 Queens Road

Figure 1-5: An OUTER JOIN supplies NULL values for missing data.

UNION of queries

Most database queries use RESTRICT and PROJECT on one or more joined tables. But sometimes you will need to combine the result of multiple queries: perhaps you want title and author from a table of books *and* title and artist from a table of CDs together in one table. That's what UNION does.

In Figure 1-6, the queries return the title and author from the books table and title and artist from a CD table; UNION combines these into one table. The only limitation is that you must choose the same number of columns from each table and they must be compatible data types.

title	author
Security Engineering	Ross Anderson
Perl the Programmers Companion	Nigel Chapman
Perl Database Programming Bible	Brent Michalski

title	artist
More Greatest Hits	Bob Dylan
Infidels	Bob Dylan
Back to mine	Morcheeba

title	author
Security Engineering	Ross Anderson
Perl the Programmers Companion	Nigel Chapman
Perl Database Programming	Brent Michalski
More Greatest Hits	Bob Dylan
Infidels	Bob Dylan
Back to mine	Morcheeba

Figure 1-6: UNION returns a table made by combining two similar tables.

All the preceding operations are used in subsequent chapters.

Designing a Database

Designing your database tables is partly an art: There are always trade-offs among simplicity, keeping data consistent, and performance. Here are some goals to aim for and guidelines to help you.

Normalization

The steps we go through in this section are called, in database jargon, *normalization*. Data is in First Normal Form (1NF) when you:

✦ Eliminate repeating groups (the different phone numbers)

✦ Create separate tables for different data: people in a people table, books in a books table, CDs in a CD table

✦ Choose a primary key for each table

The Second Normal Form (2NF) is when you:

✦ Move data that is repeated in several rows to a new table (the address table, in this case)

✦ Add the primary key of the new table to the original table, if it's not already there

Data is Third Normal Form (3NF) when you move independent data on the primary key to separate tables: the city and state tables.

Of course, you have to repeat the whole process for each of the new tables created. At the end of all this, your data should allow no duplication. You will be able to make any query (and get the same answer) that you can on the original unnormalized table.

Eliminate repeating data

Figure 1-7 is a first draft of a table with names, addresses, and phone numbers. This table is simple, but it has a problem. If you ever want to add a new type of number (a mobile phone, a pager, a FAX and so on), the structure will change. The different phone numbers are a "repeating group" that you need to get rid of somehow.

name	home	work	street	city	state
Chris	554-9992	615-6355	25 Queens Road	New York	New York
Andy	232-2123	743-4576	12 High St	Albany	New York
Brigitte			402 Sunnydale Lane	Boston	Massachusetts

Figure 1-7: A simple table

Figure 1-8 shows another version of the table. Now there is one row for each number, and we can add extra types of phone numbers easily. We've added a `phone_type` column so we can tell which number is which.

name	phone_type	phone_number	address	city	state
Chris	work	615-6355	25 Queens Road	New York	New York
Andy	mobile	722 5732-7685	12 High St	Albany	New York
Andy	work	743-4576	12 High St	Albany	New York
Andy	home	232-2123	12 High St	Albany	New York
Brigitte	mobile	722 5332-8673	402 Sunnydale Lane	Boston	Massachusetts
Chris	home	554-9992	25 Queens Road	New York	New York

Figure 1-8: Table from Figure 1-7 with repeating groups removed

Make each row uniquely identifiable

Most DBMS require that each table have a primary key: one or more columns that are unique—and not `NULL`—for each row. Uniqueness is usually enforced by creating an index on these columns.

Use primary keys to join related tables by putting the primary key of one table into a related table, where it is called a foreign key. The primary key is the `name` column in Figure 1-7 and the `name` and `phone_type` columns in Figure 1-8.

Some columns are more useful than others as primary keys. Names work only in very small tables: In one office, six people of twelve might be named Chris. Social Security Numbers are often used as primary keys: They should be unique, but apart from the privacy and security issues, you may not know the value; some people (children, foreign visitors, and so on) don't have them.

If a table doesn't have an obvious primary key, a sequential number provided by the DBMS or some other unique number such as a UUID (Universal Unique ID) is the solution.

Eliminate redundant data

The new structure solves one problem: we can add as many numbers as we want. But in many ways it's worse than we started with. Because there is no number for Brigitte, one row has a `NULL` value in a primary key column. There is also a lot of duplicated data. The duplication causes several problems:

✦ Adding new rows requires reentering existing information.

✦ If someone changes his or her name or address, we must update multiple rows.

✦ If we delete all the phone numbers for someone, we might also lose his or her address unless we're careful.

✦ Where data is duplicated, some copies of it *will* end up wrong (because of miskeying, or because a value has changed but only some of the copies have been updated).

The next step is to put data that's in multiple rows into a separate table. In Figure 1-9, the data is separated into separate tables based on addresses and the phone numbers.

name	phone_type	phone_number
Chris	work	615-6355
Andy	mobile	722 5732-7685
Andy	work	743-4576
Andy	home	232-2123
Chris	home	554-9992

name	street	city	state
Chris	25 Queens Road	New York	New York
Andy	12 High St	Albany	New York
Brigitte	402 Sunnydale Lane	Boston	Massachusetts

Figure 1-9: Repeated data placed in a separate table

Now we can have any number of phone numbers for each person — including none! We can get the original data back by joining the address and phone tables on the name column. If we want to include people without phone numbers, we must perform an OUTER JOIN.

This is probably as far as we should go with this application, but there are additional useful steps in larger systems.

Eliminate data not dependent on the key

The next step is to move to another table any data that is not *directly* related to the key of the row. In Figure 1-10, the state has nothing to do with the person's name, but the state is related to the city, so we can create a table with city and state. If all of these rules are applied to all tables recursively, we can end up with a lot of small tables.

name	street	city
Chris	25 Queens Road	New York
Andy	12 High St	Albany
Brigitte	402 Sunnydale Lane	Boston

city	state
New York	NY
Albany	NY
Boston	MA
Chicago	IL

state	name
NY	New York
IL	Illinois
MA	Massachusetts

Figure 1-10: Separate tables for address, city, and state

Because the state name is in multiple rows, it can be moved into its own table. We end up with our single name, address, and phone numbers table split into four. All the data is available; none is repeated unnecessarily, and we can recreate the original single table with joins.

De-Normalization

A problem with normalization, if you follow all the rules, is that you can end up with many small tables. This leads to complex and possibly inefficient queries with many joins. In this simple address and phone example, separate tables for city and state are overkill. Every query for an address needs to join the address, city, and state tables.

If you find yourself in this position, the answer may be de-normalization: adding some redundancy to simplify your application. In this case, putting the state column back into the address table makes the structure much simpler at the cost of typing a state name for each address.

Add indexes for performance

No one likes using a slow computer, and no one wants to wait very long for a database to find the data he or she has asked for. Apart from the DBMS and the computer it runs on, the things that affect performance are good data design and indexes.

For small tables (up to, say, a few hundred rows), indexes may not be necessary: There is an overhead in maintaining and using an index. With larger tables, indexes enable the DBMS to be much more efficient, especially when joining tables.

Add an index for each column, or each group of columns, used to join tables. Specify a unique index when you want to prevent duplicates in a column. Add an index to a column that is searched frequently, so that the DBMS does not have to search sequentially.

Summary

We've talked about the concepts and jargon you'll need to deal with databases. Though some of the details differ among vendors, everything in this chapter applies to all relational databases. Different DBMS store data in different ways, but the data is always represented as tables of rows and columns that you can join on common values. You will be using the RESTRICT, PROJECT, and JOIN operators when you start using the SQL SELECT statement in Chapter 4.

✦   ✦   ✦

Working with a Database

In This Chapter

Installed drivers

Data Source
Name (DSN)

Connecting to
a database

Disconnecting

Example program

Working with a database in Perl requires very little extra work in your programs. Since the DBI module is well written and stable, writing a database-enabled program takes minimal extra thought on the programmer's part. Sure, you need to plan what data you want to access and how to query it — but connecting to the database and executing SQL queries on it is easy.

Cross-Reference Appendix A offers instructions on how to install the DBI module and DBD driver modules. Please make sure you have these installed before continuing, since we'll be using them.

To make sure that the DBI module is installed and functioning and to see what database drivers are available on your system, let's write a short script to query the system:

```
01: #!/usr/bin/perl -w
02: # connect_test.pl
03: # Chapter 2
04: # Listing 1

05: use strict;
06: use DBI;

07: print "Available Database Drivers:\n";
08: print "*" x 40, "\n";
09: print join("\n", DBI-
>available_drivers()), "\n\n";
```

Line 1 tells the system where to find Perl and turns on warnings with the -w switch. Warnings are helpful when writing programs because they cause Perl to print additional diagnostic messages that can be helpful debugging aids. Turning warnings off in production code is perfectly acceptable once you have the program running the way you want it to. Leaving warnings on in production code can produce unneeded diagnostic messages in your server log files.

Lines 2–4 are simply comments about this program.

Line 5 turns `strict` mode on. In a program this small, `strict` is not needed, but I make it a habit to program with `strict` mode on because it can be a lifesaver when debugging. `strict` forces the programmer to declare variables and turns additional error checking on.

> **Tip**   *Always* use `strict` when you begin programming. Trying to put `strict` into an existing program is usually a major task; without `strict` mode on, Perl lets the programmer get away with a lot of sloppy coding practices. When `strict` is added, all of the sloppy code must be fixed at once.
>
> To eliminate this problem, begin programming all of your applications by using `strict` mode from the very start.

Line 6 loads the `DBI` module; this is needed for database access.

Line 7 prints a text message.

Line 8 prints a line of 40 asterisks. The x 40 tells Perl to print the quoted text 40 times. Then we have a comma and a newline to put the output onto the next line.

Line 9 uses Perl's `join` function. `join` is used to combine an array of data with a common string. The string we are joining with here is the newline \n, and the array that we are joining is actually `DBI->available_drivers()`, since this function returns an array. We follow this up with two newlines to add two blank lines to the program output.

If you enter the preceding program and the DBI is installed properly, you should get output that looks something like this:

```
Available Database Drivers:
****************************************
ExampleP
Pg
Proxy
Mysql
```

The drivers you have loaded depend on the database drivers you have loaded (DBDs). The main database drivers I am interested in here are Mysql and Pg—which are the MySQL and PostgreSQL drivers, respectively.

If all is well so far, let's move on to the next step: connecting to a database.

Connecting to a Database

To read or write a plain file in Perl, you need to open a file handle. In the same way, to access a DBI database in Perl, you need to create a database handle. A database handle is what you use to maintain a connection to a database and is how you reference a particular connection to a database when you need to call functions or make SQL queries. It is possible to have more than one database handle in a program; this means you can connect to more than one database or even to more than one database server. The servers you connect to don't even need to be on the same continent! However, due to current connectivity restrictions, the database servers *do* need to be on the same planet. Database handles are normally referenced by a variable named $dbh or by something similar such as $dbh_accounting.

Let's take a look at a program that connects to some data sources, grabs a bit of data, prints it, and disconnects. Not all data bases require disconnecting, but to make truly portable code, you should always call disconnect.

```
01: #!/usr/bin/perl -w
02: #
03: # connect_multi.pl
04: # Chapter 2
05: # Listing 2
```

Line 1 tells the system where to find Perl and turns warnings on with the -w switch. Warnings provide some extra diagnostic messages that are helpful when writing applications.

Lines 2–5 are simply comments about this program.

```
06: use strict;
07: use DBI;
```

Line 6 loads the strict module. This module enforces more stringent programming rules than coding without using strict. Using strict is *highly* recommended because it can prevent many simple programming mistakes that are hard to debug — such as misspelling a variable name.

Line 7 loads the DBI module; we need this because it provides us with an interface for database connectivity.

```
08: my $dbh_m =
       DBI->connect("DBI:mysql:quizzer:dbserver.perlguy.net",
       "bookuser",
       "password")
09:    or die("Cannot connect: $DBI::errstr");
```

Line 8 is split up a bit so that it looks nicer and is easier to explain.

The first part of **line 8** declares a new variable named $dbh_m. This is going to stand for *DataBase Handle* to *My*SQL.

The next part of **line 8** calls the connect method of the DBI. The connect method needs a few things passed to it — the *Data Source Name*, *username*, and *password*.

Line 9 is a continuation of **line 8**. This line causes the program to die (abort) if there was an error connecting to the database.

Below are two sample connect statements. The first connect statement contains all of the options/attributes you could pass. The second connect statement contains a minimal amount of options/attributes while still being a valid connect statement.

Containing everything:

```
my %attr => ( RaiseError => 0 );

$dbh =
DBI->connect("dbi:mysql:dbname=BibleBook:host.hair.net:1023",
    "username", "password", \%attr)
    or die("Error: $DBI::errstr");
```

Containing the minimum:

```
$dbh->connect("dbi:mysql:BibleBook", "username", "password")
    or die("Error: $DBI::errstr");
```

The Data Source Name (DSN)

A DSN is a string that passes all of the connect information to the database interface. It begins with DBI:. For some reason, this first part is not case-sensitive, but the rest of the DSN *is* case-sensitive. This is followed by the database driver name and a colon. For a MySQL database, we'll begin with something like this: DBI:mysql:. The database driver name *is* case-sensitive — so if you get an error but have spelled the driver name correctly, make sure the case is also correct.

Next comes the *database name*. This is where different databases require different data. For MySQL, which is what the preceding connect statement is connecting to, we simply list the database name, quizzer. With PostGreSQL, which we'll have an example of in a bit, the database name must be preceded with dbname=. For our PostgreSQL example, this becomes dbname=quizzer. With MySQL, you can use dbname= if you want, but it is not required. Other databases, such as Oracle, use different strings here, whereas the CSV driver uses the string f_dir=/*path* (where *path* leads to the directory where the data files are stored).

The server address and port number can *also* go on in the DSN! In our previous example, we list the server name, dbserver.perlguy.net; since we are using the default MySQL port (3306), we can leave it off.

A full DSN can look something like this:

DBI:mysql:dbname=quizzer:*dbserver.somewhere.com:1234*

The bold characters are required, and the italicized are optional.

Wow! That is really a lot of information, but it is definitely important to be able to connect to the database.

The next two parts of the connect string are the *username* and *password*. These are not the username and password for a normal user; they are instead the username and password for the database and/or tables being accessed. Databases typically have a permissions system of their own to restrict access to certain data — these username and password values belong to the database permission system.

Line 9 is a continuation of **line 8**. It tells the system to call the die function and to print an error message if there is an error when connecting to the database. $DBI::errstr is a variable, named $errstr in the DBI module, that gets set whenever an error is encountered. This line causes the error message to print and the program to stop execution at this point.

```
10: my $dbh_p = DBI->connect("DBI:Pg:dbname=test",
        "postgres","")
11:     or die("Cannot connect: $DBI::errstr");
```

Line 10 is the connect statement for the PostGreSQL database we are also connecting to. The DSN for this database is DBI:Pg:dbname=test. This connect statement is a lot shorter than the previous example because we do not need the *servername* or *port*, as this database server is on the same system as this program. The *username* for this database is postgres; there is no password, so we pass an empty string.

Line 11 is the same as **line 9**. It prints an error message and stops the program execution if there is a problem connecting to the database.

At this point in the program, we have *two different* connections to *two different* databases on *two different* servers! The database handle to the MySQL database is $dbh_m, and the database handle to the PostGreSQL server is $dbh_p.

```
12: my $sql = qq(select * from test_config);
```

Line 12 creates a new scalar variable named $sql and sets it to the string on the right. The qq function is nice because it acts exactly like double quotes; if your string has double quotes, you do not have to place a backslash character in front of them.

```
my $sql = qq(select * from test WHERE foo = "bar");
```

is easier to read than something like:

```
my $sql = "select * from test WHERE foo = \"bar\"";
```

Although the above example is very simple, if you start creating queries with many quoted variables, you will see how much easier and less prone to typing errors using qq() is compared to quotes and backslashes.

This $sql variable stores the SQL statement we are going to run against both databases. The SQL statement is telling the database server to select all data from the test_config table. Both databases have a table named test_config.

```
13: my $sth_m = $dbh_m->prepare($sql);
14: my $sth_p = $dbh_p->prepare($sql);
```

Lines 13–14 both declare a new scalar variable that will be used as a handle to the statement we are preparing on the right side. The prepare method takes the SQL statement and stores it in an internal, compiled format that the database can work with.

The $sth_ is similar to our database handles $dbh_. The commonly accepted way to name a statement handle is $sth or $sth_*description*.

```
15: $sth_m->execute;
16: $sth_p->execute;
```

Lines 15–16 also perform the same task. They call the execute method on the statement handle. The execute method takes the prepared SQL statement and runs it on the database engine.

```
17: while(my $p = $sth_m->fetch){
18:     print "MySQL: @$p\n";
19: }
```

Line 17 begins a while loop. This while loop fetches the data that results from the executed SQL statement on **line 15**. The fetch method you see inside the while condition grabs one row (*a.k.a. record*) of returned data and returns a reference (*a.k.a. pointer*) to an array containing this data. The pointer to this array is stored in the variable $p. (The fetch method is covered in more detail later in this book.)

Line 18 prints the row of data. We don't use special formatting here; we are just dumping the data out.

Line 19 ends the while loop that begins on **line 16**.

```
20: print "\n";
```

Line 20 simply prints a blank line. This helps separate the output from the two databases.

```
21: while(my $p = $sth_p->fetch){
22:     print "PostGreSQL: @$p\n";
23: }
```

Lines 21–23 do the same thing as **lines 17–19** but on the PostGreSQL database instead of on the MySQL database.

```
24: $dbh_m->disconnect;
25: $dbh_p->disconnect;
```

Lines 24–25 disconnect the program from the databases. Disconnecting ensures that all data is written properly to the tables. Some databases care whether or not you disconnect; others do not. Always use the disconnect method so you don't have to worry about it.

Oracle Connections

Oracle can be more of a beast to work with than other databases. Don't get me wrong; Perl still interfaces with Oracle and does an excellent job — getting everything set up can be a much more involved process though because an Oracle installation is a much greater undertaking than installing a database like MySQL.

Perl still uses the DBI for database access, as well as a DBD driver. To set up the DBD::Oracle driver, however, you need to have the Oracle client software properly installed on the system. This is why the configuration is more painful when using Perl on Oracle databases. Getting the Oracle client software set up is not nearly as easy to do as setting up MySQL or PostGreSQL.

Also, when working with Oracle databases, the user that the program is running under must have the proper Oracle environment variables set, such as the ORACLE_HOME variable. These settings should be available from your Oracle DBA.

Aside from the preceding notes, connecting to and running commands on an Oracle database is the same as working with any other database.

DBI's Error Handling

The last topic we'll cover in this chapter is error handling. The DBI->connect method can have one additional attribute passed to it. Also, you are allowed to pass a reference to a hash containing attribute values. These attribute values vary depending on the database you are connecting to. Usually, the attributes are left off, but there may be times when you will need to include the attributes. In most cases, you can leave these attributes alone since their default values are normally fine. However, if you need to, or want to, change the way errors are handled, here is how to do it.

To pass some attributes to the connect statement, do something like this:

```
my %attr => ( PrintError => 0, RaiseError => 0 );
$dbh = DBI->connect("DBI:mysql:database", "username",
                    "password", \%attr)
    or die ("Error: $DBI::errstr\n");
```

The PrintError and RaiseError attributes are used for error handling. They are set to on, 1, and off, 0, respectively by default, and should normally be left that way.

To change how PrintError and RaiseError handle errors, they can be set to 0, as they are in the preceding code. If you do this, it is up to you to catch and report all errors. If you already have the database handle created and wish to change the error-handling behavior, you can alter the values like so:

```
$dbh->{PrintError} = 1;
```

or like this:

```
$dbh->{RaiseError} = 0;
```

The PrintError attribute causes any error messages to be printed via Perl's warn method. The RaiseError attribute causes the error messages to be printed via Perl's die method — which also terminates the program execution at the point of the error.

There are valid times when you may want this functionality turned off or altered. For example, if you are on a production system and there is some sort of error with the database, you probably don't want descriptive error messages to print, enabling the user to see them. This can cause security holes because it may give detailed information to people you may not want to give it to. In cases like this, set RaiseError to 0, and handle errors via your own die messages.

For handing your own error messages, there are three DBI variables you should know about. We've used $DBI::errstr already; it shows the error string that the database returns. There are also $DBI::err and $DBI::state. $DBI::err is the error number that the database engine returns. $DBI::state is a string that contains the standard five-character SQLSTATE error string. Many database drivers do not fully support the SQLSTATE method, so it is not uncommon to not get any values returned.

Summary

At this point, you should be able to make connections to a database, perform simple queries, and set the error handling attributes. The error handling attributes that were covered are good to keep in mind, but since the default settings are good for most situations, you should not have to worry about them for now. Just remember where they are so that you can refer back to them if you find that you need them.

If you had problems with this chapter, go back and make sure that you understand the functions and code we covered since connecting to a database is a key concept that you must be able to do to continue on in this book.

Finally, if you are planning on writing code that maybe run on different platforms, don't forget to use the disconnect method. Although MySQL doesn't require disconnect to be used, it is a good habit to into.

Database-handle variables traditionally begin with $dbh, and statement-handle variables traditionally begin with $sth. Using this naming convention allows users who view this code to recognize various handles easily.

Program Listings

Listing 2-1 contains the complete and uninterrupted code from this chapter.

Listing 2-1: **connect_multi.pl**

```
01: #!/usr/bin/perl -w
02: #
03: # connect_multi.pl
04: # Chapter 2
05: # Listing 2

06: use strict;
07: use DBI;

08: my $dbh_m =
        DBI->connect("dBi:mysql:quizzer:dbserver.perlguy.net",
        "bookuser",
        "password")
09:     or die("Cannot connect: $DBI::errstr\n");

10: my $dbh_p = DBI->connect("dbi:Pg:dbname=test",
        "postgres","")
```

Continued

Listing 2-1 *(continued)*

```
11:     or die("Cannot connect: $DBI::errstr\n");

12: my $sql = qq(select * from test_config);

13: my $sth_m = $dbh_m->prepare($sql);
14: my $sth_p = $dbh_p->prepare($sql);

15: $sth_m->execute;
16: $sth_p->execute;

17: while(my $p = $sth_m->fetch){
18:   print "MySQL: @$p\n";
19: }

20: print "\n";

21: while(my $p = $sth_p->fetch){
22:   print "PostGreSQL: @$p\n";
23: }

24: $dbh_m->disconnect;
25: $dbh_p->disconnect;
```

✦   ✦   ✦

Working with Database Tables

Database tables represent a two-dimensional view of some data. I like to think of a database table as a spreadsheet page — you have rows and columns. The columns make up the database-table definition, and the rows make up each record in the table.

We'll be covering the three basic table operations in this short chapter: creating a table, modifying a table, and deleting a table. These tasks are all quite simple, but they do warrant discussion because you can't work with a database if you don't have tables.

What Is a Table?

As I mentioned previously, a database table is a two-dimensional view of a portion of database data.

Figure 3-1 is an example of what a table would look like if it were placed into a spreadsheet. The columns headings would be the table field names and a row of data in the spreadsheet would be a database record.

For smaller applications, having data stored in a single table is quite common. There is a problem with this, however, when the database starts to get larger — redundant data. For database applications that have more than a few fields where there could be redundant data, it is wiser to store the data in several different tables, each of which holds a specific set of information. Breaking the data down into tables to minimize redundant data is called normalization — a topic we cover briefly at the beginning of this book.

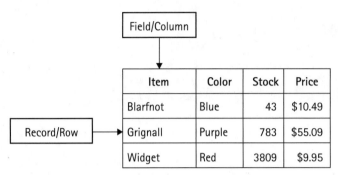

Figure 3-1: Table example

Consider a table of products that contains the product name, part number, price, vendor name, and vendor description. Even a table this small can contain a lot of redundant data! Let's say that this table has 100 products, with 10 different vendors. If we had the data all in one table, we would have the same vendor information in several records, an average of 10 times for each vendor! This is not efficient at all. A much more sensible approach is to split the vendor information into a different table and just have a vendor id number stored in the products table — a relation between the product and the vendor. Figure 3-2 shows a very small table that contains redundant vendor information.

Item	Color	Stock	Price	Vendor	Vendor Address	Vendor Phone
Blarfnot	Blue	43	$10.49	Al's Blarfnots	32 Maple Drive	312-555-3232
Grignall	Purple	783	$55.09	Stuff Inc.	132 Elm Street	816-438-3121
Smelter	Green	321	$99.95	Stuff Inc.	132 Elm Street	816-438-3121
Widget	Red	3809	$9.95	Stuff Inc.	132 Elm Street	816-438-3121

Figure 3-2: Table example with redundant data

Figure 3-3 shows that by using one table for the products and one for the vendors, you can eliminate any redundant vendor data.

Granted, the two examples above are very small but if you consider similar tables with more records, you imagine how much redundant data is reduced by using multiple tables. So, in simple terms, a relational database is a collection of tables that are related to one another.

This chapter doesn't have a lot of code examples. When you are working with tables, typically you do so from your database administration command-line or the databases' own GUI — so it is not done programmatically.

Figure 3-3: Table example with two tables

Data Types

First, we need to cover the various data types available (see Table 3-1). Data types are like variable types. In some languages, you have strings, integers, floating-point numbers, big integers, characters, and so on. The same holds true for database data types: There are different data descriptors for different types of data. Every column in the database is for storing a particular kind of data: a column for storing last names would be of type "varchar", a column for storing birthdates should be of type "date", and so on. This helps the database store the information more efficiently and helps the programmer know what kind of data to expect.

Table 3-1
Common Data Types

Name	Type	Description	Notes
INT	Numeric	Signed four-byte integer	-2147483648 to +2147483647
SMALLINT	Numeric	Signed two-byte integer	-32768 to +32767
REAL	Numeric	Variable precision	6 decimal digits precision
CHAR(n)	Character	Fixed-length char string	Holds n characters
VARCHAR(n)	Character	Variable-length char string	Holds up to n characters
BLOB	Binary	Binary Large OBject	For storing large binary data

Continued

Name	Type	Description	Notes
DATE	Date	Date storage	Ex. YYYY-MM-DD
TIME	Time	Time storage	Ex. HH:MM:SS
TIMESTAMP	Date/Time	Date & Time storage	Ex. YYYY-MM-DD HH:MM:SS

Table 3-1 *(continued)*

Creating Tables

A database must be created before a table is added. The database administrator usually creates the database through the database-administration tools or GUI. If you are also the person administering the database, create a database so that we can work with tables inside of it.

In MySQL, creating a database is easy to do from the command line. To create a database named *widgets*, this is all you need to do:

```
mysqladmin create widgets -uusername -ppassword
```

You won't get any fancy messages back if the database creation is successful; you will just return to the command-line.

Now we are ready to work with tables, so let's take a look at the SQL needed to create a table called *products*.

The SQL commands to create the *products* table are listed below. You can recreate the *products* table from the database interface or can write a short Perl script to execute the SQL for you. The SQL keywords are in all capital letters to make the SQL statement easier to read.

```
01: CREATE TABLE products(
02: Pid   INT NOT NULL,
03: Item  VARCHAR(50),
04: Descr VARCHAR(255),
05: Price REAL,
06: Vid   INT NOT NULL);
```

This SQL statement creates a table named products with five items in it.

Line 1 creates the table named `products` and opens the parenthesis for the data types.

Line 2 creates the product id field and names it `Pid`. It sets the data type to `INT` (integer) and adds a `NOT NULL` clause, which causes the database server to generate an error if someone tries to add a record but leaves this field blank.

Tip It is always a good idea to make your data types as specific as possible because the database can use that specific information to make storage and access more efficient.

Line 3 creates the item-name field and names it `Item`. This line sets the data type to `VARCHAR` with a size of 50. The `VARCHAR` data type allows up to *x* number of records.

Line 4 creates a field for the item description and names it `Descr`. This field is also set to the data type `VARCHAR` but is 255 characters long instead of 50 like the preceding `Item` field.

Note I do not abbreviate the description field `Desc` because `DESC` is a reserved word in SQL and is used for sorting items in a descending order.

Line 5 creates the item-price field and names it `Price`. This field is set to a `REAL` data type because we know that prices typically have a decimal point in them, which no integer can have. **Line 6** is the last line of this SQL statement. It creates a field named `Vid`, which stands for Vendor ID. This field is also an `INT` data type and is set so that it cannot be `NULL`.

Next, we need a vendor table so that we can link a product to a vendor.

```
01: CREATE TABLE vendors(
02: Vid     INT NOT NULL,
03: Name    VARCHAR(100),
04: Address VARCHAR(100),
05: City    VARCHAR(50),
06: State   CHAR(2),
07: Zip     VARCHAR(10),
08: Phone   VARCHAR(25));
```

Line 1 creates the table named `vendors` and opens the parenthesis for the data types.

Line 2 creates the vendor id field and names it `Vid`. It sets the data type to `INT` and adds a `NOT NULL` clause, which causes the database server to generate an error if someone tries to add a record but leaves this field blank. This is the field that we'll use to keep the relation between the product and the vendors.

Line 3 creates the name field and names it `Name`. This line sets the data type to `VARCHAR` with a size of 100.

Line 4 creates a field for the address and names it `Address`. This field is also set to the data type `VARCHAR` and is also100 characters long.

Line 5 creates a field for the city and names it `City`. This field is also set to the data type `VARCHAR` and is 50 characters long.

Line 6 creates a field for the state and names it `State`. This field is set to the data type `CHAR` and is 2 characters long. It is kept this short to allow only each state's two-letter abbreviation.

Line 7 creates a field for the ZIP code and names it `Zip`. This field is also set to the data type `VARCHAR` and is 10 characters long.

Line 8 creates a field for the phone number and names it `Phone`. This field is also set to the data type `VARCHAR` and is 25 characters long. You might think we could use a number data-type for this, but '234-1234' isn't a number, because it has a '-' in the middle, to say nothing of the parens and the space in '(719) 234-1234'.

That is all the SQL that is needed to create two tables that can be used for an item database with relations between each item and its vendor. Please note that the field sizes and names I used are very U.S.-centric. If you live somewhere that needs different field types or sizes, please adjust as necessary to accommodate for changes in address format.

Altering Tables

Altering a table is the process of making changes to an existing table. Exercise caution when modifying tables. The database *usually* tries to save any existing data, but if the modification involves changes that are not compatible, data will be lost. For example, if you have your prices stored as `REAL` numbers and decide to change them to `INT` (integers), you will either lose the data after the decimal or lose the data entirely!

Let's say we need to make some changes to the tables we've created in the previous section. We need to add a `Size` field to the products table, add an `Address2` field to the `vendors` table, and change the `Item` field in the `products` database to 100 characters instead of 50.

Here is how you go about making the preceding changes:

```
01: ALTER TABLE products ADD Size VARCHAR(20);
02: ALTER TABLE vendors ADD Address2 VARCHAR(100);
03: ALTER TABLE products MODIFY Item VARCHAR(100);
```

Lines 1–2 add a new column.

Line 3 modifies the `Item` column; it sets the new length to 100 instead of the 50 that it used to be.

Modifying the tables is something you should do only if you absolutely must. Try to design your tables properly in the first place, and you won't need to modify them later. By modifying an existing table with data in it, you risk losing data. If you have data in a table already, make sure you back the database table up before trying to modify it.

Deleting Tables

Deleting tables is the easiest database function of all of the functions we have covered. Simply use the DROP TABLE command, and the table—as well as all of the data in it—is gone. Use this command with caution!

Let's say we have sold a portion of the company and we no longer sell products. We want to get rid of our product table. We still want to keep the vendor table, however, for our birthday-card list. To get rid of the products table, we simply have to do this:

```
DROP TABLE products;
```

The table is gone, and all of its data is gone as well.

Program Example

The following small program example adds a table to an existing database. I show only one example because all we are really doing is executing a quick SQL statement that we won't use repeatedly.

```
01: #!/usr/bin/perl -w
02: # add_table.pl
03: # Chapter 3
04: # Listing 1
```

Line 1 tells the system where to find Perl and turns warnings on with the -w.

Lines 2–4 are simply comments about this program.

```
05: use strict;
06: use DBI;
```

Line 5 loads the strict module. This module is used to help the programmer. It forces the programmer to declare variables and can catch common errors that can be hard to debug.

Line 6 loads the DBI module so that we can access a database.

```
07: my $dbh = DBI->connect("DBI:mysql:widgets",
    "bookuser","testpass")
08:     or die("Cannot connect: $DBI::errstr");
```

Line 7 declares a scalar variable named $dbh and connects us to the database. The DBI->connect method is used to connect to the database; we pass the database driver and name (DBI:mysql:widgets), username (bookuser), and password (testpass) so that we can connect. The connect method returns a handle to the database if all goes well. This handle is stored in the $dbh variable.

Line 8 is a continuation of **line 7**. If there is a problem connecting to the database, this line gets executed. This line causes the program to die and to display an error message to the user.

```
09: my $sql = qq{CREATE TABLE products (
10:              Pid   INT NOT NULL,
11:              Item  VARCHAR(255),
12:              Descr VARCHAR(255),
13:              Price REAL,
14:              Vid   INT NOT NULL)};
```

Lines 9–14 are the SQL statement to add a table to the database. On **line 9**, we declare a scalar variable named $sql, which we set to the string that makes up the SQL statement. Notice that for the qq function we use curly brackets {} instead of parentheses () because we need to include parentheses inside of the quoted string.

This is the same SQL statement we use above when we create the products table. This is just a way to create a table by using Perl instead of the database command line.

```
15: my $return = $dbh->do($sql);
```

Line 15 calls the do method on the $dbh handle and passes the SQL statement, via $sql, to the method. The do method saves time when you are not expecting data to be returned because it takes the place of both the prepare and execute methods. The value the do method returns is stored in the new scalar variable named $return.

```
16: if($return) {
17:     print "Table addition successful!\n";
18: }
19: else {
20:     print "\n\nERROR! $DBI::errstr\n";
21: }
```

Lines 16–21 check to see what has happened. **Line 16** uses the if function to see if $return contains anything. If the SQL statement is successful, a value will be stored in $return. It really doesn't matter *what* value as long as a value is there.

Line 17 prints the success message if the SQL table addition is successful.

Line 18 ends the if block.

Line 19 begins the else block. This is the block of code that the program enters if there is no value in $return. If an error occurs, $return contains undef, which is not a value that evaluates to true, so the preceding if block does not execute.

Line 20 prints the error message as well as the error text that gets set in the $DBI::errstr variable.

Line 21 closes the if..else block and is also the last line of this program.

Summary

That's about it for the basics of working with tables; they're pretty simple. The Perl program we create for this example can be used for any SQL table methods you may want to do. Adding tables, dropping tables, and modifying tables can all be done by simply changing the SQL statement to perform the specific task needed.

Program Listings

Listing 3-1 contains the complete and uninterrupted code from this chapter's program example.

Listing 3-1: **Table Add**

```
01: #!/usr/bin/perl -w

02: # add_table.pl
03: # Chapter 3
04: # Listing 1

05: use strict;
06: use DBI;

07: my $dbh = DBI->connect("DBI:mysql:widgets",
       "bookuser","testpass")
08:      or die("Cannot connect: $DBI::errstr\n");

09: my $sql = qq{CREATE TABLE products (
10:               Pid   INT NOT NULL,
11:               Item  VARCHAR(255),
12:               Descr VARCHAR(255),
13:               Price REAL,
14:               Vid   INT NOT NULL)};

15: my $return = $dbh->do($sql);

16: if($return) {
17:     print "Table addition successful!\n";
18: }
19: else {
20:     print "\n\nERROR! $DBI::errstr\n";
21: }
```

✦   ✦   ✦

Fetching Data from the Database (Basics)

In Chapter 3, you learn to connect to the database and to create MySQL database tables. In this chapter, you work with data in the tables.

You'll be learning about the SQL SELECT keyword. SELECT is the SQL keyword you will use most often by far (along with FROM). All queries you perform on a database will begin with the SELECT keyword. Another keyword that will be in all of the queries you'll perform is FROM. SELECT tells the DBMS what you are looking for, and FROM tells the DBMS where to look for the data. SELECT and FROM are like Abbot and Costello—when you have one, you can always count on the other one being nearby.

When you create a query using the SQL keywords and table fields, the finished product is called a SELECT statement. Once you learn some of the basics of SELECT statements, we'll move on to some of the different ways to gain access to the data using the various methods the DBI gives us.

Following is the database structure used for this chapter, as well as the SQL statements needed to create the table if you have not yet done so. If you are using MySQL, you may want to download the code from the Web site for this book (www.wiley.com/extras). The code contains the tables and some sample data you can import into the tables—which should save you a lot of time.

```
+-----------+--------------+------+-----+---------+-------+
| Field     | Type         | Null | Key | Default | Extra |
+-----------+--------------+------+-----+---------+-------+
| isbn      | varchar(20)  | YES  |     | NULL    |       |
| title     | varchar(255) | YES  |     | NULL    |       |
| author    | varchar(255) | YES  |     | NULL    |       |
| price     | varchar(20)  | YES  |     | NULL    |       |
| format    | varchar(50)  | YES  |     | NULL    |       |
| publisher | varchar(255) | YES  |     | NULL    |       |
| pubdate   | varchar(50)  | YES  |     | NULL    |       |
| notes     | text         | YES  |     | NULL    |       |
+-----------+--------------+------+-----+---------+-------+
```

Below is the SQL to create a database in MySQL:

```
CREATE TABLE library (
    isbn varchar(20) default NULL,
    title varchar(255) default NULL,
    author varchar(255) default NULL,
    price varchar(20) default NULL,
    format varchar(50) default NULL,
    publisher varchar(255) default NULL,
    pubdate varchar(50) default NULL,
    notes text
) TYPE=MyISAM;
```

Simple SELECT Statement

Let's take a look at a short program that fetches some data from a table called *library* in our database. The library table is filled with information on many of the computer books in a personal library. In the following section, you'll see blocks of code; then you'll see an explanation of what the numbered lines mean. The numbers are added for clarity and are not part of the code.

Note   If you did not download the library data from the book's Web site, you will need to enter some sample data into the library table for these examples to work.

```
01: #!/usr/bin/perl -w
02: #
03: # select1.pl
04: # Chapter 4
05: # Listing 4-1
06: #

07: use strict;
08: use DBI;
```

Line 1 tells the system where to find Perl and turns on warnings with the -w flag.

Lines 2–6 are comments that provide information about the program.

Line 7 turns on the `strict` pragma. This forces programmers to use better pro-gramming practices, such as declaring variables before using them. Also, turning `strict` on can eliminate some hard-to-find bugs — such as using two variables with the same name.

Line 8 loads the DBI module — since we are interacting with a database, we need to load the `DataBase` interface.

```
09: my $dbh = DBI->connect
("DBI:mysql:BibleBook","bookuser","testpass")
10:     or die("Cannot connect: $DBI::errstr");
```

Lines 9–10 constitute a single Perl statement that tries to create an object of class DBI that represents a connection to the database. If the connection can't be made, our call to `DBI->connect` fails, and we abort the program with `die`. The `$dbh` stands for DataBase Handle.

```
11: my $sql = qq(SELECT * FROM library);
```

Line 11 is the SQL statement we use to fetch the data from the database table. The double quote operator (`qq`) works well when you are creating strings that may con-tain quotes. The qq operator acts just like a double quote, but you do not have to escape any double quotes that may be in the string.

This SQL statement tells the DBMS to fetch (`SELECT`) all of the data (`*`) `FROM` the requested table (library).

```
12: my $sth = $dbh->prepare($sql);
```

Line 12 calls the `prepare` method of the DBI. When you `prepare` an SQL statement, some databases store the SQL statement in an internally compiled form so that it executes faster when the `execute` method is called. MySQL does not compile the SQL statement but simply stores it. If you move from MySQL to a different database, however, you won't need to make any changes to work with the new database.

The `prepare` method returns a handle (`$sth`) used to access the DBI methods for that particular SQL statement. The `$sth` stands for Statement Handle.

```
13: $sth->execute;
```

```
14: my $counter = 1;
```

Line 13 calls the `execute` method on the SQL statement. This runs the SQL state-ment on the database — the results of the SQL call are stored as a reference in the statement handle (`$sth`).

Line 14 declares and initializes a variable named `$counter` to 1. We use this vari-able to count our records as we display the results of the SQL call.

```
15: while(my $record = $sth->fetch){
```

Line 15 begins a `while` loop that keeps returning data, one record at a time, until it runs out of data to return. The data it returns is from the result of the SQL call on **Line 13**.

Inside the `while` declaration, we declare a variable called `$record`. We use this variable as a pointer. Each time through the `while` loop, the `$sth->fetch` grabs one record from the results of the SQL call and stores a reference to an array in `$record`.

This may be a little hard to grasp at the moment, but it should click once we've gone through the next few lines of code. For now, just remember that `$record` holds a reference to an array. This is like saying `$record = \@foo;` when you are storing a reference to an array in regular Perl code.

```
16:       print "$counter: ";
```

Line 16 prints some text for our output and displays the current value in `$counter`.

```
17:       for my $field (@$record){
18:           print "$field - ";
19:       }
```

Line 17 begins a `for` loop that goes through each item in the array `@$record`. Of course, instead of "@$record" we could have written "@{$record}", which means exactly the same thing. If you aren't comfortable with either of these syntaxes, please refer to the perlreftut man page that comes free with Perl.

Line 18 prints the current field value (`$field`) from the loop and prints a dash with a space to separate the record data and make it a little easier to read. Each time through the `for` loop, the current record's field data gets stored in the `$field` variable.

Line 19 ends the `for` loop.

```
20:       $counter++;
21:       print "\n\n";
22: }
```

Line 20 increments the `$counter` variable—there is no point in having a counter if it is never incremented.

Line 21 prints two newline characters so that the output can be visually separated from one record to the next.

Line 22 ends the `while` loop as well as this program.

This program makes a connection to the database, creates an SQL statement to fetch all of the data from the library table, and then displays the results on the screen. A portion of this program's output is shown in the following code.

```
55: 1565922697 - Web Security and Commerce - Simson Garfinkel Gene Spafford
Deborah Russell (Editor) -      $34.95 - Paperback, 1st ed., 506pp. - O'Reilly
& Associates, Incorporated -  May 1997 -  -

56: 1565924924 - HTML: The Definitive Guide - Chuck Musciano Bill Kennedy Mike
Loukides (Editor) -      $34.95 - Paperback, 3rd ed., 587pp. - O'Reilly &
Associates, Incorporated -  September 1998 -  -

57: 0672308916 - PERL Programming Unleashed, with CD-ROM - Charles Salzenberg -
$34.95 -  Paperback, 800pp. -  Macmillan Computer Publishing -  February 1996 -
-

58: 1565925254 - Palm Programming: The Developer's Guide with CD-ROM - Neil
Rhodes Julie McKeehan -      $32.95 -  Paperback, 1st ed., 482pp. - O'Reilly &
Associates, Incorporated -  December 1998 -  -

59: 1565924207 - PalmPilot: The Ultimate Guide - David Pogue -      $29.95 -
Paperback, 1st ed., 489pp. -  O'Reilly & Associates, Incorporated -  May 1998 -
-

60: 0672304023 - UNIX, with CD-ROM (Unleashed) - Emmett Dulaney Susan
Christopherson Fran Hatton -      $29.95 -  Hardcover, 1st ed., 1600pp. -  Sams -
November 1993 -  -
```

SELECT statement with WHERE clause

Now we know how to get every record in a database. But if you want only some of the records, or just one, you don't want to have to sift through all of the data yourself to find what you are looking for. Instead, let the database do the work for you! We can slightly modify the first program so that it looks for only a particular record.

```
01: #!/usr/bin/perl -w
02: #
03: # select2.pl
04: # Chapter 4
05: # Listing 4-2
06: #

07: use strict;
08: use DBI;

09: my $dbh = DBI->connect
("DBI:mysql:BibleBook","bookuser","testpass")
10:     or die("Cannot connect: $DBI::errstr");
```

Lines 1–10 are exactly like the code in our first example.

```
11: my $sql = qq(SELECT * FROM library WHERE isbn =
'1565922697');
```

Line 11 has a SQL statement that causes the database to find a specific record for us.

The SQL statement starts out the same as in our first example, but now there is a WHERE statement. The entire WHERE statement is: WHERE isbn = '1565922697'. This tells the DBMS to look only for records where the isbn field is equal to 1565922697. Notice that we used a single = for a string comparison! This is because we are creating an *SQL* statement, which is different than a *Perl* statement.

In English, this is something like: *Select all records from the library table where the isbn field is equal to 1565922697.*

You are not limited to using just equals (=) in your WHERE statements. Logical operators and mathematical operators are also supported. Refer to Appendix B for some of the more common operators used with WHERE.

```
12: my $sth = $dbh->prepare($sql);

13: $sth->execute;

14: while(my $record = $sth->fetch){
15:     for my $field (@$record){
16:         print "$field\n";
17:     }
18:     print "\n\n";
19: }
```

Lines 12–19 work the same way as the code in our first example. Notice, though, that we have removed the code that acts as a counter. Since we are looking for one match only, there is no need to count how many records are returned.

The output should contain only one record, as shown in the following code.

```
1565922697
Web Security and Commerce
Simson Garfinkel Gene Spafford Deborah Russell (Editor)
    $34.95
 Paperback, 1st ed., 506pp.
 O'Reilly & Associates, Incorporated
May 1997
```

Note   If you have entered your own data into the database, instead of downloading the table information from the Web site, you will have to change the SQL statement in Line 11 so that the WHERE statement looks for something that matches your data.

SELECT statement with ORDER BY clause

The DBMS can do more than just fetch the data; it can perform operations on the data so that it is displayed exactly how you want it to.

For example, you may want the data to be returned sorted on the publisher field. To do that, use the ORDER BY clause.

```
01: #!/usr/bin/perl -w
02: #
03: # select3.pl
04: # Chapter 4
05: # Listing 4-3
06: #

07: use strict;
08: use DBI;

09: my $dbh = DBI->connect
("DBI:mysql:BibleBook","bookuser","testpass")
10:     or die("Cannot connect: $DBI::errstr");
```

Lines 1-10 are exactly like the code from our first example.

```
11: my $sql = qq(SELECT * FROM library ORDER BY publisher);
```

Line 11 contains the new SQL statement. Notice that the only difference here is the ORDER BY publisher statement. This causes the DBMS to sort the output by the specified field (publisher in this case). Determining that the program output is sorted is difficult, especially since only three of the records are shown in the following output. Run this program on your system to verify the results. If you want, change publisher to one of the other field names such as author or title to verify that the output is indeed sorted

```
12: my $sth = $dbh->prepare($sql);

13: $sth->execute;

14: my $counter = 1;

15: while(my $record = $sth->fetch){
```

Lines 12–15 are identical to the code in our first example, running the search and then looping through each record returned.

```
16:     print "Book #$counter:\n";
17:     for my $field(@$record){
18:         print "$field\n";
19:     }
```

Line 16 prints the book number and a newline.

Line 17 begins a `for` loop that iterates through all of the data for this record and stores the current data in the `$field` variable. Remember, `$record` is a *reference* to an array containing the data for the current record. By using `@$record`, we are simply looping through the array.

Line 18 prints the current item and a newline character.

Line 19 ends the `for` loop that begins on **Line 17**.

```
20:      $counter++;
21:      print "\n";
22: }
```

Line 20 increments the `$counter` variable.

Line 21 prints a newline character.

Line 22 ends the `while` loop, as well as the program.

Take a look at the output in the following code. The data should be sorted on whatever field you put in your SQL statement on **Line 11**.

```
Book #58:
0471118494
The HTML SourceBook
Ian S. Graham
     $34.95
 Paperback, 432pp.
 Wiley, John & Sons, Incorporated
 February 1995


Book #59:
0471247448
Official Guide to Programming with CGI.pm
Lincoln Stein
     $34.99
 Paperback, 1st ed., 310pp.
 Wiley, John & Sons, Incorporated
 April 1998


Book #60:
1861000723
Professional Active Server Pages
Alex Homer Richard Harrison Brian Francis Christian Gross
Darren Gill
    Bruce Hartwell Stephen Jakab Andrew Enfield Chris Ullman
(Editor) Tim
```

```
    Briggs (Editor)
       $12.95
Paperback, 641pp.
Wrox Press, Inc.
March 1997
```

Counting Your Matches

We've seen a couple different ways to select data. What if we don't want all of that data but instead want just the number of items that match? SQL has a COUNT function for this purpose.

```perl
01: #!/usr/bin/perl -w
02: #
03: # select4.pl
04: # Chapter 4
05: # Listing 4-4
06: #

07: use strict;
08: use DBI;

09: my $dbh = DBI->connect
("DBI:mysql:BibleBook","bookuser","testpass")
10:      or die("Cannot connect: $DBI::errstr");
```

Lines 1–10 are again very similar to the other program listings in this chapter.

```perl
11: my $sql = qq(SELECT COUNT(*) FROM library);
```

Line 11 is our SQL statement that uses the COUNT function. This statement tells the DBMS to count all of the records that contain data in any field in the library table. The * is a wildcard character and stands for all of the fields in this table—so if any of the fields in a record contain data, then it is counted as a match.

```perl
12: my $sth = $dbh->prepare($sql);

13: $sth->execute;

14: while(my $record = $sth->fetch){
```

Lines 12–14 are identical to our previous examples.

```perl
15:      print "You have $record->[0] books.";
16:      print "\n";
17: }
```

Line 15, however, is a bit different. We *could* have left it the same as the corresponding line in the other programs, but attempting to loop through an array with only a single item in it would be a bit wasteful. Instead, we still use the $record variable as a pointer to the array but we want only element 0 (the first item in the array) because we know that there is going to be only one element returned to us. In this case, we use the arrow operator, a.k.a. the dereferencing operator. Remember, the variable $record is a reference to an array. By using $record->[0], we dereference the array to get element 0. Another way to write this is ${$record}[0], but that is much harder to read than a simple $record->[0].

Recall that since $record holds an arrayref, we access its first element with $record->[0], not $record[0] — since $record->[0] means "element 0 in the array that $record points to," whereas $record[0] means "element 0 in the array @record." So if you get warnings from Perl that you're trying to access an undeclared variable @record, it's probably because you said something $record[0] when you meant $record->[0].

As you can see in the following code, there isn't much of an output for this program, but it does exactly what we've programmed it to do.

```
You have 60 books.
```

Grouping Your Output

Grouping (GROUP BY) your data is different from *ordering* (ORDER BY) your data. When you use the GROUP BY statement, your data is grouped together in the field(s) that you specify in the SQL statement.

Grouped together means the data is aggregated so that you do not get multiple records with the same data. Think of this like data buckets. Each bucket can hold a number of items, and we are able to count how many items are in each bucket.

Take a look at the following example; this concept should become much clearer:

```
01: #!/usr/bin/perl -w
02: #
03: # select5.pl
04: # Chapter 4
05: # Listing 4-5
06: #

07: use strict;
08: use DBI;

09: my $dbh = DBI->connect
("DBI:mysql:BibleBook","bookuser","testpass")
10:     or die("Cannot connect: $DBI::errstr");
```

Lines 1–10 reuse code from the earlier examples in this chapter.

```
11: my $sql = qq(SELECT COUNT(*), publisher FROM library GROUP
BY publisher);
```

Line 11 is our SQL statement, but it looks a bit different from the others.

This SQL statement shows a feature of the SQL SELECT statement that we have not used yet. After the SELECT and before the FROM statement, instead of putting an asterisk, we place a COUNT(*) statement *and* a database field name.

In English, this SQL statement sounds something like this: *Select the total number of matching items along with the publisher field from the library table, and then group the results by publisher.*

The COUNT(*) is the number of matches for each item we group on (publisher in this case). The publisher field is exactly that — the publisher field. We end up with the number of books from each publisher (because of the count(*) statement) and each publisher's name (because of the publisher field after the SELECT statement).

```
12: my $sth = $dbh->prepare($sql);

13: $sth->execute;

14: while(my $record = $sth->fetch){
15:     for my $field(@$record){
16:         print "$field ";
17:     }
18:     print "\n";
19: }
```

Lines 12-19 are very similar to the code we have already covered in this chapter. We have, however, removed the counter code, since we've decided to let the DBMS handle the counting for us in this example.

As you can see in the following code, this program produces an output that is very different from that of the other programs we've been working with. The first column is the total number of books from the publisher, the name of which is listed in the second column.

```
8   Addison Wesley Longman, Inc.
1   Coriolis Group
4   IDG Books Worldwide
3   Macmillan Computer Publishing
1   Manning Publications Company
5   McGraw-Hill Companies, The
1   New Riders Publishing
22  O'Reilly & Associates, Incorporated
2   Prentice Hall
8   Sams
```

```
1  Specialized Systems Consultants
3  Wiley, John & Sons, Incorporated
1  Wrox Press, Inc.
```

Why use the COUNT function instead of just setting up a counter and incrementing it? Setting up and incrementing a counter means you have to go through *each* data item and increment the counter *each* time to maintain an accurate count. If you have a small data-set, that may be no big deal. But if you have a large data-set, it can take quite a bit longer. The COUNT function in SQL is optimized internally and doesn't have to iterate through each data element to get the count. Whenever you can, use COUNT; it can definitely make a difference in program-execution speed.

Also, consider this: if you use a counter for the preceding program, you have to keep track of each publisher somehow, incrementing the counter for that publisher only. If you have books from 100 publishers, your code will get pretty unmanageable!

Other DBI Data-Retrieval Functions

Now that we have covered the basics of fetching data from a database table using the Perl DBI, we'll cover some alternative ways in Perl to fetch the data. In addition, we'll dabble with making our output look a little nicer.

With Perl and the DBI, you are not stuck using the fetch function ($sth->fetch) to get data; there are several different ways to do so. There are fetchrow_array, fetchrow_arrayref, fetchrow_hashref, and fetchall_arrayref. You can choose whichever method or methods you wish. You will probably become comfortable with one of the methods and use that one most often, which is perfectly fine. Remember that with Perl *there is more than one way to do it*.

The functions fetch and fetchrow_arrayref do the exact same thing, so we'll skip any further explanation of fetchrow_arrayref, since fetch has been covered so well in our previous examples.

fetchrow_array

Since we've been dealing with array references up to this point, working with actual arrays is now appropriate. The following code shows the fetchrow_array function.

```
01: #!/usr/bin/perl -w
02: #
03: # select6.pl
04: # Chapter 4
05: # Listing 4-6#

07: use strict;
08: use DBI;
```

```
09: my $dbh = DBI->connect
("DBI:mysql:BibleBook","bookuser","testpass")
10:    or die("Cannot connect: $DBI::errstr");
```

Lines 1–10 are very similar to the corresponding lines in the previous programs in this chapter.

```
11: my $sql = qq(SELECT isbn, price, title FROM library);
```

Line 11 is our SQL statement. This time, we fetch only the isbn, price, and title of the books instead of every field for each record. You do not have to fetch all of the data each time you perform a SELECT on a database — you can tell the DBMS exactly which fields you want by placing them after the SELECT statement instead of using a *.

```
12: my $sth = $dbh->prepare($sql);
```

```
13: $sth->execute;
```

Lines 12 and **13** are also identical to our previous examples.

```
14: while(my @array = $sth->fetchrow_array){
```

Line 14 looks similar to the previous examples, but we are now dealing with an actual array instead of a reference to an array.

Each time through the while loop, we fetch one row of data. Each field of the current record gets stored in the array. If you look at the output from this example, you can see that element 0 of the array contains the isbn, that element 1 contains the price, and that element 2 contains the title.

```
15:    no warnings;
16:    my $index = 0;
```

Line 15 turns off warnings. If we try to print the data and a field from the table we are selecting data from is empty, a warning message gets printed out each time. The warning messages generated as a result of this are no big deal; we know what is causing them. Instead of having our output littered with warnings, we simply turn them off. When warnings are turned off like this, it applies to the current block only — so once we exit that block of code, warnings are back on.

Line 16 declares a variable called $index and initializes it with a value of 0.

```
17:    for my $data(@array){
18:        print "\$array[$index] contains $data\n";
19:        $index++;
20:    }
```

Line 17 begins a for loop that loops through the @array and stores the current value from @array into the $data variable.

Line 18 prints the text shown in the program output.

Line 19 increments the $index variable.

Line 20 closes the for loop.

```
21:     print "\n";
22: }
```

Line 21 prints a final newline so that the output of each record is visually separated.

Line 22 closes the while loop. This line marks the end of the program.

The following code shows the output of this program.

```
$array[0] contains 1565922697
$array[1] contains     $34.95
$array[2] contains Web Security and Commerce

$array[0] contains 1565924924
$array[1] contains     $34.95
$array[2] contains HTML: The Definitive Guide

$array[0] contains 0672308916
$array[1] contains     $34.95
$array[2] contains PERL Programming Unleashed, with CD-ROM

$array[0] contains 1565925254
$array[1] contains     $32.95
$array[2] contains Palm Programming: The Developer's Guide with
CD-ROM

$array[0] contains 1565924207
$array[1] contains     $29.95
$array[2] contains PalmPilot: The Ultimate Guide

$array[0] contains 0672304023
$array[1] contains     $29.95
$array[2] contains UNIX, with CD-ROM (Unleashed)
```

Remember that with the fetchrow_array method, the result is an actual array rather than a pointer to an array. Depending on how you are using the data and how much data you have to access, it may be easier to deal with an array rather than a reference to an array; the choice is yours.

fetchall_arrayref

The `fetchall_arrayref` function can be a bit trickier to work with than the `fetchrow_array` function, since what you end up with is a reference to an array — where each row of the referenced array is a reference to *another* array containing the data for that row. Confused? The following example should help clear things up a bit:

```perl
01: #!/usr/bin/perl -w
02: #
03: # select7.pl
04: # Chapter 4
05: # Listing 4-7
06: #

07: use strict;
08: use DBI;

09: my $dbh = DBI->connect
("DBI:mysql:BibleBook","bookuser","testpass")
10:      or die("Cannot connect: $DBI::errstr");

11: my $sql = qq(SELECT * FROM library);

12: my $sth = $dbh->prepare($sql);

13: $sth->execute;
```

Lines 1–13 are almost identical to the previous programs. Please refer back if you are uncertain what these lines do.

```perl
14: my $ref = $sth->fetchall_arrayref;

15: my $record_idx = 0;
```

Line 14 is the call to the `fetchall_arrayref` function. Notice that we do not have to have a loop that calls the `fetch` function several times.

Line 15 declares a variable named `$record_idx` and initializes it to 0. This is our record index and is the first of two counters for this program.

```perl
16: for my $rec (@$ref){
```

Line 16 is a `for` loop that loops through the array referenced in `$ref`. Each time through the loop, `$rec` gets set to a reference to an array that holds one row of data. (This is our second reference). At this point, with `$rec`, we have data that is like the data when we use the `fetch` method.

We basically have something like this: Reference ⇨ Reference ⇨ Data

```
17:      no warnings;
18:      my $field_idx = 0;
```

Line 17 turns off warnings for this block. Several of the data elements are blank, so turning off warnings suppresses these messages when the program is run.

Line 18 declares a variable named $field_idx and initializes it to 0. This is the second counter, field index; we'll use this to keep track of where we are (what field we are at) in the arrays.

```
19:      for my $field (@$rec){
20:          print "ref[$record_idx][$field_idx] = $field\n";
21:          $field_idx++;
22:      }
```

Line 19 begins a for loop that iterates through the current array reference that we get from **Line 16**.

Line 20 prints the current data along with where it is referenced. The output of the program shows you what this looks like.

Line 21 increments $field_idx, the second counter.

Line 22 closes the inner for loop.

```
23:      $record_idx++;
24:      print "\n";
25: }
```

Line 23 increments the first counter, $record_idx.

Line 24 prints a newline character so that we can visually separate the different records in our output.

Line 25 closes the outer for loop.

```
26: print "\n";
```

```
27: print "$ref->[57][1]\n\n";
```

Line 26 prints a newline.

Line 27 is an example of how you can print a specific item from the result set. In this example, we want to print only a specific field from a specific record — namely, field 1 from record 57 from the arrayref in $ref. That is, $ref->[57][1].

The following code shows the output of this program.

```
ref[57][0] = 1565925254
ref[57][1] = Palm Programming: The Developer's Guide with
CD-ROM
ref[57][2] = Neil Rhodes Julie McKeehan
ref[57][3] =      $32.95
ref[57][4] =  Paperback, 1st ed., 482pp.
ref[57][5] =  O'Reilly & Associates, Incorporated
ref[57][6] =  December 1998
ref[57][7] =

ref[58][0] = 1565924207
ref[58][1] = PalmPilot: The Ultimate Guide
ref[58][2] = Tim O'Reilly (Editor)
ref[58][3] =      $29.95
ref[58][4] =  Paperback, 1st ed., 489pp.
ref[58][5] =  O'Reilly & Associates, Incorporated
ref[58][6] =  May 1998
ref[58][7] =

ref[59][0] = 0672304023
ref[59][1] = UNIX, with CD-ROM (Unleashed)
ref[59][2] = Emmett Dulaney Susan Christopherson Fran Hatton
ref[59][3] =      $29.95
ref[59][4] =  Hardcover, 1st ed., 1600pp.
ref[59][5] =  Sams
ref[59][6] =  November 1993
ref[59][7] =


Palm Programming: The Developer's Guide with CD-ROM
```

There are a couple important things to remember when using fetchall_arrayref.

✦ If you have a lot of data, it will *all* be loaded into memory as a result of a call with this function. If you are dealing with a large number of matching records, consider using one of the other data-access methods.

✦ The data returned from a fetchall_arrayref call is not always *all* of the matching records. Instead, it is all of the remaining matching records. So, if you have gone through the first 10 results with the fetchrow_array function, a call to fetchall_arrayref will return results 11 through the end.

fetchrow_hashref

The fetchrow_hashref method of data access is one of the best. Instead of having to deal with arrays and array indexing, you can access the data via a hash; the keys of the hash are the field names of the data.

```
01: #!/usr/bin/perl -w
02: #
```

```
03: # select8.pl
04: # Chapter 4
05: # Listing 4-8
06: #

07: use strict;
08: use DBI;

09: my $dbh = DBI->connect
("DBI:mysql:BibleBook","bookuser","testpass")
10:      or die("Cannot connect: $DBI::errstr");

11: my $sql = qq(SELECT * FROM library);

12: my $sth = $dbh->prepare($sql);

13: $sth->execute;
```

This program is also quite similar to the others we've worked with so far, but we have made a few changes because we are using the fetchrow_hashref function. If you haven't noticed yet, most of the data-access methods in the DBI are very similar.

Lines 1–13 are again nearly identical to the previous examples; if you have questions about what something is doing, please look back in this chapter for a more detailed explanation.

```
14: my $counter = 1;
```

Line 14 declares a variable named $counter and initializes it to 1. We use this variable to keep the current record number.

```
15: while(my $record = $sth->fetchrow_hashref){
```

Line 15 begins a while loop that fetches a row of data at a time. The $record inside of the while loop declaration stores a reference to a hash of the current record. This is almost identical to the fetch and fetchrow_arrayref functions, but we store a hash reference instead of an array reference.

```
16:      no warnings;
17:      print "Book #$counter\n";
```

Line 16 turns off warnings. Some of the fields in the database are empty, and if we try to use these fields in the program's output, we end up triggering a warning each time. Since we know what causes these warnings, we can safely turn them off for this block of code.

Line 17 prints the current book number.

```
18:     print "Title:      $record->{title}\n";
19:     print "Author:     $record->{author}\n";
20:     print "Publisher: $record->{publisher}\n";
21:     print "Cost:        $record->{price}\n";
```

Lines 18–21 print a label and the database-field information for the current record. Notice that the hash keys are the same as the database field names. These hash keys are taken directly from the database. They are case sensitive, so make sure you use the exact spelling you use with the database fields.

```
22:     print "\n";
23:     $counter++;
24: }
```

Line 22 prints an extra newline character so that each record is shown separately and easier to distinguish.

Line 23 increments the `$counter` variable.

Line 24 ends the `while` loop and the program.

The following code shows the output of this program.

```
Book #58
Title:     Palm Programming: The Developer's Guide with CD-ROM
Author:    Neil Rhodes Julie McKeehan
Publisher: O'Reilly & Associates, Incorporated
Cost:           $32.95

Book #59
Title:     PalmPilot: The Ultimate Guide
Author:    Tim O'Reilly (Editor)
Publisher: O'Reilly & Associates, Incorporated
Cost:           $29.95

Book #60
Title:     UNIX, with CD-ROM (Unleashed)
Author:    Emmett Dulaney Susan Christopherson Fran Hatton
Publisher: Sams
Cost:           $29.95
```

The `fetchrow_hashref` function is as easy to use, if not easier, as the array methods. The best thing about this function is that it is easy to tell exactly what database field you are dealing with, since the key value is actually the field name from the database. Working with the field names instead of with an array index also makes the code clearer for anyone who reads it or for anyone may have to come back and maintain it.

Simple Data-Retrieval Wrap-up

We've covered five methods of fetching data with the DBI. (Actually, we've covered four methods, as `fetch` and `fetchrow_arrayref` are the same.) Getting data from a database with Perl should be a breeze for you at this point, and none of our example programs have gone over 25 lines yet!

We are going to cover one final example, which uses one of the data-access methods we just learned about. But this example is going to make the output of the program a little more user friendly. This example reinforces what you've already learned, showing you another way to deal with warnings.

```
01: #!/usr/bin/perl -w
02: #
03: # select9.pl
04: # Chapter 4
05: # Listing 4-9
06: #

07: use strict;
08: use DBI;

09: my $dbh = DBI->connect
("DBI:mysql:BibleBook","bookuser","testpass")
10:     or die("Cannot connect: $DBI::errstr");

11: my $sql = qq(SELECT * FROM library);

12: my $sth = $dbh->prepare($sql);

13: $sth->execute;

14: my $counter = 1;
```

Lines 1–14 are again almost identical to our previous examples.

```
15: while(my $record = $sth->fetchrow_hashref){
```

Line 15 begins the `while` loop that fetches the data one row at a time and stores a reference to a hash containing the data in the variable `$record`.

```
16:     for my $field (keys %$record){
17:         $record->{$field} = "N/A" unless $record->{$field};
18:         $record->{$field} =~ s/^\W+//;
19:         $record->{$field} =~ s/\015?\012//g;
20:     }
```

Line 16 begins a `for` loop that loops through each of the `keys` in the hash `%$p`.

The addition of this loop is something that we have not done yet. This loop is intended to check the data and to filter some of the characters we don't want out of the data. It also helps us eliminate the warnings we get when we try to print a blank database item.

Line 17 sets the current value at `$record->{$field}` to N/A if it is currently a blank field. By doing this, we get rid of any warnings generated by trying to print blank data.

Line 18 gets rid of any nonword characters at the beginning of the string. Many of the fields originally contain spaces at the beginning. This line removes those spaces so that our output is aligned and looks much better.

The regular expression replacement `s/^\W+//;` breaks down like this:

- ✦ `^` means we are looking at the beginning of the string.

- ✦ `\W` means any nonword characters; this includes spaces and control characters.

- ✦ `+` means matching the expression one *or more* times. If there is one nonword character, or 100 nonword characters at the beginning of the line, this expression will get rid of all of them.

- ✦ `//` at the end is what we are substituting any matched characters with — nothing. This expression removes any nonword characters from the beginning of the string.

Line 19 is another regular expression. This time, the regular expression is looking for carriage-return characters or linefeed characters.

`\015` is the octal value for a carriage return, and `\012` is the octal value for a linefeed. The operating system the program is running on determines exactly what constitutes a newline. Some systems use only a linefeed, but some use both. This regular expression takes care of most situations. The `\015?\012` means the carriage return may or may not be present, but if it is, that's ok. The `\012` means the linefeed is always present.

Simply put, this regular expression removes all newlines from the string. The `g` on the end means to apply this regular expression *globally* to the string. If we eliminate the `g`, only the first instance of a newline will be removed from the string.

Line 20 ends the `for` loop that removes the characters we don't want our strings to contain.

```
21:     print "Book #$counter\n";
22:     print "Title:     $record->{title}\n";
23:     print "Author:    $record->{author}\n";
24:     print "Publisher: $record->{publisher}\n";
```

```
25:     print "ISBN:      $record->{isbn}\n";
26:     print "Cost:      $record->{price}\n";
27:     print "Pub Date:  $record->{pubdate}\n";
28:     print "\n";
29:     $counter++;
30: }
```

Line 21 prints the current book number.

Lines 22–27 print the data. All data elements should end up aligned with each other, since we have removed any leading spaces.

Line 28 prints a newline to separate each record.

Line 29 increments $counter so that our book number remains correct.

Line 30 ends the while loop as well as the program.

The output of this program, shown in the following code, looks the best yet. One thing to consider when creating database applications is that when you present data to the user, the data should be in a neat, easy-to-read format.

```
Book #58
Title:     Palm Programming: The Developer's Guide with CD-ROM
Author:    Neil Rhodes Julie McKeehan
Publisher: O'Reilly & Associates, Incorporated
ISBN:      1565925254
Cost:      32.95
Pub Date:  December 1998

Book #59
Title:     PalmPilot: The Ultimate Guide
Author:    Tim O'Reilly (Editor)
Publisher: O'Reilly & Associates, Incorporated
ISBN:      1565924207
Cost:      29.95
Pub Date:  May 1998

Book #60
Title:     UNIX, with CD-ROM (Unleashed)
Author:    Emmett Dulaney Susan Christopherson Fran Hatton
Publisher: Sams
ISBN:      0672304023
Cost:      29.95
Pub Date:  November 1993
```

Summary

This chapter deals with the basics of getting data from the database to your Perl programs. Recall that there are a number of different ways to get the data from the database: (`fetch`, `fetchrow_arrayref`, `fetchrow_array`, `fetchall_arrayref`, and `fetchrow_hashref`).

Don't forget that `fetch` and `fetchrow_arrayref` do the exact same thing. For brevity's sake, you may want to use only the `fetch` method.

Keep in mind that if you make a call to the `fetchall_arrayref` function, you should not use it if you are dealing with a large amount of data. Also, remember that it returns only the data remaining since the last fetch-type call.

Try these example programs, and try to change them so that you can get different data and see how it all works. Try things like changing the `SELECT *` statements so you get only specific fields. Or change the code so that the output from the programs is much nicer. Don't be afraid to change the code and to experiment; you won't break the computer!

Although being able to get data from the database is nice, we are ready to move to the next level — manipulating the data in the database. The next section shows you how to add records, delete records, and update existing records. Add this to your growing arsenal of Perl-database knowledge, and you'll soon be writing powerful, data-driven applications!

Program Listings

Listings 4-1 to 4-9 show the complete code for the programs in the chapter.

Listing 4-1: **select.pl**

```
01: #!/usr/bin/perl -w
02: #
03: # select1.pl
04: # Chapter 4
05: # Listing 4-1
06: #

07: use strict;
08: use DBI;

09: my $dbh = DBI->connect
("DBI:mysql:BibleBook","bookuser","testpass")
10:     or die("Cannot connect: $DBI::errstr");
```

Continued

Listing 4-1 *(continued)*

```
11: my $sql = qq(SELECT * FROM library);

12: my $sth = $dbh->prepare($sql);

13: $sth->execute;

14: my $counter = 1;

15: while(my $record = $sth->fetch){
16:     print "$counter: ";
17:     for my $field (@$record){
18:         print "$field - ";
19:     }
20:     $counter++;
21:     print "\n\n";
22: }
```

Listing 4-2: select2.pl

```
01: #!/usr/bin/perl -w
02: #
03: # select2.pl
04: # Chapter 4
05: # Listing 4-2
06: #

07: use strict;
08: use DBI;

09: my $dbh = DBI->connect
("DBI:mysql:BibleBook","bookuser","testpass")
10:     or die("Cannot connect: $DBI::errstr");

11: my $sql = qq(SELECT * FROM library WHERE isbn =
'1565924347');

12: my $sth = $dbh->prepare($sql);

13: $sth->execute;

14: while(my $record = $sth->fetch){
15:     for my $field (@$record){
16:         print "$field\n";
17:     }
18:     print "\n\n";
19: }
```

Listing 4-3: **select3.pl**

```
01: #!/usr/bin/perl -w
02: #
03: # select3.pl
04: # Chapter 4
05: # Listing 4-3
06: #

07: use strict;
08: use DBI;

09: my $dbh = DBI->connect
("DBI:mysql:BibleBook","bookuser","testpass")
10:     or die("Cannot connect: $DBI::errstr");

11: my $sql = qq(SELECT * FROM library ORDER BY publisher);

12: my $sth = $dbh->prepare($sql);

13: $sth->execute;

14: my $counter = 1;

15: while(my $record = $sth->fetch){
16:     print "Book #$counter:\n";
17:     for my $field (@$record){
18:         print "$field\n";
19:     }
20:     $counter++;
21:     print "\n";
22: }
```

Listing 4-4: **select4.pl**

```
01: #!/usr/bin/perl -w
02: #
03: # select4.pl
04: # Chapter 4
05: # Listing 4-4
06: #

07: use strict;
08: use DBI;

09: my $dbh = DBI->connect
("DBI:mysql:BibleBook","bookuser","testpass")
10:     or die("Cannot connect: $DBI::errstr");
```

Continued

Listing 4-4 *(continued)*

```
11: my $sql = qq(SELECT COUNT(*) FROM library);

12: my $sth = $dbh->prepare($sql);

13: $sth->execute;

14: while(my $record = $sth->fetch){
15:     print "You have $record->[0] books.";
16:     print "\n";
17: }
```

Listing 4-5: **select5.pl**

```
01: #!/usr/bin/perl -w
02: #
03: # select5.pl
04: # Chapter 4
05: # Listing 4-5
06: #

07: use strict;
08: use DBI;

09: my $dbh = DBI->connect
("DBI:mysql:BibleBook","bookuser","testpass")
10:     or die("Cannot connect: $DBI::errstr");

11: my $sql = qq(SELECT COUNT(*), publisher FROM library GROUP
BY publisher);

12: my $sth = $dbh->prepare($sql);

13: $sth->execute;

14: while(my $record = $sth->fetch){
15:     for my $field (@$record){
16:         print "$field ";
17:     }
18:     print "\n";
19: }
```

Listing 4-6: **select6.pl**

```
01: #!/usr/bin/perl -w
02: #
03: # select6.pl
04: # Chapter 4
05: # Listing 4-6
06: #

07: use strict;
08: use DBI;

09: my $dbh = DBI->connect
("DBI:mysql:BibleBook","bookuser","testpass")
10:     or die("Cannot connect: $DBI::errstr");

11: my $sql = qq(SELECT isbn, price, title FROM library);

12: my $sth = $dbh->prepare($sql);

13: $sth->execute;

14: while(my @array = $sth->fetchrow_array){
15:     no warnings;
16:     my $index = 0;
17:     for my $data (@array){
18:         print "\$array[$index] contains $data\n";
19:         $index++;
20:     }
21:     print "\n";
22: }
```

Listing 4-7: **select7.pl**

```
01: #!/usr/bin/perl -w
02: #
03: # select7.pl
04: # Chapter 4
05: # Listing 4-7
06: #

07: use strict;
08: use DBI;

09: my $dbh = DBI->connect
```

Continued

Listing 4-7 *(continued)*

```
("DBI:mysql:BibleBook","bookuser","testpass")
10:     or die("Cannot connect: $DBI::errstr");

11: my $sql = qq(SELECT * FROM library);

12: my $sth = $dbh->prepare($sql);

13: $sth->execute;

14: my $ref = $sth->fetchall_arrayref;

15: my $record_idx = 0;

16: for my $rec (@$ref){
17:     no warnings;
18:     my $field_idx = 0;
19:     for my $field (@$rec){
20:         print "ref[$record_idx][$field_idx] = $field\n";
21:         $field_idx++;
22:     }
23:     $record_idx++;
24:     print "\n";
25: }
26: print "\n";
27: print "$ref->[57][1]\n\n";
```

Listing 4-8: **select8.pl**

```
01: #!/usr/bin/perl -w
02: #
03: # select8.pl
04: # Chapter 4
05: # Listing 4-8
06: #

07: use strict;
08: use DBI;

09: my $dbh = DBI->connect
("DBI:mysql:BibleBook","bookuser","testpass")
10:     or die("Cannot connect: $DBI::errstr");

11: my $sql = qq(SELECT * FROM library);
```

```
12: my $sth = $dbh->prepare($sql);

13: $sth->execute;

14: my $counter = 1;

15: while(my $record = $sth->fetchrow_hashref){
16:     no warnings;
17:     print "Book #$counter\n";
18:     print "Title:     $record->{title}\n";
19:     print "Author:    $record->{author}\n";
20:     print "Publisher: $record->{publisher}\n";
21:     print "Cost:      $record->{price}\n";
22:     print "\n";
23:     $counter++;
24: }
```

Listing 4-9: **select9.pl**

```
01: #!/usr/bin/perl -w
02: #
03: # select8.pl
04: # Chapter 4
05: # Listing 4-9
06: #

07: use strict;
08: use DBI;

09: my $dbh = DBI->connect
("DBI:mysql:BibleBook","bookuser","testpass")
10:     or die("Cannot connect: $DBI::errstr");

11: my $sql = qq(SELECT * FROM library);

12: my $sth = $dbh->prepare($sql);

13: $sth->execute;

14: my $counter = 1;

15: while(my $record = $sth->fetchrow_hashref){
16:     for my $field (keys %$record){
17:         $record->{$field} = "N/A" unless $record->{$field};
18:         $record->{$field} =~ s/^\W+//;
19:         $record->{$field} =~ s/\015?\012//g;
20:     }
```

Continued

Listing 4-9 *(continued)*

```
21:     print "Book #$counter\n";
22:     print "Title:     $record->{title}\n";
23:     print "Author:    $record->{author}\n";
24:     print "Publisher: $record->{publisher}\n";
25:     print "ISBN:      $record->{isbn}\n";
26:     print "Cost       $record->{price}\n";
27:     print "Pub Date:  $record->{pubdate}\n";
28:     print "\n";
29:     $counter++;
30: }
```

✦   ✦   ✦

Making Changes to Your Data

In Chapter 4, you learn how to get data from a database, but working with databases involves much more than just getting data—it involves adding data, modifying existing data, and deleting data. This chapter covers the basics of these three essential database-manipulation skills.

Because SQL is modeled after the English language, you can count on SQL statements being quite easy to remember. For adding data to a database, use the SQL statement ADD. UPDATE modifies an existing record, and DELETE removes a record from a table.

Once we have covered those three basic data-manipulation operations, we will bring it all together into a comprehensive program that will give you a working example. This example program could then be used as a starting point for more powerful database applications.

This chapter still deals with very basic database concepts. Once we get into more advanced chapters, you will learn many shortcuts and more powerful ways to deal with the data in a database.

Before we begin walking through the example programs for this chapter, be aware that we are still using our "library" table for our examples. This is a very simple, single-table database we are using to store the book data. As we get into the advanced chapters, we will deal with some database normalization and multiple tables.

Using ADD

Our first example deals with adding data to the database. The user interface for this program is simply the command line. The program allows the user to enter one item into the database. Although the program is functional, it is not very user-friendly. We will be creating user interfaces with more features as we progress in this book.

```
01: #!/usr/bin/perl -w
02: #
03: # program 5-1
04: # Chapter 5
05: # Listing 1
06: #

07: use strict;
08: use DBI;
```

Line 1 tells the system where to find Perl and turns on warnings with the -w flag.

Lines 2–6 are comments that provide information about the program. You may notice that inside the application I use very few comments. The only reason for this is because I am providing detailed comments about the code here. Normally, I use generous comments in my code so that if anyone needs to maintain the program, or just wants to see what it does, he or she can easily do so by looking at the comments. Comments are good; use them generously.

Line 7 turns on the strict pragma. This forces the programmer to use better programming practices, such as declaring variables before they are used. Using the strict pragma helps the programmer avoid many common mistakes, like inadvertently reusing a variable name.

Line 8 loads the DBI module. The DBI module is required for programs that connect to a database. The module is well written and has become the de-facto standard in Perl database programming.

```
09: my $conn = DBI->connect
("DBI:mysql:BibleBook","bookuser","testpass")
10:    or die("Cannot connect: $DBI::errstr");
```

Lines 9–10 form a single Perl statement that tries to create an object of class DBI that represents a connection to the database. If the connection cannot be made, our call to DBI->connect will fail, and we will abort the program by using die.

```
11: my ($sql, %book, @keys);

12: Get_Data();
13: Execute_Transaction();
```

Line 11 declares some variables that we'll use in this program.

Line 12 calls the `Get_Data` subroutine. This subroutine gathers the book information from the user.

Line 13 calls the `Execute_Transaction` subroutine. This is the subroutine that writes data to the database.

```
14: sub Get_Data{
15:      $book{'isbn'}       = Get_Input("Enter ISBN #");
16:      $book{'title'}      = Get_Input("Enter Book Title");
17:      $book{'author'}     = Get_Input("Enter Book Author");
18:      $book{'price'}      = Get_Input("Enter Book Price");
19:      $book{'format'}     = Get_Input("Enter Book Format");
20:      $book{'publisher'}  = Get_Input("Enter Book Publisher");
21:      $book{'pubdate'}    = Get_Input("Enter Publish Date");
22:      $book{'notes'}      = Get_Input("Enter Notes");

23:      return 1;
24: }
```

Line 14 begins the `Get_Data` subroutine.

Lines 15–22 populate the `%book` hash. The data, which was returned from each call to `Get_Input`, is stored in the `%book` hash at the corresponding hash key.

Line 23 returns 1 from the subroutine. Returning a true value, 1 in this case, is a common Perl programming practice. Returning a true value makes it easy for a programmer to test whether or not the subroutine completed successfully.

Line 24 closes the `Get_Data` subroutine.

```
25: sub Get_Input {
26:      print $_[0], ":\n";
27:      return scalar <STDIN>;
28: }
```

Line 25 begins the `Get_Input` subroutine.

Line 26 prints the first item passed to this subroutine then a colon and a newline. The text that gets printed is the field name so that the user knows what field they are entering data for.

Line 27 returns the value that was entered by the user. The handle `<STDIN>` that you see on this line is the standard input handle. It works just like a file handle, except it reads the input from the keyboard instead of a file.

The `scalar` function that is on this line prevents `<STDIN>` from reading in all of the lines from standard input before returning the value.

Line 28 closes the `Get_Input` subroutine.

```
29: sub Execute_Transaction{
30:     @keys = keys    %book;
31:     @vals = values %book;
32:     chomp(@vals);
```

Line 29 begins the `Execute_Transaction` subroutine. This is the subroutine that reads `%book`, creates the SQL statement and adds the data to the database.

Line 30 copies the keys from the `%book` hash into the `@keys` array.

Line 31 copies the values from the `%book` hash into the `@vals` array.

Line 32 uses the `chomp` function to remove the trailing newline character off of the values in the `@vals` array. The newlines arise when the user enters the data and hits the Enter key — the Enter key is actually recorded along with the data that the user enters. `chomp` is very useful; if you pass it an array, as we do here, it will process the entire array for you!

```
33:     @vals = map{$conn->quote($_)} @vals;
```

Line 33 uses the `map` function to call the `quote` function on all of the items in the `@vals` array. `map` performs the function(s) inside of the curly bars, {}, on each member of the array that is passed to the `map` function. So, you are easily able to transform every item in an array with `map`.

```
34:     $sql = "INSERT INTO library ("
35:             . join(", ", @keys)
36:             . ") VALUES ("
37:             . join(", ", @vals)
38:             . ")";
```

This code block can be a little tricky, so please make sure you understand it before moving on.

Lines 34–38 are actually a single Perl statement; notice that the semicolon that ends the statement is on **Line 38**.

Line 34 simply stores a string of text into the scalar named `$sql`.

Line 35 begins with a dot. The dot is called the *concatenation operator* and is used to join strings together. The `join` function is used to take all of the values in an array and join them with the value passed to it — here we pass ", " so each value is joined by what is *inside* the quotes.

This line joins each value in the `@keys` array by using a comma and a space.

Line 36 adds text to the $sql string.

Line 37 does nearly the same thing **line 35** does except it acts on the values instead of the keys.

Line 38 finishes off this SQL command string by adding a trailing ').

Our finished SQL statement will look something like this:

```
INSERT INTO library (field1, field2, field3) VALUES ('item 1',
'item 2', 'item 3');

39:    my $query = $conn->prepare($sql);

40:    $query->execute or die("\nError executing SQL statement!
$DBI::errstr");
```

Line 39 uses the DBI connection object's prepare method to get the SQL statement ready to run. This returns a new object representing the query we're about to perform, which will then actually update the database.

Line 40 calls the execute method of the $query handle, which actually runs the SQL in the database. If the database returns any errors, the program will die and give us the returned error.

```
41:    print "Record added to database.\n";

42:    return 1;
43: }
```

Line 41 simply uses the print function to print a message so that the user knows that the record has been added.

Line 42 returns a true value from this subroutine.

Line 43 closes the Execute_Transaction subroutine.

There we have our first application that allows us to modify data in the database. This application adds only one record at a time, but we will soon be writing applications that offer much more functionality than this.

Using UPDATE

Once you have entries in a database, you'll eventually want to modify some of them. We'll now develop a program to alter a record in the database, given its ISBN number.

As we go through this next application, try to notice the many similarities between it and the previous program. This program uses much of the same code. I have used a few different techniques in this program, however, to show you different ways of accomplishing the same thing.

```
01: #!/usr/bin/perl -w
02: #
03: # program 5-2
04: # Chapter 5
05: # Listing 2
06: #

07: use strict;
08: use DBI;
```

Line 1 is just like the first lines of our other applications. It tells the system where to find Perl and turns on warnings with the -w.

Lines 2–6 are comments about the program.

Line 7 loads the strict pragma. This makes the programmer use better programming techniques so that common programming errors are avoided.

Line 8 loads the DBI module. This is the DataBase Interface that Perl uses to interact with databases.

```
09: my $conn->connect
("DBI:mysql:BibleBook","bookuser","testpass")
10:        or die("Cannot connect: $DBI::errstr");
```

Lines 9–10 form a single Perl statement that tries to create an object of class DBI that represents a connection to the database. If the connection cannot be made, our call to DBI->connect will fail, and we must abort the program by using die.

```
11: my $old_isbn;

12: my $book = Get_Data();
13: Change_Record($book);
```

Line 11 declares a scalar variable named $old_isbn. This variable is used so that if the ISBN of the book changes, we can still remember the old value, as it's the value that we need to query for in the database.

Line 12 calls the Get_Data subroutine. This is a bit different from the function called in the previous example. In this example, the Get_Data subroutine returns a reference to the %book hash, which we store in the scalar variable named $book.

Line 13 calls the Change_Record subroutine, and in this example we pass the hash reference (stored in $book) to the subroutine so that it can access the data.

```
14: sub Get_Data{
15:     my %book;

16:     $old_isbn           = Get_Input("Enter ISBN of Book to
Modify");
```

Line 14 begins the Get_Data subroutine.

Line 15 declares a hash variable named %book. Since we declare the variable inside of the subroutine, and use my, this variable has only a scope *inside* of this subroutine. When you declare a variable with my, that variable has a scope that exists only within the innermost enclosing block. In our previous example, %book is globally scoped, as are the other variables we declared outside of any enclosing blocks.

Keeping your variables under control gets more important as your programs grow. When you declare all of your variables as global and don't pass anything to/from subroutines, it becomes very easy to start "stepping on the toes" of the variables. By this, I mean that when everything is global and you are working with a variable named $foo, can you be absolutely sure that $foo contains the data you think it does? Not always, especially if $foo is used a lot in the program.

When, however, you declare as many variables as possible only in the scope where they are needed and pass references to/from them between subroutines, you can be much more certain that the data you *think* is in a variable actually is. Also, this can make programs easier to follow and maintain; when you look at the code, you can tell exactly where the variables/values come from.

Line 16 calls the Get_Input subroutine to print a prompt to the user. The value returned from the Get_Input subroutine is then stored in the $old_isbn variable. We do this step so to capture the ISBN number for the book that we are changing. The ISBN number uniquely identifies the book in the database. If the user is changing the ISBN of this book, we need to pass the *old* ISBN to the database because the new value is not yet known to the database.

```
17:     $book{isbn}         = Get_Input("Enter ISBN (even if not
changed)");
18:     $book{title}        = Get_Input("Enter Book Title");
19:     $book{author}       = Get_Input("Enter Book Author");
20:     $book{price}        = Get_Input("Enter Book Price");
21:     $book{format}       = Get_Input("Enter Book Format");
22:     $book{publisher}    = Get_Input("Enter Book Publisher");
23:     $book{pubdate}      = Get_Input("Enter Publish Date");
24:     $book{notes}        = Get_Input("Enter Notes")
```

Lines 17–24 use the Get_Input subroutine to prompt the user for the appropriate input and store the values returned into the %book hash.

```
25: return(\%book);
26: }
```

Line 25 returns a *reference* to the %book hash. By returning this reference, we can store the reference in a scalar variable and easily pass it among subroutines as needed. When we need to access data, we simply de-reference it and fetch it.

Line 26 ends the Get_Data subroutine.

```
27: sub Get_Input {
28:     print $_[0], ":\n";
29:     return scalar <STDIN>;
30: }
```

Line 27 begins the Get_Input subroutine.

Line 28 prints out the first item passed to this subroutine then a colon and a new-line. The text that gets printed is the field name so that the user knows what field they are entering data for.

Line 29 returns the value that was entered by the user. The handle <STDIN> that you see on this line is the standard input handle. It works just like a file handle, except it reads the input from the keyboard instead of a file.

The scalar function that is on this line prevents <STDIN> from reading all of the lines in from standard input before returning the value.

Line 30 closes the Get_Input subroutine.

```
31: sub Change_Record{
32:     my $book = shift;
```

Line 31 begins the Change_Record subroutine.

Line 32 uses the shift function to get the first (and only) value that was passed to the subroutine and stores it in the $book variable.

shift is used to take a value off of the front of an array. Since we don't pass shift an array to shift from, shift defaults to using the @_ array. The @_ array is where all data passed to a subroutine is stored; by using shift, we can easily read the values that have been passed in.

```
33: my @keys = keys    %$book;
34:     my @vals = values %$book;
35:     chomp (@vals);
```

Lines 33–34 act just like **Lines 29–32** of our previous example. The difference between these lines and the ones in the previous example is that $book is a reference to a hash, so we need to de-reference it to get the actual hash. To do this, we place a % in front of the $book. This can also be written as %{$book} for those of you who find that clearer.

Line 35 uses the chomp function to remove any trailing newlines from the values in the @vals array.

```
36:      @vals = map{$conn->quote($_)} @vals;
```

Line 36 uses the map function to call the quote function on all of the items in the @vals array. map performs the function(s) inside of the curly bars, {}, on each member of the array that is passed to the map function. So, you are easily able to transform every item in an array with map.

```
37: my $sql = "UPDATE library SET ";

38:      my $counter = 0;
39:      foreach my $key (@keys){
40:          $sql .= "$key = '$vals[$counter]', ";
41:          $counter++;
42:      }

43:      $sql =~ s{, $}{ WHERE isbn = '$old_isbn'};
```

Line 37 begins the code we use to construct the SQL statement needed to update the database. This line declares a my variable named $sql and stores the first part of the SQL statement in it.

Line 38 creates a variable named $counter and initializes it to 0. We use this as an index as we traverse through the array @vals.

Line 39 begins a foreach loop that traverses through the @keys array and stores the current value in the scalar variable named $key.

Line 40 appends (using the .= operator) the current values onto the $sql variable. If our current $key value were "title" and the current value of $vals[$counter] were "Perl Database Programming," this line would append title = 'Perl Database Programming', onto the end of whatever value were currently in the $sql variable.

Note $sql .= "foo bar blah" **is a shorthand way for writing** $sql = $sql . "foo bar blah".

Line 41 increments the $counter variable.

Line 42 closes the `foreach` loop that begins on Line 39.

Line 43 finishes off the SQL statement by replacing the last comma and space (`, `) with `WHERE isbn = 'value of old isbn'`.

Tip   I use a different syntax for this regular expression. Instead of using the /'s to delimit the regular expression, I use curly braces to enclose the parts — like this: `{look for} {replace with}`. This sometimes makes the regular expression easier to follow, in my opinion.

```
44:     my $query = $conn->do($sql)
45:          or die("\nError executing SQL statement!
$DBI::errstr");

46:     print "Record information updated in the database...\n";

47:     return 1;
48: }
```

Line 44 uses a new method for interacting with the database. Instead of having to do `$foo = $conn->prepare($sql)` and then a `$foo->execute`, if you are just doing a SQL call and don't expect any data back, you can use the `do` method to save yourself the extra `prepare` step.

Line 45 is a continuation of line 44 and causes the program to die and display an error message if an error occurs in the execution of the SQL command.

Line 46 prints out a message to the user, indicating that the update is successful.

Line 47 returns a true value from the subroutine.

Line 48 ends the `Change_Record` subroutine.

That wraps up our application that modifies existing data. Most of the code for adding and modifying is the same — the main difference is the SQL statement.

Using DELETE

Now that we can add and modify data, let's create something that allows a user to delete data from the database table. Our next application does just that; it allows the user to remove a record.

```
01: #!/usr/bin/perl -w
02: #
03: # program 5-3
04: # Chapter 5
05: # Listing 3
06: #

07: use strict;
08: use DBI;
```

Line 1 should be very familiar by now. It tells the system where to find Perl and turns on warnings.

Lines 2–6 are simply comments about the program.

Line 7 calls the `strict` pragma to force better programming style.

Line 8 loads the `DBI` module so that this program can talk to the database.

```
09: my $conn = DBI->connect
("DBI:mysql:BibleBook","bookuser","testpass")
10:     or die("Cannot connect: $DBI::errstr");
```

Lines 9–10 form a single Perl statement that tries to create an object of class `DBI` that represents a connection to the database. If the connection cannot be made, our call to `DBI->connect` will fail, and we will abort the program by using `die`.

```
11: Delete_Record(Get_ISBN());
```

Line 11 calls the `Delete_Record` subroutine and takes the value returned by the call to `Get_ISBN` as it's input.

```
12: sub Get_ISBN{
13:     print "Delete ISBN #:\n";
14:     $isbn      = <STDIN>;
15:     chomp($isbn);

16:     return($isbn);
17: }
```

Line 12 begins the `Get_ISBN` subroutine.

Line 13 prints out a prompt for the user to enter the ISBN of the book to delete.

Line 14 reads `STDIN` (the keyboard) and stores the value entered into the `$isbn` variable.

Line 15 uses the chomp function to remove any trailing newline from the $isbn variable.

Line 16 returns $isbn from the subroutine.

Line 17 ends the Get_ISBN subroutine.

```
18: sub Delete_Record{
```

Line 18 begins the Delete_Record subroutine.

```
19:    my $result = $conn->do("DELETE FROM library WHERE isbn
= '$isbn'")
20:            or die("\nError executing SQL statement!
$DBI::errstr");
```

Line 19 uses yet another method for calling an SQL statement. Here, we again use the do method, but instead of creating a variable called $sql and then storing the SQL statement string in it, we simply put the SQL string directly inside do! This is another way to save a bit of space without sacrificing clarity.

Also on this line, we declare a variable named $result and store the result of the $conn->do call. If the call is successful, 1 will be returned. If the call is not successful, 0 will be returned.

Line 20 is a continuation of Line 19. This line tells the program to die if there is a problem executing the SQL statement.

```
21:    if($result){
22:        print "Record deleted from database.\n";
23:    }
24:    else {
25:        print "Record NOT DELETED! $DBI::errstr ";
26:    }

27:    return 1;
28: }
```

Line 21 checks the $result variable to see if it contains a true value. If so, the code inside its block is executed.

Line 22 is the code that gets executed if $result contained a true value.

Line 23 ends the first part of the if..else block that begins on Line 21.

Line 24 is the else part of this if..else block. If $result does not contain a value (is false), the code inside of this block is executed.

Line 25 is the code that gets executed if `$result` is false (contained no value).

Line 26 closes the `if..else` block.

Line 27 returns a true value from the subroutine.

Line 28 closes the `Delete_Record` subroutine.

That is it for the program that deletes a record. Deleting is much easier than inserting a record or modifying an existing record because you do not have to gather all of the information about the record and then create a somewhat complex SQL statement.

Putting the Pieces Together

We have covered the main parts of a program that interact with a database. But up to this point, our user interface has been a bit minimalistic. Our next application uses the Tk libraries to draw the screens. This application is by far our most complex yet. It weighs in at almost 150 lines of code! This is a comprehensive example that should bring together all of the concepts we have covered so far.

> **Note**
>
> I originally used the Curses library to create the user interface for this program. After pumping out over 300 lines of code and getting it working how I wanted it to, I discovered that it would not run properly on a Windows system. So I had to rewrite the user-interface portion of the program! The database access stayed the same, so that code was salvageable. The new program, using Tk, is over 150 lines shorter than the Curses program, and it has a much nicer user interface. I tested this on a Windows 98 box with a current ActiveState Perl installation and on a Linux box—both ran fine and looked great.

Please note that the next program uses Tk. Since this is a database book, not a Tk book, we don't focus as much on the Tk aspect of the program so if you aren't familiar with Tk, you can safely skim those parts of the program.

Let's dive in and create a GUI database application.

```
01: #!/usr/bin/perl -w
02: #
03: # program 5-4
04: # Chapter 5
05: # Listing 4
06: #

07: use strict;
08: use DBI;
09: use Tk;
```

Line 1 should be very familiar by now. It tells the system where to find Perl and turns on warnings.

Lines 2–6 are simply comments about the program.

Line 7 calls the `strict` pragma to force better programming style.

Line 8 loads the `DBI` module so that this program can talk to the database.

Line 9 loads the Tk module. We use Tk for our user interface. Tk is a toolkit for creating graphical interfaces that work in Unix and/or Linux and Windows.

```
10: my $conn = DBI->connect
("DBI:mysql:BibleBook","bookuser","testpass")
11:      or die("Cannot connect: $DBI::errstr\n");

12: my ($sql, @keys, $record);
```

Lines 10–11 form a single Perl statement that tries to create an object of class `DBI` that represents a connection to the database. If the connection cannot be made, our call to `DBI->connect` will fail, and we will abort the program by using `die`.

Line 12 declares some variables that we globally use throughout the program.

```
13: my %fields =
14:    ('isbn'   => "ISBN: "   , 'title'     => "Title: "    ,
15:     'author' => "Author: " , 'price'     => "Price: "    ,
16:     'format' => "Format: " , 'publisher' => "Publisher: ",
17:     'pubdate'=> "Pub. Date: " );

18: my @order = qw(isbn title author publisher format pubdate
price);
```

Lines 13–17 create a hash called `%fields`. This hash is used to translate between the database field names and a more pleasing form that we display to the user. The key fields of the `%fields` hash are the same as the database row names; the values of the `%fields` hash are displayed to the user.

Line 18 creates an array called `@order`. This array contains the field names of the database table in the order that we want them to appear on the user-interface windows.

```
19: Start_TK_Interface();
20: exit;
```

Line 19 calls the `Start_Tk_Interface` subroutine. This subroutine is responsible for creating the GUI windows as well as processing all of the input.

Line 20 ends the program! Yep, that is it! Well, except for the subroutines that do all of the work. They are coming up next.

```
21: #-----------------------------------------------------
22: # Database Routines

23: sub Get_Record {
```

Lines 21–22 are just comments that make it easier to determine what the following section of the program does.

Line 23 begins the Get_Record subroutine. This subroutine is used to get a record from the database.

```
24:   my $isbn    = shift;
25:   my $sql     = qq(SELECT * FROM library WHERE isbn = $isbn);
26:   my $hdl_search = $conn->prepare($sql);
```

Line 24 creates a scalar variable called $isbn and uses the shift function to set it to the value passed to the subroutine.

Line 25 creates a scalar variable called $sql and stores a newly created SQL SELECT statement in it.

Line 26 calls the prepare function on the $sql statement and creates a variable named $hdl_search, which is a handle to the prepared-search SQL statement.

```
27:       $hdl_search->execute;
28:       $record = $hdl_search->fetchrow_hashref;

29:       return($record);
30: }
```

Line 27 uses the execute method on the $hdl_search handle. This executes the SQL statement against the database.

Line 28 calls the fetchrow_hashref function to get a value from the returned results. The result of this is stored in the $record scalar. Since all of our searches are done on ISBN, there should only be one match per ISBN search.

Line 29 returns $record, a reference to the hash containing the record data.

Line 30 closes the Get_Record subroutine.

This next subroutine is pretty short, so we'll just take a look at the whole thing without splitting it up.

```
31: sub Delete_Record {
32:     my $isbn  = shift;

33:     $sql    = qq(DELETE FROM library WHERE isbn = '$isbn');
34:     my $query = $connection->prepare($sql);

35:     $query->execute or die("\nError executing
            SQL statement! $DBI::errstr");

36:     return 1;
37: }
```

Line 31 begins the Delete_Record subroutine. This subroutine does exactly what its name says: it deletes a record from the database.

Line 32 creates a scalar variable called $isbn and uses the shift function to set it to the value passed to the subroutine when the subroutine is called.

Line 33 creates an SQL statement intended to delete a record from the database.

Note   This program does not have any real error checking. It would be a good idea here to allow only the text that you want in this box. On any production system, make sure that you always check the values that the users enter.

Line 34 prepares the SQL statement and stores the prepared query in a handle named $query.

Line 35 calls the execute function to run the query. If an error occurs, die is called, and the program exits and prints the error message.

Line 36 returns a true value from the subroutine.

Line 37 ends the Delete_Record subroutine.

```
38: sub Update_Record {
39:     my $form   = shift;
40:     my $caller = shift;
41:     $caller    -> withdraw();
```

Line 38 begins the Update_Record subroutine. This subroutine is used to update an existing record in the database.

Lines 39–40 declare scalar variables and shifts in a value passed to the subroutine. The $form variable is a reference to a hash containing references to the Tk form fields. So $form is a reference to a hash of references, yikes! Don't worry though; I'll break it down for you. The $caller variable is a handle to the window that calls this subroutine. We need the handle so that we can close the window. If we don't close the window, we will end up with a new window for each action, and our screen will soon be full of windows.

Line 41 uses the `withdraw` function to remove the calling window from the display.

```
42:     my $isbn = $form->{'isbn'}->get();
```

Line 42 gets the `isbn` that has been entered on the form.

The `get()` method comes from the Tk modules `Entry` object, which comes from the form that the user enters the data into. The `%form` hash contains a reference to each of the fields on the user entry form.

This concept is hard to grasp at first, so let me break it down even further.

Our database field names are `isbn`, `title`, `author`, and so on. When we create the form that the user can enter data on, we do so like this.

```
$form{$field} = $top_win->Entry(-object modifiers...);
```

This is in a loop, with `$field` changing each time through to the next database form field. `$top_win` is a reference to the window being created/displayed. `Entry` is an object in the `Tk` class created for entering text.

So we end up with a hash that looks something like this:

```
$form{isbn} = $ref_to_entry_field, $form{title} =
$ref_to_title_field, etc...
```

Let s get back to the code on Line 42. We are setting `$isbn` to whatever is returned from the `get()` method on the right side.

`$form->{'isbn'}` is how we de-reference the hash to get the value stored in the `isbn` key. Then, at the same time, we make a call to `get()` by using `->get()`. This causes the `get()` method to be performed on the de-referenced value in the field.

Or, if you prefer the super-short explanation: **Line 42** gets the value that is entered in the `isbn` field on the form.

This code can also been written on 2 lines, like this:

```
my $foo = $form->{'isbn'};
$isbn   = $foo->get();
```

```
43:     my @keys = keys %$form;
```

Line 43 stores all of the keys in the %$form hash into an array named @keys. This is done so that we can easily loop through the values in later code.

```
44:      my @vals = map { $$form{$_}->get() } @keys;
```

Line 44 is a fairly complex line that does a lot of work for us! The map function is used to perform something on an entire array.

Here is what this line looks like without the map function.

```
Foreach my $key (@keys){
    Push @vals $$form{$key}->get();
}
```

So **Line 44** stores all of the values into an array named @vals. We need the keys and values stored in two arrays in their proper order. The next few lines of code from the program use the join function to create the SQL statement to add a record. We want the data to go into the proper fields in the database, so we must make sure @keys and @vals are in the same order.

```
45:      my $counter = 0;
46:      $sql  = qq{UPDATE library SET };
```

Line 45 creates a scalar variable named $counter and sets it to an initial value of 0.

Line 46 begins the creation of the SQL statement we use to update the data in the database.

```
47:      foreach my $k (@keys){
48:          $sql .= qq{$k = "$vals[$counter]", };
49:          $counter++;
50:      }
```

Line 47 begins a foreach loop that traverses through the @keys array. Each time through the loop, the current value of @keys is stored in the scalar variable $k.

Line 48 appends some text to the $sql variable. The text appended is the current key and its associated value. Each time through the loop, the text added to the $sql variable looks something like this:

```
Title = "Perl Database Programming ",
```

Line 49 increments the variable named $counter. We use this variable to keep the keys and values synchronized — the first key is value 0, then value 1, and so on.

Line 50 closes the foreach loop that begins on Line 47.

```
51:      $sql  =~ s/\, $//;
52:      $sql .=  " WHERE isbn = '$isbn'";
```

Line 51 gets rid of the comma and space at the end of the value stored in $sql. Each time through the preceding loop, we add the current value plus a comma and a space. The final time through the loop also adds a comma and a space, but we don't need that one. This line takes care of removing the extra characters.

Line 52 appends the final text to the $sql variable. We now should have a complete, valid SQL statement stored in $sql. The SQL statement will look something like this:

```
UPDATE library SET format = "Hardcover", publisher = "Wiley",
title = "Brent's Book", author = "Brent", isbn = "123999",
price = "20.99", pubdate = "01-01-2001" WHERE isbn = '123456'
```

```
53:      my $query = $conn->prepare($sql);

54:      $query->execute or die("\nError executing SQL
              statement! $DBI::errstr ");

55:      return 1;
56: }
```

Line 53 creates a scalar variable named $query and stores a reference to the prepared SQL statement in it. The $conn->prepare($sql) is a call to the prepare method of the DBI, which gets an SQL statement ready for execution.

Line 54 executes the SQL statement. If there is a problem executing the SQL statement, die is called; the program terminates and prints an error message.

Line 55 returns a true value from the subroutine.

Line 56 ends the subroutine.

```
57: sub Add_Record {
58:      my $form   = shift;
59:      my $caller = shift;
60:      $caller    -> withdraw();
```

Line 57 begins the Add_Record subroutine. This subroutine is called to add records to the database.

Line 58 shifts in a reference to the hash that stores all of the form data and stores the reference in a new my variable named $form.

Line 59 shifts in a reference to the window that calls this subroutine and stores the reference in a new my variable named $caller.

Line 60 uses the withdraw() method to close the window that calls this subroutine.

```
61:      my @keys = keys %$form;
62:      my @vals = map { $conn->quote($$form{$_}->get()) }
@keys;
```

Line 61 reads all of the keys from the %$form hash and stores them in an array named @keys.

Line 62 uses the map function to get all of the form values, execute the quote function on them, and to store them in the @vals array. For each value in the %$form hash, the map function calls the get() method to retrieve the value from the form.

```
63:      $sql   = "INSERT INTO library ("
64:             . join(", ", @keys)
65:             . ") VALUES ("
66:             . join(", ", @vals)
67:             . ")";
```

Lines 63–67 are actually one line of Perl code! Notice that there is no semicolon until the end of **Line 67**.

These lines are used to create the SQL statement needed to insert new records into the database. The join function saves a lot of work. By using join, we are able to take all of the values in the @keys array and the @vals array and concatenate them into one string.

The first join uses a comma and space to join all of the values in @keys. These values do not have to be quoted, since they are the field names in the database table.

The second join does the same thing as the first, except for the @vals instead of the @keys.

These two arrays *must* have their values stored in the same order so that the correctkey=value relationship is maintained. **Lines 61** and **62** take care of this for us.

Notice the dots, . 's, at the beginning of **Lines 64–67**. The dot is the concatenation operator in Perl, for joining the many strings we have here into one large string.

```
68:      my $query = $conn->prepare($sql);

69:      $query->execute or die("\nError executing SQL
             statement! $DBI::errstr");

70:      return 1;
71: }
```

Line 68 calls the prepare method on the $sql variable and stores the reference returned in the variable named $query.

Line 69 executes the query. If an error occurs when the query executes, the program will hit `die`; then the program will exit, and an error message will be printed.

Line 70 returns a true value from the subroutine.

Line 71 ends this subroutine.

```
72: #---------------------------------------------------------
73: # Tk Interface Routines

74: my $MainWin;
```

Lines 72–73 are simply comments that let people looking at the code know that the Tk routines are below these lines.

Line 74 declares a variable named `$MainWin` that we'll be using in the next several subroutines. This variable contains a reference to a new `MainWindow` object.

```
75: sub Start_Tk_Interface {
76:     $MainWin = MainWindow->new(-title => "Choose a Database
          Action");
77:     $MainWin->MoveToplevelWindow(100,100);
```

Line 75 begins a subroutine named `Start_Tk_Interface`. This subroutine creates the first window you see and handles the button-pushes that may occur within that window.

Line 76 creates a new `MainWindow` object and stores a reference to this new object in the `$MainWin` variable. This line also sets the window's title to *Choose a Database Action*.

Line 77 moves this new window to the (X,Y) position of (100,100) on the user's screen. You can put what values you like here, but 100,100 is a safe place. Make sure you don't put the window completely out of the user's view! Use values you know are within the user's desktop.

```
78:     my $button1 = $MainWin->Button(-text => 'Add Record',
79:                 -command => [\&tk_Add_Record_Dialog, 'add']);

80:     my $button2 = $MainWin->Button(-text => 'Edit Record',
81:                 -command => [\&tk_Choose_Dialog, 'Edit']);

82:     my $button3 = $MainWin->Button(-text => 'Delete Record',
83:                 -command => [\&tk_Choose_Dialog, 'Delete']);

84:     my $button4 = $MainWin->Button(-text => 'Quit',
85:                 -command => [$MainWin => 'destroy']);
```

Lines 78–85 create the buttons that appear on the main window and associate each button with a sub to be called when it is clicked.

Line 78 creates a `my` variable called `$button1`. This variable stores a reference to the button object that is created with the `$MainWin->Button` call. This line also sets the text of the button to "Add Record".

Line 79 is a continuation of line 78. This line uses the `-command` attribute to specify that when this button is clicked, Tk should call `tk_Add_Record_Dialog('add')`.

Lines 80–83 do the same as the previous description, with the exception that a different subroutine is called and a different value is passed based upon the clicked button.

Line 84 is just like the preceding lines.

Line 85 calls the `destroy` method on the Main Window. This causes the main window and all subordinate windows to close. This exits the program.

```
86:      $button1 -> grid(-row => 0, -column => 0,
                           -padx => 10, -sticky => 'w');
87:      $button2 -> grid(-row => 0, -column => 1,
                           -padx => 10, -pady   => 40 );
88:      $button3 -> grid(-row => 0, -column => 2,
                           -padx => 10);
89:      $button4 -> grid(-row => 0, -column => 3,
                           -padx => 10, -sticky => 'e');
```

Lines 86–89 are used to position the buttons in the window. The `grid` method is one way to position items when programming a Tk application. Using `grid` to lay out the page causes the page to be divided into a logical table of rows and columns.

The `row` attribute tells the program in which row to put this item. The `column` attribute tells the program with which column this item should be positioned.

The `padx` attribute tells the program to pad 10 pixels on each side of the item. The `pady` attribute tells the program to pad the specified number of pixels on the top and bottom of the item.

The `sticky` attribute takes an argument of n, s, e, or w. These are compass directions that correspond to where this item should remain anchored. Passing an argument of w causes the item to be anchored on the left side of the window.

```
90:      MainLoop();
91: }
```

Line 90 calls the MainLoop function. This function is part of all Perl Tk applications. It keeps the program running in a loop and allows events such as button clicks to take place and be handled appropriately. By *appropriately*, I mean by the subroutines passed as they are in **Lines 78–85**.

Line 91 ends this subroutine.

```
92: sub tk_Choose_Dialog {
93:     my $type = shift;
```

Line 92 begins the tk_Choose_Dialog window. This creates the window that has the user enter the isbn and then calls the tk_Edit_or_Delete function to handle either updating or deleting the book whose isbn matches.

Line 93 creates a new scalar variable named $type and shifts in the value passed via the subroutine call. This can be either Edit or Delete. The button name is based upon this value. What happens to this record is also based upon this value.

```
94:     my $top_win = $MainWin->Toplevel(-title =>
            "Choose Record");
95:     $top_win->MoveToplevelWindow(110,110);
```

Line 94 creates a new top-level window with a title of *Choose Record*. A top-level window means the window is displayed.

Line 95 moves this new window to the (X,Y) position (110,110).

```
96:     $top_win->Label(-text => 'ISBN: ') ->
97:         grid(-row => 0, -column => 0, -sticky => 'w');

98:     my $isbn = $top_win->Entry(-width => 20) ->
99:         grid(-row => 0, -column => 1, -sticky => 'e');
```

Line 96 adds a label to the new window. This label is the **ISBN:** to the left of the text entry field on the window.

Line 97 positions this new label and anchors it to the left of the window with sticky => 'w'.

Lines 98–99 add a text-entry field to the window and anchor it to the right side of the window. Line 98 also takes a return value and stores it in the $isbn variable. This allows us to gain access to the text in this text-entry field.

```
100:     my $button = $top_win->Button(
101:         -text    => "$type Record",
102:         -command => [\&tk_Edit_or_Delete, $top_win,
                         $type, $isbn] );
```

Line 100 creates a new button on this window and stores a reference to this new button in the $button variable.

Line 101 sets the text on this new button to the value in the $type variable (*Edit* or *Delete*) and appends *Record* onto it as well. This causes the button to either say *Edit Record* or *Delete Record*.

Line 102 sets this button to call the tk_Edit_or_Delete subroutine when it is clicked. This line also passes some values to the subroutine it calls.

```
103:     $button-> grid(-row => 1, -column => 1);

104:     return 1;
105: }
```

Line 103 positions the button in row 1, column 1.

Line 104 returns a true value from this subroutine.

Line 105 ends this subroutine.

```
106: sub tk_Edit_or_Delete {
107:     my $caller = shift;
108:     my $type   = shift;
109:     my $isbn   = shift()->get();
```

Line 106 creates the tk_Edit_or_Delete subroutine.

Line 107 creates a new my variable named $caller and shifts in the first value passed to this subroutine.

Line 108 creates a new my variable named $type and shifts in the second value passed to this subroutine.

Line 109 creates a new my variable named $isbn and calls the get() function on the value we are shifting in to this variable. We shift in the third value passed to this subroutine, and we call the get() function on it at the same time.

```
110:    $caller->withdraw();

111:    Delete_Record($isbn)             if($type eq 'Delete');
112:    tk_Add_Record_Dialog("edit", $isbn) if($type eq
'Edit');

113:    return 1;
114: }
```

Line 110 calls the `withdraw` method on the window referenced in the `$caller` variable. This causes the window that calls this subroutine to close.

Line 111 calls the `Delete_Record` subroutine and passes `$isbn` to it so that the proper item is deleted from the database. The `if` statement at the end of this line checks to see if the value stored in `$type` is equal to *Delete*. This line will be executed only if the `if` statement's condition is true.

Line 112 calls the `tk_Add_Record_Dialog` subroutine and passes `"edit"` and `$isbn` to it so that the proper item is selected and displayed for editing. The `if` statement at the end of this line checks to see it the value stored in `$type` is equal to *Edit*. This line will be executed only if the `if` statement is true.

Line 113 returns a true value from this subroutine.

Line 114 ends this subroutine.

```
115: sub tk_Add_Record_Dialog {
116:     my ($record, $isbn, %form);
117:     my $type = shift;
118:     my $row  = 0;
```

Line 115 begins the `tk_Add_Record_Dialog`. This dialog is used to gather information about a book from the user so that it may be added to the database.

Line 116 declares some variables that we'll be using in this subroutine.

Line 117 declares a variable named `$type` and shifts in the first values passed to this subroutine.

Line 118 creates a new variable named `$row` and initializes it to a value of 0.

```
119:     my $top_win = $MainWin->Toplevel(-title =>
             "Add/Edit a Record");
120:     $top_win->MoveToplevelWindow(110,110);
```

Line 119 creates a new top-level window and sets its title to Add/Edit a Record.

Line 120 positions this new top-level window at (X,Y) position (110,110).

```
121:     if($type =~ /edit/){
122:         $isbn   = shift;
123:         $record = Get_Record($isbn);
124:     }
```

Line 121 checks to see if the variable `$type` contains the word *edit*. If so, the program enters the block; if not, the program continues from Line 125.

Line 122 shifts in the next value passed to this subroutine and stores the value in $isbn.

Line 123 calls the Get_Record subroutine and passes it $isbn. The results of the function are stored in the $record variable. $record will contain a reference to a hash that contains the values of the record if the Get_Record subroutine finds a matching record.

Line 124 closes this if block.

```
125:        foreach my $field (@order){
126:            my $text = $record->{$field};
```

Line 125 begins a foreach loop that traverses through the @orders array and stores the current value in $field each time through the loop. This loop creates most of the form fields in this new window.

Line 126 creates a new variable named $text and stores the value of the current field in it.

```
127:        $top_win->Label(-text => $fields{$field}) ->
128:            grid(-row => $row, -column => 0, -sticky =>
'w');
```

Line 127 creates a label for each text-entry field on this form.

Line 128 positions this label in the current row of column 0 and anchors it to the left side of the window.

```
129:        $form{$field}  = $top_win->Entry
130:            (-width => 50, -textvariable => \$text) ->
131:            grid(-row=> $row, -column=> 1, -sticky=>
'e');

132:            $row++;
133:        }
```

Lines 129–131 create the text-entry field for each item on this form. **Line 131** positions this new field and anchors the field to the right side of the window.

Line 132 increments the $row variable.

Line 133 closes this foreach loop.

```
134:        my $button;
135:        if($type =~ /edit/i){
```

Line 134 creates a new variable called $button.

Line 135 is an if statement that checks to see if the value stored in $type contains *edit*. If so, this block of code is entered. If not, this block of code is skipped.

```
136:              $button = $top_win->Button(
137:                  -text    => 'Edit Record',
138:                  -command => [\&Update_Record,\%form, $top_win] );
139:       }
```

Line 136 creates a new button on the window and stores a reference to it in $button.

Line 137 sets the text of this new button to *Edit Record*.

Line 138 sets up the action of this button to call the Update_Record subroutine when pressed and passes the subroutine a reference to the %form hash and $top_win.

```
140:       else {
141:              $button = $top_win->Button(
142:                  -text    => 'Add Record',
143:                  -command => sub{ Add_Record(\%form, $top_win)}
);
144:       }
```

Line 140 is the else part of the if..else that begins on **Line 135**.

Line 141 creates a new button on this form and stores a reference to it in $button.

Line 142 sets the text of the button to *Add Record*.

Line 143 tells the program to call the Add_Record subroutine if this button is clicked. It also passes a reference to the %form hash and $top_win variable.

Line 144 closes this if..else block.

```
145:       $button-> grid(-row => $row, -column => 1);

146:       return 1;
147: }
```

Line 145 positions the button in column 1 and at the current value of $row.

Line 146 returns a true value from this subroutine.

Line 147 ends this subroutine.

Wow, a GUI database application in fewer than 150 lines of code! This small application has a lot of potential for becoming a full-featured database GUI with error checking and extra features. Don't be afraid to expand it and even add features to it.

Summary

That is all for this chapter on making changes to your data. We have covered quite a bit in this chapter: adding data; deleting data; updating existing data; and we put it all together in a GUI application at the end!

The code in this chapter is a great starting point. If you enjoy challenges, add some error handling to the GUI. Add to the code so that the user gets back friendly error messages and handles any exceptions that may arise.

As you continue in this book, you explore more database features. All of these new features can be added to these examples. This code is meant to be built upon, not tossed aside with each new application. Expand, explore, and experiment with the code! Do not worry about "breaking" something; you won't — but if you don't try new things, you won't learn as much.

Program Listings

Listings 5-1 to 5-4 contain the complete and uninterrupted code examples from this chapter.

Listing 5-1: **Simple add**

```
01: #!/usr/bin/perl -w
02: #
03: # program 5-1
04: # Chapter 5
05: # Listing 1
06: #

07: use strict;
08: use DBI;
09: my $conn = DBI->connect
("DBI:mysql:BibleBook","bookuser","testpass")
10:     or die("Cannot connect: $DBI::errstr");
11: my ($sql, %book, @keys);

12: Get_Data();
13: Execute_Transaction();
```

```
14: sub Get_Data{
15:     $book{'isbn'}      = Get_Input("Enter ISBN #");
16:     $book{'title'}     = Get_Input("Enter Book Title");
17:     $book{'author'}    = Get_Input("Enter Book Author");
18:     $book{'price'}     = Get_Input("Enter Book Price");
19:     $book{'format'}    = Get_Input("Enter Book Format");
20:     $book{'publisher'} = Get_Input("Enter Book Publisher");
21:     $book{'pubdate'}   = Get_Input("Enter Publish Date");
22:     $book{'notes'}     = Get_Input("Enter Notes");

23:     return 1;
24: }
25: sub Get_Input {
26:     print $_[0], ":\n";
27:     return scalar <STDIN>;
28: }
29: sub Execute_Transaction{
30:     @keys = keys   %book;
31:     @vals = values %book;
32:     chomp(@vals);
33:     @vals = map{$conn->quote($_)} @vals;
34:     $sql = "INSERT INTO library ("
35:             . join(", ", @keys)
36:             . ") VALUES ("
37:             . join(", ", @vals)
38:             . ")";
39:   my $query = $conn->prepare($sql);

40:   $query->execute or die("\nError executing SQL statement! $DBI::errstr");
41:     print "Record added to database.\n";

42:     return 1;
43: }
```

Listing 5-2: **Simple update**

```
01: #!/usr/bin/perl -w
02: #
03: # program 5-2
04: # Chapter 5
05: # Listing 2
06: #

07: use strict;
08: use DBI;
09: my $conn->connect
("DBI:mysql:BibleBook","bookuser","testpass")
```

Continued

Listing 5-2 *(continued)*

```
10:        or die("Cannot connect: $DBI::errstr");
11: my $old_isbn;

12: my $book = Get_Data();
13: Change_Record($book);
14: sub Get_Data{
15:     my %book;

16:     $old_isbn        = Get_Input("Enter ISBN of Book to Modify");
17:     $book{isbn}      = Get_Input("Enter ISBN (even if not changed)");
18:     $book{title}     = Get_Input("Enter Book Title");
19:     $book{author}    = Get_Input("Enter Book Author");
20:     $book{price}     = Get_Input("Enter Book Price");
21:     $book{format}    = Get_Input("Enter Book Format");
22:     $book{publisher} = Get_Input("Enter Book Publisher");
23:     $book{pubdate}   = Get_Input("Enter Publish Date");
24:     $book{notes}     = Get_Input("Enter Notes")

25: return(\%book);
26: }
27: sub Get_Input {
28:     print $_[0], ":\n";
29:     return scalar <STDIN>;
30: }
31: sub Change_Record{
32:     my $book = shift;
33: my @keys = keys    %$book;
34:     my @vals = values %$book;
35:     chomp (@vals);
36:     @vals = map{$conn->quote($_)} @vals;
37: my $sql = "UPDATE library SET ";

38:     my $counter = 0;
39:     foreach my $key (@keys){
40:         $sql .= "$key = '$vals[$counter]', ";
41:         $counter++;
42:     }

43:     $sql =~ s{, $}{ WHERE isbn = '$old_isbn'};
44:     my $query = $conn->do($sql)
45:         or die("\nError executing SQL statement! $DBI::errstr");

46:     print "Record information updated in the database...\n";

47:     return;
48: }
```

Listing 5-3: **Simple delete**

```
01: #!/usr/bin/perl -w
02: #
03: # program 5-3
04: # Chapter 5
05: # Listing 3
06: #

07: use strict;
08: use DBI;
09: my $conn = DBI->connect("DBI:mysql:BibleBook","bookuser","testpass")
10:     or die("Cannot connect: $DBI::errstr");

11: Delete_Record(Get_ISBN());
12: sub Get_ISBN{
13:     print "Delete ISBN #:\n";
14:     $isbn     = <STDIN>;
15:     chomp($isbn);

16:     return($isbn);
17: }
18: sub Delete_Record{
19:     my $result = $conn->do("DELETE FROM library WHERE isbn = '$isbn'")
20:         or die("\nError executing SQL statement! $DBI::errstr");
21:     if($result){
22:         print "Record deleted from database.\n";
23:     }
24:     else {
25:         print "Record NOT DELETED! $DBI::errstr\n";
26:     }

27:     return;
28: }
```

Listing 5-4: **Comprehensive example**

```
01: #!/usr/bin/perl -w
02: #
03: # program 5-4
04: # Chapter 5
05: # Listing 4
06: #
```

Continued

Listing 5-4 *(continued)*

```perl
07: use strict;
08: use DBI;
09: use Tk;

10: my $conn = DBI->connect
("DBI:mysql:BibleBook","bookuser","testpass")
11:    or die("Cannot connect: $DBI::errstr");

12: my ($sql, @keys, $record);

13: my %fields =
14:    ('isbn'   => "ISBN: "   , 'title'     => "Title: "    ,
15:     'author' => "Author: " , 'price'     => "Price: "    ,
16:     'format' => "Format: " , 'publisher' => "Publisher: ",
17:     'pubdate'=> "Pub. Date: " );

18: my @order = qw(isbn title author publisher format pubdate price);

19: Start_Tk_Interface();
20: exit;

21: #-------------------------------------------------------
22: # Database Routines

23: sub Get_Record {
24:    my $isbn      = shift;
25:    my $sql       = qq(SELECT * FROM library WHERE isbn = $isbn);
26:    my $hdl_search = $conn->prepare($sql);

27:    $hdl_search->execute;
28:    $record = $hdl_search->fetchrow_hashref;

29:    return($record);
30: }

31: sub Delete_Record {
32:    my $isbn = shift;

33:    $sql      = qq(DELETE FROM library WHERE isbn = '$isbn');
34:    my $query = $conn->prepare($sql);

35:    $query->execute or die("\nError executing SQL statement! $DBI::errstr");

36:    return 1;
37: }

38: sub Update_Record {
39:    my $form   = shift;
40:    my $caller = shift;
41:    $caller    -> withdraw();
```

```
42:     my $isbn = $form->{'isbn'}->get();

43:     my @keys = keys %$form;
44:     my @vals = map { $$form{$_}->get() } @keys;

45:     my $counter = 0;
46:     $sql  = qq{UPDATE library SET };

47:     foreach my $k (@keys){
48:         $sql .= qq{$k = "$vals[$counter]", };
49:         $counter++;
50:     }

51:     $sql  =~ s/\, $//;
52:     $sql .=  " WHERE isbn = '$isbn'";

53:     my $query = $conn->prepare($sql);

54:     $query->execute or die("\nError executing SQL statement! $DBI::errstr");

55:     return 1;
56: }

57: sub Add_Record {
58:     my $form   = shift;
59:     my $caller = shift;
60:     $caller    -> withdraw();

61:     my @keys = keys %$form;
62:     my @vals = map { $conn->quote($$form{$_}->get()) } @keys;

63:     $sql  = "INSERT INTO library ("
64:             . join(", ", @keys)
65:             . ") VALUES ("
66:             . join(", ", @vals)
67:             . ")";

68:     my $query = $conn->prepare($sql);

69:     $query->execute or die("\nError executing SQL statement! $DBI::errstr");

70:     return 1;
71: }

72: #-------------------------------------------------------
73: # Tk Interface Routines

74: my $MainWin;

75: sub Start_Tk_Interface {
```

Continued

Listing 5-4 *(continued)*

```
76:    $MainWin = MainWindow->new(-title => "Choose a Database Action");
77:    $MainWin->MoveToplevelWindow(100,100);

78:    my $button1 = $MainWin->Button(-text => 'Add Record',
79:               -command => [\&tk_Add_Record_Dialog, 'add']);

80:    my $button2 = $MainWin->Button(-text => 'Edit Record',
81:               -command => [\&tk_Choose_Dialog, 'Edit']);

82:    my $button3 = $MainWin->Button(-text => 'Delete Record',
83:               -command => [\&tk_Choose_Dialog, 'Delete']);

84:    my $button4 = $MainWin->Button(-text => 'Quit',
85:               -command => [$MainWin => 'destroy']);

86:    $button1 -> grid(-row => 0, -column => 0, -padx => 10, -sticky => 'w');
87:    $button2 -> grid(-row => 0, -column => 1, -padx => 10, -pady   => 40 );
88:    $button3 -> grid(-row => 0, -column => 2, -padx => 10);
89:    $button4 -> grid(-row => 0, -column => 3, -padx => 10, -sticky => 'e');

90:    MainLoop();
91: }

92: sub tk_Choose_Dialog {
93:    my $type = shift;

94:    my $top_win = $MainWin->Toplevel(-title => "Choose Record");
95:    $top_win->MoveToplevelWindow(110,110);

96:    $top_win->Label(-text => 'ISBN: ') ->
97:        grid(-row => 0, -column => 0, -sticky => 'w');

98:    my $isbn = $top_win->Entry(-width => 20) ->
99:        grid(-row => 0, -column => 1, -sticky => 'e');

100:    my $button = $top_win->Button(
101:        -text    => "$type Record",
102:        -command => [\&tk_Edit_or_Delete, $top_win, $type, $isbn] );

103:    $button-> grid(-row => 1, -column => 1);

104:    return 1;
105: }

106: sub tk_Edit_or_Delete {
107:    my $caller = shift;
108:    my $type   = shift;
109:    my $isbn   = shift()->get();

110:    $caller->withdraw();
```

```
111:    Delete_Record($isbn)              if($type eq 'Delete');
112:    tk_Add_Record_Dialog("edit", $isbn) if($type eq 'Edit');

113:    return 1;
114: }

115: sub tk_Add_Record_Dialog {
116:    my ($record, $isbn, %form);
117:    my $type = shift;
118:    my $row  = 0;

119:    my $top_win = $MainWin->Toplevel(-title => "Add/Edit a Record");

120:    $top_win->MoveToplevelWindow(110,110);

121:    if($type =~ /edit/){
122:        $isbn   = shift;
123:        $record = Get_Record($isbn);
124:    }

125:    foreach my $field (@order){
126:        my $text = $record->{$field};

127:        $top_win->Label(-text => $fields{$field}) ->
128:          grid(-row => $row, -column => 0, -sticky => 'w');

129:        $form{$field}  = $top_win->Entry
130:            (-width => 50, -textvariable => \$text) ->
131:              grid(-row=> $row, -column=> 1, -sticky=> 'e');

132:        $row++;
133:    }

134:    my $button;
135:    if($type =~ /edit/i){
136:        $button = $top_win->Button(
137:            -text    => 'Edit Record',
138:            -command => [\&Update_Record,\%form, $top_win] );
139:    }
140:    else {
141:        $button = $top_win->Button(
142:            -text    => 'Add Record',
143:            -command => sub{ Add_Record(\%form, $top_win)} );
144:    }

145:    $button-> grid(-row => $row, -column => 1);

146:    return 1;
147: }
```

✦   ✦   ✦

Advanced Database Programming

Web Database Programming

The marriage of the Web to databases is almost a necessity for any Web site to have useful information. Users don't want to visit static pages; they want the most up-to-date information. Using a database is an excellent way to maintain and present dynamic information.

To execute programs on a Web server, we use the Common Gateway Interface (CGI). The CGI module, written by Lincoln Stein, is incredibly useful for working with Perl CGI programs. The CGI does not refer to a language; CGI programs can be written not only in Perl but also in C, C++, shell, Python, BASIC, or any other language that can run on the Web server.

This chapter gives you some tips on Web-interface design, covers some of the basic HTML form tags, and shows you how to generate pages dynamically by utilizing a database.

Cross-Reference For a more in-depth look at Web programming, including database applications, check out my other book *Writing CGI Applications with Perl* (Addison Wesley, 2001). To find out more about HTML forms and HTML in general, visit http://www.w3.org for complete specifications.

HTML Form Tags

There are a few HTML tags that you need to be familiar with before you can create a Web interface to a database. This section introduces you to the tags you will use most often. Tags used for basic HTML pages and tables are not covered. Please refer to the World Wide Web Consortium's Web site at http://www.w3.org for more information and links to tutorials.

We cover the tags used most often; then we show a couple examples to bring it all together so that you can see these items in action, gaining a better understanding of how they work together.

<form>

The HTML `<form>` tag is used to begin a form on a Web page. The `<form>` tag has two attributes we are going to cover: `action` and `method`.

<form action="/cgi-bin/foo.cgi">

The `action` attribute tells the browser where to send the request when the form is submitted. The `/cgi-bin/` directory is where CGI programs are normally located on Web servers. This path may change based on how the Web server you use is configured.

<form action="/cgi-bin/foo.cgi" method="post">

The `method` attribute tells the Web browser how data should be passed to the Web server. Two methods are used: `post` and `get`. The `post` method passes the form data via the standard input, `STDIN`. The `get` method passes the form data in the URL. Because `get` passes the data on the URL, it has some limitations that the `post` method does not. Namely, there is a limit on how much data can actually be passed on the URL. This limit varies for different browsers and Web servers. The `post` method does not have this limitation, nor does it make the information passed to the server readily visible like the `get` method does.

The `action` attribute is required by the HTML specifications: If it is left off, it is up to the browser to determine the appropriate action. To ensure compatibility, always use the action attribute. The default attribute for the `method` attribute is `get`.

When developing Web applications, use the `get` method so that you can always see what data is being passed to the program. When you are satisfied with the application, switch to the `post` method so that the URL doesn't get cluttered with all of the form data and so that you don't hit the URL-length limit.

For example, if we have a CGI application called `name.cgi` and we use the `get` method to pass the information, the URL will look something like this:

```
http://www.perlguy.net/cgi-bin/name.cgi?first=Brent&last=Michalski
```

If we use the `post` method, the URL will look like this:

```
http://www.perlguy.net/cgi-bin/name.cgi
```

The same data may have been passed, but since it is being passed via a different method, it is not visible to the user.

<input type="foo" name="field_name">

The `<input>` tag is the most popular tag for HTML forms. It is so widely used because it is so versatile and has many different attributes to modify its behavior, as we'll see in the following sections.

<input name="field_name">

The `name` attribute is used to maintain a relationship between the form data and the item on the page. It is basically a variable name used to gain access to the data stored in the field.

<input name="field_name" type="text">

The input type of `text` is the commonly seen text-entry box that appears on many forms. This type of HTML form input is used to gather text information from the user.

<input name="field_name" type="password">

The `password` type is exactly like the `text` input box. But when data is entered into this box, only the * character shows up. This field is helpful; when you type sensitive data such as passwords, this field prevents others from seeing what you have entered.

The `password` type by itself is *not* an adequate security measure; the data submitted is still passed as the user has entered it (unencrypted). If the form uses the `get` method and has a password field, the plaintext password is visible in the URL once the form is submitted and in the browser's history.

For example, if a user enters `"supersecret"` into a `password` field named `"password"` on a form that uses the `get` method, the URL may look like this once the form has been submitted:

```
http://www.perlguy.net/cgi-bin/admin.cgi?task=delete&password=supersecret
```

Notice that no encryption of the `password` field has occurred; it is exactly as the user has typed.

<input name="field_name" type="hidden" value="value_to_pass">

The `hidden` type also has a name that can be deceiving. Although the data that this field contains *is* hidden on the HTML form (it does not show up on the form as it appears on the screen), the data is visible in the HTML source. This means that sensitive data should not be passed in a `hidden` field because anyone can see the information by simply choosing View ⇨ Source in his or her browser.

The `hidden` field type can be very useful for maintaining nonsensitive data in a CGI application by passing the data in `hidden` fields between CGI program calls.

<input name="field_name" type="radio" value="val">

The `radio` input type creates radio buttons on the form. Radio buttons are the round input widgets used for lists on which only one item can be selected. For the `name` attribute, the same name is used for all radio buttons of the same type. The data in the value attribute is what gets passed to the HTML form.

\<input name="field_name" type="checkbox" value="val">

The checkbox creates the small square boxes on the form that are used for lists that can have multiple items selected. Checkboxes are similar to radio buttons, but with a checkbox, more than one item can be selected. Again, items belonging to the same list use the same name value.

Note: The radio and checkbox input items may also be passed a checked value, like so: \<input name="name" type="radio" value="yes" checked>. Passing a checked value causes the item to be initially selected when the form is loaded.

\<input type="reset" value="Reset Form">

An input type of reset is used to reset all values on the current form to their default values. The value attribute allows you to set the text that appears on the button.

\<input name="button_name" type="submit" value="Add Record">

The submit input type is used to submit data on the HTML form to the CGI program on the server. The value attribute is used to set the text on the button shown. If no value attribute is set, the default button text is "Submit Query". A form can have multiple submit buttons; on the server side, the CGI application can check to see which button has been clicked and can take appropriate action.

\<select name="list_name">

The select HTML tag is used for lists of items presented in a drop-down style.

\<option value="item_value">

The option tag goes inside of a select block. The value attribute is passed to the server if that item is currently selected when the form is submitted. For example:

```
<select name="state">
<option value="MI">Michigan</option>
<option value="MN" selected>Minnesota</option>
<option value="MS">Mississippi</option>
<option value="MO">Missouri</option>
</select>
```

In the preceding code, a drop-down list containing four states is created. By using the selected attribute, the Minnesota item is displayed on the form when it is first loaded and also when the Reset button is pressed. The full state names will be displayed in the drop-down list, but when the form is submitted, only the two-character abbreviation in the value attribute is sent to the CGI application.

<textarea name="item_name" rows="4" cols="40" wrap="physical">

A `textarea` can have quite a few attributes. The `name` attribute serves the same purpose as it does in the other HTML form tags. The `rows` and `cols` tell the browser how many rows and columns this `textarea` is supposed to be displayed as. The `wrap` attribute is used to cause the text to wrap automatically when it gets to the edge of the `textarea`.

The `textarea` tag requires a closing tag; any text in between the opening and closing tags is displayed in the `textarea` upon page load and also if the reset button is pressed.

For example:

```
<textarea name="comments" rows="2" cols="20" wrap="physical">
  This is a feedback section.
</textarea>
```

produces a `textarea` with "This is the feedback section." as the default text.

These are the only tags we will cover; these tags will be worked into our examples so that each can be seen in action.

Interface Design

When designing interfaces for Web applications, you should consider a few things to make the application friendlier to the user. For example, consider the form in Figure 6-1. Not very pretty, is it? Nothing is aligned, and it can even be hard to tell what fields go with what descriptions.

Let's use tables to clean up the interface a little. Take a look at Figure 6-2. It is the same form, except in a table format. Isn't that much better? By using tables, we were able to make the form much nicer to view. Determining what fields go with what descriptions is also easier.

This form has a bit more information than we really need for a phonebook application. The extra elements are presented to give you some familiarity with them. The HTML for this form is included on this book's Web site. Give this form a look, and play with the fields and buttons on it.

Figure 6-3 shows the actual form that we will use as our interface for inputting new records into this version of the Web phonebook application.

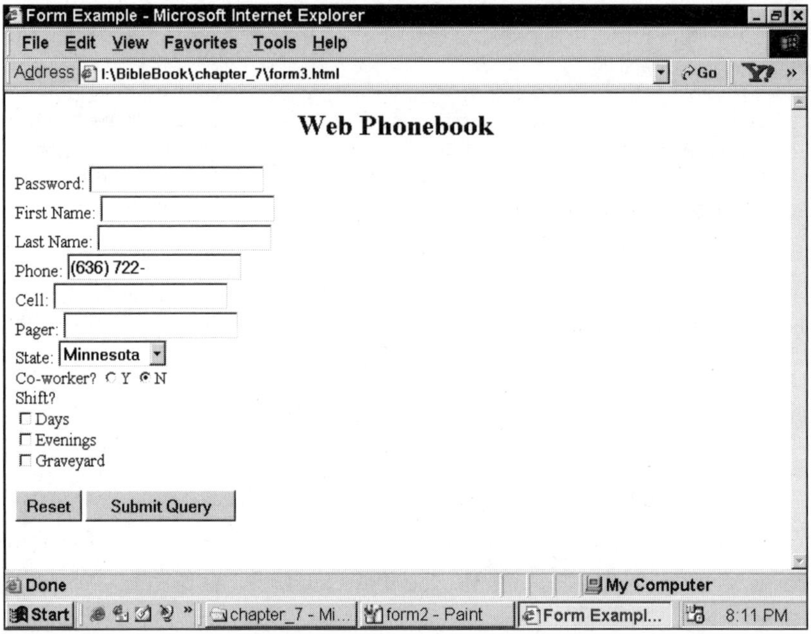

Figure 6-1: Poorly formatted HTML form

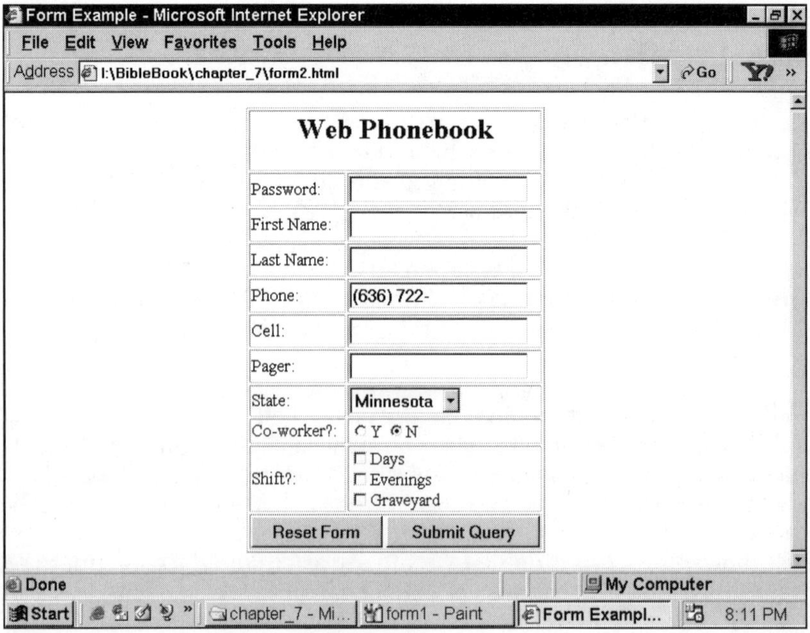

Figure 6-2: Table-formatted HTML form

Design Tips

The following are a few pointers to keep in mind when considering the design of your interface:

✦ Keep the HTML forms as clean and uncluttered as possible.

✦ Gather only the necessary information.

✦ Align fields so they are not scattered all over the form.

✦ Try to keep the form on a single screen. (Don't make the user scroll.)

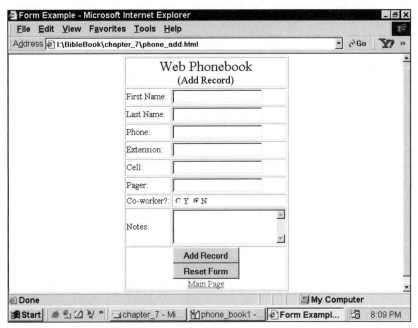

Figure 6-3: Web phonebook screen

Security issues

Security is extremely important, especially when you are dealing with the Web. There are entire books on security and Web programming. There is no way we can cover all aspects of security in Web programming in this small section. Luckily, however, there is an excellent feature of Perl that helps you make your Web programs much more secure. *Taint* mode is a switch in Perl that makes Perl treat all data that comes from an external source as *tainted.* When a variable is tainted, it cannot be used for any sort of system call. The programmer can untaint a variable by filtering it through a regular expression. By tainting variables, you cannot inadvertently execute extra shell commands from malicious user input.

To turn taint mode on, you pass the -T flag on the first line of the program.

```
#!/usr/bin/perl -T
```

The preceding line of code tells the system where to find Perl and turns taint mode on.

```
1: my $var1 = shift;          # Tainted
2: my $var2 = "Brent ";       # Not tainted
3: my $var3 = $var2 . $var1;  # Tainted

4: $var3 =~ /^([\w ]+)$/ or die "Not Cleaned!";   # Clean the
variable...
5: $var3 = $1;                # Now $var3 is untainted.
```

Line 1 $var1 is tainted because the data comes from an external source — the command line.

Line 2 is not tainted because the variable comes from inside of the program; no external data has touched this variable.

Line 3 is tainted because it has been concatenated with the first variable, which is tainted.

Line 4 runs the $var3 variable through a regular expression. This regular expression allows only word characters (alphanumerics plus the underscore) or a space. There can be any number of valid characters because we use a + in the regular expression. Because we begin the regular expression with a ^ and end it with a $, there can be no illegal data in the string. If there is any unwanted data, the regular expression will not match anything, and $1 will be empty. This line calls the die function to terminate the program if the match failed.

On **line 5**, we set $var3 to $1. $1 is the data that matches inside of the parentheses on **line 4**. If none of the data were a match, $var3 would now contain no data.

Let's say that we have a program named taint.pl with the preceding code. Let's run it like this:

```
taint.pl Michalski
```

If $var3 is then printed out, it will contain "Brent Michalski". If, however, we run the program like this:

```
taint.pl Mich-alski
```

$var3 will *not* match anything on the regular expression in **line 4**, so $var3 is now blank.

Taint checking and untainting variables can be quite confusing. The perlsec Perl document has some good information on taint. *Writing CGI Applications with Perl* (Addison Wesley, 2001) also has an entire chapter dedicated to security and all of the examples in that book use the `-T` flag. To see the perlsec document, type `perldoc perlsec` from a prompt.

Speed considerations

Perl CGI programs, without using speed-enhancing tools or methods, are not going to handle large loads and won't be lightening fast. That's ok; nothing truly is without some other tools.

Many corporations, even large financial ones, seem to think that if you want to have enterprise-class applications, you must have enterprise-class prices to handle the load. This is simply not true; many extremely busy sites—such as `http://slashdot.org`—routinely get millions of hits per day. Many of these sites use only Perl and open-source software. Yet if you ask the administrators, they are very happy with performance and the price is definitely right. Also, notice that many of these sites require a very low number of programmers to maintain the site compared with enterprise-class solutions, which typically require teams of developers for maintenance.

You have options if you want to speed Perl up on the Web-server side, but the de facto standard is mod_perl. mod_perl embeds the Perl interpreter into the Apache Web server, which eliminates the startup time of the interpreter. mod_perl can also cache subroutines for further speed enhancements.

Then there are add-ons to mod_perl to make site design even simpler. HTML::Mason is an excellent tool for creating Web sites and allows you to embed Perl right into HTML documents. eperl is another good tool; it also lets you embed Perl into the HTML. Embperl is yet another tool that allows you to embed Perl in the HTML document. All of these offer significant speed enhancements over just plain Perl programs running as CGI programs. Table 6-1 lists the URLs where these tools are available.

Table 6-1 URLs for Perl-Enabled HTML Tools	
Tool	**URL**
mod_perl (and much much more)	`http://perl.apache.org`
HTML Mason	`http://www.masonhq.com`
Embperl	`http://perl.apache.org/embperl`
eperl	`http://www.ossp.org/pkg/eperl`

Program Examples

First, let's develop a Web-based phonebook so that you can get some experience working with databases with a Web interface. The Web-database application we will create will do this:

✦ The application will show an opening screen with an add-record link and an area to enter searches.

✦ The add-record link will point to another HTML page with the form fields for entering a new record.

✦ The add-record page will take input from the user and add it to the database.

✦ The search area on the main page will take input from the user, generate an SQL query statement using data fed by the user inputs, and display a page with the matches to the query.

This is a simple Web-based phonebook; it is not as full-featured as others you may find, but this one is for learning purposes. You are free to add features whenever you want. Adding features is also an excellent way to learn more about the program and Web programming.

Web phonebook

First, let's take a look at the two HTML pages we need to create for our Web phonebook. In these HTML files, we try to use several different HTML form fields so that you can see them in action.

Main HTML page

```
01: <html>
02:   <head><title>Web Phonebook</title></head>
```

```
03:   <body>
04:    <form action="/cgi-bin/phonebook.cgi" method="post">
05:     <input type="hidden" name="form_action" value="search"
/>
06:    <table align="center" border="1" cellpadding="5">
07:     <tr>
08:      <td colspan="2" align="center">
09:       <font size="6">Web Phonebook</font>
10:      </td>
11:     </tr>
12:     <tr>
13:      <td>
14:       Add Record
15:      </td>
16:      <td>
17:       <a href="phone_add.html">Click to Add Record</a>
18:      </td>
19:     </tr>
20:     <tr>
21:      <td align="center">
22:       Search Text:<br />on<br />Field(s):
23:      </td>
24:      <td>
25:       <input type="text" name="search" /><br />
26:       <input type="checkbox" name="field"
          value="firstname" />First Name
27:       <input type="checkbox" name="field"
          value="lastname" />Last Name<br />
28:       <input type="checkbox" name="field"
          value="coworker" />Co-Worker
29:       <input type="checkbox" name="field"
          value="lastname" />Phone #
30:      </td>
31:     </tr>
32:     <tr>
33:      <td colspan="2" align="center">
34:       <input type="submit" value="Submit Search" />
35:      </td>
36:     </tr>
37:    </table>
38:   </form>
39:  </body>
40: </html>
```

The preceding HTML form contains the code needed to create the main page for our Web-based phonebook. Notice on **line 5** that we use a *hidden* form field. This field is used to determine what action to take on the database. Since this page is also the search page, the value for this hidden element is set to "search". This tells our application that the user wants to search for a record.

Add record HTML page

```
01: <html>
02:  <head>
03:   <title>
04:    Form Example
05:   </title>
06:  <head>
07:  <body>
08:   <form action="/cgi-bin/phonebook/phonebook.cgi"
          method="get">
09: <input type="hidden" name="form_action" value="addrecord"
    />
10:    <table border="1" align="center">
11:     <tr>
12:      <td colspan="2" align="center">
13:       <font size="6">Web Phonebook</font><br />
14:       <font size="4">(Add Record)</font>
15:      </td>
16:     </tr>
17:     <tr>
18:      <td>First Name:</td><td><input type="text"
         name="firstname" /></td>
19:     </tr>
20:     <tr>
21:      <td>Last Name:</td><td><input type="text"
         name="lastname" /></td>
22:     </tr>
23:     <tr>
24:      <td>Phone:</td>
25:      <td><input type="text" name="phone" /></td>
26:     </tr>
27:     <tr>
28:      <td>Extension:</td>
29:      <td><input type="text" name="extension" /></td>
30:     </tr>
31:     <tr>
32:      <td>Cell:</td><td><input type="text" name="cell"
/></td>
33:     </tr>
34:     <tr>
35:      <td>Pager:</td><td><input type="text" name="pager"
         /></td>
36:     </tr>
37:     <tr>
38:      <td>Co-worker?:</td>
39:      <td>
40:      <input type="radio" name="coworker" value="Y">Y
41:      <input type="radio" name="coworker" value="N" checked>N
42:      </td>
43:     </tr>
```

```
44:    <tr>
45:     <td>Notes:</td>
46:     <td>
47:      <textarea name="notes" cols="20" rows="3"
           wrap="physical"></textarea>
48:     </td>
49:    </tr>
50:    <tr>
51:     <td align="center" colspan="2">
52:      <input type="submit" value="Add Record" /><br />
53:      <input type="reset" value="Reset Form" /><br />
54:      <a href="phone.html">Main Page</a>
55:     </td>
56:    </tr>
57:   </table>
58:   </form>
59:  </body>
60: </html>
```

— proprietary code

Notice that on **line 9** of the preceding code we again use a hidden form field. This one contains a value of "addrecord" and is used to tell the Web application that the user wants to add a record.

Now that we have the two HTML pages that we'll use for our phonebook application, we can start coding the application and learn how it all interacts with the HTML pages we just created.

phonebook.cgi

```
01: #!/usr/bin/perl -wT
02: #
03: # program 7-1
04: # Web Phonebook Application
05: #

06: use strict;
07: use DBI;
08: use CGI qw(:standard);
09: use CGI::Carp qw(fatalsToBrowser);
```

Line 1 tells the system where to find Perl and turns on warnings with the -w; notice, however, that we now add the taint flag with the T. Turning taint checking on prevents us from using, in system calls, any data which was passed into the program that we haven't checked. This is a safety measure that no other language offers at this level.

Lines 2–5 are simply comments about this program.

Line 6 turns on strict. strict forces the programmer to declare variables and stops many simple but hard to find errors from happening (such as using the same variable name more than once in the same block).

Line 7 loads the DBI module so that we have access to the phonebook database.

Line 8 calls the CGI module and tells it to import the :standard set of features. The CGI module is an incredibly useful module, written by Lincoln Stein, for working with Perl CGI programs. Don't try to write your own subroutines to pull data from a Web form; this CGI module is written specifically for that purpose and has been updated and optimized for many years now.

Line 9 calls the CGI::Carp module and imports the fatalsToBrowser method. By using this module, you can save a lot of time debugging and can also avoid a lot of confusion. Usually, when there is anything wrong with a CGI program, the Web server simply replies with a 500 Server Error and offers no other details. Many beginning CGI programmers get lost at this point because the error message is so vague. By using the CGI::Carp module, most of the errors that occur are sent to the browser so that you get a much more descriptive error than the 500 Server Error.

```
10: print header();

11: my $action = param('form_action');

12: my $DB_Handle = DBI->connect("DBI:mysql:BibleBook",
      "bookuser", "testpass")
13:     or die("Cannot connect: $DBI::errstr\nAborting");
```

Line 10 calls the header function that is in the CGI.pm module. This function is just a shortcut that prints the "Content-Type: text/html\n\n" line for you.

Line 11 calls the param function from CGI.pm and reads in the value passed from the "form_action" field on the HTML form. Remember, this is the hidden field we use to tell the program what we want it to do.

Lines 12–13 connect to the database and store a handle to the connection in $DB_Handle. If there is a problem connecting to the database, **line 13** will print an error message and cause the program to die.

```
14: Add_Record() if($action eq 'addrecord');
15: Search_DB()  if($action eq 'search');
```

Line 14 calls the Add_Record if the value of $action equals "addrecord".

Line 15 calls Search_DB if the value of $action equals "search".

These two lines are where our program decides either to add a record to the database or to search the database for matching records. The program performs only one of these tasks at a time; it either adds a record to the database or searches the database for matching records.

```
16: sub Search_DB {
17:     my ($sql, $st_handle);
18:     my $search_for = param('search');
19:     my @field      = param('field');
```

Line 16 begins the Search_DB subroutine. This subroutine searches the database — hence the descriptive name.

Line 17 creates two variables that we use in this subroutine. By creating them as my variables, their scope is restricted to the block they are declared in.

Line 18 uses the param function from CGI.pm to read in the value passed in the search field on the HTML form and then stores the result in the $search_for variable.

Line 19 uses the param function, as in **Line 18**, but in this case we are expecting a list to be returned to us and stored in @field. The param function "does the right thing": when you ask it to return a scalar, it does; when you ask it to return a list, it does. The reason we want a list to be returned is that the field selections on the HTML form are checkboxes and there can be several values returned. This line, then, stores all of the values that are checked (and named field) on the HTML form and stores them all in the list named @field.

```
20:     @field = map { "($_ LIKE '%$search_for%')" } @field;
```

Line 20 is my favorite for this program. The map function is truly cool. It performs the block of code on each value in the array passed to it and returns the results into a new, or the same, array.

In this line, we have each of the fields we want to search stored in the array named @field. We need to incorporate these fields into a valid SQL query. This can be done using a foreach loop, but doing it this way takes more lines of code. By using map, this can be accomplished in a single line.

Inside of the braces, we have the text "($_ LIKE '%$search_for%')". This is a string, and the result of this string is what the current value that map is evaluating becomes. The $_ is the current value that map is evaluating. So, this is just like saying this:

Note The next four lines are an example, not part of the program.

```
foreach my $current  (@field) {
    $current = "($current LIKE '%$search_for%')";
    push @new_field_array, $current;
}
```

The whole task that we are trying to accomplish here is to take the field-name text that is in the array and change it to a valid portion of SQL so that we can append it to the entire SQL statement.

```
21:     $sql  = qq{SELECT * FROM phonebook WHERE (};
22:     $sql .= join ' OR ', @field;
23:     $sql .= ")";
```

Lines 21–23 generate a valid SQL query used to query the database. **Line 22** is possible because of how we set up the @field array in **line 20**.

Line 21 begins by simply setting the $sql variable to some text.

Line 22 uses the join function to take each value in the @field array and join it with OR.

Line 23 ends the SQL statement.

So, when the program gets to **line 23**, the SQL it generates may look something like this:

```
SELECT * FROM phonebook WHERE ((fname LIKE '%Brent%') OR (lname
LIKE '%Brent%') OR (phone LIKE '%Brent%'))
```

This SQL statement means we have been looking for the text "Brent" in fields fname, lname, **and/or** phone.

The %'s before and after the text we are looking for are the SQL wildcard characters. These characters act like a * in the shell. So, this translates to "find any matches that have Brent in them with any text before or after the matching text." If you want to be strict about the matching, leave off the %'s. Then the matches have to be exact.

```
24:     $st_handle =  $DB_Handle->prepare($sql);
25:     $st_handle -> execute();

26:     Display_Results($st_handle);
27: }
```

Line 24 calls the prepare method from the DBI module and passes it the SQL statement. The result of this method call is stored in $st_handle.

Line 25 takes the $st_handle statement handle and calls the execute method on it. This causes the SQL statement to be executed on the SQL database table. A pointer to the results returned is then stored in the $st_handle variable.

Line 26 calls the Display_Results subroutine and passes $st_handle to it.

Line 27 closes this subroutine.

```
28: sub Display_Results {
29:     my $handle = shift;
30:     my ($fname, $lname, $cow, $phone, $ext,
            $cell, $pager, $notes, $count);
31:     my $bgcol = "";
```

Line 28 begins the `Display_Results` subroutine. This subroutine is used to generate an HTML page of the matching records from a database search.

Line 29 creates a `my` variable named `$handle` and uses the `shift` function to read in the value. This is the value passed to the subroutine when it is called and is a handle that contains the matching records.

Line 30 declares some scalar variables we will be using in this subroutine.

Line 31 declares a variable named `$bgcol` and sets it to an initial value of an empty string.

```
32:      print<<'    HTML';
```

Line 32 begins a `here-document`. A `here-document` prints out text between the starting line and the ending tag. The ending tag is the '   HTML' on **line 32**. The only reason there are spaces before the HTML in the tag is so that we can maintain our indenting. The ending tag in a `here document` must be *exactly* what is used for creating the tag. If you have four spaces before the tag, there must be four spaces in the ending tag.

```
33:      <html><head><title>Search Results</title></head>
34:       <body>
35:        <table align="center" border="1" cellspacing="0">
36:         <tr bgcolor="#303030">
37:          <td colspan="6" align="center">
38:           <font size="5" color="white">
39:            Search Results
40:           </font>
41:          </td>
42:         </tr>
43:         <tr bgcolor="#c0c0c0">
44:          <td align="center"><b>Name</b></td>
45:          <td align="center"><b>Co-Worker?</b></td>
46:          <td align="center"><b>Phone</b></td>
47:          <td align="center"><b>Extension</b></td>
48:          <td align="center"><b>Cell</b></td>
49:          <td align="center"><b>Pager</b></td>
50:         </tr>
51:      HTML
```

Lines 33–50 are simply the HTML needed to begin the page for the search results. We are using a table to keep the data nice and formatted.

Line 51 is the ending tag for the `here document` that begins on **line 32**.

```
52:      $handle->bind_columns(undef,
53:       \($fname, $lname, $cow, $phone, $ext,
         $cell, $pager, $notes));
```

Line 52 calls the `bind_colums` method on the `$handle`. This causes the variables that we referenced to be "bound" to the query results. This means that each time we call the `fetch` method, the values are stored in the variables they are bound to. The `undef` in the first argument to `bind_columns` is not currently used by the DBI, but it is required nonetheless.

```
54:     while($handle->fetch){
55:         $bgcol = ($bgcol eq "ffffff") ? "e0e0e0": "ffffff";
```

Line 54 begins a `while` loop that calls the `fetch` method. This gets the query matches, one record at a time, until there are no more matches left. Once we are out of matches, the `while` loop terminates because the call to `$handle->fetch` is no longer true.

Line 55 makes the data more readable. This uses the `trinary` operator to alternate the background colors of each row of data. The value on the left side of the ? is evaluated; if it is true, the first item to the right of the ? is executed. It the value on the left side of the ? is false, the value to the right of the : is executed. This is an easier way to do an `if..else` block on simple expressions.

```
56:     print qq(<tr bgcolor="#$bgcol">);
57:      print qq(<td>$fname $lname</td><td
          align="center">$cow</td>);
58:      print qq(<td>$phone</td><td>$ext</td><td>$cell</td>);
59:      print qq(<td>$pager</td>);
60:     print qq(</tr>);
```

Line 56 prints the table-row tag, with the appropriate background color.

Lines 57–59 print a row of data, with each cell of data being in its own table cell. The exception to this is the name field, where we list both the first name (`fname`) and last name (`lname`) in a single table cell.

Line 60 prints the closing table row tag.

```
61:         $count++;
62:     }
```

Line 61 increments the `$count` variable. This variable is used for the sole purpose of checking to see if any data has actually returned.

Line 62 ends the `while` loop that fetches the data, row by row.

```
63:     No_Data() unless($count);

64:     print qq(</table></body></html>);
65: }
```

Line 63 calls the No_Data subroutine. This subroutine gets called if the $count variable is false. If there are no matches for the query, the while statement on **line 54** will never be entered — and the $count variable never gets incremented. This is a simple trick to see if there are any matches.

Line 64 prints the ending tags for the HTML page.

Line 65 closes this subroutine.

```
66: sub No_Data{
67:    print qq(<tr><td colspan="6" align="center">);
68:    print qq(No matches found, return to);
69:    print qq(<a href="/phonebook/phone.html">main
page</a>.);
70:    print qq(</td></tr>);
71: }
```

Line 66 begins the No_Data subroutine. This subroutine simply prints some text to let the user know that there are no matches. Without this, if there are no matches, an HTML page with a table consisting solely of headings will be displayed.

Lines 67–70 print some HTML to inform the user that there are no matches and to provide him or her with a link to the main phonebook page.

Line 71 closes this subroutine.

```
72: sub Add_Record {
73:    my $fname    = param('firstname');
74:    my $lname    = param('lastname');
75:    my $phone    = param('phone');
76:    my $ext      = param('extension');
77:    my $cell     = param('cell');
78:    my $pager    = param('pager');
79:    my $coworker = param('coworker');
80:    my $notes    = param('notes');
81:    my $sql;
```

Line 72 begins the Add_Record subroutine. This subroutine is used to gather the data entered on the HTML form, generate the appropriate SQL statement, and execute the SQL statement to add the record to the phonebook database table.

Lines 73–80 use the param function from the CGI.pm module to read in the data sent from the HTML form.

Line 81 declares a scalar variable named $sql.

```
82:    $sql  = qq{INSERT INTO phonebook (firstname,
lastname,};
83:    $sql .= qq{coworker, phone, extension, cell, pager,
              notes)};
84:    $sql .= qq{VALUES (?, ?, ?, ?, ?, ?, ?, ?)};
```

Lines 82–84 create the SQL statement needed to add a record to the database table. The ?'s on **line 84** are placeholders. They allow you to prepare an SQL statement. When you call the execute method, you pass values used to fill in the ?'s. **Line 86** shows the execute method call with the values being passed.

```
85:     my $st_handle = $DB_Handle->prepare($sql);

86:     my $rval = $st_handle->execute($fname, $lname,
$coworker,
87:             $phone, $ext, $cell, $pager, $notes);
```

Line 85 prepares the SQL statement that we create on **lines 82–84**.   Remember that when you prepare an SQL statement, it gets stored in an internally compiled format, ready to be executed against the database. The return value is a handle to that particular SQL statement that we store in the $st_handle variable in this instance.

Lines 86–87 call the execute method on the SQL statement. This line also passes the values, which we read in on **lines 73–80**, to the SQL statement. The number of values you pass in the execute call *must match exactly* the number of placeholders (?'s) in the SQL statement.

```
88:     Handle_DB_Error() unless($rval);

89:     Display_Page();
90: }
```

Line 88 calls the Handle_DB_Error subroutine if the $rval scalar is not true. On **line 86**, if for some reason the execute method call has failed, $rval remains undefined.

Line 89 calls the Display_Page subroutine. Display_Page is the subroutine that generates a simple HTML page that tells the user he or she has successfully added a record to the database.

Line 90 ends this subroutine.

```
91: sub Display_Page {
92:     print<<'    HTML';
```

Line 91 begins the Display_Page subroutine. This subroutine simply generates an HTML page to inform the user that his or her record addition has been successful.

Line 92 begins a here document. By using a here document, we save ourselves from having repeatedly to type print statements at the beginning of each line.

```
93:     <html><head><title>Record Added!</title></head>
94:      <body>
95:       <center>
96:        <font size="6">
97:         Record Added!
```

```
98:        </font>
99:        <hr />
100:       <font size="4">
101:       <a href="/phonebook/phone.html">Back to Main
Page</a>
102:         </font><br />
103:       </center>
104:      </body>
105:    </html>
```

Lines 93–105 are the HTML for the entire page we are generating.

```
106:      HTML
107: }
```

Line 106 ends the here document that we begin on **line 92**.

Line 107 closes this subroutine.

```
108: sub Handle_DB_Error {
109:     print<<'    HTML';
```

Line 108 begins the Handle_DB_Error subroutine. This subroutine is used to display an error message if there is a database error of some kind.

Line 109 begins a here document used to print the HTML for the error page.

```
110:      <html><head><title>Database Error</title></head>
111:      <body>
112:       <center>
113:        <font size="6">
114:         Error with database call.
115:        </font>
116:        <hr />
117:        <font size="4" color="red">
118:         $DBI::errstr
119:        </font><br />
120:        <font size="3">
121:         Please hit your <b>back</b> button to re-enter the
           data and try again.
122:        </font>
123:       </center>
124:      </body>
125:    </html>
```

Lines 110–125 are the HTML needed for our error page. On **line 118**, we print the $DBI::errstr variable, which is a DBI variable that contains the error message.

```
126:      HTML

127:      exit;
128: }
```

Line 126 closes the `here document` that we begin on **line 109**.

Line 127 calls the `exit` function. Since an error has occurred, we want to call the `exit` function to be absolutely sure that the program does not continue from here.

Line 128 closes this subroutine and is the end of the program as well.

So, in 128 lines of code, much of it just HTML strings, we have a Web application that can search its database table and add records to the database table. If you feel up to it, use your knowledge from this book and modify this application so that you can also modify and delete records.

Web-based quiz program

The next, and final, example for this chapter is a Web-based quiz program. It actually comprises several related programs. For this system, we take a different approach. Instead of a large program that handles everything, we now have a central module that contains the common functions and several small CGI programs that perform a specific task.

The Quizzer program allows an "administrator" to add new tests and add questions to tests. It also allows users to take the tests that have already been created. There is not much error-trapping code, nor is there a lot of code to make it look pretty. Instead, we will be working on the framework of a program that can be incorporated into a Web site and made to look very polished.

Remember that with Perl, *there is more than one way to do it!* You may find this programming style easier than one where you try to keep all of the functionality in one larger program. The idea is that if you like to program one way, do so. Perl doesn't force you to do things this way or that way. Sure, there are rules that must be followed, but the main task at hand is what is important, not how you go about handling that task.

This program is not meant for public consumption, not without a few changes. The administration programs and HTML pages are probably not something you want everyone to have access to. It is up to you to put those pages and scripts in a location that you have made safe if you don't want them to be accessible to everyone.

The SQL information for creating the tables can be found at the end of this chapter or online at this book's Web site.

The online Quizzer application consists of:

✦ A MySQL database with three tables

- Questions
- Answers
- Test_config

✦ Three HTML files for navigation

- index.html

- admin.html

- create_test.html

✦ Six Perl/CGI programs

- add_question.cgi

- create_test.cgi

- test_chooser.cgi

- take_test.cgi

- score_test.cgi

- Quizzer.pm

That seems like a lot, but with each program performing a specific task, if there is an error, this strategy can make it much easier to debug. Let's start off by looking at the HTML pages. These pages are not ornate, only functional. Also, as far as the HTML goes, only the important information is pointed out.

index.html

```
01: <html><head><title>Quizzer v0.1</title></head>
02: <body>
03:  <center><font size="6">Quizzer v0.1</font></center>
04:  <hr width="75%" />
05:  <p align="center">
06:   <font size="4">
07:    <ul>
08:     <li><a href="/cgi-bin/quizzer/test_chooser.cgi">Take
         a Test</a></li>
09:     <li><a href="admin.html">Admin Page</a></li>
10:    </ul>
11:   </font>
12:  </p>
13: </body>
14: </html>
```

This file is just a simple 14 lines of HTML. It provides you with two choices: a link to choose a test to take or a link to the administration page. For a real-world situation, you may choose to forgo this page and link directly to the "test chooser" page so that the user can only choose a test to take and not have the option to go to the administration pages.

admin.html

```
01: <html><head><title>Quizzer v0.1</title></head>
02: <body>
03:  <center><font size="6">Quizzer v0.1</font></center>
04:  <table border="1" align="center">
05:   <tr>
06:    <td>
07:     <font size="4">
08:      <ul>
09:       <li><a href="create_test.html">Create a new
            test</a></li>
10:       <li><a href="/cgi-
bin/quizzer/test_chooser?action=add">
            Add a question to a test</a></li>
11:       <li><a href="index.html">Main Page</a></li>
12:      </ul>
13:     </font>
14:    </td>
15:   </tr>
16:  </table>
17: </body>
18: </html>
```

This page simply provides test administrators with a link to create a test or to add a question to a test.

Line 10 is of interest here. On this line, we provide a link to the test_chooser.cgi program — but this time we add ?action=add to the end of the URL. We do this to tell the test_chooser.cgi program that we want to add a question, so take the appropriate actions to make sure we get to the proper pages. The test_chooser. cgi program looks for this data added to the URL. If it finds it, a different page title is shown, and the HTML form action also calls a different CGI program.

create_test.html

```
01: <html>
02: <head><title>Quizzer v0.1 - Create Test</title></head>
03: <body>
04:  <center>
05:   <font size="6">Quizzer v0.1 - Create Test</font>
06:  </center>
07:  <hr width="75%" />
08:  <form action="/cgi-bin/quizzer/create_test.cgi"
       method="post">
09:   <table border="1" align="center">
10:    <tr>
```

```
11:      <td><b>Test Name:</b></td>
12:      <td><input type="text" name="test_name"></td>
13:    </tr><tr>
14:      <td><b>Number of Questions:</b></td>
15:      <td><input type="text" name="questions"></td>
16:    </tr><tr>
17:      <td><b>Choices per Question:</b></td>
18:      <td><input type="text" name="choices"></td>
19:    </tr><tr>
20:      <td colspan="2" align="center">
21:       <input type="submit" value="Add Test to Database">
22:      </td>
23:    </tr>
24:    </table>
25:  </form>
26:  <hr width="75%" />
27:  <p align="center">
28:   <font size="4"><b>
29:    [ <a href="index.html">Main Page</a> ]
30:   </font>
31:  </p>
32: </body>
33: </html>
```

This file creates a form so that a test administrator can create a new test. There are three input fields: the test name, the number of questions that make up a test, and the maximum number of choices that each question will have.

The number of questions for a test does not mean how many questions an administrator will enter; it simply means how many questions a user needs to answer to "finish" a test. For example, a test may have 100 questions in the database, but a test may only be 10 questions long. In a case like this, the user is presented with 10 randomly chosen questions, and the test is scored.

Figure 6-4 shows what the page generated by `create_test.html` looks like.

Next, we are going to cover the Perl programs that make up the complete Quizzer application. We'll start with the administration programs so that you can get an idea how a quiz is created. Then we will cover the "user" pieces; these are the pieces that a user sees. Finally, we will cover the `Quizzer.pm` module. We are covering the `Quizzer.pm` module last because this is the piece that brings it all together; if we cover it first, you will not have the basic understanding of how the application works as a whole. By covering it last, you will have already seen what the application is supposed to do — now we'll see *how* it does it.

The following program is called by the `create_test.html` file. This program simply takes the information entered into the HTML form and stores it in the MySQL database we are using for the Quizzer application.

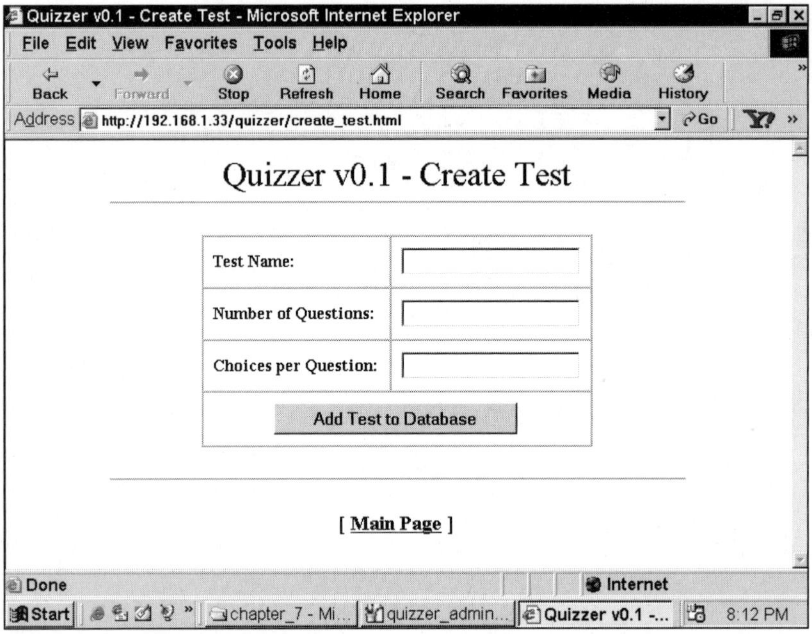

Figure 6-4: Create test HTML form

create_test.cgi

```
01: #!/usr/bin/perl -wT
02: #
03: # create_test.cgi
04: # Chapter 7
05: # Online Quizzer
06: #

07: use strict;
08: use DBI;
09: use CGI qw(:standard);
```

Line 1 tells the system where to find Perl. It also turns on warnings and taint mode with -wT.

Lines 2–6 are simply comments that give information about the program.

Line 7 turns on the strict module. The strict module forces the programmer to declare variables and enforces more rules on the programmer so that common mistakes can be avoided.

Line 8 uses the DBI module. This allows us to have access to the database that the test information is stored in.

Line 9 loads the `CGI` module and reads in the standard methods.

```
10: my $conn = DBI->connect("DBI:mysql:quizzer",
        "bookuser","testpass")
        or die("Cannot connect: $DBI::errstr\nAborting");
```

Line 10 creates a connection to the Quizzer database and returns a reference (handle) to the database, which we store in the $conn variable. If there is a problem connecting to the database, the program will call die and an error will be printed.

```
11: my $test_name = param('test_name');
12: my $questions = param('questions');
13: my $choices   = param('choices');
```

Lines 11–13 declare some variables with my and use the param function from the `CGI.pm` module to each read in the data from the HTML files form fields.

```
14: my $rval = $conn->do("INSERT INTO test_config SET
15:     NumQs=$questions, Choices=$choices,
16:     test_name='$test_name'");
```

Lines 14–16 are a single Perl statement that declares a my variable named $rval (which stands for return value, in this case) and sets it to the value returned by the do statement. The do statement here is a call to the do method on the SQL statement inside of the parentheses. Since we are not returning any data, we can skip the *prepare/execute* way of accessing the database and do it in a single call with do.

The following SQL statement takes the information passed from the HTML form in **lines 11–13** and stores it in the database.

```
17: my $val = $conn->{'mysql_insertid'};

18: print header();
```

Line 17 calls the mysql_insertid MySQL function. This function returns the value of the last autoincremented field. This feature is really not needed for our program, but I found that there really weren't any documented examples of its usage so I wanted to include an example with it in actual use. If there is a problem, undef is returned by this function call.

Line 18 prints the value/data returned by the header function. The header function is part of the `CGI.pm` module. This simply prints our Content-Type header.

```
19: if($rval) {
20:     print <<"     HTML";
21:     <html><head><title>Test Added!</title></head>
22:       <body>
23:        <font size="4">
24:         <center>
25:          Test $val Added to Database!<br>
26:         </center>
```

```
27:            </font>
28:            </body>
29:            </html>
30:      HTML
31: }
```

Line 19 checks to see if the variable $rval contains any data. If it does, we enter this block of code.

Line 20 begins a `here` document that prints the HTML message informing the user/administrator that the addition of a new test has been successful.

Note that in this `here-document`, the terminating string is surrounded by double quotes. This causes the HTML data inside of the `here` document to behave as if it were a double-quoted string. If we had used single quotes, the variable would not be interpolated on **line 25**.

Lines 21–29 are simply the HTML message we are going to display. Notice that on **line 25** we have a variable, $val, which will be interpolated with its current value when this page is displayed.

Line 30 is the ending tag for the `here` document. Since we use four spaces before the ending tag on **line 20**, we must also have four spaces before the ending tag on this line.

Line 31 closes this block of code.

```
32: else {
33:      print <<"    HTML";
34:        <html><head><title>Error!</title></head>
35:         <body>
36:          <font size="4">
37:           <center>
38:            ERROR!!! ($DBI::errstr)<br />
39:            Something unexpected happened!<br />
40:           </center>
41:          </font>
42:         </body>
43:        </html>
44:      HTML
45: }
```

Line 32 begins the `else` part of this `if..else` block. If the variable $rval contains no value, or `undef` in this case, we enter this block of code and execute it.

Line 33 begins the `here` document used to print the error message to the user.

Lines 34–43 are the HTML for the error message.

Line 44 ends the *here document* that we begin on **line 33**.

Line 45 closes the else portion of the if..else block. This is also the end of this program.

This program simply reads the three values that are entered on the HTML form, stores them into the database, and displays a message to the user, telling them that they are successful or that an error has occurred.

The following program is the CGI used to add a question to an existing test. It looks at the test-configuration file and dynamically generates an HTML form so that the test administrator can simply fill in the blanks to create a new question. Let's take a look at the code for this program.

add_question.cgi

```
01: #!/usr/bin/perl -wT
02: #
03: # add_question.cgi
04: # Chapter 7
05: # Online Quizzer
06: # Add question 2
07: #

08: use strict;
09: use CGI qw(:standard);
10: use lib qw(.);
11: use Quizzer;
```

Line 1 tells the system where to find Perl and turns on warnings and taint checking with the -wT.

Lines 2–7 are comments that give information about the program.

Line 8 turns on the strict module. strict causes the programmer to be more careful with declaring variables and also turns on other safeguards to help prevent common programming mistakes. Using strict is something you should always do.

Line 9 loads the CGI module and imports the standard set of functions. The CGI module should be used for all HTML form parsing. Writing your own HTML form parser is possible, but the CGI module is a proven and works very well. The CGI module also has been very thoroughly tested for security holes.

Line 10 tells Perl that the current directory can also be a library directory — it actually gets added to the @INC array. This means that when you load modules with use, Perl also looks in the current directory for a matching module. We need to do this because our Quizzer.pm module is in the same directory as this program.

The qw(.) is actually a bit more verbose than it could be; we could have simply used this:

```
Use lib ".";
```

There are two reasons why we didn't do that, though. First, using qw is a standard way of doing this. Second, if, at a later time, you want to add more directories to this list, you can easily do so by just adding more paths in the parentheses.

Line 11 loads the Quizzer Perl module. This is the module that contains much of the functionality of the programs for our Quizzer application.

```
12: my $test_id = param('test_id');
13: my $Qtext   = param('Qtext');
14: my $correct = param('correct');
15: my @false   = param('false');
16: my $rval;
```

Line 12 declares a my scalar variable named $test_id and reads in the value passed in from the test_id input box on the HTML form. This is the ID that the database has the test stored as.

Line 13 declares a my scalar variable named $Qtext and reads in the value passed in from the Qtext input box on the HTML form. This is the question text.

Line 14 declares a my scalar variable named $correct and reads in the value passed in from the correct input box on the HTML form. This is the text of the correct answer.

Line 15 declares a my array variable named @false and reads in the *all* of the values passed in from the text-input boxes named false on the HTML form. These are the text of each of the false answers.

Line 16 declares a my scalar variable named $rval. This is used to store a return value later on.

```
17: my ($TestID, $NumQs, $Choices, $test_name) =
       Get_Test_Config($test_id);

18: if($Qtext ne ''){
19:    $rval = Add_Question($Qtext, $test_id, $correct,
@false);
20: }

21: print header();
```

Line 17 calls the Get_Test_Config function and passes it the test ID number. This function is located in the Quizzer.pm module. It takes a test ID as its input, and returns the test ID, number of questions, number of choices for each question, and the test name. These returned values are stored in the variables $TestID, $NumQs, $Choices, and $test_name.

Line 18 checks to see if the value in $Qtext contains any data. In English, this statement is saying: *If* $Qtext *is not empty, enter this code block.* So, if $Qtext *is* empty, we don't want to add the question to the database. By not adding the question to the database, $rval remains without a value. (We'll check that in a moment.)

Line 19 calls the Add_Question function and passes $Qtext, $test_id, $correct, and @false to the function. The function returns 1 if it is successful, and that value gets stored in $rval.

Line 20 closes the small code block that we begin on **line 18**. Since we are using Perl, and the motto is *There is more than one way to do it!*, this could have been written on a single line instead. This is basically what that looks like as a single line statement:

```
$rval = Add_Question($Q, $T, $C, @F) if($Q ne '');
```

This does the same thing, but is a bit too long to fit nicely in this book (if we used the same variable names), so we opt for a regular if block.

Line 21 prints the return value of the header function. The header function is part of the CGI.pm module.

```
22: print <<HTML;
23:   <html><head><title>Add A Question</title></head>
24:   <body>
25:     <form action="add_question.cgi">
26:       <input type="hidden" name="test_id" value="$test_id">
27:       <table border="1" align="center">
28:         <tr bgcolor="#c0c0c0">
29:          <td colspan="2" align="center">
30:           <font size="6">Add question to $test_name
test.</font>
31:          </td>
32:         </tr>
33:         <tr bgcolor="#e0e0e0">
34:          <td> </td>
35:          <td align="center"><b>Question/Answer Text</b></td>
36:         </tr>
37:         <tr>
38:          <td bgcolor="#e0e0e0">
39:           <b>Question:</b>
40:          </td>
41:          <td><input type="text" size="60" name="Qtext"></td>
42:         </tr>
43:         <tr>
44:          <td bgcolor="#e0e0e0">
45:           <b>Correct Answer:</b>
46:          </td>
47:          <td><input type="text" size="60" name="correct"></td>
48:         </tr>
49: HTML
```

Lines 22–49 are a *here document* that prints the top portion of the HTML page. Notice on **line 25** that this CGI makes itself the target ('action') of the form that it produces. This is perfectly normal—when the user hits 'Submit,' it just produces another instance of this program, to carry on processing. If data is entered, and this CGI program is called, it will again display a form so that the user can enter another question—but the data that is entered is displayed at the bottom of the page, so the user can see that what he or she has entered has been added to the database.

Line 30 uses the `$test_name` variable to make the HTML page have a title in the table so that the user knows which test he or she is adding a question to.

```
50: for (1..($Choices - 1)){
51:     print qq(
52:         <tr>
53:          <td bgcolor="#e0e0e0">
54:           <b>False Answer:</b>
55:          </td>
56:          <td>
57:           <input type="text" size="60" name="false">
58:          </td>
59:         </tr>
60:     );
61: }
```

Line 50 begins a `for` loop that loops from 1 to the value of (`$Choices - 1`). We take one away from the `$Choices` variable because we already have an input item for the correct answer in **line 47**. This loop is used to create the proper number text input boxes for the false answers.

Line 51 begins a qq block. qq is yet another way to quote text. The way we are using qq here is very similar to a *here document*. **Line 51** opens the qq(block, and anything between it and the closing) on **line 60** gets printed.

qq is a nice way to print because variables still get interpolated, as in a double-quoted string, but you do not have to escape any of the quotes or double quotes that you may have inside of the block.

Lines 52–59 are simply HTML elements that make up the page we are displaying.

Line 60 closes the qq block that we began on **line 51**.

Line 61 closes the for loop that we begin on **line 50**.

```
62: print <<HTML;
63:     <tr bgcolor="#e0e0e0">
64:      <td colspan="2" align="center">
65:       <input type="submit" value="Add Question">
66:      </td>
67:     </tr>
68: HTML
```

Line 62 begins a *here document*. Again, we could have done it another way and used qq instead. These examples show you over and over that with Perl, you have a lot of freedom with how you program. If you are more comfortable with qq blocks, by all means change this to a qq block.

Lines 63–67 are HTML for the add question form.

Line 68 closes the *here document*.

```
69: if($rval){
70:     print qq(
71:         <tr><td colspan="2">
72:          <b><u>Question Added</u></b><br>
73:           <b>$Qtext</b>
74:            <ul>
75:       <li><font color="green">$correct</font> *Correct
answer
76:      );

77:      foreach my $tmp (@false){ print "<li>$tmp" if($tmp); }
78:      print qq(</ul></td>);
79: }
```

Line 69 checks to see if the scalar variable $rval contains any data. If so, this block of code is entered.

Line 70 begins a qq block for printing some HTML data.

Lines 72–75 are HTML for the resulting page we are generating.

Line 76 closes the qq block that begins on **line 70**.

Line 77 begins a foreach loop that traverses through all of the false responses and displays them in an HTML unordered list. This line just incorporates a whole foreach block of code onto a single line.

Line 78 prints some HTML tags.

Line 79 closes the if block that begins on **line 69**.

```
80: print <<HTML;
81:     </tr>
82:     <tr>
83:      <td colspan="2" align="center">
84:       <a href="/quizzer/admin.html">Admin Menu</a>
85:      </td>
86:     </tr>
87:    </table>
88:   </form></body></html>
89: HTML
```

Line 80 begins a *here document* that prints the closing HTML for this page.

Lines 81–88 are the closing HTML for this page.

Line 89 closes the *here document* and is the end of this program.

The resulting page should look something like the page in Figure 6-5.

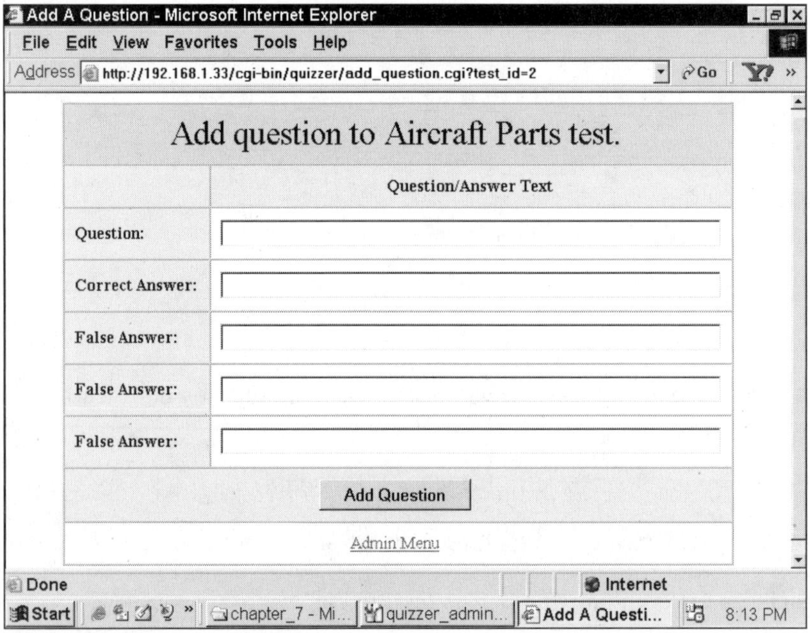

Figure 6-5: Add question form

That is it for the `add_question.cgi` program — the program that generates an HTML form based upon the test configuration, accepts the input from the test administrator, and stores the new questions in the database.

The next CGI application we look at is the `test_chooser.cgi` program. This program queries the database to get a list of all of the available tests; then it generates a page with a drop-down list for the user to choose a test from.

test_chooser.cgi

```
01: #!/usr/bin/perl -wT
02: #
03: # test_chooser.cgi
04: # Chapter 7
```

```
05: # Online Quizzer
06: # Test Chooser
07: #
```

Line 1 should be very familiar by now. This line tells the system where to find Perl and turns on warnings and taint checking.

Lines 2–7 are simply comments about the program.

```
08: use strict;
09: use lib qw(.);
10: use Quizzer;
11: use CGI qw(:standard);
```

Line 8 turns on `strict`.

Line 9 tells Perl that the current directory (.) is to be added to the @INC array. This allows modules in the current directory to be imported with the use statement.

Line 10 imports the Quizzer module.

Line 11 imports the CGI module and its :standard functions.

```
12: my $passed = param('action');
```

Line 12 declares a scalar variable named $passed and uses the param function from the CGI module to read in the value passed from the HTML form. In this case, action is actually passed only on the URL by adding ?action=add.

```
13: my $title  = "Choose a Test to Take";
14: $title     = "Add Question to?"  if($passed eq 'add');

15: my $action = "take_test.cgi";
16: $action    = "add_question.cgi"  if($passed eq 'add');
```

Line 13 declares a scalar variable named $title and sets it to an initial value.

Line 14 changes the value of $title if the value of $passed has been added. If not, it leaves the value of $title alone.

Line 15 declares a scalar variable named $action and sets it to an initial value.

Line 16 changes the value of $action if the value of $passed has been added. If not, it leaves the value of $action alone.

Lines 13–16 effectively perform an if..else, but we were able to leave off the else part by setting the variables to an initial, default, value.

```
17: my $sth_testlist = Get_Test_List();

18: print header();
```

Line 17 calls the Get_Test_List function and stores the results of the function call in the variable named $sth_testlist. This function returns a *handle* to the query results, so $sth_testlist is a handle that references the results.

Line 18 prints the data returned by a call to CGI.pm's header function.

```
19: print <<"HTML";
20:     <html><head><title>Choose A Test</title></head>
21:       <body>
22:        <form action="$action">
23:         <table border="1" align="center">
24:          <tr bgcolor="#c0c0c0">
25:           <td align="center">
26:             <font size="5">$title</font>
27:           </td>
28:          </tr>
29:          <tr>
30:           <td align="center"><select name="test_id">
31: HTML
```

Line 19 begins a *here document* that prints the beginning of the HTML page and also begins a drop-down select box named test_id.

Lines 20–30 are the beginning HTML for the page this program generates.

Line 22 places the $action value into the HTML form action tag. This gives the program the ability to dynamically change the action of the HTML form that it generates.

Line 31 ends the *here document* that begins on **line 19**.

```
32: while(my $p = $sth_testlist->fetchrow_hashref){
33:     print "<option value='$p->{TestID}'>$p-
>{test_name}</option>";
34: }
```

Line 32 begins a while block that fetches the data from the database. Notice that we are using the fetchrow_hashref function from the DBI module, but we haven't even had a use DBI statement yet. This is because the Quizzer.pm module handles all of the database functions for us, and the necessary use statements to the DBI module are contained within it.

Line 33 prints the options that make up the drop-down box on the HTML form. The value attribute of the option is the TestID, and the value shown in the drop-down box is the test_name.

Line 34 ends the while loop that begins on **line 32**.

```
35: print <<HTML;
36:             </select>
37:             </td>
```

```
38:            </tr>
39:            <tr bgcolor="#e0e0e0">
40:             <td align="center">
41:              <input type="submit" value="Choose Test">
42:             </td>
43:            </tr>
44:           </table>
45:          </form>
46:        </body></html>
47: HTML
```

Line 35 begins a *here document* that prints the closing HTML tags needed for the page we are generating.

Lines 36–46 are the HTML for the page.

Line 47 closes the *here document* and is also the last line of this program.

This wraps up the `test_chooser.cgi` program. This is a short program that displays a simple HTML form with the various tests in a drop-down box, but it is a necessary springboard to the other parts of the application because the application must know which test to work with.

The next program, `take_test.cgi`, is what a user sees when he or she takes a test. This program reads the test-configuration information, gets a random question, randomizes the order of the answer-choices, and displays it for the user. This program is doing quite a bit, but we have kept the code to a minimum by consolidating everything that we can into the `Quizzer.pm` module.

take_test.cgi

```
01: #!/usr/bin/perl -wT
02: #
03: # take_test.cgi
04: # Chapter 7
05: # Online Quizzer
06: # Test taker thing
07: #
```

Line 1 tells the system where to find Perl and turns on warnings and taint checking.

Lines 2–7 are comments about this program.

```
08: use strict;
09: use lib qw(.);
10: use CGI qw(:standard);
11: use Quizzer;
```

Line 8 turns on the `strict` module. This forces the programmer to declare variables and prevents many common programming mistakes, such as having two variables in the same scope with the same name.

Line 9 tells Perl to add the current directory (`.`) to the `@INC` array. This line *must* come before our call to the `Quizzer` module, since the `Quizzer` module is in the same directory as this program and since this directory is not in the `@INC` array yet.

Note　Remember `@INC` is an array of paths that Perl uses to find libraries and modules.

Line 10 imports the `CGI` module and its standard functions.

Line 11 imports the `Quizzer` module.

```
12: my $cookie  = cookie('Quizzer');
13: my $a_id    = param('a_id');
14: my $test_id = param('test_id');
15: my $q_id    = param('q_id');
```

Line 12 declares a scalar variable named `$cookie` and stores the results returned by a call to the `CGI` modules `cookie` function. The call to the `cookie` function passes the string `'Quizzer'` to it, so this call fetches the cookie named Quizzer if there is one stored on the users browser.

Line 13 declares a scalar variable named `$a_id` and uses `CGI.pm`'s `param` function to fetch the value from the `a_id` form field on the HTML page that calls this CGI program.

Line 14 declares a scalar variable named `$test_id` and uses `param` to get the value passed from the HTML form.

Line 15 declares a scalar variable named `$q_id` and uses the `param` function to get the value passed from the HTML form.

```
16: $test_id    = 2 unless($test_id);

17: my ($TestID, $NumQs, $Choices, $test_name) =
       Get_Test_Config($test_id);
```

Line 16 sets `$test_id` to 2 `unless` there is a value in `$test_id`. This means that if `$test_id` is empty, and nothing is passed from the HTML form, we set it to 2 as a default value. You can change the 2 to the ID of whatever test ID you want to be the default test.

Line 17 calls the `Get_Test_Config` function and passes it `$test_id`. This function returns four values that are stored in `$TestID`, `$NumQs`, `$Choices`, and `$test_name`, respectively. The `Get_Test_Config` function is located in the `Quizzer.pm` module.

```
18: # check cookies here
19: my $data = "$TestID:$q_id:$a_id";
20: $data    = $data . "*" . $cookie;
21: $data    = '' unless($a_id);
```

Line 18 is simply a comment.

Line 19 declares a scalar variable named $data and sets it to a string consisting of the values of $TestID, $q_id, and $a_id all joined by a colon. This is the correct response to the question that the user just answered. The way we encode the answers makes them look something like this 21:32:43. The first number is the test ID, then the question ID, and finally the answer ID.

Line 20 then takes the current value of $data and appends an asterisk to it and then the existing cookie. This prepends the current answer to the cookie that already exists.

Line 21 sets $data to an empty string unless an answer was provided and is in $a_id.

```
22: my $write_cookie = cookie(
23:      -name    => 'Quizzer',
24:      -value   => $data,
25: );
```

Line 22 declares a scalar variable named $write_cookie and stores the value returned by a call to CGI.pm's cookie function.

Note   We use a cookie to store the answers that the user has given to the questions. An HTTP cookie allows us to store pieces of data on the client computer.

Lines 23–24 pass some information to the cookie function.

Line 25 ends the block that contains the cookie function arguments that we opened on **line 22**.

```
26: my ($Q, $Ans, $taken) =
       Get_Question($test_id, $data, $NumQs, $write_cookie);
27: my $Qtext = $Q->{'Qtext'};
28: my $Qid   = $Q->{'Qid'};
29: $taken++;
```

Line 26 calls the Get_Question function. This function expects to be passed four items: $test_id, which is the ID of the test; $data, which is the answers of the questions already taken; $NumQs, which is the number of questions that make up a test session; and $write_cookie, which is the value of the updated cookie we need to write.

The Get_Question function returns three values: $Q, which is a reference to a hash containing the question; $Ans, which is a reference to a hash containing the answers; and $taken, which is the number of the current question.

Line 27 declares a scalar variable named $Qtext and sets it to the value stored in the Qtext key of the hash referenced in $Q.

Line 28 declares a scalar variable named $Qid and sets it to the value stored in the Qid key of the hash referenced in $Q.

Line 29 increments the $taken variable. This variable is used to show the user a count of questions they have taken so far (for example: *Question 4 of 10*).

 Tip   Using ++ is a shorthand way of saying "$x = $x + 1;"

```
30: print header(-cookie => $write_cookie);
```

Line 30 uses the header function from the CGI.pm module, as we have many times before. However, this time, we pass it a cookie that gets set on the user's system so that we can keep track of the questions that have already been answered.

```
31: print <<HTML;
32:   <html><head><title>Question $taken of
$NumQs</title></head>
33:    <body>
34:     <form action="take_test.cgi">
35:      <input type="hidden" name="test_id" value="$test_id">
36:      <input type="hidden" name="q_id"    value="$Qid">
37:      <table border="1" align="center">
38:       <tr bgcolor="#c0c0c0">
39:        <td align="center">
40:         <font size="6">Test name: $test_name</font><br>
41:         Question $taken of $NumQs.
42:        </td>
43:       </tr>
44:       <tr>
45:        <td><b>$Qtext</b></td>
46:       </tr>
47: HTML
```

Line 31 begins a *here document* that is used to print the HTML that begins the page we are generating.

Lines 32–46 contain some of the HTML for the page we are generating.

Lines 35–36 have *hidden* variables so that we can keep track of the current test_id and q_id.

On **line 40**, we display the test name. On **line 41**, we show the user what question he or she is on and how many questions are on this test. Then, on **line 45**, we display the actual question.

Line 47 is the ending tag for the *here document* we begin on **line 31**.

```
48: my @k = keys %{$Ans};
49: fisher_yates_shuffle( \@k );
```

Line 48 uses the `keys` function, which returns a list that consists of all of the keys in the hash passed to it — the hash referenced by the `$Ans` variable, in this case. This list is then stored in the new array `@k` that we also declare on this line.

Line 49 passes a reference to the `@k` array to the `fisher_yates_shuffle` subroutine, which is defined in the Quizzer.pm module. This performs a Fisher-Yates algorithm shuffle on the array, in place. The Fisher-Yates algorithm is an efficient method for randomizing the values in an array. We are merely randomizing the order in which the answers are presented to the user.

```
50: for my $key (@k){
51:     print qq(
52:         <tr>
53:           <td>
54:                
55:             <input type="radio" name="a_id"
              value="$key"> $Ans->{$key}
56:           </td>
57:         </tr>
58:     );
59: }
```

Line 50 loops through the `@k` array. Each time through the array, it sets `$key` to the current value. Notice that we use `for` and not `foreach` here — this is another *Perlism*; `for` and `foreach` are interchangeable in Perl.

Line 51 begins a `qq` block used to print the HTML needed for the page we are generating.

Lines 52–57 are the HTML for the generated page.

Line 55 creates the radio-button choices you see on the page.

Line 58 ends the `qq` block that begins on **line 51**.

Line 59 ends the `for` loop that begins on **line 50**.

```
60: print <<HTML;
61:     <tr bgcolor="#e0e0e0">
62:       <td align="center">
```

```
63:            <input type="submit" value="Submit Answer">
64:          </td>
65:        </tr>
66:        <tr>
67:          <td colspan="2" align="center">
68:            <a href="/quizzer/index.html">Home Page</a>
69:          </td>
70:        </tr>
71:      </table>
72:    </form></body></html>
73: HTML
```

Line 60 begins a *here document* that prints the HTML for the Submit button and the link to the Quizzer home page on the HTML form.

Lines 61–72 are the HTML tags needed for the table element and the Submit button.

Line 73 closes the *here document* that we begin on **line 60**.

When a user takes a test, he or she sees the questions and answers on a page like the one in Figure 6-6.

This program, in just 73 lines of code, handles page generation and maintains that answers that the user has already submitted. It is even more impressive when you consider that a majority of the 73 lines are simply HTML needed to generate the page!

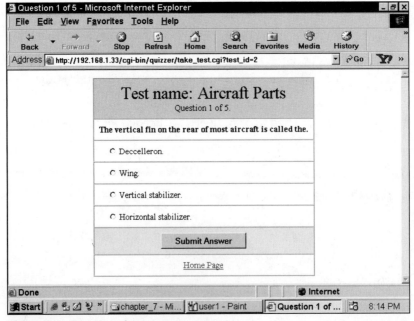

Figure 6-6: Test Question page

Well, so far we have created and taken tests, but we need some way to score the tests so that the user can see how he or she has done. The score_test.cgi is a small program that reads the cookie on the user's system, checks the database to verify the answers, and gives the user his or her score, along with the answers to the questions he or she has missed.

There is no extra "fluff" to this program. If you are going to incorporate this into a public site, you may want to work on making the output nicer looking and maybe even adding a pass/fail notification.

score_test.cgi

```
01: #!/usr/bin/perl -wT
02: #
03: # score_test.cgi
04: # Chapter 7
05: # Online Quizzer
06: # Test scoring program
07: #
```

Line 1 tells the system where to find Perl and turns on warnings and taint checking.

Lines 2–7 are comments about this program.

```
08: use strict;
09: use lib qw(.);
10: use CGI qw(:standard);
11: use Quizzer;
```

Line 8 loads the strict module. This forces the programmer to declare variables and prevents many common programming mistakes, such as having two variables in the same scope with the same name.

Line 9 tells Perl to add the current directory (.) to the @INC array. This line *must* come before our call to the Quizzer module, since the Quizzer module is in the same directory as this program and this directory is not in the @INC array.

Line 10 imports the CGI module and its standard functions.

Line 11 imports the Quizzer module.

```
12: my $cookie  = cookie('Quizzer');
13: my $test_id = param('test_id');
```

Line 12 declares a scalar variable named $cookie and calls the cookie function. The text 'Quizzer' is passed to the cookie function, and the return value of this function gets stored in the $cookie variable.

Line 13 declares a scalar variable named $test_id and sets it to the value returned by the call to the param function on the right side. This gets the value passed from the test_id field on the HTML form that calls this program.

```
14: my ($TestID, $NumQs, $Choices, $test_name) =
       Get_Test_Config($test_id);

15: my ($wrong, $score) = Score_Test($cookie);

16: print header();
```

Line 14 declares four new variables ($TestID, $NumQs, $Choices, and $test_name). Each of these new variables gets set to the values returned from the call to the Get_Test_Config function.

Line 15 declares two new scalar variables named $wrong and $score. These variables are set to the values returned from the call to the Score_Test function. In the call to the Score_Test function, we pass the value stored in the $cookie variable.

Line 16 prints the data returned from the header function.

```
17: print <<HTML;
18:  <html><head><title>Score Test</title></head>
19:   <body>
20:    <form action="take_test.cgi">
21:     <input type="hidden" name="test_id" value="$test_id">
22:     <table border="1" align="center">
23:      <tr bgcolor="#c0c0c0">
24:       <td align="center" colspan="2">
25:       <font size="5">Missed Questions:
$test_name</font><br>
26:        Score: $score\%
27:       </td>
28:      </tr>
29:      <tr bgcolor="#e0e0e0">
30:       <td><b>Question</b></td>
31:       <td><b>Correct Answer</b></td>
32:      </tr>
33: HTML
```

Line 17 begins a *here document* that prints the HTML needed to generate the top portion of the page that displays the user's test score.

Lines 18–32 are the HTML for the test score page. On **line 25**, the test name is printed. On **line 26**, the actual score is printed.

Line 33 ends the *here document* that we begin on **line 17**.

```
34: for my $item (@$wrong) {
35:     print qq(
36:         <tr>
```

```
37:            <td>
38:             $item->{'question'}
39:            </td>
40:            <td>
41:             $item->{'answer'}
42:            </td>
43:           </tr>
44:       );
45: }
```

Line 34 begins a `for` loop that traverses through each of the array elements in @$wrong. The variable $wrong is a *reference* to an array; it holds only the *address* where Perl can find the array. By putting the @ in front of it, we tell Perl that we want to get at the array that $wrong holds the address to. In other words, we *dereference* the array.

Line 35 begins a qq block that prints the questions and correct answers that the user got incorrect.

Lines 36–43 print the HTML for the page we are generating.

Line 44 closes the qq block that we begin on **line 35**.

Line 45 closes the `for` loop that we begin on **line 34**.

```
46: print <<HTML;
47:      </tr>
48:      <tr>
49:       <td colspan="2" align="center">
50:        <a href="/quizzer/index.html">Home Page</a>
51:       </td>
52:      </tr>
53:     </table>
54:    </form></body></html>
55: HTML
```

Line 46 begins a *here document* that finishes off the HTML for the page we are generating.

Lines 47–54 are the closing HTML tags for the page.

Line 55 ends the *here document* that we begin on **line 46**. This line is also the last line in this program.

When the user is finished and clicks the Score Test link, he or she sees a page like the one in Figure 6-7.

So, we have finished all of the programs needed to create tests, add answers, take tests, and score tests. Now we need to look at the module that does most of the work for us.

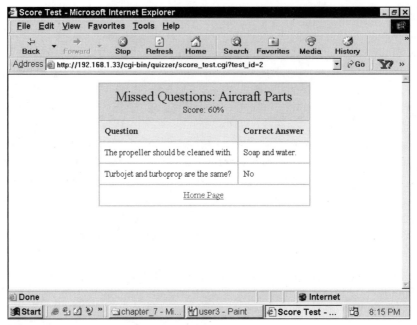

Figure 6-7: Score Test page

Quizzer.pm is the module that does most of the work for our online quiz application. We call it a module instead of an application because Quizzer.pm cannot be run on its own. Instead, it contains many of the functions we have used in the preceding programs. Quizzer.pm also contains the database routines for all of the applications, except the create_test.cgi program.

Let's dive into the Quizzer.pm code so we can bring together how all of these programs work.

Quizzer.pm

```
01: # Quizzer.pm

02: package Quizzer;
03: require Exporter;
04: use DBI;
```

Line 1 is a comment with the name of this module. Notice that this module does not have the normal #!/usr/bin/perl that all of the other programs have—that is because this module cannot be executed on its own.

Line 2 declares that this file is in the `Quizzer` namespace. This is important because it helps us separate the variables in this file from the variables in the files that import this one. For example, if we create a variable named $foo in this file and also one in our main program named $foo, how will we know which is which?

The variable in this file is actually named $Quizzer::foo, and the one in the main application is named $main::foo. If the first part is left off, and it usually is, the default is the $main:: package.

The scope of this namespace is from the point where it is declared to the end of this file. If it is declared in a block, the scope ends when the block does — just as with a `my` variable.

Line 3 brings in the `Exporter` module. We use this so that we can export functions and variables to the applications that use this module. This enables us to keep some of the functions and variables "private" to this module.

Line 4 imports the `DBI` module. We'll need this module for our database connectivity in this Quizzer.pm module.

```
05: my $conn = DBI->connect("DBI:mysql:quizzer", "bookuser",
        "testpass")
06:     or die("Cannot connect: $DBI::errstr");
```

Line 5 creates a connection to the Quizzer database and stores a handle to the connection in the variable named $conn.

This connection is being made outside of all of the functions in this module so that it is globally available to all of them in this module. This means that we need only to connect to the database once, instead of a different time for each different subroutine that calls the database.

Line 6 is a continuation of **line 5**. It tells the system to `die` if there is a problem connecting to the database.

```
07: our @ISA    = qw(Exporter);
08: our @EXPORT = qw(Add_Question Get_Test_Config Get_Question
                Score_Test fisher_yates_shuffle
Get_Test_List);
```

Line 7 tells Perl that this module is a subclass of the `Exporter` module. This is so that exporting will work right, when a program says `use Quizzer`.

Line 8 tells Perl which subroutines are okay to export by default. If you create a new subroutine, and forget to add it to your @EXPORT array, when you try to access it from a program you get an error; Perl won't be able to find the subroutine. If you are accustomed to the terms *public* and *private*, this line makes the subroutines public.

```
09: sub Get_Test_List {
10:    my $sql = qq(SELECT test_name, TestID
11:        FROM test_config ORDER BY test_name);

12:    my $sth_getlist = $conn->prepare($sql);
13:    $sth_getlist->execute() or die("Error!
$DBI::errstr\nAnborting");

14:    return($sth_getlist);
15: }
```

Line 9 begins the Get_Test_List subroutine.

Lines 10–11 are the SQL needed to get a list of test names from the database. The ORDER BY clause in the SQL statement causes the list of matches to be sorted on the field, or fields, following the clause.

Line 12 prepares the SQL statement and stores a handle to the prepared statement in the variable named $sth_getlist.

Line 13 calls the execute method on the $sth_getlist handle. If there is a problem executing this SQL query, die function is called, and an error is printed.

Line 14 returns the $sth_getlist variable, which is now a handle containing the matching data.

Line 15 closes the Get_Test_List subroutine.

That is it for the function that gets the list of available tests from the database.

```
16: sub Score_Test {
17:    my $cookie  = shift;

18:    my @data    = split(/\*/, $cookie);
19:    my $tot_q   = @data;
20:    my @wrong   = ();
```

Line 16 begins the Score_Test subroutine.

Line 17 declares a scalar variable named $cookie and shifts in the value that is passed to this subroutine when it is called.

Line 18 uses the split function to split the data in $cookie at the asterisk. When this is done, @data contains a list of data that is further split into the answers the user chooses.

Line 19 declares a scalar variable named $tot_q and stores the number of elements that are in the @data array into it.

Line 20 declares an array variable named @wrong and sets it to an initial value of ( ),ensuring that it contains no data.

```
21:   my $sth_Ans =
22:     $conn->prepare("SELECT a.Aid, a.Atext, q.Qtext
23:     FROM answers AS a, questions AS q WHERE
24:     ((q.Qid = ?) AND (a.Qid = q.Qid) AND (a.correct = 'Y'))");
```

Line 21 declares a variable named $sth_Ans; this will be used as a statement handle to this SQL query. It also sets the variable to the value returned by the prepare statement on **lines 22–24**.

Line 22 prepares the SQL inside of its block using the $conn database handle that we create at the beginning of this module.

Lines 22–24 contain the SQL statement we are dealing with for this query. It is a fairly complex SQL query that pulls data from two different tables.

The a.Aid, a.Atext values come from the *answers* table, and the q.Qtext value comes from the *questions* table. So, we are fetching the answer ID (Aid), answer text (Atext), and the question text (Qtext).

On **line 24**, we have (q.Qid = ?) —where ? is a placeholder that allows us to dynamically get data for the appropriate question just by passing the question ID in the execute statement.

Also, the (a.Qid = q.Qid) ensures that this is the proper response for this question. Qid is the *primary key* of the *questions* table and is used in the *answers* table as a *foreign key* to link a question to an answer.

Finally, notice that we have (a.correct = 'Y'), but we don't return this data. This field is used to let us know that this is the correct response for this question. If we had left this off, we would get back a list of *all* of the answers for this question (correct and incorrect). We care only about the correct response, so we limit our matches by using this statement.

```
25:       for(@data){
26:           my %rec = ();
27:           my ($TestID, $q_id, $a_id) = split(/:/);
```

Line 25 begins a for loop that traverses through all of the elements in the @data array.

Line 26 declares a hash named %rec and initializes it to an empty set.

Line 27 declares three variables $TestID, $q_id, and $a_id, and sets them equal to the values returned by the split statement. The split statement here splits on the colon but has nothing telling it what variable to split, so it splits the default variable $_. Each time through the loop, the $_variable gets set to the current value of the @data array—this is what gets split.

```
28:   $sth_Ans->execute($q_id) or die("Error!
$DBI::errstr\nAborting");
29:   my $ans = $sth_Ans->fetch;
```

Line 28 calls the `execute` method on the `$sth_Ans` handle and passes the `$q_id`. The value in `$q_id` is substituted in for the *placeholder* in the SQL statement.

Line 29 declares a scalar variable named `$ans` and sets it to the value returned by calling the `fetch` method on the `$sth_Ans` handle. The `fetch` method returns a reference to an array, so `$ans` contains a *reference* to the array returned by `fetch`.

```
30:         if($ans->[0] ne $a_id) {
31:             $rec{'answer'}   = $ans->[1];
32:             $rec{'question'} = $ans->[2];
33:             push @wrong, \%rec;
34:         }
35:     }
```

Line 30 checks the first element of the array that the `$ans` variable references to see if it is *not* equal to the value stored in `$a_id`. The `$ans->[0]` tells Perl to get the first element of the array that `$ans` references. The `$a_id` variable contains the ID of the correct answer to this question. If these two values don't match, the user has responded to the question incorrectly.

Line 31 stores the correct answer text in the hash `$rec` at *hash key* `answer`.

Line 32 stores the question text in the hash `$rec` at *hash key* `question`.

Line 33 pushes a reference to the hash `%rec` onto the `@wrong` array. The `@wrong` array contains a list of hash references to all incorrect responses.

Line 34 closes the `if` statement that is opened on **line 30**.

Line 35 closes the `for` loop that begins on **line 25**.

So, we should have now looped through all of the answers the user has chosen. All incorrect responses are stored in the `@wrong` array.

You may be wondering how we know that the answer will be array element 1 and question array element 2. (`$ans->[1]`). The `fetch` method returns an array, and the array is *always* in the order that the fields are listed in the SQL statement. So, in our SQL statement, we have "`SELECT a.Aid, a.Atext, q.Qtext`"—this makes array element 0 `Aid`, 1 `Atext`, and 2 `Qtext`.

Also, each time through this loop, we reset the hash `%rec` to `()`, so it contains nothing. However, we store a *reference* to the hash in the `@wrong` array if the response is incorrect. This reference *still exists* in the `@wrong` array, even though we have cleared the hash!

When we go through and reset the hash on **line 26**, Perl assigns that hash a memory address. As long as there is still something referencing that memory address, Perl will not reuse it. Each time through the loop, a different memory address is assigned to %rec, and we maintain a *reference* to the hash in the @wrong array.

```
36:        my $tot_w = @wrong;
37:        my $tot_s = sprintf("%2.0f", ((($tot_q-$tot_w)/$tot_q)
*
           100));
38:        return(\@wrong, $tot_s);
39: }
```

Line 36 declares a scalar variable named $tot_w and sets it to the number of items in the @wrong array. This gives us the total number of wrong responses.

Line 37 declares a scalar variable named $tot_s and sets it to the total score. We get the total score by taking the total number of questions ($tot_q) and subtracting the total number of wrong responses ($tot_w), then by dividing that by the total number of questions, finally multiplying it all by 100.

By using sprintf, we can tell Perl exactly what format we want this data in; it will round the results for us. So if the user got 10 out of 11 right, that's .9090909, which we'll multiply by a hundred, and then sprintf will round it to "91".

In this example, we set our results to at least 2 characters and 0 items after the decimal — which ends up giving us whole-number percentages. For more information, see "perldoc –f sprintf".

Line 38 returns a reference to the @wrong array and the $tot_s.

Line 39 closes the Score_Test subroutine that begins on **line 16**.

```
40: sub Get_Question {
41:        my $test_id      = shift;
42:        my $cookie       = shift;
43:        my $num_qs       = shift;
44:        my $write_cookie = shift;
```

Line 40 begins the Get_Question subroutine. This subroutine accesses the database and chooses a random question for the user. It is set up so that it will not return an answer if the user has already answered it.

Lines 41–44 declare some scalar variables and use the shift function to read in the values that are passed to the subroutine.

shift

In case you are wondering how the `shift` function works for subroutines like this, remember that the `$_` variable is the *default* variable in Perl. If you call a function that expects a scalar variable and you do not pass one to the function, Perl assumes you mean to use the `$_` variable.

The same thing goes for functions that expect to receive an array, except instead of defaulting to `$_`, they default to `@_`. `@_` is the array that all values passed to a subroutine get placed in, so by just saying `"shift"`, you end up shifting a value off of the `@_` array. *That* is how `shift` works at the beginning of all of these functions.

```
45:      my %Question;
46:      my %Answer;
47:      my %Qid;

48:      my @data = split(/\*/, $cookie);
```

Lines 45–47 declare some hashes that we'll use to keep track of the questions and answers.

Line 48 splits the `$cookie` variable at the asterisks and stores the results in the `@data` array.

```
49:      my $sth_Qlist =
50:         $conn->prepare("SELECT Qid FROM questions
                WHERE TestID = ?");

51:      $sth_Qlist->execute($test_id)
                or die("Error! $DBI::errstr\nAborting");
```

Line 49 declares a scalar variable named `$sth_Qlist` that we are going to use as a handle to the SQL statement on **line 50**.

Line 50 continues **line 49**. This is the SQL statement that we execute to get all of the questions from the database for a particular test. Notice that we use a *placeholder* so that we can prepare the SQL. Then we just pass a value in the `execute` statement to fill in the *placeholder*.

Line 51 calls the `execute` method on this handle. It passes the value in `$test_id` to the SQL statement. If there is some sort of problem executing this statement, the `die` method is called, and an error message is printed.

```
52:      my $Qnum = $sth_Qlist->fetchall_arrayref;

53:      @Questions = map { $_->[0] } @$Qnum;
```

Line 52 declares a scalar variable named $Qnum and sets it to the value returned from the fetchall_arrayref method call on the $sth_Qlist handle. This causes $Qnum to hold a *reference* to an array of all of the matching values from the SQL statement.

Line 53 uses the map function to get the first element from each match in the @$Qnum array. Since we ask only to get back one value from the SQL query, all of the matches should be stored in the first element of the array.

This simply takes the array that is referenced to by the $Qnum variable and generates a regular array named @Questions that contains all of the matching values.

```
54:     for(@data){
55:         my @tmp = split(/:/);
56:         $Qid{$tmp[1]} = 1;
57:     }
```

Line 54 begins a for loop that loops through each element in the @data array. Since we do not specify a variable for the current value to go into each time through the array, Perl's default variable, $_, is used.

Line 55 declares an array named @tmp and splits the current value of $_ at the colon. The result of this split is stored in the @tmp array. This is just a temporary array that we store the data in. It gets overwritten each time through the loop.

Each data element in the @data array looks something like this (43:31:12). Each number is an *index* to the test number, question, and answer that the user chooses. By splitting the colon, we are able to extract these elements and on the next line create a hash to maintain a list of the questions that have already been asked.

Line 56 uses the current question index, which is at $tmp[1], as a key in the $Qid hash. By setting this to 1, we are able to maintain a list of questions that have already been asked. The 1 is really irrelevant; we are looking for a duplicate key. If there is a duplicate key, we choose a different answer. (At this point, we are not choosing questions from the database, just building a hash of the questions that have already been asked.)

Line 57 closes the for loop that begins on **line 54**.

```
58:     my $taken = keys(%Qid); # Count number taken
```

Line 58 declares a scalar variable named $taken and counts the number of keys that are in the %Qid hash. This is how we get the number of questions that have been answered so far.

```
59:     while(1){
60:         my $Qcount = @Questions;
```

Line 59 creates an infinite loop! while continues looping as long as the value inside of the parentheses is true and as long as 1 *always* evaluates as true. We want to do this because inside of this loop we want to keep looping until we choose a question that has not been asked yet. Don't worry about the program getting "stuck" here, though; we will add a few ways for the program to escape from this infinite loop.

Line 60 declares a variable named $Qcount and sets it to the number of items that are in the @Questions array. This is how we get a count of how many questions there are for this test.

```
61:             No_More_Questions($test_id, $write_cookie)
62:                 if(($num_qs == $taken) or ($taken >= $Qcount));
```

Line 61 calls the No_More_Questions subroutine and passes it the $test_id and $write_cookie variables.

Line 62 limits how the subroutine on **line 61** is called. This line is actually just a continuation of **line 61**. Notice that there is no semicolon on **line 61**. This line tells Perl to call only the No_More_Questions subroutine if the conditions listed are true.

The first condition is if the number of questions for this test equals the number of questions already taken. ($num_qs == $taken). $num_qs is the question-count for a complete quiz. There may be 38 questions for this test, but a complete "quiz" could have $num_qs set to 25 so that the user is presented with only 25 questions.

The next condition checks to see if the number of questions taken is equal to or greater than the number of total questions for this test ($taken >= $Qcount). If so, we will never find a question that has not yet been asked, so we have to exit this infinite loop anyway — even if the user has not been presented enough questions to make up a complete quiz. This can be the case if there are 14 questions for this test in the database, but a complete "quiz" is set up as 25 questions in the database. This prevents the program from getting stuck in the loop under this condition.

```
63:             $Qnum = $Questions[(int(rand($Qcount)))];

64:             last unless(exists $Qid{$Qnum});
65:     }
```

Line 63 sets $Qnum equal to the value at a random location in the @Questions array. (int(rand($Qcount))) chooses a random integer between 0 and $Qcount.

Line 64 calls the last function unless the question already exists in the %Qid hash at key $Qnum. last breaks out of the current loop it is in. The unless is the same as *if not*. exists checks to see if there is data at the hash location that is passed to it. So, if nothing exists in $Qid{$Qnum}, last gets called.

Line 65 closes the infinite while loop that we begin on **line 59**.

```
66:     $sql = qq{SELECT q.Qtext, q.Qid, a.Aid, a.Atext
67:             FROM questions AS q, answers AS a
68:             WHERE ((q.Qid = a.Qid) AND (q.Qid = ?))};
```

Lines 66–68 make up the SQL statement that we use to select the question and answers that we return from this subroutine. We are selecting Qtext and Qid from the questions table and Atext and Aid from the answers table. The (q.Qid = a.Qid) ensures that we get only the answers that are tied to this question. The AS q and AS a in the SQL statement allow us to create shorter names that we can then reference the tables as in the SQL statement.

```
69:    $sth_QA = $conn->prepare($sql);
70:    $sth_QA->execute($Qnum) or die("Error!
$DBI::errstr\nAborting");
```

Line 69 prepares the SQL statement that we create on **lines 66–68**.

Line 70 executes the SQL statement and passes the value in $Qnum to take the place of the *placeholder* in the SQL statement. If there is a problem executing the SQL statement, the program dies and prints an error message.

```
71:    while(my $p = $sth_QA->fetchrow_hashref) {
72:        $Question{'Qid'}       = $p->{'Qid'};
73:        $Question{'Qtext'}     = $p->{'Qtext'};
74:        $Answer   {$p->{'Aid'}} = $p->{'Atext'};
75:    }
```

Line 71 begins a while loop that fetches one row of data returned from the SQL call. A reference to the hash returned by the fetchrow_hashref method gets stored in the scalar variable $p.

Line 72 sets the $Question hash with Qid as the key to the value in the hash returned by the fetchrow_hashref method.

Line 73 sets the $Question hash with Qtext as the key to the value in the hash returned by the fetchrow_hashref method.

Line 74 sets the $Answer hash with the answer ID (Aid) as the key to the value in the hash returned by the fetchrow_hashref method.

Line 75 ends the while loop which begins on **line 71**.

If there are 4 answers to a question in the database table, 4 rows of data will be returned. The Qid and Qtext will be the same for all 4 rows because this doesn't change. However, the answers will all have different text and different answer IDs. So, we can end up with something like this:

```
$Question{'31'} = 31;
$Question{'This is a question.'} = "This is a question. ";
$Answer{'23'} = "Answer number 1";
$Answer{'12'} = "Answer number 2";
$Answer{'78'} = "Answer number 3";
$Answer{'94'} = "Answer number 4";
```

Each time through the loop, the $Question values get set to the same thing — but that is fine. An answer is added each time through the loop as well. To end up with what is in the preceding example, the loop has to be traversed 4 times — once for each question.

```
76:      return(\%Question, \%Answer, $taken);
77: }
```

Line 76 returns a reference to the %Question hash, a reference to the %Answer hash, and the value stored in the $taken variable.

Line 77 ends the Get_Question subroutine.

```
78: sub fisher_yates_shuffle {
79:      my $array = shift;
80:      my $i;
```

Line 78 begins the fisher_yates_shuffle subroutine. This subroutine is designed to take a reference to an array as the input, and it will randomize the items in the array in place. This means that we pass a reference to an array, and the array gets randomized. This is a commonly used method for randomizing arrays, the "Fisher-Yates shuffle," named after Sir Ronald A. Fisher and Frank Yates, who introduced the algorithm in example 12 of their 1938 book Statistical Tables.

Line 79 declares a scalar variable named $array and shifts the value passed to the subroutine into it. This value should be a reference to an array.

Line 80 declares a scalar variable named $i.

```
81:      for($i = @$array; --$i;) {
82:          my $j = int rand ($i+1);
```

Line 81 begins a for loop that sets $i to the current value each time through the loop and also decrements $i. This has the effect of setting $i to the number of elements in the array @$array and then counting down one by one.

Line 82 declares a scalar variable named $j and sets it to a random integer between 1 and $i.

```
83:          next if $i == $j;
84:          @$array[$i,$j] = @$array[$j,$i];
85:      }
86: }
```

Line 83 causes the for loop to skip to the next iteration if $i and $j are equal.

Line 84 swaps the values at $array[$i] and $array[$j].

Line 85 ends the for loop that we begin on **line 81**.

Line 86 ends this subroutine.

```
87: sub No_More_Questions {
88:     my $TestID = shift;
89:     my $cookie = shift;
```

Line 87 begins the No_More_Questions subroutine. This subroutine gets called if the program runs out of questions for a quiz or if the user has answered the predetermined number of questions that make up a complete quiz.

Line 88 declares a scalar variable named $TestID and shifts in the first value that is passed in the subroutine call.

Line 89 declares a scalar variable named $cookie and shifts in the second value that is passed in the subroutine call.

```
90:     print CGI::header(-cookie => $cookie);
91:     print qq(No more questions for this test.<br>);
92:     print qq(Click
    <a href="/cgi-
bin/quizzer/score_test.cgi?test_id=$TestID">);
93:     print qq(here</a> to score test.<br>);
```

Line 90 prints the HTTP header and passes the cookie stored in the $cookie variable to the client's browser.

Line 91 prints some informational text to the user.

Line 92 prints a link to the score_test.cgi program with the $TestID included in the URL so that the program knows what to score.

Line 93 prints some more informational text to the user.

```
94:     exit;
95: }
```

Line 94 exits the program. Since the user is done with all of the questions, we want to make sure that he or she just sees the information and links to score the test — we don't want the user to try and answer more questions.

Line 95 ends this subroutine.

```
96: sub Get_Test_Config {
97:     my $test_id = shift;
```

Line 96 begins the Get_Test_Config subroutine. This is the subroutine that gets called by several of the programs to get the configuration information for the test.

Line 97 declares a scalar variable named `$test_id` and `shifts` in the value that is passed in the subroutine call.

```
98:      my $sql      = qq{SELECT * FROM test_config WHERE
                              TestID='$test_id'};
99:      my $sth_cfg = $conn->prepare($sql);
```

Line 98 declares a scalar variable named `$sql` and sets it to the SQL statement that is needed to get the test configuration information.

Line 99 declares a scalar variable named `$sth_cfg`, which will be used as a handle to the preceding SQL statement. The statement on the right calls the `prepare` method, which returns a handle to the prepared statement.

```
100:     $sth_cfg->execute() or die("Error!
$DBI::errstr\nAborting");
101:     return ($sth_cfg->fetchrow_array());
102: }
```

Line 100 calls the `execute` method on the `$sth_cfg` handle. If there is a problem with the `execute`, the program will `die` and print an error message.

Line 101 returns a pointer to the array of data that we have just fetched. This SQL statement gets only one record, so we know that the call to `fetchrow_array` contains the record we want.

Line 102 ends this subroutine.

```
103: sub Add_Question {
104:     my ($Qtext, $test_id, $correct, @false) = @_;
```

Line 103 begins the `Add_Question` subroutine. This subroutine takes the values passed to it and inserts them into the database table.

Line 104 reads in the values that passed in the subroutine call.

We don't use shift here to get the data; instead, we read in the data from the @_ array. This is another way of getting the data passed to a subroutine. In this case, it makes it easy to read in the three scalar values and then the array at the end.

```
105:     my $sql_Q = qq{INSERT INTO questions (Qtext, TestID)
106:                     VALUES ('$Qtext', '$test_id')};

107:     my $sql_F = qq{INSERT INTO answers (Qid, Atext)
108:                     VALUES (?, ?)};        # Wrong answers.

109:     my $sql_C = qq{INSERT INTO answers (Qid, Atext, correct)
110:                     VALUES (?, ?, 'Y')}; # Correct answer.
```

Lines 105–110 declare three separate scalar variables and create three separate SQL statements.

The first SQL statement, stored in the $sql_Q variable, is used to insert a question into the question database table. This SQL statement remains static, so we don't use any *placeholders*.

The second SQL statement, stored in the $sql_F variable, is used to store the wrong/false answers into the answers database table. This SQL statement uses *placeholders*.

The third SQL statement, stored in the $sql_C variable, is used to store the correct answer in the answers database table. This one also uses *placeholders* and passes a Y into the "correct" database-table field so that we know that this is the correct answer.

```
111:      my $sth_Q  = $conn->prepare($sql_Q);
112:      my $sth_F  = $conn->prepare($sql_F);
113:      my $sth_C  = $conn->prepare($sql_C);
```

Lines 111–113 prepare each of the SQL statements and store the handles returned by the prepare method in their respective scalar variables.

```
114:      $sth_Q->execute() or die("Error!
$DBI::errstr\nAborting");
115:      my $Qid = $conn->{'mysql_insertid'};
```

Line 114 executes the $sth_Q SQL statement and dies with an error message if there is a problem executing it.

Line 115 calls the mysql_insertid MySQL API function. This function call returns the value of the last autoincrement field. This value will contain the ID of the question that we've just added to the database table. The Qid is the primary key for the questions table and the foreign key for the answers table.

```
116:      $sth_C->execute($Qid, $correct)
             or die("Error! $DBI::errstr\nAborting");
```

Line 116 executes the $sth_C SQL statement and dies with an error message if there is a problem executing it.

```
117:      for my $txt (@false) {
118:          next unless($txt);
119:          $sth_F->execute($Qid, $txt)
                 or die("Error! $DBI::errstr\nAborting");
120:      }
```

Line 117 begins a `for` loop that iterates over each of the values in the `@false` array. Each time through the array, the variable `$txt` is set to the current value.

Line 118 jumps to the next iteration of the loop unless `$txt` contains some value. This means that if the current value in the `@false` array is blank, we just skip it.

Line 119 executes the `$sth_F` SQL statement that adds the false answers to the database. If there is a problem adding the record to the database, the program `dies` and displays an error message.

Line 120 closes the `for` loop that begins on **line 117**.

```
121:      return 1;
122: }

123: 1;
```

Line 121 returns 1 from this subroutine. Returning 1 from a subroutine is an easy way to determine if the subroutine has completed successfully. If you check the return value and it is 1, you know that the subroutine has made it to the end.

Line 122 closes this subroutine.

Line 123 returns 1 from this module. A module must return a true value, or Perl generates an error message.

That is it for this entire Web-based Quizzer application! Quite a bit of code, but by going through it all you should have learned a lot. We've tried to use many different techniques to maximize your exposure to some of the different ways you can do things in Perl.

If you've noticed that we used the -T, taint flag, in all of our CGI applications but never did anything with it, you are right! We have made no system calls, so there is no worry that these programs may have tried to do something with tainted data. Putting -T into *every* CGI program is a very good habit to get into; if you happen to add some code that is potentially dangerous, the taint flag should catch it and tell you about it.

Summary

In this chapter, we have covered the basics of gathering information from an HTML form. Once we have the data, we either store it in a database table or use the information to formulate an SQL query, searching the database for matching records. We also created a fairly powerful Web-based quiz application that is an excellent starting point for creating a very powerful quizzing application. Web-based applications are very popular these days, so use this knowledge and expand it.

Program Listings

Listings 6-1 to 6-8 contain the complete and uninterrupted code listings for the applications in this chapter.

Listing 6-1: **Web Phonebook Application**

```perl
01: #!/usr/bin/perl -wT
02: #
03: # program 7-1
04: # Web Phonebook Application
05: #

06: use strict;
07: use DBI;
08: use CGI qw(:standard);
09: use CGI::Carp qw(fatalsToBrowser);

10: print header();

11: my $action = param('form_action');

12: my $DB_Handle = DBI->connect("DBI:mysql:BibleBook",
    "bookuser", "testpass")
13:    or die("Cannot connect: $DBI::errstr\nAborting");

14: Add_Record() if($action eq 'addrecord');
15: Search_DB()  if($action eq 'search');

16: sub Search_DB {
17:     my ($sql, $st_handle);
18:     my $search_for = param('search');
19:     my @field      = param('field');

20:     @field = map { "($_ LIKE '%$search_for%')" } @field;

21:     $sql  = qq{SELECT * FROM phonebook WHERE (};
22:     $sql .= join ' OR ', @field;
23:     $sql .= ")";

24:     $st_handle =  $DB_Handle->prepare($sql);
25:     $st_handle -> execute();

26:     Display_Results($st_handle);
27: }

28: sub Display_Results {
29:     my $handle = shift;
30:     my ($fname, $lname, $cow, $phone, $ext, $cell, $pager,
```

Continued

Listing 6-1 *(continued)*

```
              $notes, $count);
31:     my $bgcol = "";

32:     print<<'    HTML';
33:      <html><head><title>Search Results</title></head>
34:       <body>
35:        <table align="center" border="1" cellspacing="0">
36:         <tr bgcolor="#303030">
37:          <td colspan="6" align="center">
38:           <font size="5" color="white">
39:            Search Results
40:           </font>
41:          </td>
42:         </tr>
43:         <tr bgcolor="#c0c0c0">
44:          <td align="center"><b>Name</b></td>
45:          <td align="center"><b>Co-Worker?</b></td>
46:          <td align="center"><b>Phone</b></td>
47:          <td align="center"><b>Extension</b></td>
48:          <td align="center"><b>Cell</b></td>
49:          <td align="center"><b>Pager</b></td>
50:         </tr>
51:     HTML

52:     $handle->bind_columns(undef,
53:       \($fname, $lname, $cow, $phone, $ext, $cell,
           $pager,$notes));

54:     while($handle->fetch){
55:         $bgcol = ($bgcol eq "ffffff") ? "e0e0e0"
                                    : "ffffff";

56:     print qq(<tr bgcolor="#$bgcol">);
57:      print qq(<td>$fname $lname</td><td
          align="center">$cow</td>);
58:      print qq(<td>$phone</td><td>$ext</td><td>$cell</td>);
59:      print qq(<td>$pager</td>);
60:     print qq(</tr>);

61:      $count++;
62:      }

63:     No_Data() unless($count);

64:     print qq(</table></body></html>);
65: }

66: sub No_Data{
67:    print qq(<tr><td colspan="6" align="center">);
```

```
68:    print qq(No matches found, return to);
69:    print qq(<a href="/phonebook/phone.html">main page</a>.);
70:    print qq(</td></tr>);
71: }

72: sub Add_Record {
73:    my $fname    = param('firstname');
74:    my $lname    = param('lastname');
75:    my $phone    = param('phone');
76:    my $ext      = param('extension');
77:    my $cell     = param('cell');
78:    my $pager    = param('pager');
79:    my $coworker = param('coworker');
80:    my $notes    = param('notes');
81:    my $sql;

82:    $sql  = qq{INSERT INTO phonebook (firstname, lastname,};
83:    $sql .= qq{coworker, phone, extension, cell, pager,
                  notes)};
84:    $sql .= qq{VALUES (?, ?, ?, ?, ?, ?, ?, ?)};

85:    my $st_handle = $DB_Handle->prepare($sql);

86:   my $rval = $st_handle->execute($fname, $lname, $coworker,
87:        $phone, $ext, $cell, $pager, $notes);

88:    Handle_DB_Error() unless($rval);

89:    Display_Page();
90: }

91: sub Display_Page {
92:    print<<'    HTML';
93:    <html><head><title>Record Added!</title></head>
94:     <body>
95:      <center>
96:       <font size="6">
97:        Record Added!
98:       </font>
99:       <hr />
100:       <font size="4">
101:       <a href="/phonebook/phone.html">Back to Main Page</a>
102:        </font><br />
103:       </center>
104:      </body>
105:     </html>
106:     HTML
107: }

108: sub Handle_DB_Error {
109:     print<<'    HTML';
```

Continued

Listing 6-1 *(continued)*

```
110:    <html><head><title>Database Error</title></head>
111:     <body>
112:      <center>
113:       <font size="6">
114:        Error with database call.
115:       </font>
116:       <hr />
117:       <font size="4" color="red">
118:        $DBI::errstr
119:       </font><br />
120:       <font size="3">
121:        Please hit your <b>back</b> button to re-enter the
             data and try again.
122:       </font>
123:      </center>
124:     </body>
125:    </html>
126:    HTML

127:    exit;
128: }
```

Listing 6-2: **Database tables for Quizzer application**

```
CREATE TABLE questions (
  Qid       INT NOT NULL AUTO_INCREMENT,
  Qtext     VARCHAR(255) DEFAULT NULL,
  TestID    INT DEFAULT NULL,
  PRIMARY KEY(Qid)
  );

CREATE TABLE answers (
  Aid       INT NOT NULL AUTO_INCREMENT,
  Qid       INT NOT NULL,
  text      VARCHAR(255) DEFAULT NULL,
  correct   CHAR(1) default "N",
  PRIMARY KEY(Aid)
  );

CREATE TABLE test_config (
  TestID    INT NOT NULL AUTO_INCREMENT,
  NumQs     INT NOT NULL,
  Choices   INT NOT NULL,
  PRIMARY KEY(TestID)
  );
```

Listing 6-3: **add_question.cgi**

```perl
01: #!/usr/bin/perl -wT
02: #
03: # add_question.cgi
04: # Chapter 7
05: # Online Quizzer
06: # Add question 2
07: #

08: use strict;
09: use CGI qw(:standard);
10: use lib qw(.);
11: use Quizzer;

12: my $test_id = param('test_id');
13: my $Qtext   = param('Qtext');
14: my $correct = param('correct');
15: my @false   = param('false');
16: my $rval;

17: my ($TestID, $NumQs, $Choices, $test_name) =
      Get_Test_Config($test_id);

18: if($Qtext ne ''){
19:    $rval = Add_Question($Qtext, $test_id, $correct, @false);
20: }

21: print header();

22: print <<HTML;
23:  <html><head><title>Add A Question</title></head>
24:   <body>
25:    <form action="add_question.cgi">
26:     <input type="hidden" name="test_id" value="$test_id">
27:     <table border="1" align="center">
28:      <tr bgcolor="#c0c0c0">
29:       <td colspan="2" align="center">
30:       <font size="6">Add question to $test_name test.</font>
31:       </td>
32:      </tr>
33:      <tr bgcolor="#e0e0e0">
34:       <td> </td>
35:       <td align="center"><b>Question/Answer Text</b></td>
36:      </tr>
37:      <tr>
38:       <td bgcolor="#e0e0e0">
39:        <b>Question:</b>
40:       </td>
41:       <td><input type="text" size="60" name="Qtext"></td>
42:      </tr>
```

Continued

Listing 6-3 *(continued)*

```
43:      <tr>
44:       <td bgcolor="#e0e0e0">
45:        <b>Correct Answer:</b>
46:       </td>
47:       <td><input type="text" size="60" name="correct"></td>
48:      </tr>
49: HTML

50: for (1..($Choices - 1)){
51:     print qq(
52:        <tr>
53:         <td bgcolor="#e0e0e0">
54:          <b>False Answer:</b>
55:         </td>
56:         <td>
57:          <input type="text" size="60" name="false">
58:         </td>
59:        </tr>
60:     );
61: }

62: print <<HTML;
63:      <tr bgcolor="#e0e0e0">
64:       <td colspan="2" align="center">
65:        <input type="submit" value="Add Question">
66:       </td>
67:      </tr>
68: HTML

69: if($rval){
70:     print qq(
71:  <tr><td colspan="2">
72:     <b><u>Question Added</u></b><br>
73:     <b>$Qtext</b>
74:     <ul>
75:      <li><font color="green">$correct</font> *Correct answer
76:     );

77:     foreach my $tmp (@false){ print "<li>$tmp" if($tmp); }
78:     print qq(</ul></td>);
79: }

80: print <<HTML;
81:      </tr>
82:      <tr>
83:       <td colspan="2" align="center">
84:        <a href="/quizzer/admin.html">Admin Menu</a>
85:       </td>
86:      </tr>
```

```
87:    </table>
88:   </form></body></html>
89: HTML
```

Listing 6-4: **create_test.cgi**

```perl
01: #!/usr/bin/perl -wT
02: #
03: # create_test.cgi
04: # Chapter 7
05: # Online Quizzer
06: #

07: use strict;
08: use DBI;
09: use CGI qw(:standard);

10: my $conn = DBI->connect("DBI:mysql:quizzer", "bookuser",
11:   "testpass") or die("Cannot connect: $DBI::errstr\nAborting");

12: my $test_name = param('test_name');
13: my $questions = param('questions');
14: my $choices   = param('choices');

15: my $rval = $conn->do("INSERT INTO test_config SET
16:     NumQs=$questions, Choices=$choices,
17:     test_name='$test_name'");

18: my $val = $conn->{'mysql_insertid'};

19: print header();

20: if($rval) {
21:     print <<"    HTML";
22:      <html><head><title>Test Added!</title></head>
23:       <body>
24:        <font size="4">
25:         <center>Test $val Added to Database!<br /> </center>
26:        </font>
27:       </body>
28:      </html>
29:     HTML
30: }
31: else {
32:     print <<"    HTML";
33:      <html><head><title>Error!</title></head>
34:       <body>
35:        <font size="4">
36:         <center>
```

Continued

Listing 6-4 *(continued)*

```
37:        ERROR!!! ($DBI::errstr)<br />
38:        Something unexpected happened!<br />
39:      </center>
40:      </font>
41:    </body>
42:    </html>
43:   HTML
44: }
```

Listing 6-5: **score_test.cgi**

```
01: #!/usr/bin/perl -wT
02: #
03: # score_test.cgi
04: # Chapter 7
05: # Online Quizzer
06: # Test scoring program
07: #

08: use strict;
09: use lib qw(.);
10: use CGI qw(:standard);
11: use Quizzer;

12: my $cookie  = cookie('Quizzer');
13: my $test_id = param('test_id');

14: my ($TestID, $NumQs, $Choices, $test_name) =
       Get_Test_Config($test_id);

15: my ($wrong, $score) = Score_Test($cookie);

16: print header();

17: print <<HTML;
18:   <html><head><title>Score Test</title></head>
19:   <body>
20:    <form action="take_test.cgi">
21:     <input type="hidden" name="test_id" value="$test_id">
22:     <table border="1" align="center">
23:      <tr bgcolor="#c0c0c0">
24:       <td align="center" colspan="2">
25:       <font size="5">Missed Questions:
26:        $test_name</font><br>
27:       Score: $score\%
28:      </td>
29:     </tr>
30:     <tr bgcolor="#e0e0e0">
```

```
31:       <td><b>Question</b></td>
32:       <td><b>Correct Answer</b></td>
33:     </tr>
34: HTML

35: for my $item (@$wrong) {
36:     print qq(
37:         <tr>
38:           <td>
39:       $item->{'question'}
40:       </td>
41:       <td>
42:       $item->{'answer'}
43:       </td>
44:     </tr>
45:     );
46: }

47: print <<HTML;
48:     </tr>
49:     <tr>
50:       <td colspan="2" align="center">
51:       <a href="/quizzer/index.html">Home Page</a>
52:       </td>
53:     </tr>
54:     </table>
55:   </form></body></html>
56: HTML
```

Listing 6-6: **take_test.cgi**

```
01: #!/usr/bin/perl -wT
02: #
03: # take_test.cgi
04: # Chapter 7
05: # Online Quizzer
06: # Test taker thing
07: #

08: use strict;
09: use lib qw(.);
10: use CGI qw(:standard);
11: use Quizzer;

12: my $cookie  = cookie('Quizzer');
13: my $a_id    = param('a_id');
14: my $test_id = param('test_id');
15: my $q_id    = param('q_id');
```

Continued

Listing 6-6 *(continued)*

```
16: $test_id    = 2 unless($test_id);

17: my ($TestID, $NumQs, $Choices, $test_name) =
        Get_Test_Config($test_id);

18: # check cookies here
19: my $data = "$TestID:$q_id:$a_id";
20: $data    = $data . "*" . $cookie;
21: $data    = '' unless($a_id);

22: my $write_cookie = cookie(
23:     -name    => 'Quizzer',
24:     -value   => $data,
25: );

26: my ($Q, $Ans, $taken) = Get_Question($test_id, $data,
        $NumQs, $write_cookie);
27: my $Qtext = $Q->{'Qtext'};
28: my $Qid   = $Q->{'Qid'};
29: $taken++;

30: print header(-cookie => $write_cookie);

31: print <<HTML;
32: <html><head><title>Question $taken of $NumQs</title></head>
33:  <body>
34:   <form action="take_test.cgi">
35:    <input type="hidden" name="test_id" value="$test_id">
36:    <input type="hidden" name="q_id"    value="$Qid">
37:    <table border="1" align="center">
38:     <tr bgcolor="#c0c0c0">
39:      <td align="center">
40:       <font size="6">Test name: $test_name</font><br>
41:       Question $taken of $NumQs.
42:      </td>
43:     </tr>
44:     <tr>
45:      <td><b>$Qtext</b></td>
46:     </tr>
47: HTML

48: my @k = keys %{$Ans};
49: fisher_yates_shuffle( \@k );

50: for my $key (@k){
51:     print qq(
52:        <tr>
53:         <td>
54:         
55:   <input type="radio" name="a_id" value="$key"> $Ans->{$key}
56:      </td>
```

```
57:    </tr>
58:    );
59: }

60: print <<HTML;
61:    <tr bgcolor="#e0e0e0">
62:     <td align="center">
63:      <input type="submit" value="Submit Answer">
64:     </td>
65:    </tr>
66: HTML

67: print <<HTML;
68:    </tr>
69:    <tr>
70:     <td colspan="2" align="center">
71:      <a href="/quizzer/index.html">Home Page</a>
72:     </td>
73:    </tr>
74:    </table>
75:   </form></body></html>
76: HTML
```

Listing 6-7: **test_chooser.cgi**

```
01: #!/usr/bin/perl -wT
02: #
03: # test_chooser.cgi
04: # Chapter 7
05: # Online Quizzer
06: # Test Chooser
07: #

08: use strict;
09: use lib qw(.);
10: use Quizzer;
11: use CGI qw(:standard);

12: my $passed = param('action');

13: my $title  = "Choose a Test to Take";
14: $title     = "Add Question to?"  if($passed eq 'add');

15: my $action = "take_test.cgi";
16: $action    = "add_question.cgi"  if($passed eq 'add');

17: my $sth_testlist = Get_Test_List();

18: print header();
```

Continued

Listing 6-7 *(continued)*

```
19: print <<"HTML";
20:     <html><head><title>Choose A Test</title></head>
21:      <body>
22:       <form action="$action">
23:        <table border="1" align="center">
24:      <tr bgcolor="#c0c0c0">
25:       <td align="center">
26:        <font size="5">$title</font>
27:       </td>
28:      </tr>
29:      <tr>
30:       <td align="center"><select name="test_id">
31: HTML

32: while(my $p = $sth_testlist->fetchrow_hashref){
33:     print "<option value='$p->{TestID}'>$p->{test_name}</option>";
34: }

35: print <<HTML;
36:          </select>
37:          </td>
38:      </tr>
39:      <tr bgcolor="#e0e0e0">
40:       <td align="center">
41:        <input type="submit" value="Choose Test">
42:       </td>
43:        </tr>
44:       </table>
45:       </form>
46:      </body></html>
47: HTML
```

Listing 6-8: **Quizzer.pm**

```
01: # Quizzer.pm

02: package Quizzer;
03: require Exporter;
04: use DBI;

05: my $conn = DBI->connect("DBI:mysql:quizzer", "bookuser",
06:     "testpass") or die("Cannot connect: $DBI::errstr\nAborting");

07: our @ISA    = qw(Exporter);
08: our @EXPORT = qw(Add_Question Get_Test_Config Get_Question
09:             Score_Test fisher_yates_shuffle Get_Test_List);

10: sub Get_Test_List {
```

```
11:     my $sql = qq(SELECT test_name, TestID
12:         FROM test_config ORDER BY test_name);

13:   $sth_getlist = $conn->prepare($sql);
14:   $sth_getlist->execute() or die("Error! $DBI::errstr\nAborting");

15:     return($sth_getlist);
16: }

17: sub Score_Test {
18:     my $cookie  = shift;

19:    my @data     = split(/\*/, $cookie);
20:    my $tot_q    = @data;
21:    my @wrong    = ();

22:    my $sth_Ans =
23:      $conn->prepare("SELECT a.Aid, a.Atext, q.Qtext
24:         FROM answers AS a, questions AS q WHERE
25:   ((q.Qid = ?) AND (a.Qid = q.Qid) AND (a.correct = 'Y'))");

26:    for(@data){
27:        my %rec = ();
28:        my ($TestID, $q_id, $a_id) = split(/:/);

29:        $sth_Ans->execute($q_id)
                or die("Error! $DBI::errstr\nAborting");
30:      my $ans = $sth_Ans->fetch;

31:        if($ans->[0] ne $a_id) {
32:            $rec{'answer'}   = "$ans->[1]";
33:            $rec{'question'} = "$ans->[2]";
34:        push @wrong, \%rec;
35:     }
36:     }

37:    my $tot_w = @wrong;
38:    my $tot_s = sprintf("%2.0f", ((($tot_q-$tot_w)/$tot_q) * 100));
39:    return(\@wrong, $tot_s);
40: }

41: sub Get_Question {
42:    my $test_id      = shift;
43:    my $cookie       = shift;
44:    my $num_qs       = shift;
45:    my $write_cookie = shift;

46:    my %Question;
47:    my %Answer;
```

Continued

Listing 6-8 *(continued)*

```
48:     my %Qid;

49:     my @data = split(/\*/, $cookie);

50:     my $sth_Qlist =
51:       $conn->prepare("SELECT Qid FROM questions
            WHERE TestID = ?");

52:     $sth_Qlist->execute($test_id)
            or die("Error! $DBI::errstr\nAborting");

53:     my $Qnum = $sth_Qlist->fetchall_arrayref;

54:     @Questions = map { $_->[0] } @$Qnum;

55:     for(@data){
56:         my @tmp = split(/:/);
57:         $Qid{$tmp[1]} = 1;
58:     }

59:     my $taken = keys(%Qid); # Count number taken

60:     while(1){
61:         my $Qcount = @Questions;

62:         No_More_Questions($test_id, $write_cookie)
63:         if(($num_qs == $taken) or ($taken >= $Qcount));

64:         $Qnum = $Questions[(int(rand($Qcount)))];

65:         last unless(exists $Qid{$Qnum});
66:     }

67:     $sql = qq{SELECT q.Qtext, q.Qid, a.Aid, a.Atext
68:             FROM questions AS q, answers AS a
69:             WHERE ((q.Qid = a.Qid) AND (q.Qid = ?))};

70:     $sth_QA = $conn->prepare($sql);
71:     $sth_QA->execute($Qnum)
            or die("Error! $DBI::errstr\nAborting");

72:     while(my $p = $sth_QA->fetchrow_hashref) {
73:         $Question{'Qid'}      = $p->{'Qid'};
74:         $Question{'Qtext'}    = $p->{'Qtext'};
75:         $Answer  {$p->{'Aid'}} = $p->{'Atext'};
76:     }

77:     return(\%Question, \%Answer, $taken);
78: }

79: sub fisher_yates_shuffle {
```

```
80:     my $array = shift;
81:     my $i;
82:     for($i = @$array; --$i;) {
83:         my $j = int rand ($i+1);
84:         next if $i == $j;
85:         @$array[$i,$j] = @$array[$j,$i];
86:     }
87: }

88: sub No_More_Questions {
89:     my $TestID = shift;
90:     my $cookie = shift;

91:     print CGI::header(-cookie => $cookie);
92:     print qq(No more questions for this test.<br>);
93:     print qq(Click
   <a href="/cgi-bin/quizzer/score_test.cgi?test_id=$TestID">);
96:     print qq(here</a> to score test.<br>);

97:     exit;
98: }

99: sub Get_Test_Config {
100:     my $test_id = shift;

101:     my $sql     = qq{SELECT * FROM test_config
             WHERE TestID='$test_id'};
102:     my $sth_cfg = $conn->prepare($sql);

103:     $sth_cfg->execute() or die("Error! $DBI::errstr\nAborting");

104:     return ($sth_cfg->fetchrow_array());
105: }

106: sub Add_Question {
107:     my ($Qtext, $test_id, $correct, @false) = @_;

108:     my $sql_Q = qq{INSERT INTO questions (Qtext, TestID)
109:                 VALUES ('$Qtext', '$test_id')};

110:     my $sql_F = qq{INSERT INTO answers (Qid, Atext)
111:                 VALUES (?, ?)};       # Wrong answers.

112:   my $sql_C = qq{INSERT INTO answers (Qid, Atext, correct)
113:                 VALUES (?, ?, 'Y')}; # Correct answer.

114:     my $sth_Q = $conn->prepare($sql_Q);
115:     my $sth_F = $conn->prepare($sql_F);
116:     my $sth_C = $conn->prepare($sql_C);

117:     $sth_Q->execute() or die("Error! $DBI::errstr\nAborting");
```

Continued

Listing 6-8 *(continued)*

```
118:    my $Qid = $conn->{'mysql_insertid'};

119:    $sth_C->execute($Qid, $correct)
            or die("Error! $DBI::errstr\nAborting");

120:    for my $txt (@false) {
121:        next unless($txt);
122:        $sth_F->execute($Qid, $txt)
                or die("Error! $DBI::errstr\nAborting");
123:    }

124:    return 1;
125: }

126: 1;
```

✦   ✦   ✦

Fetching Data from the Database (Advanced)

In Chapter 6, we discover how to use a Web server and browser to create a user interface. In this chapter, we build upon that concept and create a Web-based auction program! Although this isn't near what eBay is, this auction program is perfect for small fundraisers, church auctions, and so on. In fact, the idea for this chapter is taken from my "real job" at MasterCard International, where we wanted to have an internal Web-based auction for a charity we support.

To create this auction program, first we must gain an understanding of what functionality we are looking for. This auction program needs to be able to:

◆ Run several different auctions or at least have the ability for different items to have different times that bidding is allowed

◆ Store donor information

◆ Store item information

◆ Store bid information

◆ Define when bidding starts and when bidding closes

◆ List a range of items

◆ List a single item

◆ Be template-based for easy customization

The program we create in this chapter does all of the preceding.

Auction Database Tables

The first thing we need to do, now that we have some requirements, is to figure out how to design the database. Our auction database consists of four tables — auction, donor, item, and bids. This is about as normalized as we'll need to get for this small application.

The auction table looks like this:

```
+--------------+-------------+------+-----+---------+----------------+
| Field        | Type        | Null | Key | Default | Extra          |
+--------------+-------------+------+-----+---------+----------------+
| auction_id   | int(11)     |      | PRI | NULL    | auto_increment |
| name         | varchar(50) | YES  |     | NULL    |                |
| start_bidding| datetime    | YES  |     | NULL    |                |
| stop_bidding | datetime    | YES  |     | NULL    |                |
+--------------+-------------+------+-----+---------+----------------+
```

First, we have the auction_id, which is our *primary key*. This field is also set to auto_increment; each time we enter a record, the database automatically handles updating this field for us.

Next is the name field; this is the name of the auction. It is currently set to 50 characters, but if you have auctions with longer names, feel free to change this value.

start_bidding is a datetime field that contains the date and time when bidding for this auction can begin.

stop_bidding is also a datetime field. This contains the date and time when bidding ends.

Take a look at the donor table.

```
+----------+-------------+------+-----+---------+----------------+
| Field    | Type        | Null | Key | Default | Extra          |
+----------+-------------+------+-----+---------+----------------+
| donor_id | int(11)     |      | PRI | NULL    | auto_increment |
| name     | varchar(50) | YES  |     | NULL    |                |
| address1 | varchar(50) | YES  |     | NULL    |                |
| address2 | varchar(50) | YES  |     | NULL    |                |
| city     | varchar(50) | YES  |     | NULL    |                |
| state    | char(2)     | YES  |     | NULL    |                |
| zip      | varchar(10) | YES  |     | NULL    |                |
| phone    | varchar(20) | YES  |     | NULL    |                |
| contact  | varchar(50) | YES  |     | NULL    |                |
+----------+-------------+------+-----+---------+----------------+
```

The donor table is used to maintain the information about who has donated the items. Since a donor can donate many items, this table makes it so that we store as little redundant data as possible. When we enter the auction items, instead of having to enter a bunch of donor data for each item, we simply store the donor_id. That links the auction item to the proper donor.

The donor_id for this table is the *primary key*. This is also an auto_increment field, so we really don't have to do anything with it when we add data to the table. The other fields in this table should be self-explanatory. They are simply text fields that hold information about the donor.

The next table is item. This table stores the actual items that will be bid upon.

```
+--------------+--------------+------+-----+---------+----------------+
| Field        | Type         | Null | Key | Default | Extra          |
+--------------+--------------+------+-----+---------+----------------+
| item_id      | int(11)      |      | PRI | NULL    | auto_increment |
| name         | varchar(50)  | YES  |     | NULL    |                |
| description  | varchar(255) | YES  |     | NULL    |                |
| image_url    | varchar(200) | YES  |     | NULL    |                |
| donor_id     | int(11)      | YES  |     | NULL    |                |
| value        | double       | YES  |     | NULL    |                |
| min_bid      | double       | YES  |     | NULL    |                |
| min_incr     | double       | YES  |     | NULL    |                |
| auction_id   | int(11)      | YES  |     | NULL    |                |
+--------------+--------------+------+-----+---------+----------------+
```

This table also has an auto_increment field as its primary key. We have several text fields that store information about the item. Three fields are of type double; these fields contain the value of the item, the min_bid (minimum starting bid), and the min_incr (minimum bid increment).

Notice the other two int(11) (integer) fields in this table: named donor_id and auction_id. These two fields contain the donor_id and the auction_id that pertain to this item. These are called *foreign keys*. Foreign keys are fields in one table that link to the primary keys of another table. By using these foreign keys, we are able to tell exactly which donor has given this item and which auction this item is in.

Finally, we have the bids table. This table keeps track of the bids and maintains a record of all bidding activity.

```
+------------+--------------+------+-----+---------+----------------+
| Field      | Type         | Null | Key | Default | Extra          |
+------------+--------------+------+-----+---------+----------------+
| bid_id     | int(11)      |      | PRI | NULL    | auto_increment |
| item_id    | int(11)      | YES  |     | NULL    |                |
| amount     | double       | YES  |     | NULL    |                |
| bidtime    | timestamp(14)| YES  |     | NULL    |                |
| first_name | varchar(40)  | YES  |     | NULL    |                |
| last_name  | varchar(40)  | YES  |     | NULL    |                |
| phone      | varchar(20)  | YES  |     | NULL    |                |
+------------+--------------+------+-----+---------+----------------+
```

The `bids` table stores the first name, the last name, the phone number of the person bidding, and the bid amount. This table also includes an `auto_increment` field as its primary key and links to the item being bid upon via a foreign key. The one different field type you'll see here is the one for the `bidtime` field. This field is of the `timestamp` type. This is another field that automatically gets handled by the database when adding records. This field stores the time and date when the record was added.

We'll be diving into the CGI code soon. Once we are through the code for generating the pages, we will look at the module that has some additional subroutines we use for our auction site.

The Auction Application

Let's begin by looking at the code we use to generate the index page — since this is where the auction site begins. Figure 7-1 is the index page. Since we are using templates for most of the HTML, changing the look and feel of this page is very easy. This page is mostly informational; it tells about the auction and has a link that allows you to view all of the items. There is also a drop-down list that has the items listed. Obviously, if you have a lot of auction items, this drop-down list gets very large and unruly. Only use it if your list of items is of a reasonable size. You can decide what *reasonable* means to you.

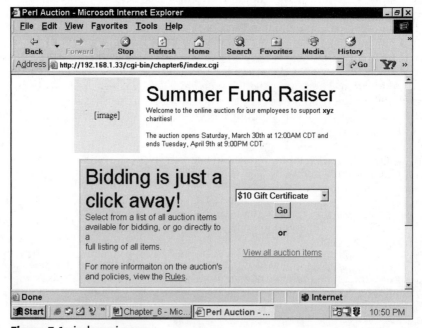

Figure 7-1: index.cgi page

Now let's take a look at the code for the index page.

index.cgi

```
01: #!/usr/bin/perl -wT
02: # index.cgi
03: # Auction program main page.
```

Line 1 tells the system where to find Perl and turns on warnings and taint checking. Warnings provide more informational messages when the program runs. Taint checking is used to keep the program from accidentally using unchecked data to perform potentially dangerous operations.

Lines 2–3 are simply comments about the program.

```
04: use strict;
05: use CGI qw(:standard);
06: use DBI;

07: use lib qw(.);
08: use SmallAuction;
```

Line 4 turns on `strict`. *Always* use `strict` in your programs. It is 100-times easier to begin *all* programs with `strict` than it is to try and go back and put `strict` into programs that are already written. `strict` forces you to follow stringent programming guidelines that are designed to help keep you from making silly programming mistakes.

For instance, if you have `strict` on and you mistype a variable name, it will generate an error. If you do not have `strict` on and you make the same mistake, Perl will automatically create the new variable and will continue happily along, using the wrong variable now. This can be very hard to troubleshoot.

Line 5 loads the `CGI` module and the `:standard` functions. This module is used to gather HTML form data and to do other CGI-related tasks.

Line 6 loads the `DBI` module. This is the module we use for database connectivity.

Line 7 uses the `lib` function to cause Perl to add the path provided to the `@INC` array. The `@INC` array is what Perl uses to search for modules. In this case, we add the dot (`.`) to the path, which means adding the current directory.

Line 8 loads the `SmallAuction` module. This module is located in the current directory—which is why we have to add it to the `@INC` array in the preceding line.

```
09: $ENV{PATH} = '';
10: my $tmpl    = "templates";
```

Line 9 sets the PATH environment variable to an empty string. Many times, when you have taint checking on, you will get an error message like this:

```
Insecure $ENV{PATH} while running -T switch at /usr/local/lib/foo line 432.
```

Simply setting the $ENV{PATH} variable in the program gets rid of this problem. If you need certain paths in the $ENV{PATH} variable, put them in place of the empty string. For example, $ENV{PATH}="/bin:/usr/bin"

Line 10 creates a scalar variable named $tmpl and sets it to the string "templates". This is the directory where the template files are located.

```
11: my $a_id = 1;  # Auction id number.
```

Line 11 creates a variable named $a_id and sets it to 1. This is the auction ID we use to get the proper auction information from the database.

```
12: my $dbh = DBI->connect("dbi:mysql:auction", "bookuser",
        "testpass")
13:     or die("Error! $!\nAborting");
```

Lines 12–13 connect us to the database. The connect method of the DBI module is what we use to create the connection. We store a handle to the connection in the variable $dbh that we declare on **line 12**. If the connection fails, **line 13** will display an error message telling us about it.

```
14: my %item = ();
```

```
15: print header;
```

Line 14 declares a hash variable named %item and initializes it to an empty set.

Line 15 prints the results of a call to the header function. The header function is part of the CGI module and is used to print a valid HTTP header.

```
16: $item{item_list}    = Drop_Down_Item_List($dbh, $a_id,
        "name");
17: $item{auction_name} = Page_Header($dbh, $tmpl, $a_id);
```

Line 16 calls the Drop_Down_Item_List function and stores the results in the %item hash under the item_list key. This function is in the SmallAuction module and is used to get all of the auction items and return them in a format to display them in an HTML "select" list. The items passed are the database handle ($dbh), the auction ID ($a_id), and the field we want to sort the data on (name).

Line 17 calls the Page_Header function used to display the HTML for the beginning of the page. This function is also part of the SmallAuction module and is passed the database handle ($dbh), the template directory ($tmpl), and the auction ID ($a_id).

```
18: Print_Page($tmpl, "index.tmpl", \%item);

19: $dbh->disconnect;
```

Line 18 calls the `Print_Page` subroutine. This subroutine is part of the `SmallAuction` module. This function is used to print the HTML pages generated by the templates. This function is passed the template directory (`$tmpl`), the template name (`index.tmpl`), and a reference to the `%item` hash. The `%item` hash is where all of the data from the database is stored so that it can be dynamically added to the HTML pages when the `Print_Page` function generates them.

Line 19 calls the `disconnect` function to disconnect the program from the database.

That is all there is to the `index.cgi` program. Most of the work is handled by the functions in the `SmallAuction` module, so this program is quite short.

The next program we'll look at is `view_all.cgi`. This program displays the data in a table format and allows the data to be shown a set number of matches at a time, as shown in Figure 7-2.

Notice that we again have a drop-down list of items. This gives the user the choice of either clicking an item from the table or selecting an item from the drop-down list.

Figure 7-2: view_all.cgi page

This program, although it also uses templates, is quite a bit longer than the
index.cgi program because there is more going on. The script for this program
shows you how to use bind_columns to make your code a bit easier. Using
bind_columns is typically a good fit when dealing with a table of data where you
are looping and filling in the table. Let's dive into the code and see how it works.

view_all.cgi

```
01: #!/usr/bin/perl -T
02: # view_all.cgi
```

Line 1 tells the system where to find Perl and turns on taint checking. *Warnings* is off
here; it was generating an irrelevant message each time the program was executed.
Because of this, it was adding a lot of unnecessary data log files. Warnings is an
excellent tool to use when creating a program, but when you move the program into
a production environment, warnings should be turned off.

Line 2 is simply a comment about this program.

```
03: use strict;
04: use CGI qw(:standard);
05: use DBI;

06: use lib qw(.);
07: use SmallAuction;
```

Line 3 loads the strict module so that we have to program more carefully and can
avoid common programming mistakes.

Line 4 loads the CGI module and it's standard functions. This is used for CGI
programming.

Line 5 loads the DBI module so that we can connect to the database.

Line 6 uses the lib method to add the current directory to the @INC variable.

Line 7 loads the SmallAuction module.

```
08: $ENV{PATH} = '';

09: my $a_id = 1;    # Auction id number.

10: my $begin_at        = param('begin_at') || 0;
11: my $num_to_display = 10;
```

Line 8 sets the $ENV{PATH} to an empty string. Again, this is to stop some insecure
dependency errors that can be caused by using taint checking. Since the $ENV{PATH}

that comes from the shell environment is set outside of this program, taint checking considers it tainted. To overcome this, we can simply set the $ENV{PATH} within the program to whatever we need it to be, "" in this case.

Line 9 declares a scalar variable named $a_id and sets it to 1. This is the ID of the auction we are running.

Line 10 declares a scalar variable named $begin_at and sets it to the value that is passed from the HTML form that calls this page. If no value was passed, the || 0 will set $begin_at to 0.

Line 11 declares a scalar variable named $num_to_display and sets it to 10. This variable is used to determine how many auction items to display on each page.

```
12: my %item = ();
13: my $tmpl = "templates";
```

Line 12 declares a hash named %item and makes sure it is empty. This is the hash we'll use to store all of the item information.

Line 13 declares a new scalar variable named $tmpl and sets it to the string "templates". This is the directory that the templates are located in.

```
14: my $dbh = DBI->connect("dbi:mysql:auction", "bookuser",
       "testpass")
15:    or die("Error! $!\nAborting");
```

Lines 14–15 create our connection to the database. On **line 14**, we call the DBI->connect method and pass it the database driver name and database name and also the username and password needed to connect to the database.

Line 15 prints an error message and halts the program if there is an error when we connect to the database.

```
16: $item{item_list}          = Drop_Down_Item_List($dbh,
       $a_id, "name");
17: my ($sth_item, $sth_bids) = Get_Item_Table($dbh,
       "name", $begin_at, $num_to_display);
```

Line 16 calls the Drop_Down_List and passes it the database handle ($dbh), the auction ID ($a_id), and the field to sort the data on ("name"). This function returns a list of items that is formatted so it can simply be dropped into an HTML drop-down list.

Line 17 calls the Get_Item_Table function. This function gets passed the database handle ($dbh), the field to sort the results on ("name"), the number to begin with ($begin_at), and the number of items to display ($num_to_display). By having the beginning number and number of items to display, this makes it very easy for us to list something like five or ten items per page.

The `Get_Item_Table` function returns two *handles* (`$sth_item`, and `$sth_bids`). These handles contain references to where the data is — just as if we were to create a statement handle for a database query. Doing this makes it very easy for us to get to the data that has been returned.

```
18: my ($name, $item_id, $descr, $min_bid, $min_incr);
19: $sth_item->bind_columns
       (\($name, $item_id, $descr, $min_bid, $min_incr));
```

Line 18 simply declares several scalar variables we'll be using shortly.

Line 19 is one we haven't seen yet. Notice that we use a new `DBI` function called `bind_columns`. This function binds the variables listed; each time we call `fetch()`, the variables are automatically populated with the current records information. Using this function is very nice because you no longer have to worry about setting the variables each time you fetch data.

```
20: print header;
21: my $auction_name = Page_Header($dbh, $tmpl, $a_id);

22: Print_Page($tmpl, "view_all.tmpl", \%item);
```

Line 20 prints the results of the `header` function. The `header` function is part of the `CGI` module. It returns the text that makes up a valid `HTTP` header.

Line 21 calls the `Page_Header` function and passes it the database handle (`$dbh`), the template directory (`$tmpl`), and the auction ID (`$a_id`). This function returns a string containing the name of the auction.

Line 22 calls the `Print_Page` function. This function gets passed the template directory (`$tmpl`), the name of the template we wish to use ("`view_all.tmpl`"), and a reference to the `%item` hash. Remember that the `%item` hash contains all of the data we need for the current record.

```
23: my %hi_bid;
24: while(my($amount, $item, $fname, $lname) =
       $sth_bids->fetchrow_array){
25:     $hi_bid{$item}->{name}   = "$fname $lname";
26:     $hi_bid{$item}->{amount} = "$amount";
27: }
```

Line 23 declares a new hash named `%hi_bid`.

Line 24 begins a `while` loop that calls `fetchrow_array` and sets several items to the values it returns. We call the `fetchrow_array` function here to get the current record.

Line 25 expands the hash to another level. At this level, the bidders first and last name is added to the new key at `$hi_bid{$item}->{name}`.

Line 26 does the same basic thing as the last line of code contained, except we call this one `amount`.

Line 27 ends the `while` loop that begins on **line 24**.

```
28: my $color = "e0e0e0";
29: my $count = 0;
```

Line 28 declares a new scalar variable named `$color` and sets it to the string "e0e0e0". We'll be using this value as a way to alternate between colors on the table we display the output on.

Line 29 declares a new scalar variable named `$count` and initializes it to 0.

```
30: while($sth_item->fetch){
31:     my $hi_bid;
32:     $count++;
33:     $color = ($color eq "e0e0e0") ? "ffffff" : "e0e0e0";
```

Line 30 begins a `while` loop that keeps fetching data until no more data is left to fetch.

Line 31 declares a new scalar variable named `$hi_bid`.

Line 32 increments the `$count` variable. This variable is used to maintain where we are when going through the data.

Line 33 checks to see if the color is equal to e0e0e0. If it is, the first item after the question mark is called — which sets the color to ffffff. If not (the color is currently ffffff), we set the color to the second value after the question mark. This is so that row colors alternate, to make reading easier.

The `(foo) ? bar : blech` operation on **line 33** is called the `trinary` or `ternary` operator. It has two names. Use whichever you like. It checks the item on the left of the ? to see if it evaluates to true. If it is true, the first item after the ? is executed. If it is false, the second item is executed.

```
34:     if(length($descr) > 40){
35:         $descr = substr($descr, 0, 37);
36:         $descr .= "...";
37:     }
```

Line 34 checks to see if the length of the value in the `$descr` variable is greater than 40. If so, we want to truncate the data so that we don't have huge item descriptions that would cause our table to look really bad.

Line 35 uses the `substr` function to take characters 0–37 and store them in the `$descr` variable. We only want 37 characters because when we append the ellipsis to the string, that will bring it up to our maximum of 40 characters.

Line 36 appends an ellipsis (. . .) to the end of the string so that the viewers of the page can see that there is more data to read in the description.

Line 37 closes the `if` block that began on **line 34**.

```
38:      $name =
    qq(<a href="/cgi-bin/auction/view_item.cgi?item=$item_id"
39:    >$name</a>);
```

Line 38 sets the `$name` variable to a link used to call the `view_item.cgi` script and view a single item.

Line 39 finishes what **line 38** begins.

```
40:      $min_bid  = sprintf("%0.2f", $min_bid);
41:      $min_incr = sprintf("%0.2f", $min_incr);
42:      $hi_bid   = sprintf("%0.2f",
             $hi_bid{$item_id}->{amount});
```

Lines 40–42 use the `sprintf` function to take the values that are fetched from the database and format them so that they have two decimal places — for the money fields.

The `"%0.2f"` tells `sprintf` to format the variable to two places after the decimal. The "f" means this is a floating-point number. This function and its use will be very familiar to C programmers.

```
43:      print qq(
44:        <tr bgcolor="#$color">
45:         <td align="left">
46:          <font class="small">$name</font>
47:         </td>
48:         <td align="center">
49:          <font class="small">$item_id</font>
50:         </td>
51:         <td align="left">
52:          <font class="small">$descr</font>
53:         </td>
54:         <td align="center">
55:          <font class="small">\$$hi_bid</font>
56:         </td>
57:         <td align="center">
58:          <font class="small">\$$min_bid</font>
59:         </td>
60:         <td align="center">
61:          <font class="small">\$$min_incr</font>
62:         </td>
63:         <td align="center">
64:          <font class="small">
```

```
                          $hi_bid{$item_id}->{name}</font>
65:          </td>
66:          </tr>
67:      );
68: }
```

Lines 43–67 form a large block that creates the HTML for one table row of data. Notice that the $name, $item_id, $descr, $hi_bid, $min_bid, and $min_incr fields are all variables that are part of the bind_columns function.

Line 68 ends the while loop that begins on **line 30**. This loop, which runs from **line 30** to **line 68**, continues looping until it runs out of data. Each time through the loop, one row of data is generated.

```
69: my ($prev, $next, $prev_link, $next_link);

70: $prev = ($begin_at - $num_to_display);
```

Line 69 declares several scalar variables.

Line 70 creates the number for the $prev variable. This variable is used in the URL to tell the program where to start listing data. $begin_at contains the value we start at, say 50, and $num_to_display contains the number of items we display per page, say 10. In this case, we have 50 - 10 to get a value of 40 for $prev. The $next variable value is derived similarly.

```
71: $prev_link = qq(&lt; View Prev $num_to_display items);
```

Line 71 sets the value of $prev_link to a default string. This default string is for when we don't have any previous data to display, so we don't make the value of $prev_link into an HTML link.

```
72: $prev_link = qq(<b><a href="?begin_at=$prev"
73:          >&lt; View Prev $num_to_display items</a></b>)
unless($prev < 0);
```

Lines 72–73 set $prev_link to a string, as does **line 71**. This time, however, we are actually setting $prev_link to an HTML link. We get to this section because there is a page to display—so, we make this a link. The unless($prev < 0) at the end tells Perl to only do this string assignment if $previous is NOT less than 0.

```
74: if($count == $num_to_display) {
75:     $next = ($begin_at + $num_to_display);
76:     $next_link = qq(<b><a href="?begin_at=$next"
77:         >View Next $num_to_display items &gt;</a></b>);
78: }
```

Line 74 begins another if..else block. This block checks to see if the value in $count is equal to the value in $num_to_display. If so, we enter the first part of this block.

Line 75 sets $next to the values of $begin_at added to $num_to_display. This is similar to what we do on **line 70**.

Line 76 creates a string of HTML and sets the $next_link variable to it. This is used to provide a link to the user so that he or she can move to the next page of data, if there is more data.

Line 77 continues what **line 76** begins.

Line 78 closes this section of the if..else block.

```
79: else {
80:    $next_link = qq(View Next $num_to_display items &gt;);
81: }
```

Line 79 begins the else portion of the if..else block. This block creates the text, but no link, for the $next_link variable.

Line 80 creates the actual text and sets $next_link to it.

Line 81 closes this block.

```
82: print qq(
83:      </table>

84:      </td>
85:      </tr>

86:      <tr>
87:      <td colspan="2" align="center">
88:       <font class="small">
89:         $prev_link
90:                 
91:         $next_link
92:       </font>
93:      </td>
94:      </tr>
95: );
```

Lines 82–95 print the rest of the code required to end the page.

```
96: Print_Page($tmpl, "footer.tmpl", \%item);

97: $dbh->disconnect;
```

Line 96 prints the footer for the page. This calls the Print_Page function, which takes three arguments: the template directory ($tmpl), the template name (footer.tmpl), and a reference to the hash containing the data that is substituted into the template when it is displayed (\%item).

Line 97 disconnects the program from the database.

That is it for the view_all.cgi program. The third, and final, CGI script for our auction program is view_item.cgi. This program is the most complex of the three programs. In this program, we'll be displaying the item information so that it can be bid on. We will also be storing the bids into the database, verifying the data, and viewing a confirmation page! Figure 7-3 shows the view_item.cgi page.

Let's walk through the code needed to do all of this.

view_item.cgi

```
01: #!/usr/bin/perl -wT
02: # view_item.cgi
```

Line 1 tells the system where to find Perl and turns on warnings and Taint checking.

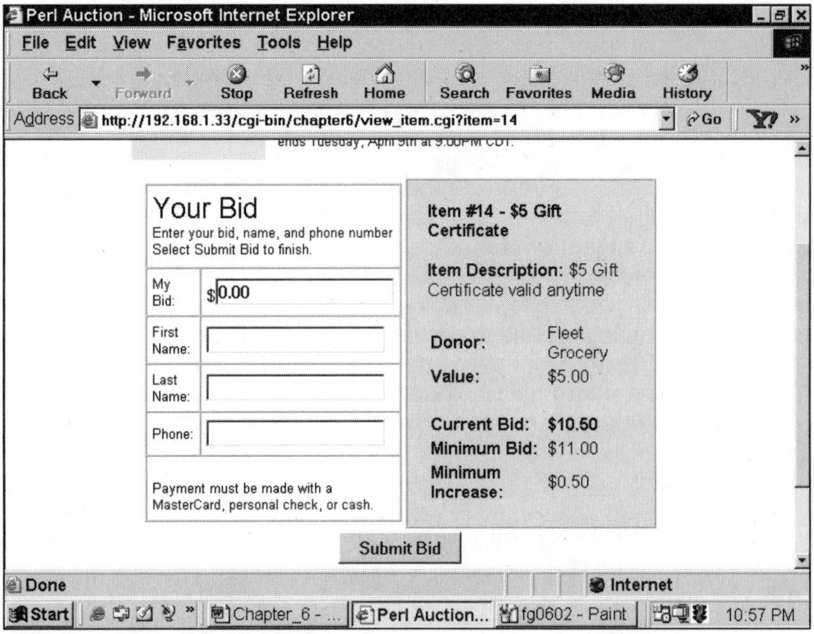

Figure 7-3: view_item.cgi page

Line 2 is just a comment about this program.

```
03: use strict;
04: use CGI qw(:standard);
05: use DBI;
```

Line 3 loads the strict module. Again, use strict in *all* of your programs.

Line 4 loads the CGI module and its :standard functions.

Line 5 loads the DBI module. We need this module so that we can connect to the database.

```
06: use lib qw(.);
07: use SmallAuction;
```

Line 6 adds the current directory, ., to the @INC array so that Perl will look in the current directory for modules.

Line 7 loads the SmallAuction module. This module contains many of the common functions that we will use, and have used, for the auction program.

```
08: my %item = ();
09: my @err  = ();
```

Line 8 declares a hash named %item and makes sure it is empty.

Line 9 declares an array named @err and makes sure it is empty.

```
10: $item{button}  = param('bid_button');
11: $item{$_}      = param($_)
12:     for( qw(item phone fname lname amount minimum) );
```

Line 10 uses the param function from the CGI module to read in the value passed in the bid_button field.

Lines 11–12 form a single Perl line that reads in the data for each of the parameters named on **line 12**. It works as follows: The for(qw(...)) on **line 12** actually creates a loop, each time through the loop $_ gets set to the current value – item, phone, etc. So as we loop, $_ gets set to the current value. **Line 11** uses the $_ to set the names of the hash key and the param value to read. Thus, these lines do exactly the same thing as this:

```
@foo = qw(item phone fname lname amount minimum);
for(@foo){
  $item{$_} = param($_);
}
```

Only the code in the program on **lines 11 and 12** does this in a more concise manner.

```
13: $ENV{PATH} = '';

14: my $a_id   = 1;    ### Auction ID
15: my $tmpl   = "templates";
16: my $count  = 0;
```

Line 13 sets the $ENV{PATH} environment variable to an empty string. This is needed to satisfy the taint checks. The Date::Manip module will cause errors to be generated if this is not done.

Line 14 declares a scalar variable named $a_id and sets it to 1. This is the auction ID.

Line 15 declares a scalar variable named $tmpl and sets it to the location of the templates directory.

Line 16 declares a scalar variable named $count and sets it to 0.

```
17: my $dbh = DBI->connect("dbi:mysql:auction", "bookuser",
       "testpass")
18:    or die("Error! $!\nAborting");
```

Line 17 uses the DBI->connect method to connect to the database. A handle to this connection is then stored in the $dbh variable.

Line 18 causes the program to die and to print an error message if the connection to the database fails.

```
19: my @money = qw(min_bid min_incr value hi_bid needed minimum
    amount);
```

Line 19 declares an array named @money and sets it to the values on the right. These fields need to be formatted in a money format.

```
20: @item{qw(name item_id desc min_bid min_incr value donor
hi_bid)} = Get_Item_Details($dbh, $item{item});
```

Line 20 loads the %item hash with the values of the list passed inside of the curly braces. Don't let the @ fool you; this is actually a hash slice which is equivalent to ($item{'name'}, $item{'item_id'}, etc...) = Get_Item_Details(...). Doing this populates the %item hash with the values returned by the Get_Item_Details function.

```
21: if($item{hi_bid} > 0) {
22:    $item{needed} = $item{hi_bid} + $item{min_incr};
23: }
```

Line 21 begins an if..else block. This block checks to see if the current high bid for the item is greater than 0. If so, we enter this block of code.

Line 22 adds the values in $item{hi_bid} and $item{min_incr} and stores the resulting value in $item{needed}. This creates a variable ($item{needed}), which stores the minimum value needed to place a bid on the item.

Line 23 closes this portion of the block.

```
24: else {
25:     $item{needed} = $item{min_bid};
26: }
```

Line 24 begins the else portion of the block that starts on **line 21**.

Line 25 sets the $item{needed} value to the value stored in the $item{min_bid} hash element.

Line 26 closes this if..else statement.

```
27: for my $val (@money) {
28:     $item{$val} = sprintf("%0.2f", $item{$val});
29: }
```

Line 27 begins a for loop that traverses through the @money array. Each time through, it sets the variable $val to the current value.

Line 28 uses the sprintf function to format the value that is currently in $item{$val} and makes sure that it contains two decimal places.

We are looping through the @money array because it contains all of the keys to the values that should be in a monetary format.

Line 29 closes this for loop.

```
30: print header;

31: my $auction_name  = Page_Header($dbh, $tmpl, $a_id);
32: my $empty_form     = 1;
33: $item{item_list}  = Drop_Down_Item_List($dbh, $a_id,
"name");
```

Line 30 prints the value returned by a call to CGI's header function.

Line 31declares a variable named $auction_name and sets it to the value returned by a call to the Page_Header function. Page_Header is passed three variables — a handle to the database ($dbh), the directory that the templates are in ($tmpl), and the auction ID ($a_id).

Line 32 declares a scalar variable named $empty_form and sets it to 1. You will see where this is used in a bit — we'll basically be using it as a boolean switch to check form status.

Line 33 sets the $item{item_list} value to the data returned by a call to the Drop_Down_Item_List function. The "name" item you see being passed to the subroutine is the name of the field that we want the results sorted on.

```
34: if($item{button} eq 'Submit Bid'){
35:     my $rval = Bidding_Open($dbh, $a_id);
```

Line 34 checks to see if the value in $item{button} is equal to 'Submit Bid'. If so, the user must be trying to submit a bid, so this block of code is entered.

Line 35 declares a variable named $rval and sets it to the data returned by the Bidding_Open subroutine. The Bidding_Open function takes a handle to the database ($dbh) and the auction ID ($a_id). This function checks to see if bidding is allowed. It returns 0 for *no* or a different value if bidding is allowed.

```
36:     unless($rval) {
37:         Print_Page($tmpl, "closed.tmpl", \%item);
38:         Print_Page($tmpl, "footer.tmpl", \%item);
39:         exit;
40:     }
```

Line 36 checks $rval to see if it is 0. The unless function in Perl means "if NOT." So, this line is checking to see if $rval is NOT true — 0 is NOT true, so this block gets entered if bidding is not allowed.

Line 37 prints the closed_tmpl template to let the bidder know that the auction is currently closed.

Line 38 prints the footer.tmpl, which is just the code to finish the HTML page.

Line 39 exits the program. We absolutely don't want the user to go any further in the program if bidding is closed — this makes sure of that.

Line 40 closes the unless block, which begins on **line 36**.

```
41:     @err          = Check_Data();
42:     $item{errors} = join('<br />', @err);
43:     $empty_form   = 0;
44: }
```

Line 41 calls the Check_Data function and stores the results into the @err array.

Line 42 uses the join function to join all of the items in the @err array with the
 HTML tag and to store the result of this action in the variable $item{errors}.

Line 43 sets the $empty_form variable to 0. This will be used to tell the program that the form is not empty.

Line 44 closes this block, which begins on **line 34**.

```
45: if(@err or $empty_form){
46:     Print_Page($tmpl, "view_item.tmpl", \%item);
47: }
```

Line 45 checks to see if @err or $empty form are true. If @err has any data in it, or if $empty_form is *not* 0, this block gets entered.

Line 46 uses the Print_Page to print the *view item* page. This function gets the template directory ($tmpl), the template file name (view_item.tmpl), and the items to populate the page with (\%item) passed to it.

Line 47 closes the if portion of this block.

```
48: else {
49:     Submit_Bid($dbh, \%item);
50:     Print_Page($tmpl, "confirmation.tmpl", \%item);
51: }
```

Line 48 is the else portion. If there are no errors and the form is not empty, we enter this block.

Line 49 calls the Submit_Bid function. This function gets passed a handle to the database ($dbh) and a reference to the item hash (\%item). This adds the bid to the database.

Line 50 calls the Print_Page subroutine. This call prints the bid confirmation page so that the bidder knows that his or her bid has been accepted.

Line 51 closes the if..else block.

```
52: Print_Page($tmpl, "footer.tmpl", \%item);

53: $dbh->disconnect;
```

Line 52 calls the Print_Page subroutine to print the page footer. This prints the ending HTML so that we don't forget any closing tags.

Line 53 disconnects us from the database. This is really the end of the program; the rest of the lines are the subroutines we call.

```
54: sub Check_Data {
55:     my @err = ();
56:     my %bid = (
```

Line 54 begins the `Check_Data` subroutine. This subroutine is used to validate the data that the bidder enters. We want to make sure that the bidder is not trying to pull anything funny on us.

Line 55 declares the `@err` array and makes sure it is empty.

Line 56 declares the `%bid` hash and opens the parentheses. We are going to load this variable up with a bunch of data that tells the program how to filter the data passed to it. The `%bid` hash is going to end up being a hash of hashes.

Each key value corresponds to a field value on the HTML form.

```
57:    phone  => { value    => $item{phone},
58:                required => 1,
59:                filter   => 'PHONE',
60:                error    => 'Error with the phone number.',
61:              },
```

Line 57 creates a hash with the key of phone. This is the `%bid{phone}` hash. We set several values here. The `value` key stores the actual data.

Line 58, the `required` key, is used to determine if this is a required field or not.

The preceding `required` key is not really put to use in this application, since we are treating all fields as required. It was left in, though, because if you want to have more fields and make some required and others not, this is a very easy way to enforce that. Simply set `required` to either 1 or 0, and check to see if the value in `value` contains any data.

Line 59 sets `filter` to a data type we'll filter on.

Line 60 stores the `error` message that gets pushed into the `@err` array if something is wrong.

Line 61 ends the phone item.

```
62:    amount => { value    => $item{amount},
63:                required => 1,
64:                filter   => 'CURRENCY',
65:                error    => 'Error with the amount.',
66:                error2   => 'Bid too low.',
67:              },
```

Lines 62–67 create the information needed to validate the `amount` field. Notice that this one has two error keys (`error` and `error2`). This is done so that we can show more descriptive error messages to the auction bidder.

```
68:    fname  => { value    => $item{fname},
69:                required => 1,
70:                filter   => 'TEXT',
```

```
71:                    error    => 'Error with the First Name.',
72:                },
73:    lname  => { value    => $item{lname},
74:                required => 1,
75:                filter   => 'TEXT',
76:                error    => 'Error with the Last Name.',
77:                },
78:    );
```

Lines 68–77 create the information needed to validate the fname and lname fields.

Line 78 closes this hash declaration, which begins on **line 56**.

```
79:        while(my($k,$v) = each %bid) {
```

Line 79 begins a while loop that iterates through the %bid hash. For each item, the current hash element and the key and value are stored in $k and $v, respectively.

```
80:            if($v->{filter} eq 'TEXT') {
81:            push @err, $v->{error}
82:                unless($v->{value} =~ /^[\w \.\']+$/);
83:            }
```

First, notice that we are using $v, the value, to reference all of these hashes. This is because %bid is a hash of hashes. For each key, the value is also a hash.

Line 80 begins the filter for all items that are set to the TEXT filter type. If the filter hash element is equal to TEXT, we enter this block.

Line 81 pushes the value in $v->{error} onto the @err array if it does not pass the test on **line 82**.

Line 82 is really a continuation of **line 81**. This line checks to see if the data in $v->{value} matches the regular expression on the right.

Let's take a closer look at what this regular expression is doing:

```
/^[\w \.\']+$/ breaks down to this.
```

The ^ anchors this regular expression to the beginning of the string. This means we are checking from the very beginning of the string; nothing can exist first. The items in the [ ] are a character class. A character class means that *any* of the items in that character class are allowed to match.

Inside the character class, the following conditions exist:

✦ The \w is the shortcut to look for *word characters*. Word characters are the letters, numbers, and underscore.

✦ Then there is a space; you can't really see it, but there is a physical space there.

✦ Next is the period \. . The period must be escaped in a regular expression — an unescaped period in a regular expression matches *any* character.

✦ Next is the single quote \'. This is also escaped.

We close the character class with the]. The + following the closing] means that the characters can match one or more times.

We have the $, which anchors this regular expression to the end of the string. By using both the ^ at the beginning and the $ at the end of the string, we anchor this regular expression to the beginning and end of the string. If we don't anchor the regular expression and it validates the data *anywhere* in the string, it considers that to be a successful match.

After all of that, it boils down to this: We check to make sure that the TEXT data type contains only *letters*, *numbers*, the *underscore*, *space*, *period* or a *single quote*.

Line 83 closes the if block.

```
84:            elsif($v->{filter} eq 'CURRENCY') {
85:            push @err, $v->{error}
86:                unless($v->{value} =~ /^\$?[\d\.\,]+$/);
87:            push @err, $v->{error2}
88:                if($item{needed} > $item{amount});
89:            }
```

Line 84 is where we go to check for items that are of the CURRENCY type.

Line 85 pushes the value in $v->{error} onto the @err array if the regular expression on **line 86** is not passed.

Line 86 checks the data to see if it contains only the data in the regular expression. This regular expression is similar to the previous one. We again have the ^ and $ to anchor the string.

The \$? means look for a dollar sign (we escape this dollar sign). If it is present, that is okay, but it does not *have* to be there. The question mark means that the character(s) can be there, but they don't have to be.

The \d means that it matches digits. Also, we have added the comma and removed the single quote and space.

Line 87 pushes the value in $v->{error2} if the condition on **line 88** is met.

Line 88 checks to see if the value in $item{needed} is greater than the value in $item{amount}.

Line 89 closes this part of the if..elsif code.

```
90:            elsif($v->{filter} eq 'PHONE') {
91:            push @err, $v->{error}
```

```
92:                    unless($v->{value} =~ /^[\d \.\-\(\)]{1,20}$/);
93:      }
94:      }
```

Line 90 is where we go to check for items that are of the PHONE type.

Line 91 pushes the value in $v->{error} onto the @err array if **line 92** returns true.

Line 92 is true if the test of the regular expression against the value in $v->{value} is true. This means we are performing an if NOT test. If the value contains only the items in the regular expression, there is no error with the data, so we don't want to push an error message onto the @err array.

This regular expression checks for *digits*, the *space*, *period*, *dash* and *parentheses*. The regular expression also limits the number of characters to 20. If the string contains characters other than these, or is blank, the test will fail, and the error message will get set.

Line 93 closes this part of the if..elsif block.

Line 94 closes the while loop that begins on **line 79**.

```
95:      return(@err);
96: }
```

Line 95 returns the @err array to the calling line of code.

Line 96 ends this subroutine.

And that wraps up the view_item CGI program. The final part of our SmallAuction application is the actual Perl module that we have many of the common subroutines in. Using a module like this one is a great way to keep all of your common subroutines together that you can avoid having redundant code.

SmallAuction.pm

```
01: package SmallAuction;
02: use strict;
03: use Date::Manip qw(UnixDate Date_Cmp);
```

Line 1 uses the package function to tell Perl that this is now the SmallAuction namespace.

Line 2 loads strict; we use strict in all of our programs.

Line 3 loads the `Date::Manip` module and imports the `UnixDate` and `Date_Cmp` functions.

```
04: use vars qw(@ISA @EXPORT);
05: use Exporter;
```

Line 4 declares `@ISA` and `@EXPORT` as global variables.

Line 5 loads the `Exporter` module.

```
06: @ISA = qw(Exporter);

07: @EXPORT = qw(Page_Header Drop_Down_Item_List Print_Page
08:              Bidding_Open Get_Item_Details Submit_Bid
09:              Get_Item_Table);
```

Line 6 adds `Exporter` to the `@ISA` array. This tells Perl that this module is going to have the ability to export functions.

Lines 7–9 push a list of functions to export onto the `@EXPORT` array. Any of the functions you want to be able to call from other programs using this module must be listed here.

```
10: sub Print_Page {
11:     my $tmpl = shift;
12:     my $page = shift;
13:     my $item = shift;
```

Line 10 begins the `Print_Page` subroutine.

Lines 11–13 declare some variables and use the `shift` function to populate them with the data that passed into the subroutine.

```
14:   open(TMPL, "$tmpl/$page") or die("ERROR: $!\nAborting");
```

Line 14 opens the `$page` file in the `$tmpl` directory. If there is an error with the open function, the `die` function is called, and an error message is displayed.

```
15:         while(<TMPL>) {
16:             s/%%(\w+)%%/$item->{$1}/g;
17:             print;
18:         }
```

Line 15 begins a `while` loop. This loop uses the file handle we create on **line 14**. This causes this block to loop through every line of the file.

Line 16 looks for elements surrounded by `%%element%%`. If it finds an element, it replaces the element with whatever is in the `%item` hash and uses the value between the %%'s as the key. This allows us to put elements into the template, having them dynamically replaced with the proper data.

Line 17 prints the current line.

Line 18 ends this while loop.

```
19:      close(TMPL);

20:      return;
21: }
```

Line 19 closes the TMPL file handle.

Line 20 returns from this function.

Line 21 ends this function.

```
22: sub Page_Header {
23:      my $dbh  = shift;
24:      my $tmpl = shift;
25:      my $a_id = shift;
```

Line 22 begins the Page_Header subroutine.

Lines 23–25 use the shift function to fetch the items passed in the function call to this function.

```
26:      my ($start, $stop, %item);
27:      my @format = qw(%A, %B %E at %i:%M%p %Z);
```

Line 26 declares some variables we'll use later on.

Line 27 sets the format for the data/time. This is needed for the Date::Manip module.

```
28:      my $sql  = qq(SELECT name, start_bidding, stop_bidding
29:                   FROM auction WHERE auction_id = ?);
```

Lines 28–29 create the SQL statement needed to get the name of the auction and the start and stop bidding times.

```
30:      my $sth  = $dbh->prepare($sql);
31:      $sth->execute($a_id);
```

Line 30 prepares the SQL statement and stores the result in the $sth statement handle.

Line 31 executes the SQL statement and passes the auction ID ($a_id) to the SQL.

```
32:      ($item{auction}, $start, $stop) =
            $sth->fetchrow_array;
33:      $item{start_date} = UnixDate($start, @format);
34:      $item{stop_date}  = UnixDate($stop, @format);
```

Line 32 fetches a row of data from the query executed previously. The results are stored in the variables on the left.

Lines 33–34 formats the date/time elements we get from the database.

```
35:     Print_Page($tmpl, "header.tmpl", \%item);

36:     return($item{auction});
37: }
```

Line 35 calls the `Print_Page` subroutine, which prints the page header.

Line 36 returns the `$item{auction}` value to the calling subroutine.

Line 37 ends this subroutine.

```
38: sub Is_Bidding_Open {
39:     my $dbh  = shift;
40:     my $a_id = shift;
```

Line 38 begins the `Is_Bidding_Open` function.

Lines 39–40 declare two variables and set them to the values passed to this subroutine.

```
41:     my $sql  = qq(SELECT start_bidding, stop_bidding
42:                   FROM auction WHERE auction_id = ?);
```

Lines 41–42 create an SQL statement that we'll use in a moment.

```
43:     my $sth  = $dbh->prepare($sql);
44:     $sth->execute($a_id);
```

Line 43 prepares the SQL statement and stores a handle to the prepared statement in your phone.

Line 44 calls the `execute` function.

```
45:     my ($start, $stop) = $sth->fetchrow_array;
```

Line 45 fetches the start time and stop time for the auction and stores them in the `$start` and `$stop` variables.

```
46:     return 0 if Date_Cmp("today", $start) == -1;
47:     return 0 if Date_Cmp($stop, "today") == -1;
```

Lines 46–47 return 0 if the value returned by the call to Date_Cmp is –1, a result of –1 means that the date comparison failed.

```
48:     return 1;
49: }
```

Line 48 returns 1; if **lines 46** or **47** did not yet return a 0, then we must be okay so we return a 1.

Line 49 ends the `Bidding_Open` subroutine.

```
50: sub Drop_Down_Item_List {
51:     my $dbh     = shift;
52:     my $auction = shift;
53:     my $sorted  = shift;
```

Line 50 begins the `Drop_Down_Item_List` subroutine. This subroutine fetches the item list and creates the HTML needed for a drop-down list.

Lines 51–53 declare some scalar variables and use the `shift` function to read in the values passed to this function.

```
54:     my $sql     = qq(SELECT item_id, name FROM item WHERE
55:                        auction_id = ?);
```

```
56:       $sql .= " ORDER BY $sorted" if $sorted;
```

Lines 54–55 make up the SQL statement we need to get the data we are looking for. We are selecting the `item_id` and `name` from the `item` table `WHERE auction id` matches that value passed in the execute command.

Line 56 appends `ORDER BY $sorted` if a value for sorting on is passed to this function when it is called. This helps us generate the SQL query statement dynamically.

```
57:     my $sth     = $dbh->prepare($sql);
58:     my $options = undef;
```

```
59:     $sth->execute($auction);
```

Line 57 uses the `prepare` method on the SQL statement and stores the result in the newly declared variable, `$sth`. By preparing the SQL, you store the database calls into a precompiled, optimized form. Not all databases take true advantage of this feature, but it needs to be called nonetheless before you `execute` the statement.

Line 58 declares a new variable named `$options` and initializes it to `undef`.

Line 59 calls the `execute` method on the `$sth` handle and passes the value in `$auction`. This value then gets substituted in place of the *placeholder* (?) in the SQL statement.

```
60:     while(my $p = $sth->fetch) {
61:         $options .=
62:             qq(<option value="$p->[0]">$p->[1]</option>\n);
    }
```

Line 60 begins a `while` loop that continues looping as long as data is being returned by the `$sth->fetch`. Each time the `fetch` method is called, the result is stored in `$p`, which ends up being a scalar variable that stores a reference to an array.

Line 61 takes the `$options` variable by using the `.=` operator.

There is really no technical term for the `.=` assignment operator. After much discussion, we've decided to call it the "*appendinate*" operator. `appendinate` is appropriate because the `.` is the concatenation operator. Together with the `=`, it concatenates and appends all at once.

By using the `appendinate` operator, we are accomplishing the same thing as a `push` onto an array, except we are "pushing" onto a scalar. This simply means that when we are done, the `$options` scalar will contain a potentially large string of data that makes up the drop-down box of auction items.

The `$p->[0]` is the *item_id*, and `$p->[1]` is the *item name*.

Line 62 closes the `while` loop that begins on **line 60**.

```
63:        return($options);
64: }
```

Line 63 returns the `$options` variable.

Line 64 ends this function.

```
65: sub Submit_Bid {
66:     my $dbh    = shift;
67:     my $item   = shift;
```

Line 65 begins the `Submit_Bid` subroutine. This subroutine is used to — you guessed it — submit a bid.

Lines 66–67 declare some scalar variables and use the `shift` function to initialize them to the values passed to this subroutine when it is called.

```
68:     my $sql_bid = qq(INSERT INTO bids
69:                   (item_id, amount, first_name,
70:              last_name, phone)
71:                   VALUES (?, ?, ?, ?, ?));
```

Lines 68–71 create an SQL statement that we use to insert a record into the bids table.

Line 68 declares the `$sql_bid` variable; then we use the qq function to create the SQL string.

Line 71 uses several *placeholders* (?); this is where the data is dynamically inserted into the statement when it is executed.

```
72:    my $sth_bid = $dbh->prepare($sql_bid);

73:    $sth_bid->execute(
                @$item{ qw(item amount fname lname phone) }
       );
```

Line 72 declares a scalar named $sth_bid and sets it to the value returned by the prepare method call. The sth_bid stands for *Statement Handle* for the *bid* SQL statement.

Line 73 executes the SQL statement by calling the execute function. The values passed into the execute function are done by using a hash slice. Since the motto of Perl is "There Is More Than One Way To Do It" (TIMTOWTDI, for short), we choose to do things a bit differently here.

This code acts the exact same way as this code:

```
$sth_bid->execute($item->{item},  $item->{amount},
                  $item->{fname}, $item->{lname},
                  $item->{phone});
```

But as you can see, our way of doing it is much shorter. Since the $item hash contains all of the data we need, and we need only a subset of that data, a hash slice makes good sense.

Note   The @ can be a little confusing because it looks like "array"; what matters here though is the { } rather than the [ ]. The documentation at perldoc perldata is quite good at explaining this. It says to consider the @ to be like *these* or *those* in English. So, it is like reading it *these hash values.*

Getting back to our %item hash, we want the item, amount, fname, lname and phone from it. We can quote each one like so:

```
@$item{ "item", "amount", "fname", "lname", "phone" }
```

But that leaves a lot of room for typing errors. Instead, we use the "quote word" function (qw). qw passes the items in a list, just like previously, but via a much cleaner method — leaving less room for error.

```
74:    return;
75: }
```

Line 74 returns us from this subroutine.

Line 75 closes the subroutine.

```
76: sub Get_Item_Details {
77:     my $dbh     = shift;
78:     my $item_id = shift;
```

Line 76 begins the Get_Item_Details subroutine. This subroutine is used to get all of the information needed to display an "item" page, which is where users go to bid on an item.

Lines 77–78 declare some scalar variables and use the shift function to initialize them to the data passed to the subroutine.

```
79:     my $sql_item  =
80:         qq(SELECT
81:         a.name, a.item_id, a.description,
82:             a.min_bid, a.min_incr, a.value, b.name
83:         FROM
84:         item AS a, donor AS b
85:         WHERE
86:         a.item_id = ?
87:         AND
88:         a.donor_id = b.donor_id
89:           );
```

Lines 79–89 make up the SQL statement to get the item information we need. It is on several lines simply to make it more readable. Nothing is worse than looking at someone's code and seeing a huge blob of text. Spread things, indent, and make generating clean code one of your goals.

Line 80 begins the SQL statement by opening a block of text with the qq function. qq is equivalent to the double quote. There is also a q operator that is equivalent to the single quote. Remember that a double-quoted string interpolates the variables within it; a single-quoted string does not.

Lines 81–82 list the fields we want to get data for. Notice that they have an a. and a b. in front of the field names. We are selecting from multiple tables and these allow us, and the database, to know which table data we are referring to.

Line 84 lists the tables we are querying in. The AS a and AS b are where we get the a. and b. on **lines 81** and **82**. Otherwise we would have to explicitly name the tables using their full names (item and donor).

Line 86 makes sure that we get to right item_id.

Line 88 makes sure that the donor_id in both tables matches.

Line 89 closes the qq block that begins on **line 79**.

```
90:      my $sql_bids  =
91:          qq(SELECT MAX(amount)
92:              FROM bids
93:             WHERE item_id = ? );
```

Line 90 declares a variable named $sql_bids. This variable contains the text that makes up the SQL statement to get the amount of the highest bid for the item we are looking at.

Line 91 uses the qq function to create the string. Here we are using the database server's MAX function to get the largest value in the amount field for the items that are returned.

Line 93 uses a *placeholder* to limit our search. We are searching on the item_id field here. Although there may be many bids on that item, only one can be the MAX bid.

```
94:      my $sth_item  = $dbh->prepare($sql_item);
95:      my $sth_bids  = $dbh->prepare($sql_bids);
```

Line 94 declares a variable named $sth_item and prepares the $sth_item SQL statement. $sth_item holds a handle to the prepared statement when finished.

Line 95 declares a variable named $sth_bids and prepares the $sth_bids SQL statement. $sth_bids holds a handle to the prepared statement when finished.

```
96:      $sth_item->execute($item_id);
97:      $sth_bids->execute($item_id);
```

Lines 96–97 execute their respective SQL statements.

```
98:      my @data = $sth_item->fetchrow_array;
99:      my $temp = $sth_bids->fetchrow_array;
```

Line 98 uses the fetchrow_array method to get the data for the current item. There are several pieces of data coming back, so we store the results into an array.

Line 99 also uses the fetchrow_array method, but only one value is being returned, so we store the results into a scalar variable instead of an array.

```
100:     push @data, $temp;
101:     return(@data);
102: }
```

Line 100 uses the push function to add the value in $temp to the @data array.

Line 101 returns the @data array.

Line 102 closes this subroutine.

```
103:  sub Get_Item_Table{
104:       my $dbh       = shift;
105:       my $sort      = shift;
106:       my $start_at  = shift;
107:       my $count     = shift;
```

Line 103 begins the Get_Item_Table subroutine. This subroutine is used to get a list of all of the items so that they can be displayed in a table.

Lines 104–107 declare scalar variables and use the shift function to initialize them with the data passed to the subroutine.

```
108:       $start_at = 0 unless $start_at;
109:       $count    = 5 unless $count;
```

Line 108 sets the value of $start_at to 0, unless $start_at already contains some data. We use the $start_at variable to determine where to start displaying data. If no starting point is sent, we set it to 0 here as the default.

Line 109 sets the value of $count to 5 unless it already contains something. We use this variable to determine how many items to display on a page.

```
110:       my $sql_item  = qq(SELECT name, item_id, description,
111:                          min_bid, min_incr FROM item
112:                    ORDER BY $sort LIMIT $start_at, $count);
```

Lines 110–112 declare a new scalar variable named $sql_item and create a string of SQL that gets stored in it. Notice that we use variables, not placeholders, in the SQL on **line 112**. This is because a placeholder cannot be used in place of the $start_at and $count variables. There is no point in using a placeholder for the $sort value but not the others.

```
113:       my $sth_item  = $dbh->prepare($sql_item);
```

Line 113 prepares the $stl_item SQL statement and stores the result of this, a handle, in the new scalar variable named $sth_item.

```
114:       $dbh->do("CREATE TEMPORARY TABLE
                    tmp(amount double, item_id int)");
```

Line 114 creates a new table that we'll use temporarily to hold some data. MySQL does not support subselects (that is, a SELECT statement within a select statement). To get around this, you can create a temporary table to store the data in and then use it as part of a query.

The temporary table we are creating here only contains two fields: amount and item_id.

```
115:       $dbh->do("LOCK TABLES bids, item read");
```

Line 115 locks out the bids table and item table. This is so we don't have people adding data when we are trying to select it.

```
116:     $dbh->do("INSERT INTO tmp SELECT MAX(amount),
117:             item_id FROM bids GROUP BY item_id");
```

Lines 116–117 are the SQL needed to insert the maximum amount and item_id from the bids table and insert them into the tmp table. This takes the place of our subselect.

There is a good reason why this has to be done: to get the high bid and high bidders from the bids table, a simple enough task — on the surface.

```
SELECT item_id, last_name, MAX(amount) FROM bids GROUP BY
item_id;
```

This *appears* to work and even returns data that looks perfectly valid. You get the proper item_id and MAX(amount) values without a problem. But the last_name is unpredictable! The reasons for this are complex and documented in MySQL. It all boils down to the fact that a subselect needs to be used to handle this task. Since MySQL doesn't support subselects, we'll use a temporary table.

```
118:     my $sql_bids = qq(SELECT bids.amount, bids.item_id,
            first_name,
119:        last_name FROM bids, tmp WHERE
120:        bids.amount=tmp.amount AND
121:        bids.item_id=tmp.item_id);
```

Lines 118–121 make up the SQL needed to get the data we are looking for. The SQL statement is stored in a new scalar variable named $sql_bids. This query selects data from the bids table and the tmp table. It uses the tmp table to ensure that we get the right data.

```
122:     my $sth_bids  = $dbh->prepare($sql_bids);

123:     $sth_item->execute;
124:     $sth_bids->execute;
```

Line 122 prepares the $sql_bids query and stores a handle to the prepared query in $sth_bids.

Lines 123–124 execute the $sth_item and $sth_bids queries.

```
125:     $dbh->do("DROP TABLE tmp");
126:     $dbh->do("UNLOCK TABLES");
```

Line 125 DROPs (deletes) the tmp table.

Line 126 unlocks the tables.

```
127:      return($sth_item, $sth_bids);
128: }

129: 1;
```

Line 127 returns the $sth_item and $sth_bids statement handles.

Line 128 closes this subroutine.

Line 129 is needed because all modules must return a true value — this ensures that by returning a 1.

Summary

That wraps up the SmallAuction module that contains the shared functions. Considering the functionality of this program, the fact that we are looking at only about 350 lines of code is truly amazing.

We have been able to cover dynamic-table generation, placeholders, limiting selections, multiple-table queries, and bind values. Those are a lot of new and exciting things for just one chapter!

You may want to add authentication and auction times to this program so that people can see exactly how much time they have to bid on an item.

Program Listings

Listings 7-1 to 7-5 contain the complete and uninterrupted code listings for the applications in this chapter. The templates for all of these pages are located on this book's companion Web site under the code for this chapter.

Listing 7-1: **MySQL tables**

```
# MySQL dump 8.16
#
# Host: localhost     Database: auction
#--------------------------------------------------------
# Server version    3.23.47

#
# Table structure for table 'auction'
```

Continued

Listing 7-1 *(continued)*

```
#
CREATE TABLE auction (
  auction_id int(11) NOT NULL auto_increment,
  name varchar(50) default NULL,
  start_bidding datetime default NULL,
  stop_bidding datetime default NULL,
  PRIMARY KEY  (auction_id)
) TYPE=MyISAM;

#
# Table structure for table 'bids'
#

CREATE TABLE bids (
  bid_id int(11) NOT NULL auto_increment,
  item_id int(11) default NULL,
  amount double default NULL,
  bidtime timestamp(14) NOT NULL,
  first_name varchar(40) default NULL,
  last_name varchar(40) default NULL,
  phone varchar(20) default NULL,
  PRIMARY KEY  (bid_id)
) TYPE=MyISAM;

#
# Table structure for table 'donor'
#

CREATE TABLE donor (
  donor_id int(11) NOT NULL auto_increment,
  name varchar(50) default NULL,
  address1 varchar(50) default NULL,
  address2 varchar(50) default NULL,
  city varchar(50) default NULL,
  state char(2) default NULL,
  zip varchar(10) default NULL,
  phone varchar(20) default NULL,
  contact varchar(50) default NULL,
  PRIMARY KEY  (donor_id)
) TYPE=MyISAM;

#
# Table structure for table 'item'
#

CREATE TABLE item (
  item_id int(11) NOT NULL auto_increment,
  name varchar(50) default NULL,
  description varchar(255) default NULL,
  image_url varchar(200) default NULL,
```

```
     donor_id int(11) default NULL,
     value double default NULL,
     min_bid double default NULL,
     min_incr double default NULL,
     auction_id int(11) default NULL,
     PRIMARY KEY  (item_id)
) TYPE=MyISAM;
```

Listing 7-2: **index.cgi**

```
01: #!/usr/bin/perl -wT
02: # index.cgi
03: # Chapter 7

04: use strict;
05: use CGI qw(:standard);
06: use DBI;

07: use lib qw(.);
08: use SmallAuction;

09: $ENV{PATH} = '';
10: my $tmpl   = "templates";

11: my $a_id = 1;  # Auction id number.

12: my $dbh = DBI->connect("dbi:mysql:auction", "bookuser",
         "testpass")
13:    or die("Error! $!\nAborting");

14: my %item = ();

15: print header;

16: $item{item_list}    = Drop_Down_Item_List($dbh, $a_id,
                  "name");
17: $item{auction_name} = Page_Header($dbh, $tmpl, $a_id);

18: Print_Page($tmpl, "index.tmpl", \%item);

19: $dbh->disconnect;
```

Listing 7-3: **view_all.cgi**

```
01: #!/usr/bin/perl -T
02: # view_all.cgi

03: use strict;
```

Continued

Listing 7-3 *(continued)*

```
04: use CGI qw(:standard);
05: use DBI;

06: use lib qw(.);
07: use SmallAuction;

08: $ENV{PATH} = '';

09: my $a_id = 1;   # Auction id number.

10: my $begin_at       = param('begin_at') || 0;
11: my $num_to_display = 10;

12: my %item = ();
13: my $tmpl = "templates";

14: my $dbh = DBI->connect("dbi:mysql:auction", "bookuser",
        "testpass")
15:     or die("Error! $!\nAborting");

16: $item{item_list}       = Drop_Down_Item_List($dbh, $a_id,
        "name");
17: my ($sth_item, $sth_bids) = Get_Item_Table($dbh, "name",
        $begin_at, $num_to_display);

18: my ($name, $item_id, $descr, $min_bid, $min_incr);
19: $sth_item->bind_columns(\($name, $item_id, $descr,
        $min_bid, $min_incr));

20: print header;
21: my $auction_name = Page_Header($dbh, $tmpl, $a_id);

22: Print_Page($tmpl, "view_all.tmpl", \%item);

23: my %hi_bid;
24: while(my($amount, $item, $fname, $lname) =
        $sth_bids->fetchrow_array){
25:     $hi_bid{$item}->{name}   = "$fname $lname";
26:     $hi_bid{$item}->{amount} = "$amount";
27: }

28: my $color = "e0e0e0";
29: my $count = 0;
30: while($sth_item->fetch){
31:     my $hi_bid;
32:     $count++;
33:     $color = ($color eq "e0e0e0") ?  "ffffff" :
            "e0e0e0";

34:     if(length($descr) > 40){
```

```
35:          $descr  = substr($descr, 0, 37);
36:          $descr .= "...";
37:      }

38:      $name = qq(<a
         href="/cgi-bin/chapter6/view_item.cgi?item=$item_id"
39:                >$name</a>);

40:      $min_bid  = sprintf("%0.2f", $min_bid);
41:      $min_incr = sprintf("%0.2f", $min_incr);
42:      $hi_bid   = sprintf("%0.2f",
             $hi_bid{$item_id}->{amount});

43:      print qq(
44:        <tr bgcolor="#$color">
45:         <td align="left">
46:          <font class="small">$name</font>
47:         </td>
48:         <td align="center">
49:          <font class="small">$item_id</font>
50:         </td>
51:         <td align="left">
52:          <font class="small">$descr</font>
53:         </td>
54:         <td align="center">
55:          <font class="small">\$$hi_bid</font>
56:         </td>
57:         <td align="center">
58:          <font class="small">\$$min_bid</font>
59:         </td>
60:         <td align="center">
61:          <font class="small">\$$min_incr</font>
62:         </td>
63:         <td align="center">
64:        <font class="small">$hi_bid{$item_id}->{name}</font>
65:         </td>
66:        </tr>
67:      );
68: }

69: my ($prev, $next, $prev_link, $next_link);

70: $prev = ($begin_at - $num_to_display);

71: $prev_link =                qq(&lt; View Prev $num_to_display
items);
72:     $prev_link = qq(<b><a href="?begin_at=$prev"
73:         >&lt; View Prev $num_to_display items</a></b>)
unless ($prev < 0);


74: if($count == $num_to_display) {
```

Continued

Listing 7-3 *(continued)*

```
75:     $next = ($begin_at + $num_to_display);
76:     $next_link = qq(<b><a href="?begin_at=$next"
77:         >View Next $num_to_display items &gt;</a></b>);
78: }
79: else {
80:     $next_link = qq(View Next $num_to_display items &gt;);
81: }

82: print qq(
83:     </table>

84:     </td>
85:     </tr>

86:     <tr>
87:      <td colspan="2" align="center">
88:       <font class="small">
89:         $prev_link
90:                 
91:         $next_link
92:       </font>
93:     </td>
94:     </tr>
95: );

96: Print_Page($tmpl, "footer.tmpl", \%item);

97: $dbh->disconnect;
```

Listing 7-4: **view_item.cgi**

```
01: #!/usr/bin/perl -wT
02: # view_item.cgi

03: use strict;
04: use CGI qw(:standard);
05: use DBI;

06: use lib qw(.);
07: use SmallAuction;

08: my %item = ();
09: my @err  = ();

10: $item{button}  = param('bid_button');
11: $item{$_}      = param($_)
```

```
12:     for( qw(item phone fname lname amount minimum) );

13: $ENV{PATH} = '';

14: my $a_id   = 1;    ### Auction ID
15: my $tmpl   = "templates";
16: my $count  = 0;

17: my $dbh = DBI->connect("dbi:mysql:auction", "bookuser",
        "testpass")
18:     or die("Error! $!\nAborting");


19: my @money = qw(min_bid min_incr value hi_bid needed
        minimum amount);

20: @item{qw(name item_id desc min_bid min_incr value donor
hi_bid)} = Get_Item_Details($dbh, $item{item});


21: if($item{hi_bid} > 0) {
22:     $item{needed} = $item{hi_bid} + $item{min_incr};
23: }
24: else {
25:     $item{needed} = $item{min_bid};
26: }

27: for my $val (@money) {
28:     $item{$val} = sprintf("%0.2f", $item{$val});
29: }

30: print header;

31: my $auction_name  = Page_Header($dbh, $tmpl, $a_id);
32: my $empty_form    = 1;
33: $item{item_list}  = Drop_Down_Item_List($dbh, $a_id,
        "name");

34: if($item{button} eq 'Submit Bid'){
35:     my $rval = Is_Bidding_Open($dbh, $a_id);

36:     unless($rval) {
37:         Print_Page($tmpl, "closed.tmpl", \%item);
38:         Print_Page($tmpl, "footer.tmpl", \%item);
39:     exit;
40:     }

41:     @err          = Check_Data();
42:     $item{errors} = join('<br />', @err);
43:     $empty_form   = 0;
44: }

45: if(@err or $empty_form){
```

Continued

Listing 7-4 *(continued)*

```
46:        Print_Page($tmpl, "view_item.tmpl", \%item);
47: }
48: else {
49:        Submit_Bid($dbh, \%item);
50:        Print_Page($tmpl, "confirmation.tmpl", \%item);
51: }

52: Print_Page($tmpl, "footer.tmpl", \%item);

53: $dbh->disconnect;

54: sub Check_Data {
55:        my @err = ();
56:        my %bid = (
57:            phone  => { value    => $item{phone},
58:                        required => 1,
59:                      filter   => 'PHONE',
60:                      error => 'Error with the phone number.',
61:                      },
62:            amount => { value    => $item{amount},
63:                        required => 1,
64:                        filter   => 'CURRENCY',
65:                        error    => 'Error with the amount.',
66:                        error2   => 'Bid too low.',
67:                      },
68:            fname  => { value    => $item{fname},
69:                        required => 1,
70:                        filter   => 'TEXT',
71:                       error => 'Error with the First Name.',
72:                      },
73:            lname  => { value    => $item{lname},
74:                        required => 1,
75:                        filter   => 'TEXT',
76:                        error => 'Error with the Last Name.',
77:                      },
78:        );

79:        while(my($k,$v) = each %bid) {
80:            if($v->{filter} eq 'TEXT') {
81:            push @err, $v->{error}
82:                unless($v->{value} =~ /^[\w \.\']+$/);
83:        }
84:            elsif($v->{filter} eq 'CURRENCY') {
85:            push @err, $v->{error}
86:                unless($v->{value} =~ /^\$?[\d\.\,]+$/);
87:            push @err, $v->{error2}
88:                if($item{needed} > $item{amount});
89:        }
90:            elsif($v->{filter} eq 'PHONE') {
91:            push @err, $v->{error}
```

```
92:                    unless($v->{value} =~ /^[\d \.\-\(\)]{1,20}$/);
93:        }
94:        }
95:        return(@err);
96: }
```

Listing 7-5: **SmallAuction.pm**

```
01: package SmallAuction;
02: use strict;
03: use Date::Manip qw(UnixDate Date_Cmp);

04: use vars qw(@ISA @EXPORT);
05: use Exporter;

06: @ISA = qw(Exporter);

07: @EXPORT = qw(Page_Header Drop_Down_Item_List Print_Page
08:              Is_Bidding_Open Get_Item_Details Submit_Bid
09:              Get_Item_Table);

10: sub Print_Page {
11:     my $tmpl = shift;
12:     my $page = shift;
13:     my $item = shift;

14:     open(TMPL, "$tmpl/$page")
            or die("ERROR: $!\nAborting");
15:         while(<TMPL>) {
16:             s/%%(\w+)%%/$item->{$1}/g;
17:             print;
18:         }
19:     close(TMPL);

20:     return;
21: }

22: sub Page_Header {
23:     my $dbh  = shift;
24:     my $tmpl = shift;
25:     my $a_id = shift;
26:     my ($start, $stop, %item);
27:     my @format = qw(%A, %B %E at %i:%M%p %Z);

28:     my $sql  = qq(SELECT name, start_bidding,
            stop_bidding
29:                     FROM auction WHERE auction_id = ?);

30:     my $sth  = $dbh->prepare($sql);
```

Continued

Listing 7-5 *(continued)*

```
31:     $sth->execute($a_id);

32:     ($item{auction}, $start, $stop) =
            $sth->fetchrow_array;
33:     $item{start_date} = UnixDate($start, @format);
34:     $item{stop_date}  = UnixDate($stop, @format);

35:     Print_Page($tmpl, "header.tmpl", \%item);

36:     return($item{auction});
37: }

38: sub Is_Bidding_Open {
39:     my $dbh  = shift;
40:     my $a_id = shift;

41:     my $sql  = qq(SELECT start_bidding, stop_bidding
42:                   FROM auction WHERE auction_id = ?);

43:     my $sth  = $dbh->prepare($sql);
44:     $sth->execute($a_id);

45:     my ($start, $stop) = $sth->fetchrow_array;

46:     return 0 if Date_Cmp("today", $start) == -1;
47:     return 0 if Date_Cmp($stop, "today") == -1;

48:     return 1;
49: }

50: sub Drop_Down_Item_List {
51:     my $dbh     = shift;
52:     my $auction = shift;
53:     my $sorted  = shift;

54:     my $sql     = qq(SELECT item_id, name FROM item WHERE
55:                   auction_id = ?);
56:      $sql .= " ORDER BY $sorted" if $sorted;

57:     my $sth     = $dbh->prepare($sql);
58:     my $options = undef;

59:     $sth->execute($auction);

60:     while(my $p = $sth->fetch) {
61:         $options .= qq(<option
                value="$p->[0]">$p->[1]</option>\n);
62:     }

63:     return($options);
```

```
64: }

65: sub Submit_Bid {
66:     my $dbh      = shift;
67:     my $item     = shift;

68:     my $sql_bid = qq(INSERT INTO bids
69:                       (item_id, amount, first_name,
70:                   last_name, phone)
71:                       VALUES (?, ?, ?, ?, ?));

72:     my $sth_bid = $dbh->prepare($sql_bid);

73:     $sth_bid->execute( @$item{ qw(item amount fname lname
             phone)});

74:     return;
75: }

76: sub Get_Item_Details {
77:     my $dbh      = shift;
78:     my $item_id = shift;

79:     my $sql_item  =
80:        qq(SELECT
81:         a.name, a.item_id, a.description,
82:             a.min_bid, a.min_incr, a.value, b.name
83:        FROM
84:         item AS a, donor AS b
85:        WHERE
86:         a.item_id = ?
87:         AND
88:         a.donor_id = b.donor_id
89:            );

90:     my $sql_bids  =
91:        qq(SELECT MAX(amount)
92:            FROM bids
93:            WHERE item_id = ?

94:     my $sth_item  = $dbh->prepare($sql_item);
95:     my $sth_bids  = $dbh->prepare($sql_bids);

96:     $sth_item->execute($item_id);
97:     $sth_bids->execute($item_id);

98:     my @data = $sth_item->fetchrow_array;
99:     my $temp = $sth_bids->fetchrow_array;

100:     push @data, $temp;
101:     return(@data);
```

Continued

Listing 7-5 *(continued)*

```
102: }

103: sub Get_Item_Table{
104:     my $dbh      = shift;
105:     my $sort     = shift;
106:     my $start_at = shift;
107:     my $count    = shift;

108:     $start_at = 0 unless $start_at;
109:     $count    = 5 unless $count;

110:     my $sql_item = qq(SELECT name, item_id,
             description,
111:                         min_bid, min_incr FROM item
112:                 ORDER BY $sort LIMIT $start_at,
                         $count);

113:     my $sth_item = $dbh->prepare($sql_item);

114:     $dbh->do("CREATE TEMPORARY TABLE tmp(amount double,
             item_id int)");
115:     $dbh->do("LOCK TABLES bids, item read");
116:     $dbh->do("INSERT INTO tmp SELECT MAX(amount),
117:             item_id FROM bids GROUP BY item_id");

118:     my $sql_bids = qq(SELECT bids.amount, bids.item_id,
                     first_name,
119:                     last_name FROM bids, tmp WHERE
120:             bids.amount=tmp.amount AND
121:             bids.item_id=tmp.item_id);

122:     my $sth_bids = $dbh->prepare($sql_bids);

123:     $sth_item->execute;
124:     $sth_bids->execute;

125:     $dbh->do("DROP TABLE tmp");
126:     $dbh->do("UNLOCK TABLES");

127:     return($sth_item, $sth_bids);
128: }

129: 1;
```

✦   ✦   ✦

Working with Binary (BLOB) Data

Databases can store more than plain text; they can store binary data as well. In database terminology, binary data is often referred to as *BLOB* (Binary Large Object). Binary data is handled a bit differently because you typically don't enter the binary data by hand for a file. Instead, an interface that allows you to choose a file to be uploaded is very helpful.

While thinking about this chapter, avoiding going back to the auction program we made in Chapter 7 was difficult. Bidding on items without seeing at least a small picture of what we are bidding on instills uneasiness. So this section builds on the auction program so that we can have images with the items.

You may ask yourself why you would want to store images in the database when the file system can hold the images just fine, and the database can hold a pointer to the files. This is a good question, and the truth of the matter is that both ways have their advantages. By storing the image location only, you save database space and don't have to deal with BLOB data. By storing image data in the database, you get the benefit of having a complete package because all data is in the database. Plus, when you back up your database, your images are backed up. Moreover, if your database is replicated across different servers, then your images will be replicated along with it.

Adding images to the auction program is quite easy. None of the existing code needs to be changed! We need only to add a program for fetching and displaying the images and to change the templates wherever we want an image to appear.

Our goal is to have images stored in the database and to be able to fetch the appropriate image when we choose. Also, we want to put a logo in the main header so that the auction program ends up looking something like Figure 8-1.

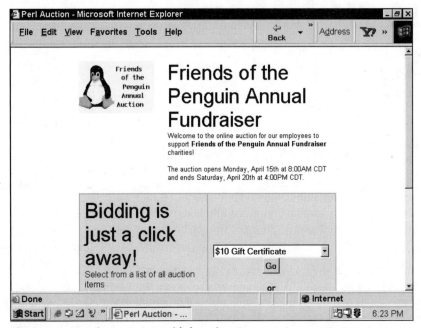

Figure 8-1: Auction program with logo image

We will create three programs in this chapter. Two of them simply make it easier for auction administers to add items to the database. The third is used to fetch/display images. The only program needed for having images in our auction program is the third — the other two programs are not needed for the actual functionality of the auction program.

Since this book focuses on databases, not user interfaces we can skimp a bit and make a simple Web interface for adding the binary data to the database table. By "skimp," we can minimize the bells-and-whistles aspect but still have the functionality we need. The Web provides a universal GUI that can be accessed regardless of the backend database or the front-end client.

Getting BLOB Data into the Database

First, we need to decide exactly what we want to store. A `logo` for the page headers can go into the Auction Table, and an `item_image` can go into the Items Table. Also, we need to store a `MIME` type for each image so that we know what type of image we are storing. The image type isn't important when storing the data, but when we want to display it, we need to tell the client what type of data we are sending.

Table structure

The new table structure for the Auction Table looks like this:

```
mysql> describe auction;
+---------------+-------------+------+-----+---------+----------------+
| Field         | Type        | Null | Key | Default | Extra          |
+---------------+-------------+------+-----+---------+----------------+
| auction_id    | int(11)     |      | PRI | NULL    | auto_increment |
| name          | varchar(50) | YES  |     | NULL    |                |
| start_bidding | datetime    | YES  |     | NULL    |                |
| stop_bidding  | datetime    | YES  |     | NULL    |                |
| logo          | mediumblob  | YES  |     | NULL    |                |
| mime          | varchar(50) | YES  |     | NULL    |                |
+---------------+-------------+------+-----+---------+----------------+
```

Notice that we've added the `logo` and mime `fields`. The data-type of `mediumblob` for the logo depends on your database. Various databases store binary data in different ways. In MySQL, using a data-type of `mediumblob` should be sufficient for just about any image file.

The new Items Table looks like this:

```
mysql> describe item;
+-------------+--------------+------+-----+---------+----------------+
| Field       | Type         | Null | Key | Default | Extra          |
+-------------+--------------+------+-----+---------+----------------+
| item_id     | int(11)      |      | PRI | NULL    | auto_increment |
| name        | varchar(50)  | YES  |     | NULL    |                |
| description | varchar(255) | YES  |     | NULL    |                |
| donor_id    | int(11)      | YES  |     | NULL    |                |
| value       | double       | YES  |     | NULL    |                |
| min_bid     | double       | YES  |     | NULL    |                |
| min_incr    | double       | YES  |     | NULL    |                |
| auction_id  | int(11)      | YES  |     | NULL    |                |
| item_image  | mediumblob   | YES  |     | NULL    |                |
| mime        | varchar(50)  | YES  |     | NULL    |                |
+-------------+--------------+------+-----+---------+----------------+
```

Again, this table is identical to the tables used in Chapter 7, except for the `item_image` field and the `MIME` field.

You can add these fields to the existing database tables, or you can make a new database; then, when you make the tables, you can add these fields. Here, we've simply made a backup of the MySQL auction database by using the `mysqldump` function and edited the output to add these fields. From there, we have used the file that `mysqldump` created and have made a new database with it.

HTML forms

The HTML forms we'll use for getting the data to the database are extremely simple.

You should be familiar with working with HTML forms, but there is one important change you must make to your `form` tag. File uploading uses multipart encoding, which is not the default, so you must set it explicitly.

Also, for file uploading you must use the POST method rather than GET.

Here is what your `form` tag might look like:

```
<form enctype="multipart/form-data" method="post"
   action="/cgi-bin/auction_up.cgi">
```

Notice that we set the encoding type (`enctype`) to `multipart/form-data`.

The other thing that may be new to you is the `input` type of `file`. To upload a file, use this input type; simply typing a file's location in a text field does not work.

Here is what your file might look like:

```
<input type="file" name="logo" size="40" />
```

Note   For security reasons, an input field of type `file` cannot be automatically populated with a value attribute. This prevents people from writing malicious programs that trick you into sending your files from your system, among other things.

The HTML form is very plain; it looks like the form in Figure 8-2. This just provides auction administrators with a simple way of creating a new auction. You can find the HTML for this page on this book's companion Web site.

The code for parsing this data is what we are really interested in here. Let's take a look at how we handle the data sent from this HTML form.

```
01: #!/usr/bin/perl -wT
02: # auction_up.cgi

03: use strict;
04: use DBI;
05: use CGI qw(:standard);

06: print header;
```

Line 1 tells the system where to find Perl and turns on warnings and taint checking.

Line 2 is simply a comment about this program.

Line 3 loads the `strict` module. This forces the programmer to adhere to stringent programming rules and helps eliminate common programming mistakes.

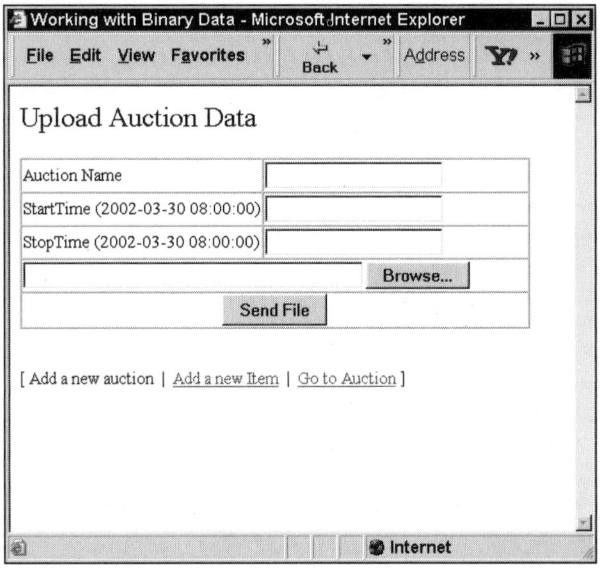

Figure 8-2: Add new auction page

Line 4 loads the `DBI` module so that we can have database access.

Line 5 loads the `CGI` module, which is a great help when dealing with HTML forms and especially with file uploads.

Line 6 prints the standard HTTP header. The `header` function is part of the `CGI` module's standard functions.

```
07: my ($image_data, $data, %fd);

08: my $image  = param('logo');
09: die unless $image;
10: my $mime   = CGI::uploadInfo($image)->{'Content-Type'};
11: my @fields = qw(auction_name start_bid stop_bid);
```

Line 7 declares a couple of variables we'll be using shortly.

Line 8 uses `CGI.pm`'s `param` function to get the value passed in the `logo` field on the HTML form. This is the field in which the file was passed. `CGI.pm` handles files as well, so working with file uploads is easy!

Line 9 calls `die` if `$image` contains no data.

Line 10 uses `uploadInfo` from the `CGI` module to get the `MIME` type of the file that was just uploaded.

Line 11 declares a new array named @fields that contains the names of the HTML form fields we will be working with.

```
12: for(@fields){ $fd{$_} = param($_); }
```

Line 12 takes the values in the @fields array and stores them into a hash named %fd (for Form Data). Reading the data this way gives you a nice, easy hash to deal with, containing only the HTML form data you want.

```
13: my $dbh = DBI->connect("dbi:mysql:auction_img",
                           "bookuser", "testpass")
14:     or die("Error! $!\nAborting");
```

Line 13 uses the connect method from the DBI to initiate a connection to the database. We use the mysql driver to connect to the auction_img database; our username is bookuser, with a password of testpass.

Line 14 prints an error message if there is a problem connecting to the database; then it terminates the program.

```
15: while( read($image, $data, 2048) ) {
16:     $image_data .= $data;
17: }
```

Line 15 begins a while loop that reads the uploaded file 2048 bytes at a time and stores the data in the $image_data variable via the appendination operator.

Note The .= operator is named appendination. The .= does not have a formal name. This is a fit because .= both *appends* and *concatenates* in the same operation.

Each time through the loop, the read function is executed. When it executes, the first argument is the *file handle*; the second argument is the *temporary storage variable*, and the last argument is the *number of bytes to read* in at a time. read returns true each time it finds data; once it runs out, it returns false so the while loop can exit. If there are less than 2048 bytes left to read, Perl will read in the remaining data and *do the right thing.* You won't cause any out-of-bounds errors or anything like that. *The right thing* is that Perl just reads what is left and returns that data.

Line 16 uses the appendination operator to concatenate the data in the $data variable onto the end of the $image_data variable.

Line 17 ends the while loop.

```
18: $image_data = $dbh->quote($image_data);
19: $mime       = $dbh->quote($mime);
```

Lines 18–19 use the `quote` function from the `DBI` to quote the strings of data in `$image_data` and `$mime`. This should really be done on all variables to make sure no weird data is trying to get sent to the database. These are the only two variables we'll worry about in this administrative program, though.

Note

Using the `quote` function on all data being passed to a query is recommended when you are getting data from unknown people. If you do not quote your data properly and if someone sends a quote in a query, it might cause the query to fail—sometimes these query-failure messages contain more information about the database server than you may want the users to see.

```
20: my $sql = qq{INSERT INTO auction
21:   (name, start_bidding, stop_bidding, logo, mime)
22:     VALUES
23:   (?, ?, ?, $image_data, $mime) };
```

Lines 20–23 create the SQL statement needed to add the new record to the database. Notice on **Line 22** that although we have placeholders, we also have regular variables. Placeholders don't work very well with binary data—extra data is sent. For the `image_data` field and `mime` field, using variables makes sense.

```
24: my $sth   = $dbh->prepare($sql);

25: $sth->execute($fd{auction_name},$fd{start_bid},
                   $fd{stop_bid})
26:   or die("Error: $DBI::errstr \nAborting");

27: print "SUCCESS!!!\nMIME type: $mime\n";
```

Line 24 calls the `prepare` method to get the SQL statement ready to run by the database.

Line 25 calls the `execute` method and sends the data for the placeholders to the database.

Line 26 causes the program to abort and to send an error message to the screen if there is a problem executing the query.

Line 27 prints a message to the user, informing him or her that the actions have been successful.

That is it for the program that adds a new auction to the database table. There isn't a whole lot to this program; it simply takes a few form fields and adds the appropriate data to a database table.

The next program adds items to the database. Again, this program contains a simple interface because auction administrators will use it. We need a few more fields for the items because we need to enter more data about each item. Take a look at Figure 8-3 to see what this page looks like. Again, the HTML for this page can be found at this book's Web site.

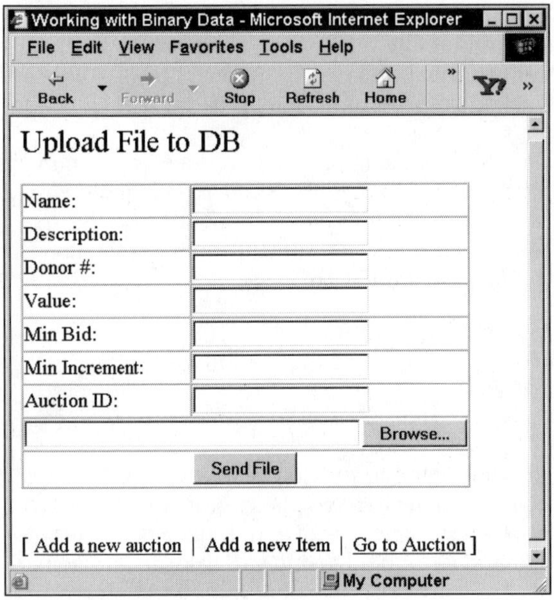

Figure 8-3: Add auction item form

```
01: #!/usr/bin/perl -wT
02: # upload.cgi

03: use strict;
04: use DBI;
05: use CGI qw(:standard);

06: print header;
```

Line 1 tells the system where to find Perl and turns on warnings and taint checking.

Line 2 is a comment about this program.

Line 3 loads the strict module.

Line 4 loads the DBI module for database access.

Line 5 loads the CGI module and imports its :standard functions.

Line 6 prints the results of a call to CGI.pm's header function. This simply prints the HTTP header.

```
07: my ($image_data, $data, %fd);

08: my $image_handle = param('image1');
09: my $mime =
        CGI::uploadInfo($image_handle)->{'Content-Type'};
```

Line 7 simply declares a few scalar variables.

Line 8 creates a new variable named $image_handle and sets it to the value returned by a call to the param function. This is simply reading in the data that was passed from the HTML form in the image1 field.

Line 9 uses the CGI::uploadInfo function to determine the content-type of the file that was just uploaded.

```
10: my @fields  = qw(item_name description donor_id
11:                   value min_bid min_incr auction_id);

12: for(@fields){ $fd{$_} = param($_); }
```

Lines 10–11 create a new array named @fields and use the qw (quote word) function to populate the new array with the values of the fields we want to work with.

Line 12 takes the newly created array and traverses through it. While traversing through the array, this line reads in each value using the param function and stores the results in the %fd hash. (The fd stands for Field Data.)

```
13: my $dbh = DBI->connect("dbi:mysql:auction_img",
        "bookuser", "testpass")
14:     or die("Error! $!\nAborting");
```

Line 13 uses the connect method from the DBI module to initiate a connection to the database.

Line 14 prints the error message and aborts the program if there is a problem connecting to the database.

```
15: while( read($image_handle, $data, 2048) ) {
16:     $image_data .= $data;
17: }
```

Line 15 begins a while loop that reads data from the $image_handle filehandle until there is no more data left to read. The read function uses the $image_handle variable as a filehandle and uses the $data variable as the temporary storage location. 2048 is the number of bytes read each time through the loop.

Line 16 uses the appendination operator, .=, to take the data in $data and to append it to the end of the $image_data variable.

Line 17 closes the while loop.

```
18: $image_data = $dbh->quote($image_data);
19: $mime       = $dbh->quote($mime);
```

Lines 18-19 uses the quote function to quote the data in $image_data and $mime.

Note   To be as portable as possible, use the quote function; it is designed to work properly for the specific database that the DBI is connected to.

```
20: my $sql = qq{INSERT INTO item
21:    ( name, description, donor_id, value, min_bid,
22:       min_incr, auction_id, item_image, mime)
23:    VALUES
24:       (?, ?, ?, ?, ?, ?, ?, $image_data, $mime) };
```

Lines 20–24 make up the SQL to insert an auction item into the database table. More items are in this SQL statement than in the SQL statement for our former program, but the concept is the same. The $image_data and $mime are sent as data right in the SQL statement, because of the "?" bug with BLOBs that we mentioned earlier. The $mime item, since it is just text, is probably acceptable, but we're being cautious.

```
25: my $sth    = $dbh->prepare($sql);
```

Line 25 calls the prepare function and passes it $sql. The result of the call to prepare is stored in $sth, the statement handle.

```
26: $sth->execute( @fd{ qw(item_name description donor_id
27:                        value min_bid min_incr auction_id) })
28:    or die("Error: $DBI::errstr \nAborting");
```

Lines 26–27 use a hash slice to send the appropriate %fd hash values to the execute function.

Note   A slice is a very useful way to access a portion of an array or hash. Although it may look like an array because of the @, it can be either a portion of an array or a hash.

You can recognize an array or hash slice by the {} or [] symbols. @fd{} indicates a hash slice of %fd. @fd[] indicates an array slice.

The qw inside of this slice simply takes the place of quotes around the strings and the commas separating the strings. That is, qw(a b c) is just shorthand for ('a', 'b', 'c').

Line 28 causes the program to exit if there is a problem executing the statement.

```
29: print "Success!\n";
30: print "MIME type: $mime\n";
```

Lines 29–30 print a simple message so that the user knows the task has been successful.

The next program is used in the HTML image tags to display an image. To use the program, simply put something like this in your HTML file:

```
<img src="/cgi-bin/display_image.cgi?item_id=34">
```

The preceding line of code displays the image for item 34. As you can see, this is exactly like a regular image link, except we point to a program that returns an image rather than pointing to an image file itself. One key benefit here is that you can easily vary the item_id dynamically and can change images without changing code.

One thing we'll use in this program is a 1×1 pixel graphic. If the image data is not present in the database for the particular item we are looking for, the program will send the 1×1 graphic instead. This prevents the broken image graphic from displaying as would happen if a HTTP request for an image didn't actually successfully return an image file. So, if you had <img src="foo" /> and foo returned HTML saying '404 Not Found', then you'd just see a broken image.

Let's take a look at our program; it is actually very simple.

```
01: #!/usr/bin/perl -wT
02: # display_image.cgi

03: use strict;
04: use DBI;
05: use CGI qw(:standard);
```

Line 1 tells the system where to find Perl and turns on warnings and taint checking.

Line 2 is simply a comment about this program.

Line 3 loads the strict module.

Line 4 loads the DBI module for database access.

Line 5 loads the CGI module and its :standard functions.

```
06: my $a_id    = param("a_id");
07: my $item_id = param("item_id");

08: my ($sth, $sql, $item);
```

Lines 6–7 declare a scalar variable and read in the value passed from the HTML form via the param function. The a_id is an item from the Auction Table, the logo. The item_id is an item from the Item Table. Only one of these should be passed at a time.

Line 8 declares some scalar variables that we'll use in a bit.

```
09: my $dbh = DBI->connect("dbi:mysql:auction_img",
        "bookuser", "testpass")
10:     or die("Error! $DBI::errstr\nAborting");
```

Line 9 creates a connection to the database and stores a handle to that connection in $dbh.

Line 10 causes the program to abort and to display an error message if there is a problem connecting to the database.

```
11: if($a_id) {
12:     die "No valid a_id?" unless $a_id =~ m/\A\d+\z/;
13:     $sql = qq{SELECT logo, mime FROM auction
                    WHERE auction_id = ? };
14:     $item   = $a_id;
15: }
```

Line 11 begins an if..else block. This part checks to see if there is any data in $a_id. If there is, a value is passed via a_id to this variable, so the user is looking for the auction logo. If something is in $a_id, this block of code gets entered.

Line 12 calls the die function and displays an error message if the value in $a_id contains anything other than numbers.

Line 13 simply sets the $sql variable to the SQL statement needed to select the logo for the current auction from the Auction Table.

Line 14 sets the scalar variable $item equal to the value in $a_id.

Line 15 ends this block of the if.else statement.

```
16: else {
17: die "No valid item_id?"
        unless $item_id and $item_id =~ m/\A\d+\z/;
18:     $sql = qq(SELECT item_image, mime FROM item WHERE
item_id = ?);
19:     $item   = $item_id;
20: }
```

Line 16 begins the else portion of this if..else block. If no data is passed into $a_id, we enter this block and use it for handling the default case.

Line 17 calls the die function and displays an error message if $item_id is empty or contains anything other than numbers.

Line 18 is the SQL for selecting the item_image and mime values from the Item Table.

Line 19 sets the scalar variable $item equal to the value in $item_id.

Line 20 ends this if..else block.

```
21: $sth = $dbh->prepare($sql);
22: $sth->execute($item);

23: my ($image, $mime) = $sth->fetchrow_array;
```

Line 21 prepares the SQL statement stored in $sql. $sth holds a handle to this prepared statement.

Line 22 executes the SQL statement and passes the value of $item to the SQL statement so that it can take the place of the placeholder (?).

Line 23 calls the fetchrow_array method on the $sth handle. This returns one row of data in a list. By putting the parenthesis around the $image and $mime values, we make them into a list context — so they are populated with the first and second items returned. We know that we will get no more than one record returned to us because the field that we are basing our search of the database table on is a primary key.

```
24: if($mime) {
25:     print header(-type => $mime);
26:     print $image;
27: }
```

Line 24 checks to see if the $mime variable contains anything. If it is not empty, data is returned from our SQL call, and we need to handle the output accordingly — so we enter this part of the if..else block.

Line 25 uses the CGI module's header function to print an HTTP header with the proper MIME type for this image.

Line 26 prints the data in $image.

Line 27 closes this part of the if..else block.

```
28: else {
29:     $mime = "image/jpeg";
30:     print header(-type => $mime);
```

Line 28 is entered if there is not a value in $mime.

Line 29 sets the value of $mime to image/jpeg. This line can actually be skipped, the text substituted into **Line 30**, where we have the variable; it remains, in this case, for consistency of the code — so that it looks like the header function in the preceding block.

Line 30 prints the HTTP header with the appropriate MIME type.

```
31:     open(PX, "templates/pixel.jpg")
            or die("Error: $!\nAborting");
32:         binmode(PX);

33:     while( read(PX, my $data, 1024) ) {
34:         print $data;
35:     }
36: }
```

Line 31 opens the 1×1 pixel image at the location specified. This is used to display a blank area so that you don't get a broken-image picture if nothing is returned from the database.

Line 32 calls the binmode function to ensure that binary mode is used on this filehandle.

Line 33 reads the file in, using the $data variable as the temporary storage.

Line 34 prints the data.

Line 35 closes the while loop that begins on **Line 33**.

Line 36 ends this program.

See, in just 36 lines of code, we have a program that can return graphical images from a database!

Summary

We hope that once you are all done, you can create something like Figure 8-4.

The only other things that need to be done to generate an auction site that looks like the one in the preceding figure is to modify the template code for generating the HTML.

To generate an image for an auction item, we have something like this in the template:

```
<img src="/cgi-bin/display_image.cgi?item_id=%%item_id%%
height="100" width="100">
```

Because of how we handle the templating, the item_id will get filled in with the value of the item the user is looking for.

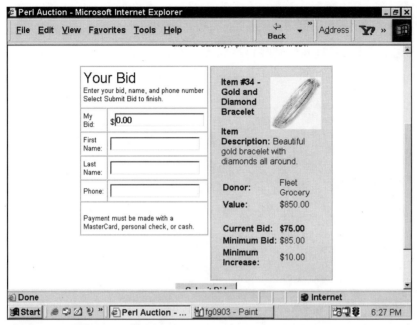

Figure 8-4: Bid page with picture

Working with BLOB data is not all that difficult. The most difficult aspect is getting the data into the database. To do that, we have to create a program to help us work with the data. Once we have the BLOB data in the database, getting it back is really just as easy as getting any other data.

Program Listings

Listings 8-1 to 8-3 contain only the code for the new programs. If you need the old programs and templates, a visit to this book's Web site is the easiest way to obtain them.

Listing 8-1: **auction_up.cgi**

```
01: #!/usr/bin/perl -wT
02: # auction_up.cgi

03: use strict;
04: use DBI;
```

Continued

Listing 8-1 *(continued)*

```
05: use CGI qw(:standard);

06: print header;

07: my ($image_data, $data, %fd);

08: my $image  = param('logo');
09: my $mime   = CGI::uploadInfo($image)->{'Content-Type'};
10: my @fields = qw(auction_name start_bid stop_bid);

11: for(@fields){ $fd{$_} = param($_); }

12: my $dbh = DBI->connect("dbi:mysql:auction_img",
        "bookuser", "testpass")
13:    or die("Error! $!\nAborting");


14: while( read($image, $data, 2048) ) {
15:     $image_data .= $data;
16: }

17: $image_data = $dbh->quote($image_data);
18: $mime       = $dbh->quote($mime);

19: my $sql = qq{INSERT INTO auction
20:   (name, start_bidding, stop_bidding, logo, mime)
21:    VALUES
22:   (?, ?, ?, $image_data, $mime) };

23: my $sth   = $dbh->prepare($sql);

24: $sth->execute($fd{auction_name},
        $fd{start_bid},$fd{stop_bid})
25:    or die("Error: $DBI::errstr \nAborting");

26: print "SUCCESS!!!\nMIME type: $mime\n";
```

Listing 8-2: **upload.cgi**

```
01: #!/usr/bin/perl -wT
02: # upload.cgi

03: use strict;
04: use DBI;
```

```
05: use CGI qw(:standard);

06: print header;

07: my ($image_data, $data, %fd);

08: my $image_handle = param('image1');
09: my $mime
        = CGI::uploadInfo($image_handle)->{'Content-Type'};

10: my @fields  = qw(item_name description donor_id
11:                  value min_bid min_incr auction_id);

12: for(@fields){ $fd{$_} = param($_); }

13: my $dbh = DBI->connect("dbi:mysql:auction_img",
        "bookuser", "testpass")
14:     or die("Error! $!\nAborting");

15: while( read($image_handle, $data, 2048) ) {
16:     $image_data .= $data;
17: }

18: $image_data = $dbh->quote($image_data);
19: $mime       = $dbh->quote($mime);

20: my $sql = qq{INSERT INTO item
21:   ( name, description, donor_id, value, min_bid,
22:     min_incr, auction_id, item_image, mime)
23:   VALUES
24:     (?, ?, ?, ?, ?, ?, ?, $image_data, $mime) };

25: my $sth   = $dbh->prepare($sql);

26: $sth->execute( @fd{ qw(item_name description donor_id
27:                     value min_bid min_incr auction_id) })
28:     or die("Error: $DBI::errstr \nAborting");

29: print "Success!\n";
30: print "MIME type: $mime\n";
```

Listing 8-3: **display_image.cgi**

```
01: #!/usr/bin/perl -wT
02: # display_image.cgi

03: use strict;
04: use DBI;
```

Continued

Listing 8-3 *(continued)*

```
05: use CGI qw(:standard);

06: my $a_id    = param("a_id");
07: my $item_id = param("item_id");

08: my ($sth, $sql, $item);

09: my $dbh = DBI->connect("dbi:mysql:auction_img",
        "bookuser", "testpass")
10:     or die("Error! $DBI::errstr\nAborting");

11: if($a_id) {
12:     die "No valid a_id?" unless $a_id =~ m/\A\d+\z/;
13:     $sql = qq{SELECT logo, mime FROM auction
        WHERE auction_id = ? };
14:     $item   = $a_id;
15: }
16: else {
17:   die "No valid item_id?"
        unless $item_id and $item_id =~ m/\A\d+\z/;
18:     $sql = qq(SELECT item_image, mime FROM item
        WHERE item_id = ?);
19:     $item   = $item_id;
20: }

21: $sth = $dbh->prepare($sql);
22: $sth->execute($item);

23: my ($image, $mime) = $sth->fetchrow_array;

24: if($mime) {
25:     print header(-type => $mime);
26:     print $image;
27: }
28: else {
29:     $mime = "image/jpeg";
30:     print header(-type => $mime);

31:     open(PX, "templates/pixel.jpg")
            or die("Error: $!\nAborting");

32:     binmode(PX);

33:     while( read(PX, my $data, 1024) ) {
34:         print $data;
35:     }
36: }
```

✦   ✦   ✦

Session Management with Tied Hashes

✦   ✦   ✦   ✦

In This Chapter

Tracking a user with
a session cookie

Understanding tied
hashes

Building a
personalized Web
page

✦   ✦   ✦   ✦

Often, you want to keep track of a user as he or she
moves through your Web site. A database can be the
perfect tool for this job. When you combine the database with
HTTP cookies, you have the ideal method of keeping track of
individual users.

Many Web sites keep track of who you are and even personal-
ize the content based upon your user preferences. Typically,
they do this by using a database to store your preferences
and by using cookies to store your unique identity.

Cookies are valuable in tasks such as this. Cookies have had
some bad press, mainly due to the insecurities in Internet
Explorer. The fact is, however, that cookies are a safe way to
store information on a Web browser. Also, to boost security
even more, we can store all of the information in a database
on the Web-server side. Only the user ID is stored in a cookie
on the browser side.

At the lowest level, the HTTP server sees just unrelated
requests for pages, without any idea of who's really request-
ing them. But only by using cookies can we properly support
the idea of a 'session' in HTTP.

Using Tied Hashes

What are tied hashes? How do they fit into all of this? You are familiar with a regular hash—an array that uses not just a number as an index, but instead any sort of string (and typically a non-numeric one). When a variable is tied in Perl, all methods that access that variable can be changed. If you have tied a scalar variable named $counter, for example, you can change the behavior of that scalar variable so that it increments each time it is accessed. The following code:

```
print "$counter\n";
print "$counter\n";
print "$counter\n";
```

actually prints:

```
1
2
3
```

This is because the variable is tied. With a scalar, there are only a few ways to access it. You can FETCH data from it, you can STORE information into it, or you can DESTROY it. Things are a bit more complex with a hash, which is good because it gives us even more power to do what we need to do.

Besides FETCH, STORE, and DESTROY, tied hashes also have DELETE to delete a value in the hash, CLEAR to clear the entire hash, EXISTS to see if a key exists, FIRSTKEY to get the first key in the hash, and NEXTKEY to fetch the next key.

We'll be tying a hash to a database. This allows us to change how the hash behaves and causes it to manipulate a database, simply by modifying values in the hash!

At the moment, this is probably all pretty confusing. Since true learning happens by doing, not just reading, we'll create an example program that ties a hash to a database so that we can track user preferences.

Program Example

The program we'll be creating is a two-page Web site. One page is used for "user registration," and the other page is the index for a registered user. A real-world Web site has many more pages, but as you'll see from our example, adding pages to this site is easy.

Figure 9-1 shows the "user registration" screen of our Web site. We are going to collect some data to generate a personalized Web page. Some of this data is required information, so there is a * next to the mandatory fields.

Figure 9-1: Sign-up/Registration

For our example, we'll be taking the *first name*, *last name*, three *favorite links*, a *favorite image*, *favorite quote*, *page text color*, *page background color,* and how long we should store this information.

signup.cgi

```
01: #!/usr/bin/perl -wT
02: # signup.cgi

03: use strict;
04: use lib qw(.);
05: use BasicSession;
06: use CGI qw(:standard);
```

Line 1 tells the system where to find Perl and turns on warnings and taint checking.

Line 2 is a comment about this program.

Line 3 loads the strict module. The strict module keeps the programmer from making simple mistakes such as redeclaring variables or mistyping a variable name. All variables must be declared before they are used — if a variable name is mistyped, an error will occur, warning the programmer of this.

Line 4 makes Perl search in the current directory (.) for modules.

Line 5 loads the BasicSession.pm module. This is a module we'll create that has the session-tracking code as well as the code for tying our hash to the database.

Line 6 loads the CGI.pm module and its :standard set of functions.

```
07: my  (%item, $errors);

08: my $remember_for = param('remember');
```

Line 7 declares a hash named %item and a scalar named $errors.

Line 8 declares a scalar variable named $remember_for and sets it to the value passed in the remember variable from the HTML form. The CGI.pm param function is used to get this value and decode it

```
09: if(my $clear = param('clear')) {
10:     our $sess     = Get_Session("clear");
11: }
```

Line 9 declares a variable named $clear and sets it to the value returned by param('clear'). If a value is passed from the Web page in the clear variable, this block will get entered.

Line 10 is executed if something is passed in the clear variable. This declares an our variable named $sess and sets it to the value returned by the Get_Session function. By declaring the variable as our, we are declaring it as a *global* variable. By passing the value "clear" to the Get_Session function, we are clearing the cookie on the user's system.

Line 11 closes this block.

```
12: else {
13:     our $sess     = Get_Session($remember_for);
14: }
```

Line 12 is the else section of this if..else block. It gets entered if the statement on **line 9** is false (that is, no value is passed in the clear variable).

Line 13 declares an our variable named $sess and passes the Get_Session function the value in $remember_for. This causes a cookie to be set on the users system and the "session value" to be returned and stored in the $sess variable. The $sess variable is the key value we use to determine who this user is throughout this program. $sess is therefore very important.

Line 14 closes this `if..else` block.

```
15: my  @fields    = qw(first_name last_name link1 link2
16:                      link3 image text_color bg_color
17:                      remember fav_quote);
```

Lines 15–17 declare an array named `@fields` and sets it to the HTML form-field names.

```
18: my  @required = qw(first_name last_name link1
19:                     image text_color bg_color);
```

Lines 18–19 declare an array named `@required` and set it to the values we are considering required.

```
20: tie %item, 'BasicSession';
```

Line 20 uses the tie function to tie the `%item` hash to a new object of the class BasicSession. For this to work, the BasicSession class has to provide special methods for the tied-hash interface (as described in perldoc perltie). The tie function takes the syntax `tie variable, Classname, parameters...;` where "parameters" is a list of whatever optional parameters the given class needs. Some classes need no parameters, some need several.

```
21: if(param()) {
22:     $errors = Check_Fields();
```

Line 21 checks to see if the `param()` function returns any data. If it does, it must have had some data sent to it, so we enter this block of code.

Line 22 calls the `Check_Fields` function and sets `$errors` to the value returned. `Check_Fields` checks the required fields to see that they contain data.

```
23:     if($errors) {
24:         $item{"ERROR_MESSAGE"} = "* A required item is
            missing...";
25:     }
```

Line 23 checks to see if the variable `$errors` contains anything. If it does, this block is entered.

Line 24 sets the ERROR_MESSAGE value to the string on the right.

Line 25 closes this portion of the `if..elsif..else` block.

```
26:     elsif (param('clear')){
27:         $item{"ERROR_MESSAGE"} = "";
28:     }
```

Line 26 checks to see if the `clear` HTML form variable has been set to 1. If so, we enter this code block.

Line 27 sets the `ERROR_MESSAGE` value to an empty string. This causes the cookie to be cleared from the user's browser, enabling him or her to sign in again. This is useful if someone is on an already signed-in system but is not the user who originally signed in.

Line 28 closes this portion of the `if..elsif..else` block.

```
29:      else {
30:          $item{"ERROR_MESSAGE"}
31:          = "Data Updated!<br /> Click
32:              <a
                href=\"/cgi-bin/index.cgi\">here</a>
33:              to go to main site.";
34:      }
```

Line 29 is the `else` part of the `if..elsif..else` block. We get here if the preceding two conditions are not true.

Lines 30–33 simply set the `ERROR_MESSAGE` to a successful message that gives the user a link he or she can click to get to the main page.

Line 34 closes the last part of this `if..elsif..else` block.

```
35:      for(@fields) {
36:          if(defined param($_)) {
37:              $item{$_} = param($_);
38:          }
39:            else {
40:              delete($item{$_});
41:          }
42:      }
43: }
```

Line 35 begins a loop that iterates through all of the items in the `@fields` array.

Line 36 checks to see if the current item has HTML form data passed. The `param` function will return true if so.

Line 37 adds the value passed from the HTML form to the `%item` hash. The key value of the hash is actually the name of the item from the HTML form. So, for example, if you had an `<input type="text" name="foo_bar">` in your HTML, whatever the user entered there will appear in `$item{"foo_bar"}`

Line 38 ends the `if` statement that begins on **line 36**.

Line 39 is the else block that we get to if the statement on **line 36** is false.

Line 40 deletes the current item.

All of the HTML form items that we care about have their names stored in the @fields array. So, as we iterate through all of the values in @fields, we go through all of the HTML form values too. If an item contains data, we need to store that data. But, if an item does not contain data, we need to make sure the item is blank in the hash. Otherwise, we end up having extra data we may not want.

Line 41 closes the if..else block.

Line 42 closes the loop that begins on **line 35**.

One thing to remember as we manipulate this %item hash is that because we tie the hash to the BasicSession module, it does not behave like a normal hash. In fact, as we add data to or remove data from this hash, we are adding to and deleting from a MySQL database.

Line 43 closes the if block that begins on **line 21**.

```
44: Wrap_Page("./templates", "signup.tmpl", \%item);
```

Line 44 calls the Wrap_Page function and passes it three values. The *template directory*, the *file to display*, and a *reference to the %item* hash.

All of the pages we display by using this program are merely HTML templates. We use this function to print the page header, to read and display the template file, and to display the page footer.

```
45: sub Check_Fields {
46:     return if(param('clear') == 1);
```

Line 45 begins the Check_Fields function.

Line 46 returns if the clear parameter is set to 1. If it is, we do not want to proceed in this function.

```
47:     for my $fld (@required) {
48:         next if(param($fld));
49:         $errors++;
50:     }
```

Line 47 iterates through all of the items in the @required array. These are the items that must contain data.

Line 48 calls next to jump to the next iteration of this loop if data is found.

Line 49 increments $errors if we've gotten here. The only way to get this far is to have an empty, required, value.

Line 50 closes this for loop.

```
51:     return $errors;
52: }
```

Line 51 returns whatever is in $errors. Let's hope it's empty!

Line 52 closes the Check_Fields function.

This is the end of our signup.cgi program. This is the program that reads all of the data from the signup screen and sets it in the %item hash (and therefore the database).

Once you fill in the values and click the submit button, you will see something like Figure 9-2.

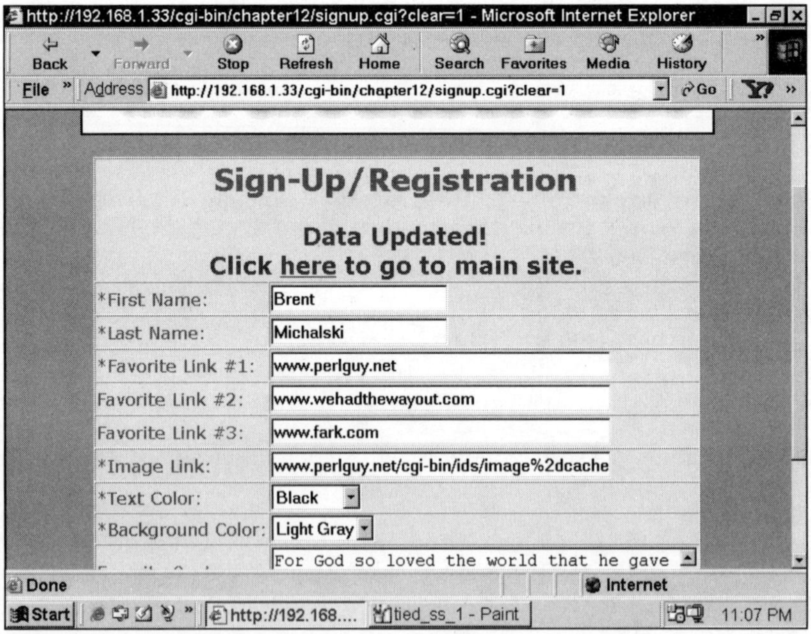

Figure 9-2: Sign-up clicked

From here, click the link to get to the index.cgi page, shown in Figure 9-3 (note the additional text in the second screen).

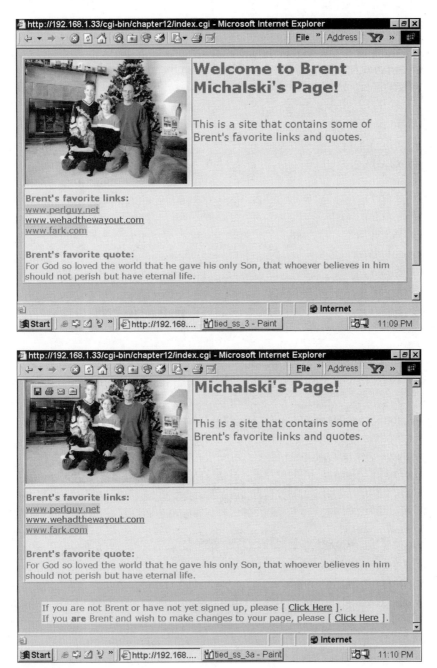

Figure 9-3: index.cgi page

But how does it know what values to put where? Well, by using templates for the HTML pages, we can dynamically substitute values. By surrounding the "variables" that we want with %%, we can create an easy-to-substitute variable. For example, if we want to place the first_name somewhere on the HTML page, we simply place %%first_name%% where we want it to go.

Lets take a closer look at a template.

index.tmpl

```
01: <div align="center">
02:  <table border="1">
03:   <tr>
04:    <td>
05:     <img src="http://%%image%%" width="320" height="240" alt="">
06:    </td>
07:    <td valign="top">
08:     <h2>Welcome to %%first_name%% %%last_name%%'s Page!</h2><br />
09:     <font class="medium">
10:      This is a site that contains some of %%first_name%%'s favorite
         links and quotes.
11:     </font>
12:    </td>
13:   </tr>
14:   <tr>
15:    <td valign="top" colspan="2">
16:     <font class="big">
17:      <b>%%first_name%%'s favorite links:</b>
18:     </font>
19:     <br />
20:     <font class="small">
21:      <a href="http://%%link1%%">%%link1%%</a><br />
22:      <a href="http://%%link2%%">%%link2%%</a><br />
23:      <a href="http://%%link3%%">%%link3%%</a><br />
24:     <br />
25:     <font class="big">
26:      <b>%%first_name%%'s favorite quote:</b>
27:     </font><br />
28:     <font class="small">
29:      %%fav_quote%%
30:     </font><br />
31:     </font>
32:    </td>
33:   </tr>
34:  </table>

35:  <br /><br />
36:  <table border="0">
37:   <tr>
38:    <td>
39:     <font class="small">
```

```
40:     If you are not %%first_name%% or have not yet signed up, please
41:     [ <a href="/cgi-bin/chapter9/signup.cgi?clear=1">Click Here</a> ].
42:     <br />
43:     If you <b>are</b> %%first_name%% and wish to make changes to
        your page, please
44:     [ <a href="/cgi-bin/chapter9/signup.cgi">Click Here</a> ].
45:     </font>
46:   </td>
47:  </tr>
48: </table>
49: </div>
```

We won't go through this template line by line, since it is just HTML. But take a look at the bold areas. Each "variable" we are going to replace is surrounded by %% and bold. The bolding is just to make it easier to spot; the %% are important. Inside of our BasicSession module, we have a function called Print_Page that handles the variable substitution and printing of the HTML.

Before we get to the BasicSession module, we'll take a look at index.cgi. The index.cgi script calls the preceding template file. As you'll see, generating personalized pages using templates and tied hashes is quite easy once you've set it up.

index.cgi

```
01: #!/usr/bin/perl -wT

02: use strict;
03: use lib qw(.);
04: use BasicSession;
05: use CGI qw(:standard);
```

Line 1 tells the system where to find Perl and turns on warnings and taint checking.

Line 2 loads the strict module.

Line 3 tells Perl that it can use the current directory (the .) also when looking for modules. This is necessary because BasicSession is not in the normal path on which Perl looks for modules.

Line 4 loads the BasicSession Perl module.

Line 5 loads the CGI module and imports its :standard functions.

```
06: our $sess;
07: my  %item;

08: $sess = Get_Session();
09: tie %item, 'BasicSession';

10: Wrap_Page("./templates", "index.tmpl", \%item);
```

Line 6 declares the $sess variable by using the our declaration. Using our makes the variable globally scoped so that we can share it with the functions in the BasicSession module.

Line 7 declares the %item hash.

Line 8 sets the $sess variable to the value returned by a call to the Get_Session function.

Line 9 ties the %item variable to the BasicSession module.

Line 10 calls the Wrap_Page function. This function expects three arguments; the *template directory*, the *name of the file to display*, and a *reference to the %item hash*. This hash reference is used to fill in the "variables" in the HTML template.

Also, notice that we call Wrap_Page, not the Print_Page function. This is because we want all of our pages to be wrapped with a header and footer. By calling Wrap_Page, we have it do the calls to the header template, then to the index.tmpl template, and finally to the footer template.

And that is it for the index.cgi program. Simply 10 lines and a template file and you have a personalized page!

Now that we've seen all of the easy stuff, let's take a look at the workhorse. The BasicSession.pm Perl module is a little bigger than the other files we've worked with so far. This module handles the cookies, the getting session, and all of the database transactions. Yet, this file is still under 125 lines of Perl.

BasicSession.pm

```
01: package BasicSession;

02: use Tie::Hash;
03: use DBI;
04: use CGI qw(cookie header);
05: use strict;
```

Line 1 sets the package for this module to BasicSession. This causes Perl to change to the BasicSession namespace rather than using the default main name-space you are in when you begin a Perl program.

Line 2 loads the Tie::Hash library, which defines the classes Tie::Hash and Tie::StdHash. We'll use the Tie::StdHash class.

Line 3 loads the DBI module for our database access.

Line 4 loads the CGI module and imports the :standard functions.

Note You might notice that this module loads the `CGI` module; the programs that call this module might also load the `CGI` module. Perl is smart enough to know if the `CGI` module is already loaded and will not load it if it is already present.

Line 5 loads the `strict` module. We do *all* of our programming under `strict` mode to avoid having to debug common errors that might creep into our program.

```
06: use vars qw(@ISA @EXPORT $sess);

07: @ISA = qw(Tie::StdHash Exporter);

08: use Exporter;

09: @EXPORT = qw(Wrap_Page Get_Session);
```

Line 6 declares the variables @ISA, @EXPORT, and $sess so that `strict` won't complain about them.

Line 7 loads the @ISA array by using `Tie::StdHash` and `Exporter`. The @ISA array is used for inheritance. This tells Perl that this module is a descendent of the `Tie::StdHash` and `Exporter` classes.

Line 8 calls the `Exporter` module. This allows us to export the functions we choose so that other Perl programs may use them.

Line 9 adds the functions that are to be exported to the @EXPORT array.

```
10: my $dbh = DBI->connect("DBI:mysql:user_prefs",
        "bookuser", "testpass")
11:   or die "Error: $DBI::errstr\nAborting";

12: my ($sql, @KEYS);
```

Line 10 creates our connection to the database by using the `DBI` module. The result of the connection is stored as a handle in $dbh.

Line 11 is part of **line 10**. If the connection to the database has failed, **line 11** will cause the program to abort and display an error message.

Line 12 declares some variables that we'll be using.

```
13: sub STORE {
14:     my ($self, $key, $val) = @_;

15:     $val =~ s#^http://##;  # Get rid of http://

16:     my $exists = $self->EXISTS($key);
```

Line 13 begins our `STORE` subroutine.

Note   Remember that when a hash is tied to a class, certain subroutines must be created so that Perl knows what to do for each possible way the hash is accessed. Because of this, we need to have TIEHASH; STORE, FETCH; EXISTS; CLEAR; DELETE; FIRSTKEY; NEXTKEY, and DESTROY methods.

Luckily, someone has done all of the initial work for us. The Tie::Hash module we have imported contains default methods for each of these actions. So, if you want to stick with the default behavior, you don't have to worry about creating a method for it; it has already been done. Since our hash is tied directly to a database, however, we'll need to create our own methods for most of these actions.

Line 14 reads in the values passed to the subroutine. The first value is always a reference to itself, so we'll call it $self. The next two are the key and value pair that will be the key and value of the hash item.

Line 15 examines the $val variable and removes any http:// that may be at the beginning of the string. This occurs so that any links that the users enter will not have the http:// in them.

Line 16 checks to see if the value we are setting already exists. The EXISTS method expects the session and $key to be passed to it. If it does exist, the $exists variable will be set to a true value.

```
17:      if($exists) {
18:          $sql = qq{ UPDATE session
19:                  SET
20:              name  = '$key',
21:              value = '$val'
22:              WHERE
23:              (user_id = '$main::sess'
24:                  AND name = '$key') };
25:      }
```

Line 17 begins an if..else block. This section checks to see if the $exists variable contains a true value. If so, this block is entered.

Lines 18–24 create the SQL statement needed to update the value in the database. Since the value already exists, we cannot do an INSERT; we must do an UPDATE instead. This sets the $key and $val to the new value, where the user_id is $main::sess and the name is $key.

Line 25 ends this part of the if..else block.

```
26:      else {
27:          $sql = qq{INSERT INTO session
28:                  (name, value, user_id)
29:              VALUES
30:              ('$key', '$val', '$main::sess') };
31:      }
```

Line 26 is where we end up if the $exists variable does not contain a true value. This means that the item we are trying to add to the hash does not yet exist.

Lines 27–30 create the SQL statement needed to insert this new value into the database.

Line 31 ends this block and the if..else statement.

```
32:     my $sth = $dbh->prepare($sql);

33:     $sth->execute or die $DBI::errstr;
34: }
```

Line 32 prepares the $sql statement that we just created and stores a handle to the prepared statement in $sth.

Line 33 executes the SQL statement. If there is a problem executing it, the program will abort, and an error message will be displayed.

Line 34 ends the STORE subroutine.

```
35: sub EXISTS {
36:     my ($self, $sess, $key) = @_;
37:     my $sql = qq{ SELECT * FROM session
38:                   WHERE user_id = ? AND
39:                   name = ?};
```

Line 35 begins the EXISTS subroutine. This subroutine simply has to check the database to see if the key already exists. If it does, it simply has to return some data (true); if not, it returns 0 (false).

Line 36 gets the arguments passed to the subroutine ($sess and $key, in this case, since the $self value is passed automatically).

Lines 37–39 create the SQL statement that selects all data from the session table, where the user_id = *(the session id)* and the name = *(the key value)*.

```
40:     my $sth = $dbh->prepare($sql);

41:     $sth->execute($sess, $key) or die $DBI::errstr;

42:     my $tmp = $sth->fetch;
```

Line 40 prepares the SQL statement we just created and stores a handle, or reference, to that statement in $sth.

Line 41 executes the SQL statement and passes the values in $sess and $key to the statement to fill in the placeholders (?) used in the SQL statement. If, for some reason, the execute fails, the die statement will cause the program to terminate and display an error message.

Line 42 creates a variable named $tmp and stores the result of a call to $sth->fetch. If any data is returned, $tmp should contain a reference to an array of the data now.

```
43:      return $tmp->[0] ? $tmp->[0] : 0;
44: }
```

Line 43 checks to see if element [0] contained any data. If so, this item existed. This line uses the trinary operator to return the proper value. If $tmp->[0] is true (it contained data), the first item after the ? will be returned ($tmp->[0]). If not ($tmp->[0] was false), the value after the : is returned, 0 in our case.

Line 44 ends the EXISTS subroutine.

```
45: sub DELETE {
46:      my ($self, $key) = @_;
```

Line 45 creates the DELETE subroutine. This is used to delete a value from the hash and database. It corresponds to a call to Perl's delete function on a hash value.

Line 46 gets the values passed in to this subroutine. This subroutine simply needs to be passed the $key of the value being deleted.

```
47:      my $sql = qq{ DELETE FROM session
48:                    WHERE user_id = ? AND
49:                    name = ?};
```

Lines 47–49 create the SQL statement needed to delete the value from the database.

```
50:      my $sth = $dbh->prepare($sql);

51:      $sth->execute($main::sess, $key) or die $DBI::errstr;
52: }
```

Line 50 prepares the SQL statement and stores a reference to the prepared statement in the $sth variable.

Line 51 executes the SQL statement. We pass the values $main::sess and $key to fill in the placeholders in the SQL statement. If the execute fails for some unlikely reason, say the database is no longer available, the die statement will cause the program to abort and display an error message.

Line 52 ends the DELETE subroutine.

```
53: sub FIRSTKEY {
54:      my $self = shift;
```

Line 53 begins the FIRSTKEY subroutine. This subroutine is used when a call to each or keys is made. It typically needs the NEXTKEY subroutine as well to work properly.

Line 54 shifts in a reference to itself; nothing is passed to this subroutine.

```
55:      my $sql = qq{ SELECT name FROM session
56:                    WHERE user_id = ? };
```

Lines 55–56 create the SQL statement to select all of the name items from the session table, where user_id = *(the session id)*.

```
57:      my $sth = $dbh->prepare($sql);

58:      $sth->execute($main::sess) or die $DBI::errstr;
59:      $self->{DATA}  = $sth->fetchall_arrayref;
```

Line 57 prepares the SQL statement and stores a reference to the prepared statement in the $sth variable.

Line 58 executes the SQL statement and passes $main::sess to fill the placeholder. If a problem occurs during this statement's execution, the die function will cause the program to abort and display an error message.

Line 59 sets $self->{DATA} to the value returned by the call to $sth->fetchall_arrayref. $sth->fetchall_arrayref returns a reference to an array containing all values returned by the SQL call.

```
60:      for(@{$self->{DATA}}) {
61:          $_ = $_->[0];
62:          $_ = '' unless defined $_;
63:      }
```

Line 60 begins a for loop that iterates over all of the elements in the array referenced by $self->{DATA}.

Line 61 sets the current item, $_, to the value of the current array, element [0].

Line 62 sets the current value of $_ to an empty string if it is not defined. We can't return undef as a key, or we will get an error.

Line 63 closes this for loop.

```
64:      return shift @{ $self->{DATA} };
65: }
```

Line 64 returns the first key, or undef.

Line 65 ends this FIRSTKEY subroutine.

```
66: sub NEXTKEY {
67:     my ($self) = @_;

68:        return shift @{ $self->{DATA} };
69: }
```

Line 66 begins the NEXTKEY subroutine. This is the second half of the subroutines that handle the each and keys calls for tied hashes.

Line 67 gets the value passed to the subroutine.

Line 68 returns the same thing we return in the FIRSTKEY subroutine. Perl knows how to handle this though and takes the next key of the hash.

Line 69 ends the NEXTKEY subroutine.

```
70: sub FETCH {
71:     my ($self, $key) = @_;
```

Line 70 begins the FETCH subroutine. This is the subroutine that gets called when someone tries to get a value from a tied hash, like so:

```
my $foo = $item{first_name};
```

This is considered fetching the value of the %item hash with the first_name key. The result is a call to the FETCH subroutine.

Line 71 gets the values passed to the subroutine.

```
72:     my $sql = qq{ SELECT value FROM session
73:                 WHERE user_id = ? AND
74:                 name = ?};
```

Lines 72–74 create the SQL needed to fetch an item from the database. Here we need the item name (which is the key). The user_id is just the $main::sess variable stored as a cookie on the user's browser.

```
75:     my $sth = $dbh->prepare($sql);

76:     $sth->execute($main::sess, $key) or die $DBI::errstr;
```

Line 75 prepares the SQL and stores a reference to the prepared SQL statement in $sth.

Line 76 executes the SQL statement and passes the $main::sess and $key values to fill in the placeholders in the SQL statement. If there is a problem executing the SQL statement, the die function is called, and an error message displayed.

```
77:     my $tmp = $sth->fetch;

78:     return $tmp->[0];
79: }
```

Line 77 creates a variable named $tmp and sets it to the value returned by a call to $sth->fetch.

Line 78 returns the value at element [0] of $tmp. Since the SQL statement is looking for a specific item, and using the primary key (user_id) to find the value, no more than one value should ever be returned. This is why we can rely on using element [0] — if there is an item, it will be at this element and if there isn't, then the value of $tmp->[0] is undef, which is what you get when you try to call $something{"stuff"} and there's no such entry in that hash.

Line 79 closes the FETCH subroutine.

```
80: sub DESTROY {
81:     $dbh->disconnect();
82: }
```

Line 80 begins the DESTROY subroutine. This is the subroutine called when the tie-hash object is no longer used and Perl is garbage collecting.

Line 81 disconnects from the database.

Line 82 ends the DESTROY subroutine.

That was the last of the subroutines related to the tied hash.

```
83: sub Get_Session {
84:     my $expires = shift;
85:     my $sess    = cookie("user_id");
86:     my $cookie;

87:     $sess = time() . $$ unless($sess);
```

Line 83 begins the Get_Session subroutine. This subroutine is used to get the cookie from the user, if the cookie exists.

Line 84 shifts in the expiration date. These functions do not automatically pass a reference to themselves, so you don't see the $self variable anymore.

Line 85 calls the cookie function and tells it to get the user_id cookie. The value returned is stored in $sess.

Line 86 declares a variable named $cookie.

Line 87 sets $sess to the value returned by a call to time() plus the current process id $$. The unless($sess) tells Perl to set $sess only if it does not yet contain any data. This means that if data has already been set by the call to the cookie function on **line 85**, this line will be ignored.

Note   The session value is the current time plus the process ID. This should be a unique string and safe for most applications.

```
88:      if($expires eq "clear") {
89:          $cookie = cookie( -name    => 'user_id',
90:                            -value   => '',
91:                            -expires => "now",
92:                          );
93:      }
```

Line 88 checks to see if the variable $expires is equal to *clear*. If so, we enter this block of code and expire the users cookie.

Lines 89–92 are the call to the cookie function. The cookie function is very handy and versatile. Notice that we call it previously and pass it a name and that it returns the cookie to us. Now, we are calling it and passing it some values. We pass it the cookie name, the value to store, and when the cookie should expire. The properly formatted cookie is then stored in the variable named $cookie.

Line 93 closes this part of the if..else block.

```
94:      else {
95:          $cookie = cookie( -name    => 'user_id',
96:                            -value   => $sess,
97:                            -expires => $expires,
98:                          );
99:      }
```

Line 94 begins the else block; we get here if the value of $expires is not *clear*.

Lines 95–98 again create a cookie. This time, though, we set the value to $sess and expires to $expires.

Line 99 ends the if..else block.

```
100:     print header( -cookie => $cookie );
101:     return $sess;
102: }
```

Line 100 prints the HTTP header and passes the cookie to the header function. Passing the cookie to the header function causes the header function to pass not only the HTTP header information, but also the properly formatted cookie information.

Line 101 returns the $sess.

Line 102 ends the Get_Session subroutine.

```
103: sub Wrap_Page {
104:     my $tdir = shift;
105:     my $tmpl = shift;
106:     my $item = shift;
```

Line 103 beings the Wrap_Page subroutine. This subroutine is used to wrap a header and footer around the page we want to print.

Lines 104–106 shift in the information needed for this function. $tdir is the template directory, $tmpl is the template of the file we wish to display, and $item is a reference to the hash that contains the data, dynamically displayed on the page.

```
107:     Print_Page($tdir, "header.tmpl", $item);
108:     Print_Page($tdir, $tmpl, $item);
109:     Print_Page($tdir, "footer.tmpl", $item);
110: }
```

Lines 107–109 are simply calls to the Print_Page subroutine. Print_Page handles the details of substituting in the dynamic variables and displaying the HTML.

Line 110 ends the Wrap_Page subroutine.

```
111: sub Print_Page {
112:     my $tdir = shift;
113:     my $tmpl = shift;
114:     my $item = shift;
```

Line 111 begins the Print_Page subroutine. This is the one that substitutes the dynamic variables and prints the HTML.

Lines 112–114 shift in the values passed to the subroutine. These are the same values passed to the Wrap_Page subroutine.

```
115:     local $^W = 0;

116:     open(TMPL, "$tdir/$tmpl")
             or die("ERROR: $!\nAborting");
117:         while(<TMPL>) {
118:             s/%%(.*?)%%/$item->{$1}/g;
119:             print;
120:         }
121:     close(TMPL);
```

Line 115 turns warnings off for this block. Turning warnings off will suppress `undef` warning messages that may occur if we try to replace an item `%%foo%%` and there's no `$item->{"foo"}`.

Line 116 opens the template file and stores the filehandle in `TMPL`.

Line 117 loops through the filehandle, one line at a time.

Line 118 replaces for the `%%varname%%` strings in the template with the appropriate values. The parentheses capture the variable name between the %%'s and stores it in $1. Then, on the right side of the substitution it calls `$item->{$1}` so to get the value of that key in the `%$item` hash. So `"In %%city%%, I bet it's hot!"` looks up `$item->{'city'}`, producing `"In Springfield, I bet it's hot!"`. If there is no `"city"` entry in the `%$item` hash, an empty-string is interpolated, like `"In , I bet it's hot!"`. **Line 119** prints the current line.

Line 120 closes the `while` loop that begins on **line 115**.

Line 121 closes the `TMPL` filehandle.

```
122:     return;
123: }

124: 1;
```

Line 122 returns from the subroutine.

Line 123 closes this subroutine.

Line 124 is needed because all modules must return a true value to signal that it has been properly loaded—this returns 1, so it satisfies that requirement.

Summary

You have now seen how to manipulate user sessions with tied hashes and cookies. You have also created the framework for a simple Web portal. To further your learning, make some enhancements to the portal, such as additional links, a blogging area, or even add the ability for more images. You are well on your way to having a fun, personalized Web site.

Program Listings

Listings 9-1 to 9-6 show the complete listings of the programs what we covered in this chapter.

Listing 9-1: **signup.cgi**

```
01: #!/usr/bin/perl -wT
02: # signup.cgi

03: use strict;
04: use lib qw(.);
05: use BasicSession;
06: use CGI qw(:standard);

07: my  (%item, $errors);

08: my $remember_for = param('remember');

09: if(my $clear = param('clear')) {
10:     our $sess    = Get_Session("clear");
11: }
12: else {
13:     our $sess    = Get_Session($remember_for);
14: }

15: my  @fields   = qw(first_name last_name link1 link2
16:                    link3 image text_color bg_color
17:                  remember fav_quote);

18: my  @required = qw(first_name last_name link1
19:                    image text_color bg_color);

20: tie %item, 'BasicSession';

21: if(param()) {
22:     $errors = Check_Fields();

23:     if($errors) {
24:         $item{"ERROR_MESSAGE"} =
                "* A required item is missing...";
25:     }
26:     elsif (param('clear') == 1){
27:         $item{"ERROR_MESSAGE"} = "";
28:     }
29:     else {
30:         $item{"ERROR_MESSAGE"}
31:          = "Data Updated!<br /> Click
32:         <a href=\"/cgi-bin/ index.cgi\">here</a>
33:             to go to main site.";
34:     }

35:     for(@fields) {
36:         if(defined param($_)) {
37:             $item{$_} = param($_);
```

Continued

Listing 9-1 *(continued)*

```
38:         }
39:     else {
40:          delete($item{$_});
41:         }
42:     }
43: }

44: Wrap_Page("./templates", "signup.tmpl", \%item);

45: sub Check_Fields {
46:     return if(param('clear') == 1);

47:     for my $fld (@required) {
48:         next if(param($fld));
49:      $errors++;
50:     }

51:     return $errors;
52: }
```

Listing 9-2: index.cgi

```
01: #!/usr/bin/perl -wT

02: use strict;
03: use lib qw(.);
04: use BasicSession;

05: use CGI qw(:standard);

06: our $sess;
07: my  %item;

08: $sess = Get_Session();
09: tie %item, 'BasicSession';

10: Wrap_Page("./templates", "index.tmpl", \%item);
```

Listing 9-3: BasicSession.pm

```
01: package BasicSession;

02: use Tie::Hash;
03: use DBI;
04: use CGI qw(cookie header);
05: use strict;
```

```perl
06: use vars qw(@ISA @EXPORT $sess);

07: @ISA = qw(Tie::StdHash Exporter);

08: use Exporter;

09: @EXPORT = qw(Wrap_Page Get_Session);

10: my $dbh = DBI->connect("DBI:mysql:user_prefs",
                                 "bookuser", "testpass")
11:    or die "Error: $DBI::errstr\nAborting";

12: my ($sql, @KEYS);

13: sub STORE {
14:    my ($self, $key, $val) = @_;

15:    $val =~ s#^http://##;  # Get rid of http://

16:    my $exists = $self->EXISTS($key);

17:    if($exists) {
18:        $sql = qq{ UPDATE session
19:                    SET
20:             name  = '$key',
21:             value = '$val'
22:              WHERE
23:               (user_id = '$main::sess'
24:                  AND name = '$key') };
25:    }
26:    else {
27:        $sql = qq{INSERT INTO session
28:              (name, value, user_id)
29:            VALUES
30:              ('$key', '$val', '$main::sess') };
31:    }

32:    my $sth = $dbh->prepare($sql);

33:    $sth->execute or die $DBI::errstr;
34: }

35: sub EXISTS {
36:    my ($self, $sess, $key) = @_;
37:    my $sql = qq{ SELECT * FROM session
38:                WHERE user_id = ? AND
39:            name = ?};

40:    my $sth = $dbh->prepare($sql);

41:    $sth->execute($sess, $key) or die $DBI::errstr;
```

Continued

Listing 9-3 *(continued)*

```
42:     my $tmp = $sth->fetch;

43:     return $tmp->[0] ? $tmp->[0] : 0;
44: }

45: sub DELETE {
46:     my ($self, $key) = @_;

47:     my $sql = qq{ DELETE FROM session
48:                     WHERE user_id = ? AND
49:             name = ?};

50:     my $sth = $dbh->prepare($sql);

51:     $sth->execute($main::sess, $key) or die $DBI::errstr;
52: }

53: sub FIRSTKEY {
54:     my $self = shift;

55:     my $sql = qq{ SELECT value FROM session
56:                     WHERE user_id = ? };

57:     my $sth = $dbh->prepare($sql);

58:     $sth->execute($main::sess) or die $DBI::errstr;
59:     $self->{DATA}  = $sth->fetchall_arrayref;

60:     for(@{$self->{DATA}}) {
61:         $_ = $_->[0];
62:         $_ = '' unless defined $_;
63:     }

64:     return shift @{ $self->{DATA} };
65: }

66: sub NEXTKEY {
67:     my ($self) = @_;

68:     return shift @{ $self->{DATA} };
69: }

70: sub FETCH {
71:     my ($self, $key) = @_;
72:     my $sql = qq{ SELECT value FROM session
73:                     WHERE user_id = ? AND
74:             name = ?};

75:     my $sth = $dbh->prepare($sql);

76:     $sth->execute($main::sess, $key) or die $DBI::errstr;
```

```
77:      my $tmp = $sth->fetch;

78:      return $tmp->[0];
79: }

08: sub DESTROY {
81:      $dbh->disconnect();
82: }

83: sub Get_Session {
84:      my $expires = shift;
85:      my $sess    = cookie("user_id");
86:      my $cookie;

87:      $sess = time() . $$ unless($sess);

88:      if($expires eq "clear") {
89:          $cookie = cookie( -name    => 'user_id',
90:                            -value   => '',
91:                            -expires => "now",
92:                          );
93:      }
94:      else {
95:          $cookie = cookie( -name    => 'user_id',
96:                            -value   => $sess,
97:                            -expires => $expires,
98:                          );
99:      }

100:     print header( -cookie => $cookie );
101:     return $sess;
102: }

103: sub Wrap_Page {
104:      my $tdir = shift;
105:      my $tmpl = shift;
106:      my $item = shift;

107:      Print_Page($tdir, "header.tmpl", $item);
108:      Print_Page($tdir, $tmpl, $item);
109:      Print_Page($tdir, "footer.tmpl", $item);
110: }

111: sub Print_Page {
112:      my $tdir = shift;
113:      my $tmpl = shift;
114:      my $item = shift;

115:      local $^W = 0;

116:      open(TMPL, "$tdir/$tmpl")
```

Continued

Listing 9-3 *(continued)*

```
                 or die("ERROR: $!\nAborting");
117:         while(<TMPL>) {
118:             s/%%(.*?)%%/$item->{$1}/g;
119:             print;
120:         }
121:     close(TMPL);

122:     return;
123: }

124: 1;
```

Listing 9-4: **header.tmpl**

```
01: <html><head><title>%%title%%</title>
02: <style type="text/css">
03: <!--
04: body { background: %%bg_color%% }
05: hr   { color:      #c0c0c0 }

06: td   { background: #e0e0e0;
07:        color:      #000000;
08:        font-size:  10pt;
09:        font-family: Lucida, Verdana, Helvetica, Arial; }

10: a:link    { color:      #4444ff;
11:             background: #c0c0c0 }

12: a:visited { color: #333377 }

13: a:active  { color: #0000dd }

14: i, p, ul, li
15: { font-family: Lucida, Verdana, Helvetica, Arial;
16:   font-size:   10pt;
17:   color:       %%text_color%% }

18: b
19: { font-family: Lucida, Verdana, Helvetica, Arial;
20:   font-size:   10pt;
21:   color:       %%text_color%% }

22: .small
23: { font-family: Lucida, Verdana, Helvetica, Arial;
24:   font-size:   10pt;
25:   color:       %%text_color%% }

26: .medium
```

```
27: { font-family: Lucida, Verdana, Helvetica, Arial;
28:   font-size:    12pt;
29:   color:        %%text_color%% }

30: .big_error
31: { font-family: Lucida, Verdana, Helvetica, Arial;
32:   font-size:    14pt;
33:   font-weight: bold;
34:   color:        #ff0000 }

35: .big
36: { font-family: Lucida, Verdana, Helvetica, Arial;
37:   font-size:    14pt;
38:   color:        %%text_color%% }

39: h2
40: { font-family: Lucida, Verdana, Helvetica, Arial;
41:   font-size:    18pt;
42:   color:        %%text_color%% }

43: h1
44: { font-family: Lucida, Verdana, Helvetica, Arial;
45:   font-size:    24pt;
46:   color:        %%text_color%% }
47: -->
48: </style>
49: </head>
50: <body>
```

Listing 9-5: **index.tmpl**

```
01: <div align="center">
02:   <table border="1">
03:     <tr>
04:       <td>
05:         <img src="http://%%image%%" width="320" height="240"
alt="">
06:       </td>
07:       <td valign="top">
08:         <h2>Welcome to %%first_name%% %%last_name%%'s
            Page!</h2><br />
09:         <font class="medium">
10:           This is a site that contains some of
            %%first_name%%'s favorite links and quotes.
11:         </font>
12:       </td>
13:     </tr>
14:     <tr>
15:       <td valign="top" colspan="2">
16:         <font class="big">
```

Continued

Listing 9-5 *(continued)*

```
17:     <b>%%first_name%%'s favorite links:</b>
18:    </font>
19:    <br />
20:    <font class="small">
21:     <a href="http://%%link1%%">%%link1%%</a><br />
22:     <a href="http://%%link2%%">%%link2%%</a><br />
23:     <a href="http://%%link3%%">%%link3%%</a><br />
24:    <br />
25:    <font class="big">
26:     <b>%%first_name%%'s favorite quote:</b>
27:    </font><br />
28:    <font class="small">
29:     %%fav_quote%%
30:    </font><br />
31:    </font>
32:   </td>
33:  </tr>
34: </table>

35: <br /><br />
36: <table border="0">
37:  <tr>
38:   <td>
39:    <font class="small">
40:     If you are not %%first_name%% or have not yet signed
       up, please
41:     [ <a href =
    "/cgi-bin/chapter9/signup.cgi?clear=1">Click Here</a> ].
42:     <br />
43:     If you <b>are</b> %%first_name%% and wish to make
       changes to your page, please
44:     [ <a href="/cgi-bin/chapter9/signup.cgi">Click
       Here</a> ].
45:    </font>
46:   </td>
47:  </tr>
48: </table>
49: </div>
```

Listing 9-6: **footer.tmpl**

```
01: </body>
02: </html>
```

✦   ✦   ✦

Using Database Transactions

This chapter introduces the concept of transactions, one of the core features of SQL and an easy way to increase the reliability of any database-backed system. Transactions are a set of SQL queries that are "grouped" together. Then if any, or all, of the SQL queries fails for any reason, the entire group can be reversed so the database is exactly the way we left it before we began the transaction. We'll be discussing transactions, their methods, and finally look at a small example that shows a transaction in action.

Using Transactions

MySQL has only recently introduced transactions, and they apply only to some table types (InnoDB and BDB); these are slower than other table types and take more memory and disc space. Other SQL databases such as PostgreSQL or Oracle support transactions; even in these cases, however, the code becomes somewhat more complex. Why, then, you might be wondering, should you introduce complexity and overhead?

Transactions are a means of ensuring data integrity. Data integrity is just a fancy term that means keeping your data intact, and correct. Many database operations are implemented as multiple SQL statements; for example, a payment system for online purchase might include the following:

✦ Decrement customer's account by purchase amount

✦ Increment merchant's account by purchase amount

✦ Order goods to be shipped

Obviously, if the first step fails, the error-checking routine should abort the remaining steps. However, what if the latter steps fail? Even assuming the system is perfectly reliable, perhaps the merchant's account has been closed or the goods are no longer available. In this case, the customer must receive a refund; but undoing all of these steps is time-consuming and prone to error. (What happens if an error occurs during the undo process?) If only there were a way to perform these tasks atomically: if an error occurs, all changes are rejected.

Naturally, there is such a way: the entire operation is wrapped in transaction statements and treated as a single process. If any stage fails, the whole procedure can be aborted and the database reset to its initial state.

In essence, transactions allow a multistatement process to be treated by the database as if it contains only a single statement. Everything works, or everything is rejected.

As shown, failures can occur even with a perfectly reliable system. In practice, system failures also occur. The front-end querying machine or the database server itself may fail, or communication between them may be lost. In any of these cases, the database server aborts the entire transaction and the database is restored to the state it was in before the transaction began.

Even if no failures occur, transactions can still be useful in a system with multiple simultaneous client accesses; in the modern computing environment, this includes almost any Web-based system. Use of transactions can effectively create a "snapshot" of the database for the exclusive use of a client. This is unaffected by changes made elsewhere. This allows the client software to treat the database as a single consistent data source, rather than constantly checking to avoid race conditions. Race conditions occur when two or more processes try to read or write the same record/table/data at the same time. The degree of isolation does vary somewhat among databases, and the client often controls it. Check the database system's documentation for specifics.The ideal solution for a multiuser system is the heavy use of both transactions and explicit locks (which enable you to lock others from modifying the data); neither is sufficient alone.

In SQL, transactions are controlled with three keywords:

✦ BEGIN initiates a transaction.

✦ COMMIT ends a transaction, requiring the database to store all changes that have been made since the beginning of that transaction.

✦ ROLLBACK aborts a transaction, restoring the database to the state that the database was in before the first statement in the transaction. If connectivity to the client is lost before a COMMIT is issued, ROLLBACK is implicitly executed.

Many databases allow transactions to be nested: one can BEGIN a transaction; perform operations on the database; BEGIN a subsequence of statements that are part of the main transaction; COMMIT that, then continue with the main transaction. Consult your database server documentation to see if the database you are using supports nested transactions.

Transactions and Perl

Transactions in the context of the Perl DBI are slightly restricted, in that it is not possible for a transaction to persist for longer than the duration of a single connection to the database. In general, this does not present a problem. When it does present a problem, the problem can be solved by reformulating the flow of control or by using persistent database handles.

In fact, this can be advantageous. Since it is possible to have multiple connections to the same database, UPDATEs and INSERTs can be taking place in a transactional environment while SELECTs are treated through a different database handle. This is useful when the program is looping through the results of a SELECT statement and making changes to the database based on those results. Many databases terminate active SELECTs when a transaction is committed on the same database handle. Using a separate handle, although doing so may increase program startup time, solves this problem.

When a connection is established by using the DBI->connect method, the AutoCommit parameter defaults to 1 (that is, each database command exists in its own transaction and takes effect immediately). This is not guaranteed to be the case in future versions of the DBI module, however. It is a good habit to specify AutoCommit explicitly. This parameter is specified as a hash reference in the fourth position of the connect function:

```
my $dbh = DBI->connect
   ("DBI:mysql:BibleBook","bookuser","testpass",
                    {AutoCommit => 1})
         or die("Cannot connect: $DBI::errstr");
```

AutoCommit can also be changed after the connection has been made:

```
$dbh->{AutoCommit}=1;
```

To enable transactions, simply set AutoCommit to 0 either in the DBI->connect call or in a later explicit call.

The actual transaction controls are as follows.

BEGIN

The BEGIN statement is rarely, if ever, explicitly required in a transactional database. However, since the DBI module makes transaction use optional, it is required that all clients initiate transactional statements with the begin_work method:

```
$dbh->begin_work
     or die("Database does not support transactions");
```

If `AutoCommit` is on, it will be turned off until the next commit or rollback call (see the following). If the database does not support transactions, `begin-work` returns a fatal error.

Some databases may, separately, require a `BEGIN` statement; check the documentation. For PostgreSQL, send:

```
$dbh->do('BEGIN');
```

COMMIT

A `COMMIT` is explicitly required when operating in transactional mode. `COMMIT` defines the successful end of the transaction (and, if `AutoCommit` is 0, a return to single-statement mode). It is implemented with the `commit` method of DBI:

```
$dbh->commit;
```

It is well worth ensuring that all possible checks have been performed before issuing a `COMMIT`; otherwise, many of the advantages of the transactional system are lost.

If for some reason the `COMMIT` fails, such as the database has suddenly crashed, the standard `DBI->errstr` method will show the error. (This will also happen if a `COMMIT` is issued while the database connection is in single-statement mode.)

ROLLBACK

Often, client software issues a `ROLLBACK` when part of a transaction has failed. It is implemented with DBI's `ROLLBACK` method:

```
$dbh->rollback;
```

As with the `COMMIT` method, issuing a rollback returns the database connection to single-statement mode if `AutoCommit` is 0. If the `ROLLBACK` fails, which should only happen if the database is already in single-statement mode (or, in MySQL, if some nontransaction-safe tables are involved in the transaction), an error will be raised.

If connectivity is lost during a transaction, the database server assumes a `ROLLBACK`. There is one exception to this: if the program disconnects explicitly (using the `DBI->disconnect` method) with a transaction outstanding, some databases (notably Oracle and Ingres) will automatically commit outstanding statements; others, such as Informix, will roll back instead. Always specify explicitly what should be done with an outstanding transaction before disconnecting.

Note If the program disconnects due to an error condition, the database driver will always send a ROLLBACK.

Transactions in Practice

The most convenient way to use transactions with the Perl DBI is to enclose all of the Perl constructs associated with the transaction in a single eval{} block and to call die if any failures occur. In this way, both database errors and other failures of the program can be treated together without further effort from the programmer.

Note that not all undesired conditions constitute database or Perl errors. Selecting rows from a table will not fail even if no rows match the selection criteria, for example. In cases such as this, it is most convenient to check for problems explicitly with Perl code and to raise an error deliberately with die if they are detected. This then invokes the error handling procedure, which (as you will see) can take appropriate action.

The objective of this example program is to build a list of publishers, and the number of books in the library by each publisher, in the table pubslist (which should contain "publisher" and "count" fields).

```
01: #! /usr/bin/perl -w
02: #
03: # transaction.pl
04: # Chapter 11
05: # Listing 1
06: #

07: use strict;
08: use DBI;
```

Lines 1–8 are standard for a database program.

```
09: my $dbh = DBI->connect
("DBI:mysql:BibleBook","bookuser","testpass",
10:          {AutoCommit => 0, RaiseError => 1})
11:   or die("Cannot connect: $DBI::errstr");
```

Lines 9–11 extend the connection command to allow the setting of AutoCommit (as discussed previously) and RaiseError, which causes the DBI to return a fatal error when a database command fails.

```
12: $dbh->begin_work;
```

Line 12 informs the database that a transaction is about to take place.

```
13:   eval {
```

Line 13 is the most important innovation. Within this block, fatal errors do not take effect as normal (causing the program to terminate immediately); instead, the block is terminated, and program flow continues.

```
14:   $dbh->do("DELETE FROM pubslist");
```

Line 14 drops the old list of publishers.

```
15:    my $sth=$dbh->prepare("SELECT COUNT(*),publisher FROM library
16:                          GROUP BY publisher");
17:    $sth->execute;
```

Lines 15–17 should be familiar by now. Note that there is no need to trap specific errors. Any problem, be it a database error or resource exhaustion on the client, raises a fatal error, which is dealt with automatically.

```
18:    while (my ($count,$publisher)=$sth->fetchrow_array) {
19:      my $publisherq=$dbh->quote($publisher);
20:      $dbh->do("INSERT INTO pubslist (publisher,count)
21:                VALUES ($publisherq,$count)");
22:    }
```

Lines 18–22 insert each data point in the other table. Again, this should be familiar material.

```
23:    $sth->finish;
```

Line 23 cleans up after the statement.

```
24: };
```

Line 24 is the end of the `eval` block. Errors that occur after this point are treated normally.

```
25: if ($@) {
```

Line 25 determines whether any errors have occurred. Whenever you have an eval block, if there were any errors, the $@ variable gets set to a true value.

```
26:   $dbh->rollback;
```

Line 26, if errors have occurred, abandons the entire operation. This is also the point at which to provide any other error-recovery code the program requires, based on the type of error that has occurred. Something like an email notification or writing to an error log.

```
27: }
28: else {
29:    $dbh->commit;
```

Line 27 ends the if portion of the if..else block.

Line 28 begins the else portion of the if..else block. This block gets entered if there were no errors in the eval block.

Line 29 otherwise commits all changes to the database.

```
30: }
31: $dbh->disconnect;
```

Line 30 ends the if..else block.

Line 31 shuts down the database connection.

An alternative method of handling transactions is not to set the RaiseError attribute but to test for errors after each call:

```
$dbh->prepare($sql) or die $dbh->errstr;
```

This is useful only when some database calls are expected to return errors and when these errors are not fatal to the processing of the transaction.

It is also not necessary to use the eval{} block construct. Test each call with:

```
my $errorstatus=0;
$dbh->prepare($sql) or $errorstatus=1;
```

Then check $errorstatus when the transaction has been completed. However, this means that fatal errors elsewhere in the code have not been handled normally; they cause an implicit rollback, as the program has disconnected automatically on termination, but do not allow for any other clean up.

As a general rule, eval{} block and RaiseError are the cleanest methods for using transactions and should be used unless there is an overpowering reason to do otherwise.

Transaction Caveats

Some commands are intrinsically impossible to undo; issuing them causes an immediate and permanent change to the database. In MySQL, these commands are:

✦ ALTER TABLE

✦ BEGIN

✦ CREATE INDEX

✦ DROP DATABASE

✦ DROP TABLE

✦ LOCK TABLES

✦ RENAME TABLE

✦ TRUNCATE

Issuing these commands in transactional mode immediately terminates the current transaction as if a COMMIT command has been issued. (Note, in particular, the presence in the list of BEGIN; it is not possible to "nest" transactions in MySQL.) Users of other databases will find similar restrictions and should consult their database documentation for details.

Summary

So, in this section you have seen how to create basic transactions using BEGIN, COMMIT, and ROLLBACK. Remember that not all databases support transactions, and some support transactions different than others. So consult your database server documentation before you jump into a big database project.

Special Note for MySQL Users

Since MySQL does not support transactions on all table types, some tables in a database are transaction-safe, but others (that need to be accessed faster) are not. If a transaction includes data from nontransaction-safe tables, an attempt to ROLLBACK will cause an error. Always be aware of the underlying database structure when writing code to use transactions in MySQL. Code intended to be portable to a variety of systems, possibly where older versions of MySQL are in use, should not use transactions.

Program Listing

Listing 10-1 is the complete, uninterrupted code example from this chapter.

Listing 10-1: **Transactions in practice**

```
01: #! /usr/bin/perl -w
02: #
03: # transaction.pl
04: # Chapter 11
05: # Listing 1
06: #

07: use strict;
08: use DBI;

09: my $dbh = DBI->connect
("DBI:mysql:BibleBook","bookuser","testpass",
10:                    {AutoCommit => 0, RaiseError => 1})
11:          or die("Cannot connect: $DBI::errstr\n");

12: $dbh->begin_work;
13: eval {
14:    $dbh->do("DELETE FROM pubslist");
15:    my $sth=$dbh->prepare("SELECT COUNT(*),publisher FROM library
16:                        GROUP BY publisher");
17:    $sth->execute;
18:    while (my ($count,$publisher)=$sth->fetchrow_array) {
19:      my $publisherq=$dbh->quote($publisher);
20:      $dbh->do("INSERT INTO pubslist (publisher,count)
21:               VALUES ($publisherq,$count)");
22:    }
23:    $sth->finish;
24: };
25: if ($@) {
26:    $dbh->rollback;
27: }
28: else {
29:    $dbh->commit;
30: }
31: $dbh->disconnect;
```

✦   ✦   ✦

Perl and
Web Services

Perl, XML, and Databases

XML is a hot topic in just about any computing circle
these days. The thing that most people don't realize,
buzzwords aside, is that XML is not a magic bullet. Instead,
XML is simply a data format that many programs know how
to read and/or write. By itself, XML is nothing more than text.
But, interwoven with the hundreds (if not thousands) of tools
available, XML is a powerful medium for data exchange.

XML's strength lies in the fact that once you have your data in
XML format, you are free of the burdens of proprietary file formats and can slice and dice the data any way you want to.

This book is about databases, not about what you can and
can't do with XML. So, instead of throwing a bunch of XML-
type applications at you, we cover a short, simple application
that dumps one of our databases into an XML format.

When you are ready to transform your XML data into whatever
you need to, get Elliotte Rusty Harold's *XML Bible* (Hungry
Minds [now Wiley Publishing], 2001, ISBN 0-7645-4760-7). It's a
great resource that shows you the true power of what you can
do with XML data.

The Photo Dumper Application

This program takes the data from our photo-album script,
which comes from the Web-Based Photo Album you'll be reading about later in the book. (Yes, this is only Chapter 11, but
the data derived from the photo album is ideal for dumping
into the XML format.)

This program is designed to be fairly generic; it should be
able to work with other simple databases with minimal
changes. This is not an end-all XML dumper however. It is
just very simple.

photo_dumper.pl

```
01: #!/usr/bin/perl -w

02: use strict;
03: use DBI;
```

Line 1 tells the system where to find Perl and turns on the warning flag.

Line 2 loads the strict module.

Line 3 loads the DBI module so that we can connect to the database.

```
04: my $dbh = DBI->connect("DBI:mysql:photoalbum",
                  "bookuser","testpass")
05:     or die("Cannot connect: $DBI::errstr\n");
```

Line 4 declares a scalar variable named $dbh that is used to store a handle to the database connection. The DBI->connect method passes the arguments to the DBI and makes a connection to the database.

Line 5 is a continuation of **line 4** and causes the program to abort if there is a problem connecting to the database.

```
06: my %db;

07: $db{name}  = "photoalbum";
08: $db{album} = "album_id";
09: $db{photo} = "img_id";
10: $db{f_key} = "album_id";
```

Line 6 declares a hash named %db.

Lines 7–10 populate the %db hash with some data we'll be using shortly.

```
11: my $main_table = "album";
12: my @sub_tables = qw{photo};
```

Line 11 declares a scalar variable named $main_table and sets it to the string album.

Line 12 declares an array and adds one item to it: photo. This array can be populated with more tables to loop through, if your database has more tables.

```
13: Gen_Output();
```

Line 13 is simply a call to the `Gen_Output` function. This function begins gathering the data and printing the results.

```
14: sub Gen_Output {
15:     print qq(<?xml version="1.0"?>\n);
16:     print start_tag($db{name}), "\n";
```

Line 14 begins the `Gen_Output` function.

Line 15 prints the XML header tag. This is needed for the output to be a valid XML document.

Line 16 prints the value returned by the `start_tag` subroutine with $db{name} being passed to it. This is the tag that wraps the entire document.

The `start_tag` and `end_tag` subroutines are used to ensure that we create valid XML tags.

```
17:     my @albums = Get_Keys($main_table);

18:     for my $tmp (@albums) {
19:         print start_tag($main_table), "\n";
```

Line 17 calls the `Get_Keys` function and passes the value in $main_table. This function queries the database and gets all of the index fields for the $main_table, storing them in the array @albums. This causes the array @albums to contain a list of all of the photo albums in the database.

Line 18 begins a `for` loop that iterates through each of the albums; the current album index is stored in the $tmp variable.

Line 19 prints the value returned by the start_tag subroutine with $main_table being passed to it. This wraps each album with the tag <album>.

```
20:         Print_Data($main_table, $tmp, 3);

21:         for my $sub_tbl (@sub_tables){
22:             Do_SubTable($sub_tbl, $tmp);
23:         }
```

Line 20 calls the `Print_Data` function and passes it three values, $main_table, $tmp, and 3. 3 is the number of spaces to indent the output (which is optional, but makes the file easier to look at when printed).

Line 21 begins a loop. This loop iterates through all of the values in the array @sub_tables. Each time through the loop, the current table name is stored in the $sub_tbl scalar variable.

Line 22 calls the `Do_SubTable` subroutine and passes the `$sub_tbl` and `$tmp` values.

Line 23 ends the loop that begins on **line 21**.

```
24:            print end_tag($main_table),"\n";
25:        }

26:        print end_tag($db{name}), "\n";
27: }
```

Line 24 prints the value returned by the `end_tag` subroutine when it is passed `$main_table`. The `end_tag` subroutine returns a closing tag to match the tag we begin on **line 19**.

Line 25 closes the block that begins on **line 18**.

Line 26 uses the `end_tag` subroutine to close the tag that wraps the entire output.

Line 27 ends this subroutine.

```
28: sub Do_SubTable {
29:     my $table = shift;
30:     my $rel   = shift;
```

Line 28 begins the `Do_SubTable` subroutine. This subroutine handles getting the data from the subordinate tables and printing their values.

Lines 29–30 declare some scalar variables and use the `shift` function to store the values passed to this function into these variables.

```
31:     my @keys = Get_Keys($table, $rel);
```

Line 31 calls the `Get_Keys` function and stores the result into the `@arr` array.

```
32:     for my $key (@keys) {
33:         print " ", start_tag($table), "\n";
34:         Print_Data($table, $key, 4);
35:         print " ", end_tag($table), "\n\n";
36:     }
37: }
```

Line 32 begins a loop that iterates through all of the values in the `@keys` array. The current value is stored in the `$key` variable.

Line 33 prints an XML tag with the value in the `$table` variable.

Line 34 calls the `Print_Data` function to print the data for this item. The values `$table`, `$key`, and 4 are passed to `Print_Data`.

Line 35 prints the closing XML tag to correspond to the tag we print on **line 33**.

Line 36 closes this `for` loop.

Line 37 closes this subroutine.

```
38: sub Get_Keys {
39:     my $table    = shift;
40:     my $index    = shift;
41:     my @values   = ();
```

Line 38 begins the `Get_Keys` subroutine.

Lines 39–40 declare a scalar variable and use the `shift` function to read in the first two values passed to this subroutine.

Line 41 declares an array named `@values` and ensures that it is empty by setting it to `()`.

```
42:     my $sql = qq{SELECT $db{$table} FROM $table};
43:     $sql   .= qq{ WHERE $db{f_key} = $index} if($index);
44:     my $sth = $dbh->prepare($sql);
```

Line 42 declares a scalar variable named `$sql` and fills it with a string that makes up the SQL statement we want to execute.

Line 43 adds a `WHERE` clause to the SQL statement if the `$index` variable contains data.

Line 44 prepares the SQL statement and stores a handle to the prepared statement in the new scalar variable `$sth`.

```
45:     $sth->execute();

46:     while(my @arr = $sth->fetchrow_array)
            { push @values, @arr; }

47:     return(@values);
48: }
```

Line 45 calls the `execute()` method on the statement handle to run the SQL query.

Line 46 is a `while` loop that loops through the values returned by the SQL call and stores all of the results into the array named `@values`. The first part of this line calls the `fetchrow_array` method on the data returned by the SQL query and stores the array of data in the `@arr` array. Then, the push `@values`, `@arr` takes the data in `@arr` and pushes it onto the `@values` array. This effectively concatenates the data onto the array. So, after this line has executed, all of the data returned by the SQL query should be in the `@values` array.

Line 47 returns the @values array.

Line 48 closes this subroutine.

```
49: sub Print_Data {
50:     my $table   = shift;
51:     my $key     = shift;
52:     my $indent  = shift;
53:     my @values  = ();
```

Line 49 begins the Print_Data subroutine.

Lines 50–52 declare new scalar variables and use the shift function to read in the data passed to the subroutine.

Line 53 declares an array named @values and ensures it is empty by setting it to ().

```
54:     my $sql = qq{SELECT * FROM $table WHERE $db{$table}
            = ?};
55:     my $sth = $dbh->prepare($sql);

56:     $sth->execute($key);
```

Line 54 creates the SQL query needed to get all of the data from the table and stores the SQL query string in $sql.

Line 55 uses the prepare method to get the SQL statement ready for execution. The result of the prepare call is stored in $sth.

Line 56 executes the query and passes the value in $key to replace the placeholder (?).

```
57:     while(my $data = $sth->fetchrow_hashref){
58:         for(keys(%$data)){

59:             $data->{$_} = "" unless defined $data->{$_};

60:             print " " x $indent, start_tag($_),
61:               xml_esc($data->{$_}), end_tag($_), "\n";
62:         }
63:     }
```

Line 57 begins a while loop that gets one row of data and passes that row back as a reference to a hash. We store this hash reference in $data.

Line 58 begins a for loop that iterates through each of the keys in the hash referenced by $data.

Line 59 sets the value in $data->{$_} to an empty string if it is not yet defined.

Line 60 prints $indent number of spaces and then, using the start_tag subroutine to generate a valid XML tag, prints out the next starting XML tag. **Line 61** is a continuation of **line 60**. At this point, we should have a valid XML opening tag. Next we use the xml_esc subroutine to print the data that $data->{$_} holds. The call to xml_esc ensures that we will not have and invalid characters in our output. Finally, we make a call to the end_tag subroutine to create a valid XML closing tag for us.

So, **lines 60 and 61** create something like this:

```
<valid_tag>valid xml data</valid_tag>
```

Line 62 ends the for loop that begins on **line 58**.

Line 63 ends the while loop that begins on **line 57**.

```
64:        return 1;
65: }
```

Line 64 returns a true value.

Line 65 closes this subroutine.

```
66: sub start_tag { "<"  . xml_esc_name($_[0]) . ">" }
67: sub end_tag   { "</" . xml_esc_name($_[0]) . ">" }
```

Lines 66 and 67 are two different subroutines that are used to create a beginning and an ending XML tag, respectively. These subroutines simply take the value that is passed to them ($_[0]), and pass it to the xml_esc_name subroutine. The value returned by xml_esc_name is a valid XML tag. This valid XML tag is then wrapped in the <> or </> characters to create the entire, valid, XML tag.

```
68: sub xml_esc_name {
69:        my $name = shift;
70:        return '_' unless length $name;
```

Line 68 begins the xml_esc_name subroutine. This subroutine processes the string passed to it and ensures that it is a valid name for an XML tag.

Line 69 creates a my variable called $name and uses the shift function to load it with the value that was passed to this subroutine.

Line 70 returns an underscore if there was no data passed to this subroutine. This ensures that even though no data was passed, a valid XML tag is still generated. (A lone underscore is a valid XML tag.)

```
71:        $name =~ s/[^-\._a-zA-Z0-9]/_/g;
72:        $name =~ s/^(\d)/_$1/;
```

Line 71 checks to see if $name contains anything that is not a dash, period, underscore, or an alphanumeric character; the caret ^ means not. Any characters that do not meet this criteria are replaced with an underscore character.

Line 72 then checks to see if $name begins with a digit. If so, we add an underscore to the beginning of $name. The caret ^ in this context means *the beginning of the string.* And, since we placed parentheses around the character we are matching, any matching data gets captured and stored in the $1 variable.

```
73:     return $name;
74: }
```

Line 73 returns the value stored in $name.

Line 74 ends this subroutine.

```
75: sub xml_esc {
76:     my $it = shift;
```

Line 75 begins the xml_esc subroutine. This subroutine is used to turn anything even remotely odd into &#nnn; entities.

Line 76 creates a my variable named $it and uses the shift function to load it with the data that was passed to this subroutine.

```
77:     $it =~ s{([^\x20\x21\x23-\x25\x28-\x3b\x3d\x3F-
\x5B\x5D-\x7E])}
78:             {'&#'.(ord($1)).';'}eg;
```

Lines 77 and 78 are a single Perl line, split onto two lines. This substitution command looks for any characters that do not match those listed in between the square brackets []. Anything that does not match gets changed into an &#nnn; entity. The ord($1) command returns the numeric value of the item passed to it. The value that was returned is wrapped between the &# and the ; characters. The e at the end of the substitution command tell Perl to evaluate the right side as an expression (execute the ord()), and the g means to make the substitutions globally to all values that match the criteria.

```
79:     return $it;
80: }
```

Line 79 returns the current value stored in $it.

Line 80 ends this subroutine.

The output of this program should look something like this:

```xml
<?xml version="1.0"?>
<photoalbum>
<album>
  <album_id>1020740752</album_id>
  <comments>BOKTWD, round "2".</comments>
  <name>BOKTWD 2</name>
 <photo>
   <img_date>2002-04-25 09:37:58</img_date>
   <album_id>1020740752</album_id>
   <img_title>untitled</img_title>
   <focal_length>6.6</focal_length>
   <aperture>2.83</aperture>
   <width>1600</width>
   <fnumber>2.5</fnumber>
   <iso_speed>100</iso_speed>
   <img_location>/photos/Family_Photos_1/24250020.jpg</img_location>
   <height>1200</height>
   <img_id>200204250937581020740773</img_id>
   <exposure>10/881</exposure>
   <resolution>375/1 dpi</resolution>
   <make>SEIKO EPSON CORP.</make>
   <flash>Yes</flash>
   <model>PhotoPC 850Z</model>
 </photo>

 <photo>
   <img_date>2002-04-25 09:38:38</img_date>
   <album_id>1020740752</album_id>
   <img_title>untitled</img_title>
   <focal_length>6.6</focal_length>
   <aperture>2.83</aperture>
   <width>1600</width>
   <fnumber>2.5</fnumber>
   <iso_speed>100</iso_speed>
   <img_location>/photos/Family_Photos_1/24250021.jpg</img_location>
   <height>1200</height>
   <img_id>200204250938381020740795</img_id>
   <exposure>10/1113</exposure>
   <resolution>375/1 dpi</resolution>
   <make>SEIKO EPSON CORP.</make>
   <flash>Yes</flash>
   <model>PhotoPC 850Z</model>
 </photo>
</album>
</photoalbum>
```

That is it for this simple database-to-XML dumper. Once this program is run, you should have a nice XML output. You can then use other XML applications to transform the data, convert the data, or do whatever you wish with it.

Summary

This is all we are going to cover for this chapter. Most database-dumping to XML that you may want to do is very similar to this application — so there is no point writing and walking through several nearly identical applications.

You may want to add a Web interface to this application, structuring the interface so that you can pass different databases and table structures to it. This application should give you a starting framework for something like this.

Program Listing

Listing 11-1 contains the complete and uninterrupted code for `photo_dumper.pl`. You can also find the code on this book's companion Web site.

Listing 11-1: **photo_dumper.pl**

```perl
01: #!/usr/bin/perl -w

02: use strict;
03: use DBI;

04: my $dbh = DBI->connect
("DBI:mysql:photoalbum","bookuser","testpass")
05:     or die("Cannot connect: $DBI::errstr\n");

06: my %db;

07: $db{name}  = "photoalbum";
08: $db{album} = "album_id";
09: $db{photo} = "img_id";
10: $db{f_key} = "album_id";

11: my $main_table = "album";
12: my @sub_tables = qw{photo};

13: Gen_Output();

14: sub Gen_Output {
15:     print qq(<?xml version="1.0"?>);
16:     print start_tag($db{name}), "\n";

17:     my @albums = Get_Keys($main_table);

18:     for my $tmp (@albums) {
```

```
19:          print start_tag($main_table), "\n";

20:          Print_Data($main_table, $tmp, 3);

21:          for my $sub_tbl (@sub_tables){
22:               Do_SubTable($sub_tbl, $tmp);
23:          }

24:          print end_tag($main_table), "\n";
25:     }

26:     print end_tag($db{name}), "\n";
27: }

28: sub Do_SubTable {
29:     my $table = shift;
30:     my $rel   = shift;

31:     my @keys = Get_Keys($table, $rel);

32:     for my $key (@keys) {
33:          print " ", start_tag($table), "\n";
34:          Print_Data($table, $key, 4);
35:          print " ", end_tag($table), "\n\n";
36:     }
37: }

38: sub Get_Keys {
39:     my $table    = shift;
40:     my $index    = shift;
41:     my @values   = ();

42:     my $sql = qq{SELECT $db{$table} FROM $table};
43:     $sql    .= qq{ WHERE $db{f_key} = $index} if($index);
44:     my $sth = $dbh->prepare($sql);

45:     $sth->execute();

46:     while(my @arr = $sth->fetchrow_array){ push @values,
@arr; }

47:     return(@values);
48: }

49: sub Print_Data {
50:     my $table    = shift;
51:     my $key      = shift;
52:     my $indent   = shift;
53:     my @values   = ();
```

Continued

Listing 11-1 *(continued)*

```
54:     my $sql = qq{SELECT * FROM $table WHERE $db{$table} =
?};
55:     my $sth = $dbh->prepare($sql);

56:     $sth->execute($key);

57:     while(my $data = $sth->fetchrow_hashref){
58:         for(keys(%$data)){
59:             $data->{$_} = "" unless defined $data->{$_};

60:             print " " x $indent, start_tag($_),
61:             xml_esc($data->{$_}), end_tag($_), "\n";
62:         }
63:     }

64:     return;
65: }

66: sub start_tag { "<"  . xml_esc_name($_[0]) . ">" }
67: sub end_tag   { "</" . xml_esc_name($_[0]) . ">" }

68: sub xml_esc_name {
69:     my $name = shift;

70:     return '_' unless length $name;

71:     $name =~ s/[^-\._a-zA-Z0-9]/_/g;
72:     $name =~ s/^(\d)/_$1/;

73:     return $name;
74: }

75: sub xml_esc {
76:     my $it = shift;

77:     $it =~ s{(([^\x20\x21\x23-\x25\x28-\x3b\x3d\x3F-
\x5B\x5D-\x7E]))}
78:             {'&#'.(ord($1)).';'}eg;

79:     return $it;
80: }
```

✦   ✦   ✦

Creating a SOAP-Based Catalog

Web services are a hot topic these days. Everyone seems to be talking about Web services this and Web services that. It's nearly impossible to pick up a trade magazine without having to read about Web services to some degree or other.

This chapter covers one aspect of Web services: the SOAP protocol. SOAP is our focus because it is fairly common and well documented at w3.org; also, some decent Perl modules are already available for it.

Before I explain my interpretation of SOAP, I want to make sure that you know where to get the complete documentation. You can find the SOAP protocol, and all of its definitions, explanations, and standards, by going to http://www.w3.org and clicking the SOAP link. The w3.org site is *the* place to go if you need detailed, technical documentation about the protocols governing the World Wide Web.

What Is SOAP?

The World Wide Web Consortium describes the latest version of SOAP as follows:

> SOAP version 1.2 provides a simple and lightweight mechanism for exchanging structured and typed information between peers in a decentralized, distributed environment using XML. SOAP does not itself define any application semantics such as a programming model or implementation specific semantics; rather it defines a simple mechanism for expressing application semantics

by providing a modular packaging model and mechanisms for encoding application defined data. This allows SOAP to be used for a large variety of purposes ranging from messaging systems to remote procedure call (RPC) invocations. In previous versions of this specification the SOAP name was an acronym. This is no longer the case.

Wow, that sounds as if it were written by a committee; it actually *was* written by a committee. But we can decipher it into something meaningful to us.

SOAP allows us to create a "SOAP server," which processes requests and returns the results. It also allows us to create a "SOAP client," which makes requests and gathers the data a SOAP server returns. This all should sound very familiar at the moment — almost like a Web server and a Web browser. Simply put, however, a SOAP server serves functions, not pages.

What does *serving functions* mean? Just as you can make calls to specific functions, the same is true of SOAP servers. They contain functions that have been opened so that other programs can access them. These servers can operate over HTTP, SMTP, FTP, and so on.

The great thing about all of this is that SOAP is a standard interface, and as long as you follow the standard specifications for sending and receiving data, the language you use makes no difference! So, if I write a SOAP server in C++, that doesn't mean I am limited to calling its functions in C++; you can use Perl, Tcl, BASIC, C, or whatever you want to use — as long as you follow the established guidelines.

I've provided a very simplistic overview of what SOAP is. SOAP is potentially quite complex. Luckily, the SOAP-Lite Perl module takes care of 99 percent of the details for us; we just have to do a bit of Perl to implement a SOAP client or server.

We are going to cover how to create a simple SOAP server and SOAP client to implement a Web-based catalog system. The catalog system provides a list of products; when a user clicks a product-part number, the system provides detailed information about that product.

Building a SOAP Server

The SOAP server we'll create is going to expose two functions for SOAP clients to access. One function returns a list of all the products in the database; this function expects nothing to be passed to it and returns an array of array references (also known as a "list of lists"). The other function expects a part number to be passed to it and returns an XML document that we'll parse to create a page of detailed information about a product.

We'll begin by taking a look at the code that makes up the SOAP server. This is actually just a CGI program that has a few things added to get it to behave like a SOAP server.

```
01: #!/usr/bin/perl -w
02: # A simple, SOAP server

03: use strict;
04: use DBI;
05: use LWP::Simple ();
06: use HTML::LinkExtor;
07: use SOAP::Transport::HTTP;
```

Line 1 tells the system where to find Perl and turns warnings on.

Line 2 is simply a comment about this program.

Line 3 loads the `strict` module. This module causes Perl to be more picky about what it allows and makes the programmer give more thought to the programming process. Always use `strict`; it can prevent many common programming mistakes.

Line 4 loads the `DBI` module. We need to access a database for this program, so we use the `DBI` module, which is the DataBase Interface for Perl.

Line 5 loads the `LWP::Simple` module and the `()` makes sure none of the methods get loaded into our namespace. We explicitly call LWP::Simple::get in our program, so it does not have to be loaded at this point. Our program uses this module for fetching a document from a remote Web server.

Line 6 loads the `HTML::LinkExtor` module. This module extracts links from an HTML document. We'll be parsing a large HTML document inside of this program; this module makes parsing extremely easy for us.

Line 7 loads the `SOAP::Transport::HTTP` module. This is how we can easily create a SOAP server that uses the HTTP protocol for its communications.

```
08: package Catalog;

09: my $dbh = DBI->connect
("DBI:mysql:books:switch.perlguy.net",
      "bookuser","")
10:     or die("Cannot connect: $DBI::errstr\nAborting.");

11: my @imgs;
```

Line 8 declares that we are now inside of the `Catalog` package. Packages are used to declare different namespaces in Perl.

Line 9 connects us to the database and returns a handle with the connection. When the handle is returned, we store it in the newly declared variable named $dbh (meaning DataBase Handle).

Notice that with this connection string, we provide the driver name (mysql), database (books), and server name (switch.perlguy.net). The database happens to be on a completely different machine than this program.

Line 10 is a continuation of **line 9**; the die function causes the program to die and to display an error message if there is a problem connecting to the database.

Line 11 declares a new array named @imgs. This newly declared array and the variable named $dbh on **line 9** are available to all functions within the Catalog package (namespace), since they are declared outside of any of the subroutines.

```
12: SOAP::Transport::HTTP::CGI
13:   -> dispatch_to('Catalog')
14:   -> handle;
```

Lines 12–14 create a wrapper around the Catalog package.

The first part, **line 12**, tells the system that we are creating a SOAP server using the HTTP protocol and that this is going to be run like a CGI-based server. This is all part of the SOAP::Lite package.

The second part, **line 13**, tells this SOAP server that when someone tries to access a method, he or she must request it to be dispatched to the Catalog package.

The last part, **line 14**, simply passes control to the handle method so that the requests are handled properly.

These preceding three lines are what make this CGI program a SOAP server.

```
15: sub Get_Product_List {
16:     my $sql = qq(SELECT title, isbn FROM library);
17:     my $sth = $dbh->prepare($sql);
18:     $sth->execute;
```

Line 15 begins a subroutine named Get_Product_List. This subroutine is one of the two that we are making available as SOAP services. Get_Product_List takes no arguments; it simply queries the database and returns a list of products.

Line 16 creates a new variable named $sql and stores in it the SQL statement needed to get the data from the database.

Line 17 prepares the SQL statement and stores the prepared statement in the new variable named $sth. STH stands for *StatemenT H*andle.

Line 18 calls the `execute` method on the `$sth` handle. This causes the SQL statement to be run against the database, the results of which are also stored as a reference in the `$sth` handle.

```
19:      my @products;
20:      while(my $ptr = $sth->fetch){
21:          push (@products, [ @$ptr ]);
22:      }
```

Line 19 declares a new array named `@products`.

Line 20 begins a `while` loop that loops as long as the `$sth->fetch` call returns data. Once the `fetch` call runs out of data to retrieve, `$ptr` is set to `undef` and the `while` loop terminates.

Line 21 pushes a reference to a new anonymous array holding the current values onto the `@products` array. Each time it goes through the loop, `$ptr` stores a reference to an array that contains the current values. To get the array values, you can prefix the reference with @. The brackets (`[]`) around `@$ptr` cause the current values of the array to be copied into a new anonymous array. A reference to the new anonymous array gets pushed onto the `@products` array. Each new anonymous array is its own array and occupies its own memory.

If we try to pass a reference to the array by using `$ptr`, we will overwrite the data each time through the loop, as we are storing it in the same array memory address each time. At the end of the loop, we then end up with a bunch of arrays that all point to the last record we have accessed — which is not what we want to do.

Line 22 ends the `while` loop, which begins on **line 20**.

```
23:      return(\@products);
24: }
```

Line 23 returns a reference to the `@products` array. And that's what any SOAP client calling this routine will get back: a list of lists.

Line 24 ends the `Get_Product_List` subroutine.

```
25: sub Get_Product_Data {
26:      my $rval;
27:      my ($class, $input) = @_;
28:      die "Bad ISBN Number."
             unless($input =~ m/^[\dXx-]{10,13}$/);
29:      $Catalog::input    = $input;
```

Line 25 begins the `Get_Product_Data` subroutine. This subroutine is also accessible through the SOAP server. This subroutine expects to be passed a part number of the item that the user wants more details about. This part number is stored in the `$input` variable.

Line 26 declares a new scalar variable named $rval.

Line 27 declares two new scalar variables. $class is a reference to the package itself; this value is automatically passed. The $input variable is the value that the function call passes; it should contain the part number of the item we are looking for.

Line 28 calls the die function unless the value passed to the $input variable matches the regular expression. The regular expression checks to ensure that only digits, dashes, and the letter X appear in the $input variable. The regular expression also checks to ensure the value in $input is between 10 and 13 characters long. This allows us to validate that we got the type of input that we expected. Allowing any arbitrary data would be a security risk, so we want to avoid that.

Line 29 sets a package-wide variable named $Catalog::input to the value $input. The $input variable we declare on **line 27** has a scope of this current subroutine only. But, by declaring the variable $Catalog::input, we effectively create a new variable that is accessible within the Catalog package.

```
30:     my $sql   = "SELECT * FROM library WHERE isbn =
'$input'";
31:     my $p          = $dbh->selectrow_hashref($sql);
32:     $p->{image} = _get_image($input);
```

Line 30 declares a new scalar variable named $sql and sets it equivalent to the SQL statement on the right side.

Line 31 creates a new scalar variable named $p, which we use as a pointer to the value the selectrow_hashref method call returns. selectrow_hashref is yet another way to get data from a database by using the DBI. Notice that we do not have to prepare and execute this statement. Since we are getting only one item back, and we know this ahead of time, we can use the selectrow_hashref method. This method is referenced directly from the database handle ($dbh), and the SQL statement is passed directly to it. Once the selectrow_hashref does its magic, the variable $p will contain a reference to a hash, which contains the data that has been returned.

Line 32 sets the hash item at key image to the value that a call to the _get_image subroutine returns.

```
33:     if($p){
34:         $rval  = qq(<?xml version="1.0"?>\n);
35:         $rval .= qq( <catalog_item>\n);
```

Line 33 checks to see if the variable $p contains some sort of data. If it does, this block is entered.

Line 34 stores some text in the $rval variable. This text is the XML header for the data being returned.

Line 35 adds the XML tag `<catalog_item>` to the `$rval` variable.

```
36:            while(my($k,$v) = each %$p) {
37:                if($v) {
38:                    $v      =~ s/^ +//;
39:                    $v      =~ s/(\015?\012)$//;
40:                    $rval .= "    <$k>$v</$k>\n";
41:                }
42:            }
```

Line 36 begins a `while` loop that traverses through each hash element in the hash that the `$p` variable references. For each hash element, the `$k` and `$v` variables are set to the key and value, respectively.

Line 37 uses an `if` condition to check if the current value of the hash (`$v`) contains any data. If there *is* data, the program continues into the block of code.

Line 38 uses a regular expression to remove any leading spaces in `$v`. The ^ means *at the beginning of the string*; then we have a space, which is what we are looking for, and finally a +, which means *one or more*. So this regular expression roughly translates to *remove all spaces from the beginning of the string*.

Line 39 removes the carriage returns and/or linefeeds from the end of the string. The \015 is the octal value for a carriage return. The ? means that there may or may not be a carriage return — if there is, remove it; if there is not, that is ok too. The \012 is the octal value for a linefeed. The $ at the end means remove them only if they are at the end of the string.

Line 40 creates a new XML element that contains the value of the current hash element. The XML element name is the key value, `$k`. So if the current key were *name* and the current value were *Logan*, the tag generated would be `<name>Logan</name>`.

Line 41 closes the `if` block, which begins on **line 37**.

Line 42 closes the `while` block, which begins on **line 36**.

```
43:            $rval .= qq(  </catalog_item>\n);
44:        }

45:        $dbh->disconnect;
46:        return($rval);
47: }
```

Line 43 adds a closing tag to the string contained in `$rval`.

Line 44 closes the block of code that begins on **line 33**.

Line 45 disconnects the program from the database.

Line 46 returns $rval. $rval contains the XML document as a large string. The XML document in $rval is the data for the product information.

Line 47 ends the Get_Product_Data subroutine.

```
48: sub _get_image {
49:     my $input = $Catalog::input;
50:     my $url = "http://www.amazon.com/exec/obidos/ASIN/" .
             $input;
```

Line 48 begins the _get_image subroutine. This subroutine is prefixed with an underscore, and the name is in lowercase because this subroutine is only used internally by other subroutines in this program. This is a common practice so that you can easily see which subroutines are "private" and which subroutines are "public."

Line 49 declares a new scalar variable named $input and sets it to the value that is in $Catalog::input.

Line 50 declares a new scalar variable named $url and creates a URL based upon a fixed string and the value that is in the $input variable. The value in the $input variable should be the part number.

```
51:     my $p = HTML::LinkExtor
52:               ->new(\&_callback)
53:               ->parse(LWP::Simple::get($url));
```

Line 51 creates a new scalar variable named $p and sets it to the value returned by the call to HTML::LinkExtor. This call to HTML::LinkExtor spans **lines 51–53**.

Line 52 calls the new method from HTML::LinkExtor and passes it a reference to the _callback function. The _callback function is called when we pass data to the $p reference.

Line 53 calls the parse method of HTML::LinkExtor. This method is passed the value that is returned from the call to LWP::Simple::get($url). LWP::Simple::get($url) goes out on the Internet and fetches the HTML file that $url points to. The HTML page that this call returns is parsed by the LinkExtor module.

The _callback function, which we will cover shortly, determines what data to retrieve from the HTML page we have just fetched.

```
54:     return($imgs[0]);
55: }
```

Line 54 returns the value of the first element in the @imgs array. This value should contain a link to the picture of the book on the Amazon Web site.

Line 55 ends the _get_image subroutine.

```
56: sub _callback {
57:     my($tag, %attr) = @_;
58:     return if $tag ne 'img';
```

Line 56 begins the _callback subroutine. This subroutine is used to filter out the data we don't want from the HTML page that the _get_image subroutine has fetched.

The LinkExtor module parses all of the links out of the Web page. These links are then passed along to the _callback function, along with any attributes that are in the HTML tag.

Line 57 declares a scalar variable and a hash and stores the values passed to the subroutine. $tag contains the current tag, and %attr contains the attributes that are in that tag on the HTML page.

Line 58 returns from the subroutine if the current tag is not an image tag.

```
59:     my @foo = values %attr;
60:     return if($foo[0] !~ /$Catalog::input/i);

61:     push(@imgs, values %attr);
62: }
```

Line 59 declares a new array named @foo and stores the values from the %attr array in it.

The %attr hash would contain a key of src and a value of /images/foo.png if we had an image tag like this: <img src="/images/foo.png">.

Line 60 returns if the first element of the @foo array doesn't contain the data stored in $Catalog::input. The value in $Catalog::input is the part number (or ISBN in the case of this example).

Line 61 pushes the current values into the @imgs array.

Line 62 ends the _callback subroutine.

That is it! It takes 62 lines of code to make up a SOAP server that contains two useful commands.

Listing All Items

Next, we cover the catalog program. This program creates a Web page that contains a listing of all of the products, along with their part numbers. The products for this example are a list of books, and the part numbers are actually the ISBNs of these books. In reality, the parts and part numbers can be for any type of product. I just happen to have a database of books already populated, so it's easy for me to create an example based upon already existing data.

The catalog page this program creates is not designed to look pretty; it is designed to be a simple example to work with. For a real-world application, you would most likely want to make the user interface look much nicer for your customers. Figure 12-1 shows an example of what this program produces.

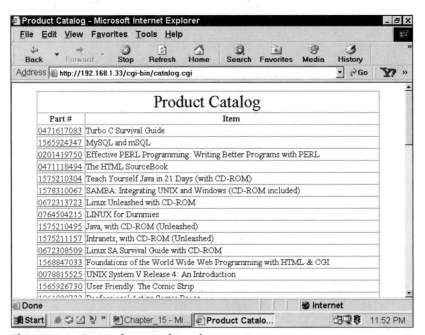

Figure 12-1: Output from catalog.cgi

```
01: #!/usr/bin/perl -wT

02: use strict;
03: use SOAP::Lite;
04: use CGI qw(:standard);
```

Line 1 tells the system where to find Perl and turns on warnings and taint checking. Since this is a CGI program, turning taint checking on is a good idea for safety sake. By turning taint checking on, if I try to perform a system command with data read in by the program, this will warn me that it may be unsafe.

Line 2 loads the strict module. strict should be used for all programs so that you can avoid common errors and also so that you are forced to program carefully.

Line 3 loads the SOAP::Lite module. We use this module to access the functions on the SOAP server.

Line 4 loads the CGI module and its standard features.

```
05: my $rval = SOAP::Lite
06:    -> uri('http://goliath.perlguy.net/Catalog')
07:    -> proxy('http://goliath.perlguy.net/cgi-
   bin/soap_server.cgi')
08:    -> Get_Product_List()
09:    -> result;
```

Line 5 declares a scalar variable named $rval and assigns it to the value that the call to the SOAP::Lite module returns. Since the Get_Products_List SOAP method returns a reference to an array of references, a reference will be stored in $rval.

Lines 5–9 are actually several methods from the SOAP::Lite module concatenated. These commands make up a SOAP client that retrieves data from the SOAP server.

Line 6 tells the SOAP client the URI, or namespace, of the service we are calling.

Line 7 is the address of the SOAP server we are contacting.

Line 8 is the remote function we are calling on the SOAP sever.

Line 9 calls the result method, which returns the results of the function we have called.

```
10: print header;
```

Line 10 prints the data returned by a call to the header function. The header function is part of the standard set of functions in the CGI module. This simply prints the HTTP header information.

```
11: print<<HTML;
12: <html>
13:   <head><title>Product Catalog</title></head>
```

```
14:  <body>
15:   <table border="1" cellspacing="0" align="center">
16:    <tr>
17:     <td colspan="2" align="center">
18:      <font size="6">
19:       Product Catalog
20:      </font>
21:     </td>
22:    </tr>
23:    <tr>
24:     <td align="center">
25:      <b>Part #</b>
26:     </td>
27:     <td align="center">
28:      <b>Item</b>
29:     </td>
30:    </tr>
31: HTML
```

Lines 11–31 are a *here document* that prints the beginning HTML needed to gener-ate the top of the page that displays all of the items.

```
32: for (@$rval){
33:     print qq(    <tr><td>);
34:     print qq(<a href="/cgi-bin/item_details.cgi?item_num=
          $_->[1]">$_->[1]</a>);
35:     print qq(    </td><td>$_->[0]);
36:     print qq(    </td></tr>\n);
37: }
```

Line 32 begins a `for` loop that iterates through each of the items in the array `@$rval`.

Line 33 prints a table row and table-column tag.

Line 34 prints a link to the `item_details.cgi` program as well as the item number (ISBN).

Line 35 prints a closing table-column tag and begins a new column containing the item name.

Line 36 prints a closing table column and closing table row tag.

Line 37 ends the `for` loop that begins on **line 32**.

```
38: print<<HTML;
39:   </table>
40:  </body>
41: </html>
42: HTML
```

Lines 38–42 are a *here document* that prints the remaining HTML needed for the product display page.

We now have our SOAP server and the program that calls one of the SOAP functions. Next we'll take a look at the program that displays the detailed information about an item that has been clicked.

Showing Item Details

This next program does a couple different things to show you how even a small program can do several different things and become part of a fairly sophisticated system.

The `item_details.cgi` program for this example is run on one server, connects to a SOAP server that fetches the product information from a totally different server, and returns the results as an XML document. The SOAP server also fetches a Web page from Amazon.com and parses the page so that the only thing we keep is the URL to an image of the product, or book.

In this small program, we connect to a SOAP service that connects to two other servers, and we pull all of this data into a single page—totally seamless to the user!

Figure 12-2 shows what a detailed product page looks like.

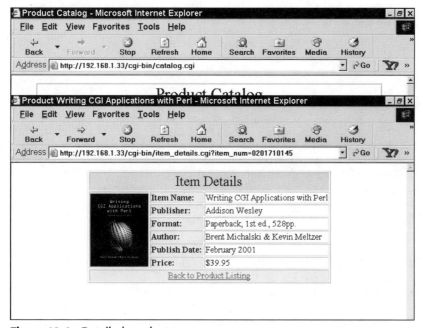

Figure 12-2: Detailed product page

```
01: #!/usr/bin/perl -wT

02: use strict;
03: use CGI qw(:standard);
04: use SOAP::Lite;
05: use XML::Simple;
```

Line 1 tells the system where to find Perl and turns on warnings and taint checking.

Line 2 loads the strict module.

Line 3 loads the CGI module and its standard functions.

Line 4 loads the SOAP::Lite module.

Line 5 loads the XML::Simple module.

```
06: print header;
07: my $input = param('item_num');
```

Line 6 prints the data that a call to the header function returns. The header function is part of the CGI module.

Line 7 declares a new variable named $input and sets it to the value that a call to the param function returns. The param function in this case is looking for the value passed in the URL as an HTML GET.

```
08: my $data = SOAP::Lite
09:    -> uri('http://goliath.perlguy.net/Catalog')
10:    -> proxy('http://goliath.perlguy.net/cgi-
    bin/soap_server.cgi')
11:    -> Get_Product_Data($input)
12:    -> result;
```

Line 8 declares a scalar variable named $data and assigns it to the value that the call to the SOAP::Lite module returns. The value that Get_Product_Data returns is a string that makes up an XML document.

Lines 8–12 are actually several methods from the SOAP::Lite module concatenated. These commands make up a SOAP client that retrieves data from the SOAP server.

Line 9 tells the SOAP client the URI, or namespace, of the service we are calling.

Line 10 is the address of the SOAP server we are contacting.

Line 11 is the remote function we are calling on the SOAP server; we pass the value in $input to the Get_Product_Data function.

Line 12 calls the `result` method, which returns the results of the function we have called.

```
13: $data =~ s/\&amp;|\&/\&amp;/g;
14: my $item = XMLin($data);
```

Line 13 replaces any ampersands HTML markups (&) or lone ampersands (&) in the XML document that was returned, with their equivalent HTML markup (&). A plain ampersand in an XML document causes an error when the document is parsed. We included & in our search to ensure that we don't change an already marked-up ampersands from & to &amp;.

Line 14 declares a scalar variable named $item. This new scalar variable is set to the value that a call to the XMLin function returns. XMLin is part of the XML::Simple module, and it returns a reference to a hash containing the parsed XML document.

```
15: print<<HTML;
16: <html>
17:  <head><title>Product $item->{title}</title></head>
18:  <body>
19:   <table border="1" align="center">
20:    <tr bgcolor="#c0c0c0">
21:     <td colspan="3" align="center">
22:      <font size="5">Item Details</font>
23:     </td>
24:    </tr>
25:    <tr>
26:     <td rowspan="6" bgcolor="#e0e0e0"><img
         src="$item->{image}"></td>
27:     <td bgcolor="#e0e0e0"><b>Item Name:</b></td>
28:     <td>$item->{title}</td>
29:    </tr>
30:    <tr>
31:     <td bgcolor="#e0e0e0"><b>Publisher:</b></td>
32:     <td>$item->{publisher}</td>
33:    </tr>
34:    <tr>
35:     <td bgcolor="#e0e0e0"><b>Format:</b></td>
36:     <td>$item->{format}</td>
37:    </tr>
38:    <tr>
39:     <td bgcolor="#e0e0e0"><b>Author:</b></td>
40:     <td>$item->{author}</td>
41:    </tr>
42:    <tr>
43:     <td bgcolor="#e0e0e0"><b>Publish Date:</b></td>
44:     <td>$item->{pubdate}</td>
45:    </tr>
46:    <tr>
47:     <td bgcolor="#e0e0e0"><b>Price:</b></td>
```

```
48:      <td>$item->{price}</td>
49:      </tr>
50:      <tr bgcolor="#e0e0e0">
51:       <td colspan="3" align="center">
52:        <a href="/cgi-bin/catalog.cgi">Back to Product
                  Listing</a>
53:       </td>
54:      </tr>
55:     </table>
56:    </body>
57:   </html>
58:  HTML
```

Lines 15–58 are a *here document* that prints the HTML that generates the detailed item-listing page.

Each item from the XML document is simply referenced as a hash element in the hash that the $item variable points to.

In just 14 lines of code (the code before the here document), we connect to a SOAP server, connect to a remote database, and also connect to the servers at Amazon.com, pulling all of this data back and forming a nice Web page from it!

I find it just amazing that so much is going on and that we are able to pull it all together with such small programs. Because of this power and simplicity, Web services should really take off. You will no longer have to write all of the code for each application yourself—instead, you will just need to know where the Web services are that you need to connect to and put the pieces together to make your new, larger, application work.

Summary

This chapter shows you how to create a fairly simple SOAP server. We've also covered a couple of different ways to access the SOAP server. The SOAP server we created is simply running as a CGI program. A SOAP server running as a CGI program is not a speed-demon. If you are thinking of setting up a SOAP server for a site that has high traffic volumes, you will want something more powerful. Don't fear; there are several tools that allow you to embed the SOAP server directory into Apache, which helps make the server run very fast. Do a quick Google search for mod_soap, and you will find links to several tools that can make your SOAP server scream!

Program Listings

Listings 12-1 to 12-3 show the complete and uninterrupted code from this chapter.

Listing 12-1: **soap_server.cgi**

```perl
01: #!/usr/bin/perl -w
02: # A simple, SOAP server

03: use strict;
04: use DBI;
05: use LWP::Simple;
06: use HTML::LinkExtor;
07: use SOAP::Transport::HTTP;

08: package Catalog;

09: my $dbh = DBI-
>connect("DBI:mysql:books:switch.perlguy.net",
     "bookuser","")
10:     or die("Cannot connect: $DBI::errstr\n");

11: my @imgs;

12: SOAP::Transport::HTTP::CGI
13:   -> dispatch_to('Catalog')
14:   -> handle;

15: sub Get_Product_List {
16:     my $sql = qq(SELECT title, isbn FROM library);
17:     my $sth = $dbh->prepare($sql);
18:     $sth->execute;

19:     my @products = ();
20:     while(my $ptr = $sth->fetch){
21:         push (@products, [ @$ptr ]);
22:     }

23:     return(\@products);
24: }

25: sub Get_Product_Data {
26:     my $rval;
27:     my ($class, $input) = @_;
28:     $Catalog::input     = $input;
```

Continued

Listing 12-1 *(continued)*

```
29:     my $sql    = "SELECT * FROM library WHERE isbn
          = '$input'";
30:     my $p      = $dbh->selectrow_hashref($sql);
31:     $p->{image} = _get_image($input);

32:     if($p){
33:         $rval  = qq(<?xml version="1.0"?>\n);
34:         $rval .= qq( <catalog_item>\n);
35:         while(my($k,$v) = each %$p) {
36:             if($v) {
37:                 $v      =~ s/^ +//;
38:                 $v      =~ s/(\015?\012)$//;
39:                 $rval .= "  <$k>$v</$k>\n";
40:             }
41:         }
42:         $rval .= qq( </catalog_item>\n);
43:     }

44:     $dbh->disconnect;
45:     return($rval);
46: }

47: sub _get_image {
48:     my $input = $Catalog::input;
49:     my $url   = http://www.amazon.com/exec/obidos/ASIN/
          . $input;

50:     my $p  = HTML::LinkExtor
51:      ->new(\&_callback)
52:      ->parse(LWP::Simple::get($url));

53:     return($imgs[0]);
54: }

55: sub _callback {
56:     my($tag, %attr) = @_;
57:     return if $tag ne 'img';

58:     my @foo = values %attr;
59:     return if($foo[0] !~ /$Catalog::input/i);

60:     push(@imgs, values %attr);
61: }
```

Listing 12-2: **catalog.cgi**

```
01: #!/usr/bin/perl -wT

02: use strict;
03: use SOAP::Lite;
04: use CGI qw(:standard);

05: my $rval = SOAP::Lite
06:    -> uri('http://goliath.perlguy.net/Catalog')
07:    -> proxy('http://goliath.perlguy.net/cgi-
    bin/soap_server.cgi')
08:    -> Get_Product_List()
09:    -> result;

10: print header;

11: print<<HTML;
12: <html>
13:  <head><title>Product Catalog</title></head>
14:  <body>
15:   <table border="1" cellspacing="0" align="center">
16:    <tr>
17:     <td colspan="2" align="center">
18:      <font size="6">
19:       Product Catalog
20:      </font>
21:     </td>
22:    </tr>
23:    <tr>
24:     <td align="center">
25:      <b>Part #</b>
26:     </td>
27:     <td align="center">
28:      <b>Item</b>
29:     </td>
30:    </tr>
31: HTML

32: for (@$rval){
33:     print qq(   <tr><td>);
34:     print qq(<a href="/cgi-bin/item_details.cgi?item_num=$_
        ->[1]">$_->[1]</a>);
35:     print qq(    </td><td>$_->[0]);
36:     print qq(   </td></tr>\n);
37: }

38: print<<HTML;
39:   </table>
40:  </body>
41: </html>
42: HTML
```

Listing 12-3: **Item_details.cgi**

```perl
01: #!/usr/bin/perl -wT

02: use strict;
03: use CGI qw(:standard);
04: use SOAP::Lite;
05: use XML::Simple;

06: print header;
07: my $input = param('item_num');

08: my $data = SOAP::Lite
09:   -> uri('http://goliath.perlguy.net/Catalog')
10:   -> proxy('http://goliath.perlguy.net/cgi-
    bin/soap_server.cgi')
11:   -> Get_Product_Data($input)
12:   -> result;

13: $data =~ s/\&amp;|\&/\&amp;/g;
14: my $item = XMLin($data);

15: print<<HTML;
16: <html>
17:  <head><title>Product $item->{title}</title></head>
18:  <body>
19:   <table border="1" align="center">
20:    <tr bgcolor="#c0c0c0">
21:     <td colspan="3" align="center">
22:      <font size="5">Item Details</font>
23:     </td>
24:    </tr>
25:    <tr>
26:     <td rowspan="6" bgcolor="#e0e0e0"><img src="$item
       ->{image}"></td>
27:     <td bgcolor="#e0e0e0"><b>Item Name:</b></td>
28:     <td>$item->{title}</td>
29:    </tr>
30:    <tr>
31:     <td bgcolor="#e0e0e0"><b>Publisher:</b></td>
32:     <td>$item->{publisher}</td>
33:    </tr>
34:    <tr>
35:     <td bgcolor="#e0e0e0"><b>Format:</b></td>
36:     <td>$item->{format}</td>
37:    </tr>
38:    <tr>
39:     <td bgcolor="#e0e0e0"><b>Author:</b></td>
40:     <td>$item->{author}</td>
41:    </tr>
```

```
42:    <tr>
43:     <td bgcolor="#e0e0e0"><b>Publish Date:</b></td>
44:     <td>$item->{pubdate}</td>
45:    </tr>
46:    <tr>
47:     <td bgcolor="#e0e0e0"><b>Price:</b></td>
48:     <td>$item->{price}</td>
49:    </tr>
50:    <tr bgcolor="#e0e0e0">
51:     <td colspan="3" align="center">
52:    <a href="/cgi-bin/catalog.cgi">Back to Product
Listing</a>
53:      </td>
54:     </tr>
55:    </table>
56:   </body>
57:  </html>
58: HTML
```

✦   ✦   ✦

Sending Automatic E-mail Reports

◆　◆　◆　◆

In This Chapter

Sending e-mail
automatically

Simple reports

More complex
reports

◆　◆　◆　◆

Although a Web-based reporting interface can be a helpful tool, an e-mail-based system is much more so. E-mail can be downloaded and moved off-line; it may be archived more readily than a Web page, and it may serve as the basis for reports to be sent to others who do not necessarily have administrative access to the system.

Perl is very well-suited to the construction of this type of report. This chapter demonstrates some of the flexibility Perl offers in this regard — from simple text-based notes to complex reports incorporating graphics.

The examples in this chapter deal with the reporting of user sessions. The relevant tables are the session table, which can be created as follows:

```
CREATE TABLE session (
  user_id integer unsigned,
  first_used datetime,
  last_used datetime,
  valid tinyint unsigned,
  ip varchar(20)
);
```

and the user table:

```
CREATE TABLE user (
  id integer unsigned primary key
auto_increment,
  username varchar(20)
);
```

Obviously, in a real-world application, the tables would contain other fields (a password for the user table and an authentication token for the session table), but those are not relevant here. The operation of this session system is simple: when a user logs on, he or she is presented by a randomly generated authentication token (which might be stored in a cookie or encoded in the URL of the page), which is valid for the current session. This creates a new entry in the session table, setting user_id, first_used, valid, and ip. Each page the user accesses updates the last_used field. When the user logs out, or attempts to access a page after the session has expired due to inactivity, valid is set to 0 to indicate that the session is no longer active.

Sending E-mail Automatically

Before we can generate reports, it is necessary to find out how to send e-mail from within a Perl program. There are, as one might expect, many ways to do this, ranging from opening a pipe to sendmail to more complex, fully featured systems; the solution presented here is toward the lower end of the complexity scale but can perform most e-mail tasks quickly and securely.

The MIME::Lite module

MIME::Lite is a simple, stand-alone module for generating and sending MIME e-mail messages. MIME is the mail protocol you need for mailing HTML or graphics, or anything other than just ASCII plaintext. It does not deal with message parsing (an entirely separate task), nor does it require any other modules apart from those already installed in the base Perl distribution. But it does automatically handle any necessary encoding.

The only problem occurs on Windows-based systems or on those that do not have their own mail servers; MIME::Lite uses a pipe to sendmail as its default means of getting mail off the systems. Very few Windows systems have this available. The usual approach in this case is to specify an external SMTP server. To make MIME::Lite use this function, just add:

```
MIME::Lite->send('smtp','hostname');
```

(replacing 'hostname' with the name of the external server, of course) to the beginning of each script that will send mail. Alternatively, if there is a program on the system that acts similarly to sendmail, set:

```
MIME::Lite->send('sendmail',"d:\\programs\\sendmail.exe");
```

The preceding line is not used in the examples in this chapter.

crontab

The cron program covers the "automatic" part of this chapter's title. This is a standard Unix function that causes a program to be run at specified times. Often, the reporting program runs under the same user id as the Web server; this might be Apache, www-data, or nobody. For this example, we use www-data.

You need shell access to set up the crontab listing for the report program, either as root or as the www-data user. Run the command:

```
crontab -u www-data -e
```

to edit the listing of tasks to be carried out automatically by the www-data user; add the new line at the end.

The format of the crontab entries can be a bit tricky, see the manual page for crontab(5) for detailed information about the format of the crontab file. The most common cases, though, are a program to be run once a day, once a week, or once a month. This can be executed by the following entries:

```
15 8 * * * /path/to/daily/program_name
15 8 * * 1 /path/to/weekly/program_name
last:15 8 1 * * /path/to/monthly/program_name
```

In each case, the daily program is run at 8:15 A.M. (local time). The weekly program is run only on Monday; the monthly program is run on the first of the month. Note that, if the program produces output on STDOUT or STDERR, the output will be e-mailed to the local user that owns the crontab entry (*www-data* in this case). This is rarely useful. Try to ensure that programs running under cron in this way do not produce such output. Under Windows, the Task Scheduler can be used to similar ends.

Creating a Simple Report

The simplest report is a plain-text e-mail, constructed on the basis of a few SQL queries. In this case, we report the total number of sessions in the last week, the number of distinct users, and the number of sessions each user starts.

```
01: #! /usr/bin/perl -w
02: #
03: # report_text.pl
04: # Chapter 13
05: # Listing 1
06: #

07: use strict;
08: use DBI;
09: use MIME::Lite;
```

Line 1 tells the system where to find Perl and turns warnings on.

Lines 2–6 are comments about the program.

Line 7 loads the strict module.

Line 8 loads the DBI module, for our database access.

Line 9 loads the MIME::Lite module for our e-mail functionality.

```
10: my $dbh=DBI->connect
('DBI:mysql:UserTrack','user','password')
11:          or die("Cannot connect: $DBI::errstr");

12: my $messagebody;
```

Line 10 uses the DBI->connect method to create a connection to the database server. The result of the connection attempt are returned as a reference to the database connection object and stored in the $dbh variable.

Line 11 is a continuation of **line 10**. This line calls the die method and prints an error message if there was a problem obtaining a database connection.

Line 12 contains the $messagebody scalar variable we use to build up the body of the e-mail.

```
13: my ($totalusers)=
14:    $dbh->selectrow_array("SELECT COUNT(DISTINCT user_id)
15:                          FROM session
16:                          WHERE first_used >
17:                          DATE_SUB(SYSDATE(),INTERVAL 7 DAY)");
18: $messagebody = "Total users: $totalusers\n\n";
```

Line 13 declares a scalar variable.

Lines 14–17 are a continuation of **line 13** that create and execute the SQL statement listed on these lines. The result of the query is stored in the $totalusers variable.

There are parenthesis around the $totalusers variable to force it into *list mode*. By forcing the variable into list mode, the variable captures the first array element that is returned by the selectrow_array method call. If you had left off the parenthesis, the value that would get stored into $totalusers would be the number of elements in the array that the selectrow_array method call had returned, which is definitely not what we want.

Line 18 stores the text Total users: along with the value stored in $totalusers into the $messagebody variable.

So now $messagebody contains the first report—a simple count of distinct user_id values. MySQL handles the date calculations, which avoids the need for date manipulation within the Perl program; see the documentation of date functions for more detail. By looking at the SQL statement, we can see that this is a weekly report.

```
19: my ($totalsessions)=
20:    $dbh->selectrow_array("SELECT COUNT(*)
21:                            FROM session
22:                            WHERE first_used >
23:                            DATE_SUB(SYSDATE(),INTERVAL 7 DAY)");
24: $messagebody .= "Total sessions: $totalsessions\n\n";
```

Lines 19–24 perform the same basic function as **lines 13-18**, but this time our SQL command searches for the total number of items that match our criteria rather than the DISTINCT user_id as before.

```
25: my $sth = $dbh->prepare("SELECT count(*),username
26:                           FROM session, user
27:                           WHERE first_used >
28:                              DATE_SUB(SYSDATE(),INTERVAL 7 DAY)
29:                           AND user_id=user.id
30:                           GROUP BY username");
```

Lines 25–30 prepare an SQL statement and store a handle to the prepared statement in the $sth variable. The result of the SQL statement for this report is a sorted list of users who have logged in during the period and the number of times each has done so.

```
31: $sth->execute;
```

Line 31 calls the execute method on the statement handle ($sth) to execute the SQL statement.

```
32: while (my ($count, $user) = $sth->fetchrow_array) {
33:    my $s = ($count == 1) ? '' : 's';
34:    $messagebody .= "$user: $count login$s\n";
35: }
36: $sth->finish;
```

Line 32 begins a while loop. Each time through this while loop the $sth->fetchrow_array method is called and the result of the call is stored into the $count and $user variables.

Line 33 checks to see if $count is equal to 1. If this is true, then $s gets set to nothing. If false, then $s gets set to the letter s.

Line 34 appends the username and the number of logins that the user had onto our $messagebody variable.

Line 35 ends the `while` loop that began on **line 32**.

Line 36 calls the `finish` method to clean up the `$sth` statement handle.

```
37: $dbh->disconnect;
```

Line 37 calls the `disconnect` method to disconnect us from the database.

```
38: my $message=MIME::Lite->new(
39:              From    => 'reports@example.com',
40:              To      => 'you@example.com',
41:              Subject => 'Weekly report',
42:              Data    => $messagebody
43:            );
```

Lines 38–43 create and configure the `MIME::Lite` object. Obviously, greater complexity is possible, but this is all that is necessary to send a report.

```
44: $message->send;
```

Line 44 sends the message.

Creating a More Complex Report

The first example shows how quickly a simple report can be generated; but it also shows some of the problems that arise. Very little formatting is possible within plain-text mail, and tables, in particular, are used infrequently or are ugly in appearance. Moreover, changing the order of the entries in the report, or the layout, requires editing the program code.

One solution to the layout problem is using a template module. As with sending mail, many of these are available for Perl; for the purposes of this chapter, `HTML::Template` is used as a reasonable compromise between capability and ease of use. (Other modules that deserve investigation are `Text::Template`, at the low end of the capability scale, and `Template::Toolkit`, at the high end. Resist the temptation to invent your own template module. It has been done many times before, and most of the standard pitfalls have been overcome in the code that is already available.)

The template (which, in spite of the module's name, can be any form of text, not just HTML) is stored in a separate file from the program. Interspersed with the normal layout commands are special tags, into which will be placed data that the program generates. This allows layout changes to be made without editing the main program file and (more important) allows reports in multiple formats to be generated from the same software.

As for a solution to the formatting problem, one convenient approach is the use of HTML e-mail. HTML has the advantage of allowing greater control over layout than plain text; in particular, the `<table>` structure is very useful.

Naturally, some of the intended audience of a report might not have HTML-enabled mail readers. It is generally a good idea to include a plain-text version of the report as well, in a multipart/alternative (HTML) structure, as we shall see. A templating system makes this very easy.

Essentially, this example produces the same report as the preceding example, but in both text and HTML formats, by use of `HTML::Template`.

```
01: #! /usr/bin/perl -w
02: #
03: # report_html.pl
04: # Chapter 13
05: # Listing 2
06: #
```

Lines 1–6 tell the system where to find Perl, turn warnings on, and give some comments about the program.

```
07: use strict;
08: use DBI;
09: use HTML::Template;
10: use MIME::Lite;
```

Line 7 loads the `strict` module.

Line 8 loads the `DBI` module, for database access.

Line 9 loads the `HTML::Template` module.

Line 10 loads the `MIME::Lite` module.

```
11: my $dbh = DBI->connect('DBI:mysql:UserTrack','user','password')
12:          or die("Cannot connect: $DBI::errstr ");
```

Lines 11–12 create a connection to the database and store a handle in the `$dbh` variable. If there is a problem connecting to the database, then the `die` method is called and the program aborts and displays an error message.

```
13: my @template;
14: $template[0]=HTML::Template->new(filename => 'template_2.txt');
15: $template[1]=HTML::Template->new(filename => 'template_2.html');
```

Line 13 declares an array named `@template`.

Lines 14–15 create two separate `HTML::Template` objects, one for each of the formats to be used. These are based on separate files, which can be edited independently. Although the same data is put into each, different processing creates different output. (Check `perldoc HTML::Template` for documentation on the `HTML_TEMPLATE_ROOT` environment variable and for other ways of specifying the location of template files.) For simplicity, you may want to use an absolute filename. By default, though, the program looks first in the directory in which it resides.

```
16: my ($totalusers)=
17:    $dbh->selectrow_array("SELECT COUNT(DISTINCT user_id)
18:                           FROM session
19:                           WHERE first_used >
20:                               DATE_SUB(SYSDATE(),INTERVAL 7 DAY)");
```

Line 16 declares a scalar variable named `$totalusers` and, using the parentheses to force it into a list context, gets loaded with the value returned by the `$dbh->selectrow_array` method on **line 17**.

Lines 17–20 create and execute an SQL statement to get out report data.

```
21: foreach my $tmpl (@template) {
22:    $tmpl->param(totalusers => $totalusers);
23: }
```

Lines 21–23 extract information from the database just as before. However, the `param` method of `HTML::Template` is used to indicate that the `totalusers` template variable should be replaced by the value just extracted. This is done for each template.

```
24: my ($totalsessions)=
25:    $dbh->selectrow_array("SELECT COUNT(*)
26:                           FROM session
27:                           WHERE first_used >
28:                               DATE_SUB(SYSDATE(),INTERVAL 7 DAY)");
```

Line 24 declares a scalar variable named `$totalsessions` and stores the result of the `$dbh->selectrow_array` method from **line 25** into it.

Lines 25–28 create and execute the SQL statement needed for this part of our report.

```
29: foreach my $tmpl (@template) {
30:    $tmpl->param(totalsessions => $totalsessions);
31: }
```

Line 29 begins a `foreach` loop that loops through the different templates in the `@template` array. Each time through the loop, the current value is set in the `$tmpl` variable.

Line 30 passes the totalsessions parameter and it's value to the current template referenced by $tmpl.

Line 31 ends the foreach loop.

```
32: my $sth = $dbh->prepare("SELECT count(*),username
33:                     FROM session, user
34:                       WHERE first_used >
35:                         DATE_SUB(SYSDATE(),INTERVAL 7 DAY)
36:                         AND user_id=user.id
37:                       GROUP BY username");
```

Lines 32–37 prepare the SQL statement for our next report item and store a reference to the prepared statement in the newly defined $sth variable.

```
38: $sth->execute;
39: my @usersession;
```

Line 38 executes the SQL statement we prepared above.

Line 39 declares a new array named @usersession.

```
40: while (my ($count, $user) = $sth->fetchrow_array) {
41:   push @usersession, {user  => $user,
42:                     count => $count};
43: }
```

Line 40 begins a while loop that continues as long as the $sth->fetchrow_array method keeps returning data. Each time through the loop, the current values from the $sth->fetchrow_array method get stored in the $count and $user variables.

Lines 41–42 push a reference to an anonymous hash containing the user and the count onto the @usersession array.

{user => $user, count => $count} actually creates a hash with no name. A reference to this hash is then pushed into the @usersession array so that we can easily retrieve it.

Line 43 closes the while loop.

```
44: foreach my $tmpl (@template) {
45:   $tmpl->param(usersession => \@usersession);
46: }
```

Line 44 begins a foreach loop that loops through the different templates in the @template array. Each time through the loop, the current value is set in the $tmpl variable.

Line 45 passes the usersession parameter and a reference to an array containing it's values to the current template referenced by $tmpl.

Line 46 ends the foreach loop.

```
47: $sth->finish;
48: $dbh->disconnect;
```

Line 47 calls the finish method to clean up the $sth statement handle.

Line 48 calls the disconnect method to disconnect from the database.

```
49: my $message = MIME::Lite->new(
50:              From    => 'reports@example.com',
51:              To      => 'you@example.com',
52:              Subject => 'Weekly report',
53:              Type    => 'multipart/alternative'
54:            );
```

Lines 49–54 prepare the e-mail message. Rather than including text directly in the message constructor as before, here we specify that this message is to take advantage of the power of the MIME standard by setting the Type parameter to multipart/alternative (in this case, text and HTML).

```
55: $message->attach(Type => 'text/plain',
56:                  Data => $template[0]->output);
57: $message->attach(Type => 'text/html',
58:                  Data => $template[1]->output);
```

```
59: $message->send;
```

Lines 55–58 convert each of the template objects, using its output method, to a scalar containing the original template — with the interpolated data that the program adds. These are then passed to the attach method of MIME::Lite, which adds them to the message under construction.

Line 59 sends the message exactly as before.

The two template files are as follows:

template_2.txt

```
Total users: <tmpl_var name=totalusers>

Total sessions: <tmpl_var name=totalsessions>
```

```
Sessions per user:
<tmpl_loop name=usersession><tmpl_var name=user>: <tmpl_var
name=count>
</tmpl_loop>
```

The `<tmpl_var>` tag introduces a variable to be interpolated in the final output. `<tmpl_loop>` introduces a loop; note that variables defined outside the loop are not automatically present within the loop and need to be defined explicitly if they are required. Since `HTML::Template` always passes through every new line , the `usersession` loop is kept on one line, avoiding extra line breaks in the final output.

template_2.html

```
<html>
<head>
<title>Weekly report</title>
</head>
<body>
<p>Total users: <tmpl_var name=totalusers escape=html></p>
<p>Total sessions: <tmpl_var name=totalsessions
escape=html></p>
<p>Sessions per user:
<table>
<tr><td>User</td><td>Logins</td></tr>
<tmpl_loop name=usersession>
<tr>
<td><tmpl_var name=user escape=html></td>
<td><tmpl_var name=count escape=html></td>
</tr>
</tmpl_loop>
</table></p></body></html>
```

The preceding HTML-mode template is more complex than the plain-text template, though the HTML-mode template contains more noninterpolated text. Note the `escape=html` argument to the `<tmpl_var>` tag; this causes any body text that might be interpreted specially, such as the symbols <, >, or &, to be automatically converted to an encoded equivalent that can safely be sent to a Web browser. Although it should not be necessary in this particular case, using `escape=html` is a good habit to get into.

Creating Graphical Reports

The final refinement to e-mail reporting, which is dealt with here, is the use of dynamic graphical content. It is, of course, possible to write custom-graphing packages by using the GD module. The GD module is a powerful interface to Thomas Boutell's gd graphics library. In most cases, however, all that is needed is a simple graph; here, the GD::Graph module becomes useful.

GD::Graph is capable of moderately complex graph generation, but operation of the basic functions is very simple: just provide an array of arrayrefs, each the same size. The first arrayref contains data-row labels, and later ones contain data (GD::Graph doesn't support true X-Y graph plotting). Three-dimensional graphing, although provided by a separate module dependent on GD::Graph, is essentially similar.

Creating a graph consists of multiple stages:

1. Create the graph object (specifying the type of graph and the size).

2. Set the parameters of the graph (axis labels, scaling, and so on).

3. Populate the data array; then use the plot function to convert it to a GD object (an image).

4. Use one of GD's output functions to convert the GD object to a usable image.

The following example generates a summary of session lengths, in both graphical and HTML table format.

```
01: #!/usr/bin/perl -w
02: #
03: # report_graphic.pl
04: # Chapter 13
05: # Listing 3
06: #
```

Lines 1–6 tell the system where to find Perl, turn on warnings and list some comments about this program.

```
07: use strict;
08: use DBI;
09: use HTML::Template;
10: use MIME::Lite;
11: use GD::Graph::bars3d;
```

Lines 7–10 load some common modules.

Line 11 causes the GD::Graph module to import only the graph types it is explicitly told to use. In this case, we are drawing a three-dimensional bar chart.

```
12: my @buckets=(0, 60, 300, 3600);
13: my @description=('0', '60 sec', '5 min', '1 hour', '');
14: my ($w, $h)=(400, 300);
```

Lines 12–14 set various configuration options, allowing them to be conveniently changed later (should this be necessary). The @buckets array contains the boundaries between the different session durations (in seconds); @description contains the corresponding textual descriptions.

```
15: my $graph=new GD::Graph::bars3d($w, $h);
```

Line 15 creates the GD::Graph::bars3d object by using the basic parameters: pixel width and height.

```
16: $graph->set(x_label => 'Session duration',
17:              y_label => 'Number of sessions');
```

Lines 16–17 set other properties of the graph (in this case, just the axis labels). If automatic scaling produces odd results because of the nature of the data, or if colors are changed, further parameters to the set method can achieve the desired results.

```
18: my $dbh = DBI->connect('DBI:mysql:UserTrack','user','password')
19:          or die("Cannot connect: $DBI::errstr");

20: my $template= HTML::Template->new(filename => 'template_3.html');

21: my @data;
22: my @loop;
```

Lines 18–19 create the database connection and store a reference to the connection in $dbh. If there is a problem connecting to the database, then the die method is called and the program aborts.

Line 20 creates a new template object and stores a reference to the object in the $template variable.

Lines 21–22 declare a couple arrays named @data and @loop that we'll be using to store data in the appropriate format for the graph and for the HTML table, respectively.

```
23: foreach my $b (0..$#buckets) {
24:   my %loopdata;
25:   my @where;
26:   my @desc;
```

Line 23 begins a foreach loop that loops from 0 to the number of the last element in the @buckets array. Each time through the loop, the current value gets stored in $b.

Lines 24–26 declare some variables that we'll be using.

```
27:    if ($b > 0) {
28:        my $low = $buckets[$b];
29:        push @where,
       "(unix_timestamp(last_used)-unix_timestamp(first_used)) > $low";
30:    }
```

Line 27 checks to see if $b is greater than 0 and if so, this code block is entered.

Line 28 declares a variable named $low and sets it to the value stored in $buckets[$b].

Line 29 pushes a string onto the @where array. This string will become part of the SQL command.

Line 30 closes this if block.

```
31:    push @desc, $description[$b];
```

Line 31 pushes the current value in $description[$b] into the @desc array.

```
32:    if ($b < $#buckets) {
33:        my $high = $buckets[$b+1];
34:        push @where,
      "(unix_timestamp(last_used)-unix_timestamp(first_used)) <= $high";
```

Line 32 checks to see if $b is less than $#buckets (the index of the last element in the @buckets array).

Line 33 declares a variable named $high and stores the value in $buckets[$b+1] into it.

Line 34 pushes a string into the @where array. This string will become part of the SQL command.

```
35:        push @desc, $description[$b+1];
```

Line 35 pushes the value stored in $description[$b+1] into the @desc array.

```
36:    } else {
37:        $desc[0] .= '+';
38:    }
```

Line 36 closes the first part of the if block, and opens an else portion.

Line 37 appends a plus sign to the first element of the @desc array.

Line 38 closes this if..else block.

```
39:    my $desc = join('-', @desc);
40:    push @{$data[0]}, $desc;
41:    $loopdata{desc} = $desc;
42:    my $where = join(' AND ', @where);
```

Line 39 declares a scalar variable named $desc and uses the join function to store all of the values in @desc array joined together with a dash into it.

Line 40 uses the push function to push the $desc string into the array referenced by $data[0].

Line 41 sets $loopdata{desc} to the value in $desc.

Line 42 declares a scalar variable named $where and uses the join function to store all of the values in the @where array joined together with ' AND '. The $where variable will become our WHERE clause in the SQL statement.

So, **lines 24–42** automatically generate a description of the time period from the @description list; this time period is then stored in the first @data arrayref (for the graph) and in %loopdata (for the table). Also, a sequence of restriction clauses based on the time period is assembled here, then concatenated into a form usable in the actual SELECT statement.

```
43:    my $sql="SELECT COUNT(*)
44:           FROM session
45:           WHERE first_used >
46:            DATE_SUB(SYSDATE(),INTERVAL 7 DAY)
47:           AND $where";
```

Lines 43-47 create the SQL statement needed to get the report data from the database.

```
48:    my ($value) = $dbh->selectrow_array($sql);
```

Line 48 executes the SQL statement and then returns the first row that was returned from the database. This data is then stored into the $value variable.

```
49:    push @{$data[1]}, $value;
50:    $loopdata{count} = $value;
51:    push @loop, \%loopdata;
```

Lines 49–51, once the value has been retrieved, store it in the second @data arrayref and in %loopdata. The latter is then appended to the template-loop structure.

```
52: }
53: $dbh->disconnect;
54: $template->param(width    => $w,
55:                   height   => $h,
56:                   duration => \@loop);
```

Line 52 ends the `foreach` loop.

Line 53 disconnects us from the database.

Lines 54–56 send some parameters to the template so that they can be filled in for our final report.

```
57: my $gd = $graph->plot(\@data);
```

Line 57 plots the graph. `$gd` now holds a GD bitmap image object.

```
58: my $message=MIME::Lite->new(
59:            From    => 'reports@example.com',
60:            To      => 'you@example.com',
61:            Subject => 'Weekly report',
62:            Type    => 'multipart/mixed'
63:          );
```

Lines 58–63 prepare the new message.

```
64: $message->attach(Type => 'text/html',
65:                 Data => $template->output);
```

Lines 64–65 attach the HTML file to the e-mail message.

```
66: $message->attach(Type     => 'image/png',
67:                 Filename => 'graph1.png',
68:                 Data     => $gd->png);
```

Lines 66–68 convert the GD object to raw PNG data (the GD library no longer supports GIFs due to licensing issues) and add it to the message. The filename parameter does not refer to an actual file; rather, it gives the name under which the image should be saved when it is received, which matches the name of the image-source tag given in the template.

```
69: $message->send;
```

Line 69 sends the message.

The template used for this report is very similar to that used with report HTML; the sole difference is the IMG tag, with height and width inserted automatically as a courtesy to the eventual viewer.

template_3.html

```
<html>
<head>
<title>Weekly report</title>
</head>
```

```
<body>
<p>Sessions per user:</p>
<img src="graph1.png" alt="sessions_graph" width=<tmpl_var
name=width> height=<tmpl_var name=height>>
<table>
<tr><td>Duration</td><td>Sessions</td></tr>
<tmpl_loop name=duration>
<tr>
<td><tmpl_var name=desc escape=html></td>
<td><tmpl_var name=count escape=html></td>
</tr>
</tmpl_loop>
</table></body></html>
```

Code very similar to this can be used to generate a report on the Web site itself; the only change necessary is that both the HTML page and the image are written to files rather than incorporated into an e-mail message.

The results should look something like Figure 13-1.

Duration	Sessions
0–60 sec	3
60 sec – 5 min	6
5 min – 1 hour	9
1 hour +	12

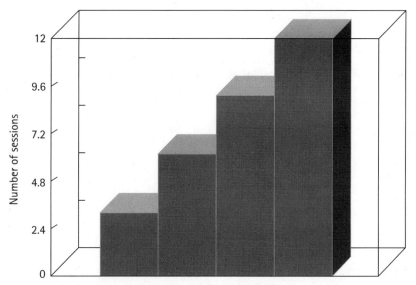

Figure 13-1: Output of template3.html

Summary

In this chapter you have learned how to create basic reports and send them as both plaintext e-mail messages and as graphical attachments in e-mail. This chapter was an excellent starting point, now it is up to you to take it to the next level. You can create just about any sort of report you want from databases or even log files, and then set them up to automatically e-mail you! If you are a systems administrator, you should realize that this kind of utility can make your job much easier!

Program Listings

Listings 13-1 to 13-3 contain the complete and uninterrupted code for the programs developed in this chapter.

Listing 13-1: **Plain-text report**

```
01: #! /usr/bin/perl -w
02: #
03: # report_text.pl
04: # Chapter 13
05: # Listing 1
06: #

07: use strict;
08: use DBI;
09: use MIME::Lite;

10: my $dbh=DBI->connect('DBI:mysql:UserTrack','user','password')
11:        or die("Cannot connect: $DBI::errstr");

12: my $messagebody;
13: my ($totalusers)=
14:   $dbh->selectrow_array("SELECT COUNT(DISTINCT user_id)
15:                          FROM session
16:                          WHERE first_used >
17:                          DATE_SUB(SYSDATE(),INTERVAL 7 DAY)");

18: $messagebody, "Total users: $totalusers\n\n";

19: my ($totalsessions)=
20:   $dbh->selectrow_array("SELECT COUNT(*)
21:                          FROM session
22:                          WHERE first_used >
23:                          DATE_SUB(SYSDATE(),INTERVAL 7 DAY)");

24: $messagebody .= "Total sessions: $totalsessions\n\n";
```

```
25: my $sth=$dbh->prepare("SELECT count(*),username
26:                        FROM session, user
27:                         WHERE first_used >
28:                          DATE_SUB(SYSDATE(),INTERVAL 7 DAY)
29:                         AND user_id=user.id
30:                        GROUP BY username");

31: $sth->execute;

32: while (my ($count,$user)=$sth->fetchrow_array) {
33:   my $s=($count==1)?'':'s';
34:   $messagebody .= "$user: $count login$s\n";
35: }

36: $sth->finish;

37: $dbh->disconnect;

38: my $message=MIME::Lite->new(
39:             From    => 'reports@example.com',
40:             To      => 'you@example.com',
41:             Subject => 'Weekly report',
42:             Data    => $messagebody
43:             );
44: $message->send;
```

Listing 13-2: **HTML report**

```
01: #! /usr/bin/perl -w
02: #
03: # report_html.pl
04: # Chapter 13
05: # Listing 2
06: #

07: use strict;
08: use DBI;
09: use HTML::Template;
10: use MIME::Lite;

11: my $dbh=DBI->connect('DBI:mysql:UserTrack','user','password')
12:        or die("Cannot connect: $DBI::errstr");

13: my @template;
14: $template[0]=HTML::Template->new(filename => 'template_2.txt');
```

Continued

Listing 13-2 *(continued)*

```
15: $template[1]=HTML::Template->new(filename => 'template_2.html');

16: my ($totalusers)=
17:   $dbh->selectrow_array("SELECT COUNT(DISTINCT user_id)
18:                          FROM session
19:                          WHERE first_used >
20:                            DATE_SUB(SYSDATE(),INTERVAL 7 DAY)");

21: foreach my $tmpl (@template) {
22:   $tmpl->param(totalusers => $totalusers);
23: }

24: my ($totalsessions)=
25:   $dbh->selectrow_array("SELECT COUNT(*)
26:                          FROM session
27:                          WHERE first_used >
28:                            DATE_SUB(SYSDATE(),INTERVAL 7 DAY)");

29: foreach my $tmpl (@template) {
30:   $tmpl->param(totalsessions => $totalsessions);
31: }

32: my $sth=$dbh->prepare("SELECT count(*),username
33:                        FROM session, user
34:                        WHERE first_used >
35:                          DATE_SUB(SYSDATE(),INTERVAL 7 DAY)
36:                        AND user_id=user.id
37:                        GROUP BY username");

38: $sth->execute;
39: my @usersession;

40: while (my ($count,$user)=$sth->fetchrow_array) {
41:   push @usersession,{user => $user,
42:                      count => $count};
43: }

44: foreach my $tmpl (@template) {
45:   $tmpl->param(usersession => \@usersession);
46: }

47: $sth->finish;
48: $dbh->disconnect;

49: my $message=MIME::Lite->new(
50:             From    => 'reports@example.com',
51:             To      => 'you@example.com',
52:             Subject => 'Weekly report',
```

```
53:                Type    => 'multipart/alternative'
54:            );

55: $message->attach(Type => 'TEXT',
56:                    Data => $template[0]->output);

57: $message->attach(Type => 'text/html',
58:                    Data => $template[1]->output);

59: $message->send;
```

Listing 13-3: **Graphical report**

```
01: #! /usr/bin/perl -w
02: #
03: # report_graphic.pl
04: # Chapter 13
05: # Listing 3
06: #

07: use strict;
08: use DBI;
09: use HTML::Template;
10: use MIME::Lite;
11: use GD::Graph::bars3d;

12: my @buckets     = (0, 60, 300, 3600);
13: my @description = ('0', '60 sec', '5 min', '1 hour','');
14: my ($w, $h)     = (400, 300);

15: my $graph = new GD::Graph::bars3d($w, $h);

16: $graph->set(x_label => 'Session duration',
17:             y_label => 'Number of sessions');

18: my $dbh = DBI->connect('DBI:mysql:UserTrack','user','password')
19:         or die("Cannot connect: $DBI::errstr");

20: my $template = HTML::Template->new(filename => 'template_3.html');

21: my @data;
22: my @loop;

23: foreach my $b (0..$#buckets) {
24:    my %loopdata;
25:    my @where;
```

Continued

Listing 13-3 *(continued)*

```
26:    my @desc;

27:    if ($b > 0) {
28:      my $low = $buckets[$b];
29:      push @where, "(unix_timestamp(last_used)-unix_timestamp(first_used)) >
$low";
30:    }

31:    push @desc,$description[$b];

32:    if ($b < $#buckets) {
33:      my $high = $buckets[$b+1];
34:      push @where, "(unix_timestamp(last_used)-unix_timestamp(first_used)) <=
$high";

35:      push @desc, $description[$b+1];

36:    } else {
37:      $desc[0] .= '+';
38:    }

39:    my $desc = join('-', @desc);
40:    push @{$data[0]}, $desc;
41:    $loopdata{desc} = $desc;
42:    my $where = join(' AND ', @where);

43:    my $sql = "SELECT COUNT(*)
44:             FROM session
45:             WHERE first_used >
46:              DATE_SUB(SYSDATE(),INTERVAL 7 DAY)
47:             AND $where";

48:    my ($value) = $dbh->selectrow_array($sql);

49:    push @{$data[1]}, $value;
50:    $loopdata{count} = $value;
51:    push @loop, \%loopdata;

52: }
53: $dbh->disconnect;
54: $template->param(width => $w,
55:                  height => $h,
56:                  duration => \@loop);

57: my $gd=$graph->plot(\@data);

58: my $message=MIME::Lite->new(
59:              From    => 'reports@example.com',
```

```
60:                To      => 'you@example.com',
61:              Subject => 'Weekly report',
62:              Type    => 'multipart/mixed'
63:            );

64: $message->attach(Type => 'text/html',
65:               Data => $template->output);

66: $message->attach(Type     => 'image/png',
67:               Filename => 'graph1.png',
68:               Data     => $gd->png);

69: $message->send;
```

✦   ✦   ✦

Perl and General Web Programming

◆ ◆ ◆ ◆

◆ ◆ ◆ ◆

Creating a Phonebook

This chapter uses many of the skills covered earlier to create some fully functional and useful programs:

✦ A command-line program for adding people and numbers to person and phone tables

✦ A short phone number lookup program

✦ A large maintenance program for the person and phone tables

The programs are intended to be easy to change and extend. In these programs, the prompts, the SQL, and some of the validation are dependent on data; change the data, and the program changes.

Understanding the Program Table Structure

The tables are based on the person and phone number tables used in the first chapter. Here's the structure of the `person` table and the SQL to create it:

```
+------------+-------------+------+-----+---------+----------------+
| Field      | Type        | Null | Key | Default | Extra          |
+------------+-------------+------+-----+---------+----------------+
| id         | int(11)     |      | PRI | NULL    | auto_increment |
| first_name | varchar(30) |      |     |         |                |
| last_name  | varchar(30) | YES  |     | NULL    |                |
| greeting   | varchar(30) | YES  |     | NULL    |                |
+------------+-------------+------+-----+---------+----------------+

CREATE TABLE person (
  id int(11) NOT NULL auto_increment,
  first_name varchar(30) NOT NULL default '',
  last_name varchar(30) default NULL,
  greeting varchar(30) default NULL,
  PRIMARY KEY  (id)
) TYPE=MyISAM;
```

The `phone` table uses the `person.id` and the `phone_type` as the primary key:

```
+--------------+-------------+------+-----+---------+-------+
| Field        | Type        | Null | Key | Default | Extra |
+--------------+-------------+------+-----+---------+-------+
| id           | int(11)     |      | PRI | 0       |       |
| phone_type   | varchar(10) |      | PRI |         |       |
| phone_number | varchar(30) |      |     |         |       |
| note         | varchar(30) | YES  |     | NULL    |       |
+--------------+-------------+------+-----+---------+-------+

CREATE TABLE phone (
  id int(11) NOT NULL default '0',
  phone_type varchar(10) NOT NULL default '',
  phone_number varchar(30) NOT NULL default '',
  note varchar(30) default NULL,
  PRIMARY KEY  (id, phone_type)
) TYPE=MyISAM;
```

Creating a Phonebook from the Command Line

Sometimes it is useful to prototype with command-line programs before getting involved with user-interface details. This program offers a simple way of adding records. It loops prompting for data about a person. For each person, it loops prompting for phone data. Each loop ends when no data is entered for a required field.

Here's the code.

```
01: #!/usr/bin/perl -w
02: #
03: # program 14-1, Chapter 14, Listing 1
04: #

05: use DBI;
06: use strict;
07: my $Connection = DBI->connect
    ('DBI:mysql:test','bookuser','testpass')
08:    or die "Can't connect to database\nError: $DBI::errstr\nExiting";
```

Lines 1–8 start the program in the usual way, loading the DBI module and enabling warnings and the strict pragma. Then they get a connection to the database or exit with an informative error message.

```
09: my $Query_statement = undef;
10: my $Person_insert_statement = undef;
11: my $Phone_insert_statement = undef;
```

Lines 9–11 define global variables used to store statement handles. You'll see why they are global later on.

```
12: my %Fields = (
13:    id           => {required => 1, label => 'ID'          },
14:    first_name   => {required => 1, label => 'First Name'  },
15:    last_name    => {required => 0, label => 'Last Name'   },
16:    greeting     => {required => 0, label => 'Greeting'    },
17:    phone_type   => {required => 1, label => 'Number Type'},
18:    phone_number => {required => 1, label => 'Number'      },
19:    note         => {required => 0, label => 'Note'        },
20: );
```

Lines 12–20 define another global that holds useful information about the data the program uses. In addition to keeping a nice label for each column, this version stores whether or not the field is required; we'll use this for validating the input. The advantage of variables like this is that, if you add more columns to the database and to this variable, the program should just work with the new variables.

```
21: my @Person_prompts = qw(first_name last_name greeting);
22: my @Phone_prompts = qw(phone_type phone_number note);

23: my @Phone_cols = ('id', @Phone_prompts);
```

Lines 21–23 define more globals that control how the program works: the list of columns to prompt for and the columns to INSERT into the phone table.

```
24: while ( my %person = input_person() ) {
25:     while ( my %phone = input_phone() ) {
26:         $phone{id} = $person{id};
27:         add_phone( %phone );
28:     }
29: }
```

Lines 24–29 are the heart of the program. While the user provides another set of `person` data and `while` he or she types more `phone` details, these lines make sure the `person.id` is copied to the `phone.id`; then they `INSERT` the phone record. There's slightly more than that happening, but it's hidden away in the `input_person` and `input_phone` subroutines. Both subroutines are expected to return a hash of the data the user types. Each `while` condition is true if the hashes contain data. The condition ends when the hash is empty, such as when the user simply hits enter without any data.

```
30: $Connection->disconnect;
31: exit 0;
```

Lines 30–31. When the user has finished entering numbers and people, close the connection to the database and end the program.

```
32: sub input_person {
33:     my %person;

34:     print "Enter person details, (Fields marked with * are required).\nTo
exit program, hit CTRL-D.\n";
```

Line 32 starts the routine to collect the information needed for the `person` table.

Line 33 declares a hash used to store the data using the column names as keys.

Line 34 prints out some basic instructions to the user.

```
35:     foreach my $col ( @Person_prompts ) {
36:         my $req = $Fields{$col}{'required'} ? '*' : '';
37:         print "$Fields{$col}{'label'}$req:\t";
38:         my $line = <STDIN>;
39:         return    unless defined $line;    # no input
40:         chomp( $line );
41:         if ( $Fields{$col}{'required'} and $line !~ /\S+/ ) {
42:             warn "Required field missing, please re-enter\n";
43:             return;
44:         }
45:         $person{$col} = $line;
46:     }
```

Lines 35–46 make up the loop that prompts for, reads, validates, and saves user input for each column of the `person` table.

Line 36 checks whether the current field requires a value, and sets a variable that we'll show the user.

Lines 37 and 38 print the prompt and read a line of input.

Line 39 deals with undefined input, which happens when the user presses the EOF character (usually control-D), by returning no value from the subroutine. This ends the `while` loop in the main program and the program.

Lines 40–44 remove the line delimiter and, if the column is required, check that the input contains one or more nonspace (`\S+`) characters. If required fields are missing, the program returns rather abruptly.

Line 45 (finally!) stores the data we've just collected into the person hash.

Line 46 ends the loop that began on **line 35**.

```
47:     unless ( defined($person{id} = get_person_id(%person)) ) {
```

Line 47 checks whether the person already exists in the database. `get_person_id` returns the ID if it finds a person matching the values in the `person` hash.

```
48:         $person{id} = add_person( %person );
49:         return undef    unless $person{id};
50:     }
```

Line 48 adds the person if `get_person_id` doesn't find one.

Line 49 returns `undef` if, for some unknown reason the `add_person` had failed to add the person to the database table.

Line 50 closes the `unless` block that began on **line 47**.

```
51:     return %person;
52: }
```

Line 51 returns the validated input to the main program.

Line 52 ends the `input_person` subroutine.

```
53: sub get_person_id {
54:     my %person = @_;
55:     my $person_query_sql = qq(SELECT * FROM person
56:         WHERE first_name = ? AND last_name = ?);
```

Lines 53 begins the `get_person_id` subroutine. The `get_person_id` subroutine looks in the database for a row matching the name passed in. It returns the ID if found or `undef` if not.

Line 54 makes a local copy of the parameters, storing them into the %person hash.

Lines 55 and 56 create the SQL query string. The query has two placeholders for the values we are looking for.

```
57:     $Query_statement ||= $Connection->prepare( $person_query_sql )
58:         or die "Can't prepare query\nError: $DBI::errstr\nExiting";
```

Lines 57 and 58 prepare the SQL statement and get a statement handle, but only once. The first time the subroutine is called, the global $Query_statement is undefined, so the or-equals assignment operator executes the prepare method and stores the result. Once $Query_statement has a value, prepare is not repeated. We only need to prepare the statement once because we used placeholders. Each time we execute this SQL statement, we can pass different values and the placeholders dynamically change in the SQL.

We could have prepared the statement in the main program, but the SELECT statement would have been a long way away from where it's used. It's convenient to keep the SQL near where it's needed, if only so that you don't forget which columns and parameters it uses.

```
59:     if ($Query_statement->execute($person{first_name},$person{last_name})){
60:         my $href = $Query_statement->fetchrow_hashref();
61:         return undef    unless $href;
62:         return $href->{id};
63:     }
```

Line 59 executes the query passing in the names we get from the user.

Line 60 fetches a reference to a hash containing column:value pairs of the first matching person. (An enhancement would be to deal with multiple matches.)

Line 61 returns undef if the $href reference is undef, there are no matching records.

Line 62 returns the ID, we must have found a match.

Line 63 closes the if statement that began on **line 59**.

```
64:     else {
65:         warn "Can't execute query\nError: $DBI::errstr";
66:         return;
67:     }
68: }
```

Line 64 begins an else block. This block gets entered if, for some reason, the execute on **line 59** failed.

Line 65 prints an error message, informing the user of the problem.

Line 66 returns nothing back to the program.

Line 67 ends the if..else block which began on **line 59**.

Line 68 ends the get_person_id subroutine.

The add_person subroutine adds a row to the person table and returns the person ID or undef if the INSERT fails.

```
69: sub add_person {
70:     my %person = @_;
71:     my $person_insert_sql = 'INSERT INTO person('
72:         . join(',', @Person_prompts) . ') VALUES(
73:         . join(',', map {'?'} @Person_prompts) . ')';
```

Line 69 begins the add_person subroutine. The add_person subroutine adds a row to the person table and returns the person ID or undef if the INSERT fails.

Line 70 makes a private copy of the parameters and stores them into the %person hash.

Lines 71–73 define the INSERT statement we'll use. Rather than hard-code the column names, it uses the list defined near the start of the program. We use the same list to generate the placeholders with map.

```
74:     $Person_insert_statement ||= $Connection->prepare($person_insert_sql)
75:         or die "Can't prepare insert: $DBI::errstr";
```

Line 74 prepares the SQL statement and store the result in the global variable $Person_insert_statement.

Line 75 is a continuation of line 74, an error here is fatal, so we call the die method and inform the user.

```
76:     unless ($Person_insert_statement->execute(@person{@Person_prompts})) {
77:         warn "Can't execute insert: $DBI::errstr";
78:         return undef;
79:     }
```

Lines 76 executes the SQL INSERT. We wrapped the execute method inside of an unless statement so that we know if the statement executed or failed. The parameters to execute, which will be substituted for the placeholders in the SQL statement, are accessed as a "hash-slice", with @foo{keylist} syntax. In this case, the key list is a list of values corresponding to the keys from the @Person_prompts array.

Line 77 prints a warning if for some reason the execute statement on **line 76** failed.

Line 78 returns undef.

Line 79 ends the unless block from **line 76**.

Because we're using the same array to generate the SQL and supply the values, we need to change only the array if the number or order of fields changes.

```
80:     # and return the id    ***MySQL specific attribute****
81:     return $Person_insert_statement->{'mysql_insertid'};
82: }
```

Line 80 is a comment.

Line 81 uses a MySQL-specific attribute of the statement handle to get the value that MySQL assigns to the autoincrementing id column and returns it to signify success.

Other DBMS's do this in different ways. For instance, PostgreSQL uses "sequence generators" with nextval and currval functions. You can create a generator for person-IDs and use SQL like this:

```
INSERT INTO person(id,first_name,last_name,greeting)
VALUES(nextval('person_id'),?,?,?)
```

This stores the next value from the generator in id; then SELECT currval('person_id') to get the current value of the generator.

The input_phone subroutine is similar to input_person but is a little simpler because it doesn't check whether a matching record already exists.

```
83: sub input_phone {
84:     my %phone;

85:     print "Enter phone details, (Fields marked with * are required)\n";
86:     foreach my $col ( @Phone_prompts ) {
87:         my $req = $Fields{$col}{'required'} ? '*' : '';
88:         print "$Fields{$col}{'label'}$req:\t";
89:         my $line = <STDIN>;
90:         return    unless defined $line;    # no input
91:         chomp( $line );
92:         if ( $Fields{$col}{'required'} and $line !~ /\S+/ ) {
93:             warn "Required field missing, please re-enter\n";
94:             return;
95:         }
96:         $phone{$col} = $line;
97:     }
98:     return %phone;
99: }
```

Lines 83–99 are basically the same as **Lines 32–46** except that the data is stored in the %phone hash and we use the @Phone_prompts list of field-names to prompt for.

```
100: sub add_phone {
101:     my %phone = @_;
102:     my $phone_insert_sql = 'INSERT INTO phone('
103:         . join(',', @Phone_cols) . ') VALUES('
104:         . join(',', map {'?'} @Phone_cols) . ')';

105:     $Phone_insert_statement ||= $Connection->prepare($phone_insert_sql)
106:         or die "Can't prepare insert\nError: $DBI::errstr\nExiting";

107:     $Phone_insert_statement->execute(@phone{@Phone_cols})
108:         or warn "Can't execute insert\nError: $DBI::errstr";
109: }
```

Lines 100–109 are the add_phone subroutine. The add_phone subroutine corresponds to add_person except that it uses the @Phone_cols array for the column list.

One difference from add_person is that duplicate records are possible. The primary key of the phone table is id+phone_type, so if the user enters an existing value for phone_type, the execute will fail.

When the program runs, it looks like this:

```
Enter person details, (Fields marked with * are required)
To exit the program, hit CTRL-D.
First Name*:      Harry
Last Name:        Hotspur
Greeting:      Sir
Enter phone details, (Fields marked with * are required)
Number Type*:   work
Number*:        020s 555 1515
Note:
Enter phone details, (Fields marked with * are required)
Number Type*:
Required field missing, please re-enter
Enter person details, (Fields marked with * are required)
Forename*:
Required field missing, please re-enter
```

That's it! The program should be easy to change to allow for more columns; just change the %Fields hash and the arrays holding column names. There are a couple of changes you can make:

✦ Allow reinput of required fields without losing existing input.

✦ Check for duplicate keys in the phone table before adding a phone number, or allow the user to edit the values after an error.

Creating a Phone Number Lookup Program

Getting information into a database is a good thing, but the point of databases is to make the data easily available. The next program is the sort in which Perl excels. The program is intended to find phone numbers quickly. It runs from the command-line but can be run from macros. It looks like this:

```
$ phone
phone: please supply a name!
usage:      ./phone name
example:    ./phone Smith
$ phone chris
Chris Chalmers (Chris)
        home: (555) 232-5676
        mobile: 7746 654-2323
$
```

And here's the code:

```
01: #!/usr/bin/perl -w
02: #
03: # program 14-2, Chapter 14, Listing 2
04: #

05: use DBI;
06: use strict;
```

Lines 1–6 start in the usual way: warnings, strict, and the DBI module.

```
07: # check the user gave a search term
08: my $name = shift(@ARGV);
09: unless ($name) {
10:     die "$0: please supply a name!
11: usage:      $0 name
12: example:    $0 Smith\n";
13: }
```

Line 7 is simply a comment.

Line 8 uses the shift function to get a value from the @ARGV array. The @ARGV array is populated with the values that the user passed on the command line.

Line 9 checks to see if $name contains any data. If not, then this block of code is entered.

Lines 10–12 use the die function to print out a message to the user and program usage instructions. This causes the program to stop right here because it cannot go on unless it has data to search for.

Line 13 ends the unless block which began on **line 9**.

```
14: # connect to DBMS and get a database handle
15: my $dsn = 'DBI:mysql:BibleBook';
16: my $connection = DBI->connect($dsn, 'bookuser', 'testpass')
17:    or die "Can't connect to database: $dsn\nError: $DBI::errstr\nExiting";
```

Line 14 is a comment.

Line 15 creates a string named $dsn that is our data source name.

Line 16 creates a connection to the database and stores the result in the $connection string.

Line 17 calls the die function and prints out an error message telling the user that there was a problem connecting to the database.

This time the data source name string is in a separate variable so it can be reused in the error message. A school of thought says you shouldn't give out information unnecessarily — for example your database names — but since users can read the Perl source to see database and usernames and passwords, it seems harmless in this case. It would be different if this were used as a CGI program.

```
18: $name =~ /(\w+)/;
19: $name = $connection->quote("%$1%");
```

Lines 18 and 19 do some simple validation on the name. Because we don't entirely trust our users, we select only the first string of "word" characters; then we add SQL wildcard characters to it so that matches don't have to be complete. The DBI quote function properly quotes the resulting string.

```
20: # prepare the statement and get a statement handle
21: my $sql = <<EOS;
22: SELECT first_name,last_name,greeting,phone_type,phone_number,note
23: FROM person, phone
24: WHERE person.id = phone.id
25: AND (first_name   LIKE $name
26:      OR last_name LIKE $name
27:      OR greeting  LIKE $name)
28: EOS
```

Line 20 is a comment.

Line 21 begins a *here-document* that uses EOS as it's terminator. This means that anything between this line, and the EOS on **line 28** is treated as a string and will be stored in the $sql variable.

Lines 22–27 define the SELECT statement. The statement joins the person and phone tables on their common column and looks for the entered name in any of the name fields. Because the statement is used only once and the name has been quoted, $name is plugged straight into the SQL.

Line 28 ends the *here-document* that began on **line 21**.

```
29: my $query = $connection->prepare($sql)
30:    or die "$0: can't prepare '$sql'\nError: $DBI::errstr\nExiting";

31: # run the query
32: $query->execute();
```

Lines 29–30 `prepare` the query and call the `die` method if there's a problem.

Line 31 is a comment.

Line 32 executes the query. No parameters are necessary.

```
33: # get/display the results
34: my $current_name = '';
```

Line 33 is a comment.

Line 34 defines the variable used to keep track of when the name changes, and initially sets it to an empty string.

```
35: while (my @data = $query->fetchrow()) {
```

Line 35 begins a `while` loop that is the core of this program. This `while` loop will continue as long as `fetchrow` returns more data.

```
36:    if ($current_name ne "$data[0] $data[1]") {
37:        print "$data[0] $data[1] ($data[2])\n";
38:        $current_name = "$data[0] $data[1]";
39:    }
```

Line 36 checks to see if the value in `$current_name` is not equal to the values in `"$data[0] $data[1]"`. If not, then the name has changed so we need to print out the new contact name. If the name is the same, we don't print out the name again, instead we move on and print out the next phone number.

Line 37 prints out the current contact's name and greeting.

Line 38 stores the first name (`$data[0]`) and last name (`$data[1]`) into the `$current_name` string.

Line 39 ends the `if` block.

```
40:    print "\t$data[3]: $data[4]\t$data[5]\n";
41: }
```

Line 40 prints the phone data.

Line 41 ends the `while` loop that began on **line 35**.

```
42: # tidy up
43: $query->finish();
44: $connection->disconnect();
45: exit 0;
```

Line 42 is a comment.

Lines 43–45 release any resources the statement and database handles hold before exiting.

This was a simple program with no subroutines and one single purpose.

Creating a Graphical Phonebook Application

This program uses a lot of the techniques we've already used to build a "full-function" maintenance program for the person and phone tables. It uses the Tk module to make it a cross-platform graphical application. If you know Tk well, you'll find this application simple. But if you don't know Tk well, you'll have to pay close attention to the explanation of the code.

```
01: #!/usr/bin/perl -w
02: # program 14-3
03: # Chapter 14
04: # Listing 3

05: use strict;
06: use DBI;
07: use Tk;
```

Lines 1–7 start in the usual way, with the addition of the Tk module.

```
08: my $Connection = DBI->connect
   ('DBI:mysql:BibleBook', 'bookuser', 'testpass')
09:          or die "Can't connect to database: $DBI::errstr";
```

Lines 8–9 connect to the database and get a database handle. We call the die method and print an error message if we can't connect.

```
10: my %Fields = (
11:     id            => {required => 1, label => 'ID'          },
12:     first_name    => {required => 1, label => 'Forename'    },
13:     last_name     => {required => 0, label => 'Surname'     },
14:     greeting      => {required => 0, label => 'Greeting'    },
15:     phone_type    => {required => 1, label => 'Number Type'},
16:     phone_number  => {required => 1, label => 'Number'      },
17:     note          => {required => 0, label => 'Note'        },
18: );

19: my @Person_prompts = qw(first_name last_name greeting);
```

```
20: my @Phone_prompts  = qw(phone_type phone_number note);
21: my @Phone_cols     = ('id', @Phone_prompts);
22: my $Main_win;

23: my ($pr_lst, $ph_lst);
```

Lines 10–21 reuse some of the global variables code from the earlier command-line program that make the program easy to extend.

Line 22 is a new global variable, $Main_win, which holds the object representing the program's main window.

Line 23 declares a couple variables that we'll be using.

```
24: show_main_form();
25: MainLoop();
26: $Connection->disconnect();
27: exit 0;
```

Line 24 calls the show_main_form subroutine to build and display the main program window.

Line 25 starts TK's main event-loop. MainLoop() finishes when the user closes the main program window.

Line 26 cleanly disconnects us from the database.

Line 27 exits the program.

```
28: sub show_main_form {
```

Line 28 begins the show_main_form subroutine which is the largest single subroutine in the program. It creates and displays the main window (with list boxes for people and phone numbers and buttons to add) and updates and deletes people and phone records. The buttons and list boxes are the jumping-off points for the rest of the code in the program.

```
29:     $Main_win = MainWindow->new(-title => 'Perl/Tk PhoneBook');
```

Line 29 creates the main window and gives it a title. A reference to the main window is stored in a global variable because it's needed whenever we create a window.

```
30:     my $person_frame = $Main_win->Frame();

31:     $pr_lst = $person_frame->Scrolled('Listbox',
32:         -scrollbars => 'oe', -height => 10,
33:         -selectmode => 'browse');

34:     my $phone_frame = $Main_win->Frame();
```

```
35:      $ph_lst = $phone_frame->Scrolled('Listbox',
36:          -scrollbars => 'oe', -height => 4,
37:          -selectmode => 'browse');
```

Lines 30–37 create frames and list boxes for people and phone numbers. We use frames to group and control the placement of related widgets. The frames are children of the main window, the list boxes children of the frames. Tk list boxes don't, by default, have scrollbars. We've used the Scrolled constructor to create a list box with a scrollbar attached. The scrollbar attribute 'oe' means the scrollbar is "optional"—only displayed when necessary—and is attached to the east (right-hand) side of the list box.

```
38:      my $person_add_b =
             $person_frame->Button(-text => 'Add Person',
39:          -command => sub {
40:              show_person_form('Add Person');
41:              fill_person_list();
42:          }
43:      );
```

Line 38 creates a variable named $person_add_b and begins the code that will create an "Add Person" button in the $person_frame.

Line 39 declares an anonymous subroutine that gets executed whenever this button is pressed.

Line 40 is a call to the show_person_form subroutine. The "Add Person" text that is passed in the function call is used as the title of the window.

Line 41 is a call to the fill_person_list subroutine which fills the person listbox with data.

Line 42 ends the anonymous subroutine.

Line 43 ends the $person_add_b button declaration.

```
44:      my $person_upd_b =
             $person_frame->Button(-text => 'Update Person',
45:          -state => 'disabled',
46:          -command => sub {
47:              show_person_form('Update Person',
48:                  $pr_lst->get('active'));

49:              fill_person_list();

50:          }
51:      );
```

Line 44 creates a variable named $person_upd_b and begins the code that will create an "Add Person" button in the $person_frame.

Line 45 sets the initial state of this button to be disabled.

Line 46 declares an anonymous subroutine that gets executed whenever this button is pressed.

Lines 47–48 are a call to the show_person_form subroutine. The "Update Person" text that is passed in the function call is used as the title of the window. The $pr_lst->get('active') gets the "active" person in the list (the last person that was selected) and passes this value to the show_person_form subroutine so that when the new window pops up, it is pre-populated with the selected user's data.

Line 49 is a call to the fill_person_list subroutine which fills the person listbox with data.

Line 50 ends the anonymous subroutine.

Line 51 ends the $person_upd_b button declaration.

```
52:     my $person_del_b =
            $person_frame->Button(-text => 'Delete Person',
53:         -state => 'disabled',
54:         -command => sub {
55:             chk_del_person($pr_lst->get('active'));

56:             fill_person_list();


57:         }
58:     );
```

Line 52 creates a variable named $person_del_b and begins the code that will create a "Delete Person" button in the $person_frame.

Line 53 sets the initial state of this button to be disabled.

Line 54 declares an anonymous subroutine that gets executed whenever this button is pressed.

Line 55 is a call to the chk_del_person subroutine. The $pr_lst->get ('active') gets the "active" person in the list (the last person that was selected) and passes this value to the chk_del_person subroutine so that we can pop up a window to verify that the user really wants to delete this person.

Line 56 is a call to the fill_person_list subroutine, which fills the person listbox with data.

Line 57 ends the anonymous subroutine.

Line 58 ends the $person_del_b button declaration.

```
59:     my $phone_add_b = $phone_frame->Button(-text => 'Add Phone',
60:         -state => 'disabled',
61:         -command => sub {
62:             show_phone_form('Add Phone');
63:         }
64:     );
```

Line 59 creates a variable named $phone_add_b and begins the code that will create an "Add Phone" button in the $phone_frame.

Line 60 sets the initial state of this button to be disabled.

Line 61 declares an anonymous subroutine that gets executed whenever this button is pressed.

Line 62 is a call to the show_phone_form subroutine. The "Add Phone" text that is passed in the function call is used as the title of the window. This subroutine call will display a blank "add phone" window.

Line 63 ends the anonymous subroutine.

Line 64 ends the $phone_add_b button declaration.

```
65:     my $phone_upd_b = $phone_frame->Button(-text => 'Update Phone',
66:         -state => 'disabled',
67:         -command => sub {
68:             show_phone_form('Update Phone', $ph-lst->get($ph_lst-
>curselection()));
69:         }
70:     );
```

Line 65 creates a variable named $phone_upd_b and begins the code that will create an "Update Phone" button in the $phone_frame.

Line 66 sets the initial state of this button to be disabled.

Line 67 declares an anonymous subroutine that gets executed whenever this button is pressed.

Line 68 is a call to the show_phone_form subroutine. The "Update Phone" text that is passed in the function call is used as the title of the window. The $ph_lst->get($ph_lst->curselection()) gets the phone number in the list that is selected and passes this value to the show_phone_form subroutine so that when we can pop up the phone number editing window the data is pre-populated.

Line 69 ends the anonymous subroutine.

Line 70 ends the $phone_upd_b button declaration.

```
71:        my $phone_del_b = $phone_frame->Button(-text => 'Delete Phone',
72:            state => 'disabled',
73:          -command => sub {
74:              chk_del_phone(
75:                        $ph_lst->get($ph_lst->curselection()));
76:              fill_phone_list($pr_lst->get($pr_lst->curselection()));
77:          }
78:      );
```

Line 71 creates a variable named `$phone_del_b` and begins the code that will create a "Delete Phone" button in the `$phone_frame`.

Line 72 sets the initial state of this button to be disabled.

Line 73 declares an anonymous subroutine that gets executed whenever this button is pressed.

Lines 74 and 75 are a call to the `chk_del_phone` subroutine. The `$pr_lst->get($pr_lst->curselection())` and the `$ph_lst->get` `($ph_lst->curselection())` get the "active" person and phone number in the list and pass these values to the `chk_del_phone` subroutine so that we can pop up a window to verify that the user really wants to delete this phone number.

Line 76 is a call to the `fill_phone_list` subroutine, which fills the phone listbox with data.

Line 77 ends the anonymous subroutine.

Line 78 ends the `$person_del_b` button declaration.

```
79:        $person_frame->pack( -side => 'top', -fill => 'both', -expand => 1);
80:        $person_list->pack( -side => 'top', -fill => 'both', -expand => 1);

81:        foreach my $button ($person_add_b, $person_upd_b, $person_del_b) {
82:            $button->pack(-side => 'left');
83:        }

84:        $phone_frame->pack( -side => 'top', -fill => 'both', -expand => 1);
85:        $phone_list->pack( -side => 'top', -fill => 'both', -expand => 1);

86:        foreach my $button ($phone_add_b, $phone_upd_b, $phone_del_b) {
87:            $button->pack(-side => 'left');
88:        }
```

Lines 79–88 use the pack geometry manager to display the widgets we've created.

The packer works by placing each widget against one side of the parent widget, optionally expanding the child widget to fill a rectangle. The next widget is placed against one side of the (reduced) space in the parent widget.

```
89:       $Main_win->Button( -text => 'Exit', -command => sub {
90:            $Connection->disconnect();
91:            $Main_win->withdraw();
92:            exit 0;
93:         } )->pack();
```

Lines 89–93 create one more widget: a button that's immediately packed at the bottom of the main window. This is our "Exit" button that ends the program.

```
94:       $pr_lst->bind( '<Button-1>',
95:          sub {
96:             return  unless defined $pr_lst->curselection();
97:             $person_upd_b->configure(-state => 'active');
98:             $person_del_b->configure(-state => 'active');
99:             $phone_add_b->configure(-state => 'active');
100:             fill_phone_list($pr_lst->get($pr_lst->curselection()));
101:          }
102:       );
```

Lines 94–102 bind actions — anonymous subroutines — to mouse clicks. A single click with the first mouse button on the list boxes checks whether anything has been selected and, if so, activates the buttons.

Line 94 binds these actions on the person list ($pr_lst object) to mouse button 1.

Line 95 declares an anonymous subroutine that is executed when an item on the person list listbox is clicked.

Line 96 returns unless a person was selected.

Lines 97–99 set the person update, person delete, and phone add buttons to their active state.

Line 100 populates the phone list with the selected persons phone numbers.

Line 101 ends the anonymous subroutine.

Line 102 ends the button 1 click declaration.

```
103:      $ph_lst->bind( '<Button-1>',
104:         sub {
105:            return  unless defined $ph_lst->curselection();
106:            $phone_upd_b->configure(-state => 'active');
107:            $phone_del_b->configure(-state => 'active');
108:         }
109:      );
```

Line 103 binds a button 1 single click to the phone list ($ph_lst object).

Line 104 declares an anonymous subroutine that is executed when an item on the phone list listbox is clicked.

Line 105 returns unless a phone number was selected.

Lines 106 and 107 set the phone update, and phone delete buttons to their active state.

Line 108 ends the anonymous subroutine.

Line 109 ends the button 1 click declaration.

```
110:     $pr_lst->bind( '<Double-Button-1>',
111:         sub {
112:             return  unless defined $pr_lst->curselection();
113:             show_person_form('Update Person',
114:                     $pr_lst->get($pr_lst->curselection()));
115:             fill_person_list();
116:             fill_phone_list($pr_lst->curselection());
117:         }
118:     );
```

Line 110 binds these actions on the person list ($pr_lst object) to a mouse button 1 double-click.

Line 111 declares an anonymous subroutine that is executed when an item on the person list listbox is double-clicked.

Line 112 returns unless a person was selected.

Lines 113 and 114 calls the show_person_form subroutine and passes in the title "Update Person" and the current userid.

Line 115 populates the person list.

Line 116 populates the phone list with the selected person's phone numbers.

Line 117 ends the anonymous subroutine.

Line 118 ends the button 1 double-click declaration.

```
119:     $ph_lst->bind( '<Double-Button-1>',
120:         sub {
121:             return  unless defined $ph_lst->curselection();
122:             show_phone_form('Update Phone', $pr_lst->get('active'),
123:                     $ph_lst->get('active'));
124:             fill_phone_list($ph_lst, $pr_lst->get('active'));
125:         }
126:     );
```

Line 119 binds these actions on the phone list ($ph_lst object) to a mouse button 1 double-click.

Line 120 declares an anonymous subroutine that is executed when an item on the phone number list listbox is double-clicked.

Line 121 returns unless a person was selected.

Lines 122 and 123 calls the show_phone_form subroutine and passes in the title "Update Phone", the current userid, and the current phone list selection.

Line 124 populates the phone list with the selected person's phone numbers.

Line 125 ends the anonymous subroutine.

Line 126 ends the button 1 double-click declaration.

So, a single click with the first mouse button on the list boxes checks whether anything has been selected and, if so, activates the buttons. Clicking a person also runs the subroutine to fill in the phone list box. Actually, the way list boxes work is that a click selects the nearest item so; if there are any items in the list box, clicking will select one of them.

A double click with the first button runs the update function on the selected item and refills the list box in case it has changed.

```
127:      fill_person_list();
128:         return;
129: }
```

Line 127 fills the person list box for the first time before the subroutine returns to the main program.

Line 128 returns us to where the program called.

Line 129 ends this subroutine.

When the main program calls MainLoop(), the main form is displayed and the program waits for clicks on buttons or list boxes and runs the related code.

Most of the remaining functions are called from buttons or bind commands set up in show_main_form. The first of these is show_person_form. Its job is to draw the form for adding new person records or updating existing ones.

So, at this point, you have created the main program form, which should look something like Figure 14-1.

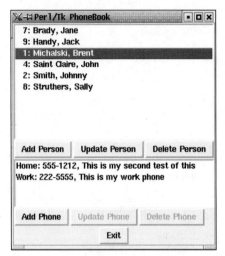

Figure 14-1: Main program form

```
130:   sub show_person_form{
131:       my $label = shift;
132:       my $person = shift;
133:       my %person;
```

Line 130 begins the show_person_form subroutine.

Lines 131 and 132 declare a couple scalar variables and shift that values passed to this subroutine into them.

Line 133 declares a hash that we'll be using.

```
134:       if ($person) {
135:           $person{'id'} = get_person_id($person);

136:           my $sql = 'SELECT * FROM person WHERE id = ?';
137:           my $array_ref = $Connection->selectall_arrayref($sql, undef,
138:         $person{'id'});

139:           my $i = 1;
140:           foreach my $col ( @Person_prompts ) {
141:               $person{$col} = $array_ref->[0]->[$i];
142:               $i++;
143:           }
144:       }
```

Line 134 checks to see if $person contains a value, if so, the code block is entered.

Line 135 sets the id key in the %person hash ($person{'id'}) to the value returned by the call to the get_person_id subroutine.

Line 136 creates the SQL needed to get all of the data from the person table which matches the id value we pass to the placeholder.

Line 137 declares a variable named $array_ref which stores the result of the $Connection->selectall_arrayref call.

Line 138 continues **line 137**, the $person{'id'} is the value that will replace the placeholder in the SQL statement.

Line 139 creates a scalar variable named $i that we'll use for an array index counter.

Line 140 is a foreach loop that loops through each of the values in the @Person_prompts array. Each time through the loop, the current value is stored in the $col variable.

Line 141 sets $person{$col} to the value that was returned from the SQL call. $array_ref->[0]->[$i] is the current column value. We know this because since we searched on the primary key value in the table (the id field), there can only be one record returned to us, it will be at $array_ref->[0]. The extra ->[$i] will be each field from the record that was returned to us.

Line 142 increments the $i variable.

Line 143 ends for foreach loop.

Line 144 ends the if code block.

If the query fails (it shouldn't, because the data we're looking for comes from the database), we end up filling the person hash with undefined values. An alternative is to warn the user, asking him or her to try again.

```
145:    my $person_form = $Main_win->Toplevel( -title => $label );
```

Line 145 creates a new top-level window to hold the person add/update form.

```
146:    my $row = 0;
147:    my %entry;
```

Line 146 declares a variable named $row and sets it to 0.

Line 147 declares a hash named %entry.

```
148:    foreach my $col ( @Person_prompts ) {
149:        my $req = $Fields{$col}{'required'} ? '*' : '';
```

Line 148 begins a foreach loop that loops through all of the values in @Person_prompts. Each time through the loop the current value gets stored in the $col variable.

Line 149 creates a variable named $req and, if the current field is a required field, stores a * into $req. If the field is not required, $req is set to an empty string.

```
150:        $person_form->Label( -text => "$Fields{$col}{'label'}$req ")->
151:            grid( -row => $row, -column => 0, -sticky => 'e');
```

Lines 150 and 151 create the field label for the current field and place it on the form.

```
152:        $entry{$col} = $person_form->Entry( -width => 20,
153:            -textvariable => \$person{$col} )->
154:            grid(-row => $row++, -column => 1, -sticky => 'w');
155:    }
```

Lines 152–154 create the text entry fields and place them on the form.

Line 155 closes the foreach loop which began on **line 148**.

```
156:    $person_form->Button( -text => 'Close',
157:        -command => sub { $person_form->withdraw() })->
158:            grid(-row => $row, -column => 0, -sticky => 'w');
```

Lines 156–158 create a "Close" button on the form.

Line 157 sets the action for the button to the anonymous subroutine on this line — which simply closes the window. The action of the close button is a method call. It's easier to put the call in an anonymous subroutine.

```
159:    $person_form->Button( -text => $label,
160:        -command => [ \&add_upd_person, $label, $person_form, \%entry])->
161:            grid(-row => $row, -column => 1, -sticky => 'w');
```

Lines 159–161 create a button on the page, with the value from $label as the button label.

Line 160 sets the command for this button and passes the %entry hash so that the data can pre-populate the form.

```
162:    return;
163: }
```

Line 162 returns.

Line 163 ends this subroutine.

The person form should look similar to Figure 14-2.

Figure 14-2: Person form

The show_phone_form does the same job as show_person_form but has to do more checking.

```
164: sub show_phone_form {
165:     my $label = shift;
166:     my $person = get_person_id($pr_lst->get('active'));
167:     my $phone = shift;
168:   my %phone;
```

Lines 165–168 declare some variables and use the shift function to read them in from the values passed to the subroutine.

Line 166 declares the $person variable and uses the get_person_id subroutine to get the value of the currently selected person.

```
169:     unless ($person) {
170:         $Main_win->messageBox(-icon => 'error', -type => 'OK',
171:             -title => 'Select a Person',
172:             -message => 'Please select a person and retry.');
173:         return;
174:     }
```

Lines 169–174 confirm that a person item has been supplied. If not, the subroutine can't do anything useful except tell the user and return. This should never happen, but it doesn't hurt to check.

```
175:     if ($phone) {
176:         $phone =~ /^(.*?): (.*?), (.*)/;
177:         @phone{@Phone_prompts} = ($1, $2, $3);
178:     }
```

Lines 175–178 pick the phone information out of the phone list-box entry. The three fields the match operation selects are assigned to a hash slice that uses the

Phone_prompts array. This time, it just saves typing. If the format of the phone list-box entry changes, we'll have to change the regular expression and the assignment.

```
179:    elsif ($label =~ /Update/) {
180:        $Main_win->messageBox(-icon => 'error', -type => 'OK',
181:            -title => 'Select a Phone',
182:            -message => 'Please select a phone and retry.');
183:        return;
184:    }
```

Lines 179–184 deal with the case of no phone item when we're supposed to be updating. Again, this shouldn't happen; if it does, we throw up a message box to tell the user and return to the main form.

```
185:    my $phone_form = $Main_win->Toplevel( -title => $label );
186:    my $row = 0;
187:    my %entry;

188:    foreach my $col ( @Phone_prompts ) {
189:        my $req = $Fields{$col}{'required'} ? '*' : '';

190:        $phone_form->Label( -text => "$Fields{$col}{'label'}$req ")->
191:            grid( -row => $row, -column => 0, -sticky => 'e');

192:        $entry{$col} = $phone_form->Entry( -width => 20,
193:                -textvariable => \$phone{$col} )->
194:            grid(-row => $row++, -column => 1, -sticky => 'w');
195:    }
196:    $phone_form->Button( -text => 'Close',
197:        -command => sub { $phone_form->withdraw() })->
198:            grid(-row => $row, -column => 0, -sticky => 'w');

199:    $phone_form->Button( -text => $label,
200:        -command => [ \&add_upd_phone, $label, $phone_form, \%entry,
201:                get_person_id($person) ])->
202:            grid(-row => $row, -column => 1, -sticky => 'w');

203:    return;
204: }
```

Lines 185–204 create a form and buttons in the same way as show_person_form.

The phone from should look like Figure 14-3.

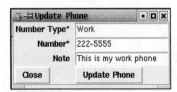

Figure 14-3: Phone form

```
205: sub fill_pr_lst {
```

Line 205 begins the `fill_pr_lst` subroutine, which gets a list box, deletes any items in it, and fills it with data from the `person` table.

```
206:     my $sql = 'SELECT id,last_name,first_name FROM person '
207:            . 'ORDER by last_name,first_name';
```

Lines 206 and **207** define the SQL query, hard coded this time.

```
208:     my $ptr = $Connection->selectall_hashref($sql, undef);
```

Line 208 executes the query and fetches all the data, once again in the form of a reference to an array of hashes. If the fetch fails, it returns `undef`.

```
209:     $pr_lst->delete(0, 'end');
210:     $pr_lit->insert('end', map { sprintf "%4d: %-s",
211:                      $_->{id}, "$_->{last_name}, $_->{first_name}" } @{$ptr}
);
212: }
```

Line 209 deletes any values already in the list-box.

Lines 210–211 inserts into the list-box the result of the query. Since the `insert` method can add a list of items, we've used `map` to generate the list. `map` runs `sprintf` on each element of the list we get from dereferencing `$plist_ref`. Each element is a hash, so it is dereferenced again (`$_->{id}`) to get the actual values.

Line 212 ends the `fill_pr_lst` subroutine.

```
213: sub fill_ph_lst {
214:     my $person_id = get_person_id( shift );

215:     my $sql = 'SELECT phone_type,phone_number,note FROM phone '
216:            . 'WHERE id = ? '
217:            . 'ORDER by phone_type';

218:     my $ptr = $Connection->selectall_arrayref($sql, undef, $person_id);

219:     $ph_lst->delete(0, 'end');
220:     $ph_lst->insert('end', map {
221:                      "$_->[0]: $_->[1], $_->[2] "} @{$ptr} );
222:     return;
223: }
```

Lines 213–223 repeat the functionality for the phone list box. This time, we're interested only in numbers for a particular person's ID. Code in the `show_phone_form` subroutine depends on the format of the string added to the list box, so this shouldn't be changed separately.

```
224: sub get_person_id {
225:     my $person = shift;
226:     $person =~ /^\s*(\d+):?/;
227:     return $1;
228: }
```

Lines 224–228 define a helper function that gets passed the person data from the person list-box. Then, on **line 226**, we filter out everything but the person ID.

The add_upd_person and add_upd_phone subroutines run from the confirm button on the corresponding form.

```
229: sub add_upd_person {
230:     my $label       = shift;
231:     my $person_form = shift;
232:     my $id          = shift;
233:     my $form_entry  = shift;
```

Line 229 begins the add_upd_person subroutine.

Lines **230–233** declare several scalar variables and load them with the values that were passed to the subroutine.

```
234:     my (%person, $sql);
```

```
235:     my $missing_fields = 0;
```

Lines 234–235 define a hash to store the person data, a scalar for the SQL statement, and a flag to set if required fields are missing.

```
236:     foreach my $col ( @Person_prompts ) {
237:         $person{$col} = $form_entry->{$col}->get();
238:         $missing_fields = 1
239:             if $Fields{$col}{'required'} && ! length $person{$col};
240:     }
```

Lines 236–240 get the values from the entry widgets and store them in the person hash. If the field is required and has zero length we set the $missing_fields flag to 1. This curious construction exists because the get() method returns a zero length, but defined, string when the field is empty. A test for defined always succeeds; a test for "Truth" fails with an input of 0, which might be a valid value.

```
241:     if ($missing_fields) {
242:         $Main_win->messageBox(-icon => 'error', -type => 'OK',
243:             -title => 'Required Fields Missing',
244:             -message => "Please fill fields marked '*'");
245:         return;
246:     }
```

Lines 241–246 display a message box if there are missing fields. The immediate return means that the person form stays active and the user can correct his or her entry.

```
247:      if ($label =~ /^Add/) {
248:          $sql = 'INSERT INTO person('
249:              . join(',', @Person_prompts) . ') VALUES('


250:              . join(',', map {'?'} @Person_prompts) . ')';

251:          unless ( $Connection->do( $sql, undef,
252:                          @person{@Person_prompts}) ) {
253:              $Main_win->messageBox(-icon => 'error', -type => 'OK',
254:                  -title => 'Error Adding Person',
255:                  -message => "$DBI::errstr, please correct and retry.");

256:              return;
257:          }
258:      }
```

Line 247 checks to see if $label begins with "Add". If so, the code block is entered.

Lines 248–250 create the SQL statement needed to insert a person into the database.

Lines 251–257 are the SQL do statement that actually executes the SQL statement. If an error occurs, then this code block is entered and we display a message box informing the user of the problem. Once again, an immediate return leaves the person form visible.

Line 258 ends the if portion of this if..else block.

```
259:      else {  # assume we're updating
260:          $sql = 'UPDATE person SET '
261:              . join(',', map {"$_ = ?"} @Person_prompts)
262:              . ' WHERE id = ?';

263:          unless ( $Connection->do($sql, undef,
264:                  @person{@Person_prompts}, $id) ) {
265:              $Main_win->messageBox(-icon => 'error', -type => 'OK',
266:                  -title => 'Error Updating Person',
267:                  -message => "$DBI::errstr, please correct and retry.");
268:              return;
269:          }
270:      }
```

Lines 259–270 performs the same basic function as the block above where we inserted a new person. In this block, however, we are updating an existing person.

```
271:    fill_pr_list();
272:    $person_form->withdraw();
273:    return;
274: }
```

Line 271 calls the `fill_pr_list` subroutine to refresh the person list-box with the new, updated information.

Line 272 removes the person `form`, since the operation has succeeded.

Line 273 returns us to where the subroutine was called.

Line 274 ends the `add_upd_person` subroutine.

```
275: sub add_upd_phone {
276:     my (%phone, $sql);
277:     my $missing_fields = 0;

278:     my $label      = shift;
279:     my $phone_form = shift;
280:     my $form_entry = shift;
281:     $phone{'id'}   = shift;
```

Line 275 begins the `add_upd_phone` subroutine.

Lines 276–277 define a hash to store the person data, a scalar for the SQL statement, and a flag to set if required fields are missing.

Lines **278–281** declare several scalar variables and load them with the values that were passed to the subroutine.

```
282:     foreach my $col ( @Phone_prompts ) {
283:         $phone{$col} = $form_entry->{$col}->get();
284:         $missing_fields = 1
285:             if $Fields{$col}{'required'} && ! length $phone{$col};
286:     }
```

Lines 282–286 get the values from the entry widgets and store them in the phone hash. If the field is required and has zero length we set the `$missing_fields` flag to 1.

This curious construction exists because the `get()` method returns a zero length, but defined, string when the field is empty. A test for `defined` always succeeds; a test for "Truth" fails with an input of 0, which might be a valid value.

```
287:     if ($missing_fields) {
288:         $Main_win->messageBox(-icon => 'error', -type => 'OK',
289:             -title => 'Required Fields Missing',
290:             -message => "Please fill fields marked '*'");
291:         return;
292:     }
```

Lines 287–292 display a message box if there are missing fields. The immediate return means that the `person` form stays active and the user can correct his or her entry.

```
293:    if ($label =~ /^Add/) {
294:        $sql = 'INSERT INTO phone('
295:            . join(',', @Phone_cols) . ') VALUES('
296:            . join(',', map {'?'} @Phone_cols) . ')';

297:        unless ( $Connection->do($sql, undef, @phone{@Phone_cols}) ) {
298:            $Main_win->messageBox(-icon => 'error', -type => 'OK',
299:                -title => 'Error Adding Phone',
300:                -message => "$DBI::errstr, please correct and retry.");
301:            return;
302:        }
303:    }
```

Line 293 checks to see if `$label` begins with "Add". If so, the code block is entered.

Lines 294–296 create the SQL statement needed to insert a phone number into the database.

Lines 297–302 are the SQL do statement that actually executes the SQL statement. If an error occurs, then this code block is entered and we display a message box informing the user of the problem. Once again, an immediate return leaves the `phone` form visible.

Line 303 ends the `if` portion of this `if..else` block.

```
304:    else {  # assume we're updating
305:        $sql = 'UPDATE phone SET '
306:            . join(',', map {"$_ = ?"} @Phone_prompts)
307:            . ' WHERE id = ? AND phone_type = ?';

308:        unless ( $Connection->do($sql, undef, @phone{@Phone_prompts},
309:                $phone{'id'}, $phone{'phone_type'}) ) {
310:            $Main_win->messageBox(-icon => 'error', -type => 'OK',
311:                -title => 'Error Updating Phone',
312:                -message => "$DBI::errstr, please correct and retry.");
313:            return;
314:        }
315:    }

316:    fill_pr_lst();
317:    fill_ph_lst($phone{'id'});
318:    $phone_form->withdraw();
319:    return;
320: }
```

Lines 304–320 performs the same basic function as the block above where we inserted a new phone number. In this block, however, we are updating an existing phone number.

The `chk_del_person` and `chk_del_phone` subroutines below are called when the Delete buttons on the main window are pressed. Both prompt for confirmation before attempting the delete.

```
321: sub chk_del_person {
322:     my $person = shift;
323:     my $person_id = get_person_id($person);
```

Line 321 begins the `chk_del_person` subroutine.

Line 322 creates a scalar variable named `$person` and uses the `shift` function to store the value passed to the subroutine into it.

Line 323 uses the `get_person_id` subroutine to extract the person ID from the value passed to it. This value is then stored in the `$person_id` variable.

```
324:     my $button = $Main_win->messageBox(-icon => 'question',
325:         -type => 'YesNo', -title => 'Delete Person',
326:         -message => "Delete $person and related phone numbers?");
```

Lines 324–326 display a message window with Yes and No buttons. The return value of the `messageBox` method is the label on the button pressed.

```
327:     if ($button eq 'Yes') {
```

Line 327 looks for the Yes button.

```
328:         eval {
329:             my $sql = 'DELETE FROM phone where id = ?';
330:             $Connection->do($sql, undef, $person_id)
331:                 or die $DBI::errstr;

332:             $sql = 'DELETE FROM person where id = ?';
333:             $Connection->do($sql, undef, $person_id)
334:                 or die $DBI::errstr;
335:         };
```

Lines 328–335 delete all the phone numbers for the person ID and delete the person. Both the SQL commands `die` on errors, but the surrounding `eval` catches `die`. This means that if the first delete fails, we don't attempt the second.

```
336:         if ($@) {
337:             $Main_win->messageBox(-icon => 'error', -type => 'OK',
338:                 -title => 'Error Deleting Person',
339:                 -message => $DBI::errstr);
340:         }
341:     }
342:     return;
343: }
```

Lines 336–343 check whether eval has failed by looking at $@. If either of the delete commands has failed, $@ will hold the message from die. We then display an error message to the user to tell them that the delete failed.

The delete confirmation window should look something like Figure 14-4.

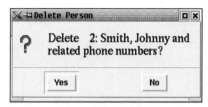

Figure 14-4: Delete confirmation window

If the program has used transactions (and the DBMS supported them), this is where it issues a rollback to undo changes to the database. Since we're not using transactions, the program just shows the error in another message window.

```
344: sub chk_del_phone {
345:     my $person = shift;
346:     my $phone = shift;
347:     my $person_id = get_person_id($person);

348:     $phone =~ /^(.*?):/;
349:     my $phone_type = $1;

350:     my $button = $Main_win->messageBox(-icon => 'question',
351:         -type => 'YesNo', -title => 'Delete Phone',
352:         -message => "Delete the number $phone for $person?");

353:     if ($button eq 'Yes') {
354:         eval {
355:             my $sql = 'DELETE FROM phone where id = ? AND phone_type = ?';
356:             $Connection->do($sql, undef, $person_id, $phone_type)
357:                 or die $DBI::errstr;
358:         };
359:         if ($@) {
360:             $Main_win->messageBox(-icon => 'error', -type => 'OK',
361:                 -title => 'Error Deleting Phone Number',
362:                 -message => $DBI::errstr);
363:         }
364:     }
365:     return;
366: }
```

Lines 344–366 delete the selected phone record. This subroutine is almost identical to the chk_del_person subroutine.

Lines 348–349 get the `phone_type` out of the phone list-box entry.

That completes the phonebook program — a cross-platform application to maintain `person` and `phone` tables in fewer than 400 lines of code!

Summary

There we have it — a quick, command-line, data-load program, an even quicker number lookup, and a full-featured GUI application (all with error checking, all able to be modified quite easily).

Try them out, and try adding columns to the tables and the data structure in the program. It's a thrilling experience to have simple changes to data, changing what programs do!

Program Listings

Listings 14-1 to 14-3 show the complete and uninterrupted code for the applications in this chapter.

Listing 14-1: **Command-line phonebook code**

```
01: #!/usr/bin/perl -w
02: #
03: # program 14-1, Chapter 14, Listing 1
04: #

05: use DBI;
06: use strict;
07: my $Connection = DBI->connect
    ('DBI:mysql:test','bookuser','testpass')
08:     or die "Can't connect to database\nError: $DBI::errstr\nExiting";

09: my $Query_statement = undef;
10: my $Person_insert_statement = undef;
11: my $Phone_insert_statement = undef;

12: my %Fields = (
13:     id             => {required => 1, label => 'ID'          },
14:     first_name     => {required => 1, label => 'First Name'  },
15:     last_name      => {required => 0, label => 'Last Name'    },
16:     greeting       => {required => 0, label => 'Greeting'     },
17:     phone_type     => {required => 1, label => 'Number Type'},
```

```
18:     phone_number => {required => 1, label => 'Number'    },
19:     note          => {required => 0, label => 'Note'      },
20: );

21: my @Person_prompts = qw(first_name last_name greeting);
22: my @Phone_prompts = qw(phone_type phone_number note);
23: my @Phone_cols = ('id', @Phone_prompts);

24: while ( my %person = input_person() ) {
25:     while ( my %phone = input_phone() ) {
26:         $phone{id} = $person{id};
27:         add_phone( %phone );
28:     }
29: }

30: $Connection->disconnect;
31: exit 0;

32: sub input_person {
33:     my %person;

34:     print "Enter person details, (Fields marked with * are required).\nTo
exit program, hit CTRL-D.\n";

35:     foreach my $col ( @Person_prompts ) {
36:         my $req = $Fields{$col}{'required'} ? '*' : '';
37:         print "$Fields{$col}{'label'}$req:\t";
38:         my $line = <STDIN>;
39:         return    unless defined $line;    # no input
40:         chomp( $line );
41:         if ( $Fields{$col}{'required'} and $line !~ /\S+/ ) {
42:             warn "Required field missing, please re-enter\n";
43:             return;
44:         }
45:         $person{$col} = $line;
46:     }

47:     unless ( defined($person{id} = get_person_id(%person)) ) {
48:         $person{id} = add_person( %person );
49:         return undef    unless $person{id};
50:     }

51:     return %person;
52: }

53: sub get_person_id {
54:     my %person = @_;
55:     my $person_query_sql = qq(SELECT * FROM person
56:         WHERE first_name = ? AND last_name = ?);

57:     $Query_statement ||= $Connection->prepare( $person_query_sql )
```

Continued

Listing 14-1 *(continued)*

```perl
58:            or die "Can't prepare query\nError: $DBI::errstr\nExiting";

59:        if ($Query_statement->execute($person{first_name},$person{last_name})){
60:            my $href = $Query_statement->fetchrow_hashref();
61:            return undef    unless $href;
62:            return $href->{id};
63:        }

64:        else {
65:            warn "Can't execute query\nError: $DBI::errstr";
66:            return;
67:        }
68: }

69: sub add_person {
70:        my %person = @_;
71:        my $person_insert_sql = 'INSERT INTO person('
72:            . join(',', @Person_prompts) . ') VALUES('
73:            . join(',', map {'?'} @Person_prompts) . ')';

74:        $Person_insert_statement ||= $Connection->prepare($person_insert_sql)
75:            or die "Can't prepare insert: $DBI::errstr";

76:        unless ($Person_insert_statement->execute(@person{@Person_prompts})) {
77:            warn "Can't execute insert: $DBI::errstr";
78:            return undef;
79:        }

80:        # and return the id    ***MySQL specific attribute****
81:        return $Person_insert_statement->{'mysql_insertid'};
82: }

83: sub input_phone {
84:        my %phone;

85:        print "Enter phone details, (Fields marked with * are required)\n";
86:        foreach my $col ( @Phone_prompts ) {
87:            my $req = $Fields{$col}{'required'} ? '*' : '';
88:            print "$Fields{$col}{'label'}$req:\t";
89:            my $line = <STDIN>;
90:            return    unless defined $line;    # no input
91:            chomp( $line );
92:            if ( $Fields{$col}{'required'} and $line !~ /\S+/ ) {
93:                warn "Required field missing, please re-enter\n";
94:                return;
95:            }
96:            $phone{$col} = $line;
97:        }
```

```
98:     return %phone;
99: }

100: sub add_phone {
101:     my %phone = @_;
102:     my $phone_insert_sql = 'INSERT INTO phone('
103:         . join(',', @Phone_cols) . ') VALUES('
104:         . join(',', map {'?'} @Phone_cols) . ')';

105:     $Phone_insert_statement ||= $Connection->prepare($phone_insert_sql)
106:         or die "Can't prepare insert\nError: $DBI::errstr\nExiting";

107:     $Phone_insert_statement->execute(@phone{@Phone_cols})
108:         or warn "Can't execute insert\nError: $DBI::errstr";
109: }
```

Listing 14-2: **Phone number lookup program**

```
01: #!/usr/bin/perl -w
02: #
03: # program 14-2, Chapter 14, Listing 2
04: #

05: use DBI;
06: use strict;

07: # check the user gave a search term
08: my $name = shift(@ARGV);
09: unless ($name) {
10:     die "$0: please supply a name!
11: usage:      $0 name
12: example:    $0 Smith\n";
13: }

14: # connect to DBMS and get a database handle
15: my $dsn = 'DBI:mysql:BibleBook';
16: my $connection = DBI->connect($dsn, 'bookuser', 'testpass')
17:     or die "Can't connect to database: $dsn\nError: $DBI::errstr\nExiting";

18: $name =~ /(\w+)/;
19: $name = $connection->quote("%$1%");

20: # prepare the statement and get a statement handle
21: my $sql = <<EOS;
22: SELECT first_name,last_name,greeting,phone_type,phone_number,note
23: FROM person, phone
```

Continued

Listing 14-2 *(continued)*

```
24: WHERE person.id = phone.id
25: AND (first_name   LIKE $name
26:       OR last_name LIKE $name
27:       OR greeting  LIKE $name)
28: EOS

29: my $query = $connection->prepare($sql)
30:     or die "$0: can't prepare '$sql'\nError: $DBI::errstr\nExiting";

31: # run the query
32: $query->execute();

33: # get/display the results
34: my $current_name = '';

35: while (my @data = $query->fetchrow()) {
36:     if ($current_name ne "$data[0] $data[1]") {
37:         print "$data[0] $data[1] ($data[2])\n";
38:         $current_name = "$data[0] $data[1]";
39:     }

40:     print "\t$data[3]: $data[4]\t$data[5]\n";
41: }

42: # tidy up
43: $query->finish();
44: $connection->disconnect();
45: exit 0;
```

Listing 14-3: **Graphical phonebook code**

```
01: #!/usr/bin/perl -w
02: # program 14-3
03: # Chapter 14
04: # Listing 3

05: use strict;
06: use DBI;
07: use Tk;

08: my $Connection = DBI->connect
    ('DBI:mysql:BibleBook', 'bookuser', 'testpass')
09:         or die "Can't connect to database: $DBI::errstr";

10: my %Fields = (
```

```
11:     id            => {required => 1, label => 'ID'          },
12:     first_name    => {required => 1, label => 'Forename'    },
13:     last_name     => {required => 0, label => 'Surname'     },
14:     greeting      => {required => 0, label => 'Greeting'    },
15:     phone_type    => {required => 1, label => 'Number Type'},
16:     phone_number  => {required => 1, label => 'Number'      },
17:     note          => {required => 0, label => 'Note'        },
18: );

19: my @Person_prompts = qw(first_name last_name greeting);
20: my @Phone_prompts  = qw(phone_type phone_number note);
21: my @Phone_cols     = ('id', @Phone_prompts);
22: my $Main_win;
23: my ($pr_lst, $ph_lst);

24: show_main_form();
25: MainLoop();
26: $Connection->disconnect();
27: exit 0;

28: sub show_main_form {
29:     $Main_win = MainWindow->new(-title => 'Perl/Tk PhoneBook');
30:     my $person_frame = $Main_win->Frame();
31:     $pr_lst = $person_frame->Scrolled('Listbox',
32:         -scrollbars => 'oe', -height => 10,
33:         -selectmode => 'browse');

34:     my $phone_frame = $Main_win->Frame();
35:     $ph_lst = $phone_frame->Scrolled('Listbox',
36:         -scrollbars => 'oe', -height => 4,
37:         -selectmode => 'browse');

38:     my $person_add_b =
39:         $person_frame->Button(-text => 'Add Person',
40:           -command => sub {
41:             show_person_form('Add Person');
42:             fill_person_list();
43:           }
        );

44:     my $person_upd_b =
45:         $person_frame->Button(-text => 'Update Person',
46:           -state => 'disabled',
47:           -command => sub {
48:             show_person_form('Update Person',
                    $pr_lst->get('active'));

49:             fill_person_list();

50:           }
```

Continued

Listing 14-3 *(continued)*

```perl
51:     );

52:     my $person_del_b =
          $person_frame->Button(-text => 'Delete Person',
53:         -state => 'disabled',
54:         -command => sub {
55:             chk_del_person($pr_lst->get('active'));

56:             fill_person_list();


57:         }
58:     );

59:     my $phone_add_b = $phone_frame->Button(-text => 'Add Phone',
60:         -state => 'disabled',
61:         -command => sub {
62:             show_phone_form('Add Phone');
63:         }
64:     );

65:     my $phone_upd_b = $phone_frame->Button(-text => 'Update Phone',
66:         -state => 'disabled',
67:         -command => sub {
68:             show_phone_form('Update Phone', $ph-lst->get($ph_lst-
>curselection()));
69:         }
70:     );

71:     my $phone_del_b = $phone_frame->Button(-text => 'Delete Phone',
72:         -state => 'disabled',
73:         -command => sub {
74:             chk_del_phone(
75:                     $ph_lst->get($ph_lst->curselection()));
76:             fill_phone_list($pr_lst->get($pr_lst->curselection()));
77:         }
78:     );

79:     $person_frame->pack( -side => 'top', -fill => 'both', -expand => 1);
80:     $person_list->pack( -side => 'top', -fill => 'both', -expand => 1);
81:     foreach my $button ($person_add_b, $person_upd_b, $person_del_b) {
82:         $button->pack(-side => 'left');
83:     }
84:     $phone_frame->pack( -side => 'top', -fill => 'both', -expand => 1);
85:     $phone_list->pack( -side => 'top', -fill => 'both', -expand => 1);
86:     foreach my $button ($phone_add_b, $phone_upd_b, $phone_del_b) {
87:         $button->pack(-side => 'left');
88:     }

89:     $Main_win->Button( -text => 'Exit', -command => sub {
```

```
90:              $Connection->disconnect();
91:              $Main_win->withdraw();
92:              exit 0;
93:          } )->pack();

94:     $pr_lst->bind( '<Button-1>',
95:         sub {
96:             return  unless defined $pr_lst->curselection();
97:             $person_upd_b->configure(-state => 'active');
98:             $person_del_b->configure(-state => 'active');
99:             $phone_add_b->configure(-state => 'active');
100:            fill_phone_list($pr_lst->get($pr_lst->curselection()));
101:         }
102:     );

103:    $ph_lst->bind( '<Button-1>',
104:        sub {
105:            return  unless defined $ph_lst->curselection();
106:            $phone_upd_b->configure(-state => 'active');
107:            $phone_del_b->configure(-state => 'active');
108:        }
109:    );

110:    $pr_lst->bind( '<Double-Button-1>',
111:        sub {
112:            return  unless defined $pr_lst->curselection();
113:            show_person_form('Update Person',
114:                      $pr_lst->get($pr_lst->curselection()));
115:            fill_person_list();
116:            fill_phone_list($pr_lst->curselection());
117:        }
118:    );

119:    $ph_lst->bind( '<Double-Button-1>',
120:        sub {
121:            return  unless defined $ph_lst->curselection();
122:            show_phone_form('Update Phone', $pr_lst->get('active'),
123:                      $ph_lst->get('active'));
124:            fill_phone_list($ph_lst, $pr_lst->get('active'));
125:        }
126:    );

127:    fill_person_list();
128:       return;
129: }

130: sub show_person_form{
131:     my $label = shift;
132:     my $person = shift;
133:     my %person;

134:     if ($person) {
```

Continued

Listing 14-3 *(continued)*

```
135:        $person{'id'} = get_person_id($person);

136:        my $sql = 'SELECT * FROM person WHERE id = ?';
137:        my $array_ref = $Connection->selectall_arrayref($sql, undef,
138:     $person{'id'});

139:        my $i = 1;
140:        foreach my $col ( @Person_prompts ) {
141:            $person{$col} = $array_ref->[0]->[$i];
142:            $i++;
143:        }
144:    }

145:    my $person_form = $Main_win->Toplevel( -title => $label );
146:    my $row = 0;
147:    my %entry;

148:    foreach my $col ( @Person_prompts ) {
149:        my $req = $Fields{$col}{'required'} ? '*' : '';

150:        $person_form->Label( -text => "$Fields{$col}{'label'}$req ")->
151:            grid( -row => $row, -column => 0, -sticky => 'e');

152:        $entry{$col} = $person_form->Entry( -width => 20,
153:                -textvariable => \$person{$col} )->
154:            grid(-row => $row++, -column => 1, -sticky => 'w');
155:    }

156:    $person_form->Button( -text => 'Close',
157:        -command => sub { $person_form->withdraw() })->
158:            grid(-row => $row, -column => 0, -sticky => 'w');

159:    $person_form->Button( -text => $label,
160:        -command => [ \&add_upd_person, $label, $person_form, \%entry])->
161:            grid(-row => $row, -column => 1, -sticky => 'w');

162:    return;
163: }

164: sub show_phone_form {
165:     my $label = shift;
166:     my $person = get_person_id($pr_lst->get('active'));
167:     my $phone = shift;
168:     my %phone;

169:     unless ($person) {
170:         $Main_win->messageBox(-icon => 'error', -type => 'OK',
171:             -title => 'Select a Person',
172:             -message => 'Please select a person and retry.');
```

```
173:            return;
174:        }

175:        if ($phone) {
176:            $phone =~ /^(.*?): (.*?), (.*)/;
177:            @phone{@Phone_prompts} = ($1, $2, $3);
178:        }

179:        elsif ($label =~ /Update/) {
180:            $Main_win->messageBox(-icon => 'error', -type => 'OK',
181:                -title => 'Select a Phone',
182:                -message => 'Please select a phone and retry.');
183:            return;
184:        }

185:        my $phone_form = $Main_win->Toplevel( -title => $label );
186:        my $row = 0;
187:        my %entry;
188:        foreach my $col ( @Phone_prompts ) {
189:            my $req = $Fields{$col}{'required'} ? '*' : '';

190:            $phone_form->Label( -text => "$Fields{$col}{'label'}$req ")->
191:                grid( -row => $row, -column => 0, -sticky => 'e');

192:            $entry{$col} = $phone_form->Entry( -width => 20,
193:                    -textvariable => \$phone{$col} )->
194:                grid(-row => $row++, -column => 1, -sticky => 'w');
195:        }
196:        $phone_form->Button( -text => 'Close',
197:            -command => sub { $phone_form->withdraw() })->
198:                grid(-row => $row, -column => 0, -sticky => 'w');
199:        $phone_form->Button( -text => $label,
200:            -command => [ \&add_upd_phone, $label, $phone_form, \%entry,
201:                    get_person_id($person) ])->
202:                grid(-row => $row, -column => 1, -sticky => 'w');

203:        return;
204: }

205: sub fill_pr_lst {
206:        my $sql = 'SELECT id,last_name,first_name FROM person '
207:            . 'ORDER by last_name,first_name';

208:        my $ptr = $Connection->selectall_hashref($sql, undef);
209:        $pr_lst->delete(0, 'end');
210:        $pr_lit->insert('end', map { sprintf "%4d: %-s",
211:                    $_->{id}, "$_->{last_name}, $_->{first_name}" } @{$ptr}
);
212: }

213: sub fill_ph_lst {
```

Continued

Listing 14-3 *(continued)*

```
214:    my $person_id = get_person_id( shift );
215:    my $sql = 'SELECT phone_type,phone_number,note FROM phone '
216:        . 'WHERE id = ? '
217:        . 'ORDER by phone_type';
218:    my $ptr = $Connection->selectall_arrayref($sql, undef, $person_id);
219:    $ph_lst->delete(0, 'end');
220:    $ph_lst->insert('end', map {
221:            "$_->[0]: $_->[1], $_->[2] "} @{$ptr} );
222:    return;
223: }

224: sub get_person_id {
225:    my $person = shift;
226:    $person =~ /^\s*(\d+):?/;
227:    return $1;
228: }

229: sub add_upd_person {
230:    my $label       = shift;
231:    my $person_form = shift;
232:    my $id          = shift;
233:    my $form_entry  = shift;

234:    my (%person, $sql);

235:    my $missing_fields = 0;

236:    foreach my $col ( @Person_prompts ) {
237:        $person{$col} = $form_entry->{$col}->get();
238:        $missing_fields = 1
239:            if $Fields{$col}{'required'} && ! length $person{$col};
240:    }

241:    if ($missing_fields) {
242:        $Main_win->messageBox(-icon => 'error', -type => 'OK',
243:            -title => 'Required Fields Missing',
244:            -message => "Please fill fields marked '*'");
245:        return;
246:    }

247:    if ($label =~ /^Add/) {
248:        $sql = 'INSERT INTO person('
249:            . join(',', @Person_prompts) . ') VALUES('

250:            . join(',', map {'?'} @Person_prompts) . ')';
251:        unless ( $Connection->do( $sql, undef,
252:                        @person{@Person_prompts}) ) {
253:            $Main_win->messageBox(-icon => 'error', -type => 'OK',
254:                -title => 'Error Adding Person',
```

```
255:                       -message => "$DBI::errstr, please correct and retry.");
256:               return;
257:           }
258:     }

259:     else {   # assume we're updating
260:         $sql = 'UPDATE person SET '
261:             . join(',', map {"$_ = ?"} @Person_prompts)
262:             . ' WHERE id = ?';
263:         unless ( $Connection->do($sql, undef,
264:                   @person{@Person_prompts}, $id) ) {
265:             $Main_win->messageBox(-icon => 'error', -type => 'OK',
266:                 -title => 'Error Updating Person',
267:                 -message => "$DBI::errstr, please correct and retry.");
268:             return;
269:         }
270:     }

271:     fill_pr_list();
272:     $person_form->withdraw();
273:     return;
274: }

275: sub add_upd_phone {
276:     my (%phone, $sql);
277:     my $missing_fields = 0;

278:     my $label      = shift;
279:     my $phone_form = shift;
280:     my $form_entry = shift;
281:     $phone{'id'}   = shift;

282:     foreach my $col ( @Phone_prompts ) {
283:         $phone{$col} = $form_entry->{$col}->get();
284:         $missing_fields = 1
285:             if $Fields{$col}{'required'} && ! length $phone{$col};
286:     }

287:     if ($missing_fields) {
288:             $Main_win->messageBox(-icon => 'error', -type => 'OK',
298:                 -title => 'Required Fields Missing',
290:                 -message => "Please fill fields marked '*'");
291:             return;
292:     }

293:     if ($label =~ /^Add/) {
294:         $sql = 'INSERT INTO phone('
295:             . join(',', @Phone_cols) . ') VALUES('
296:             . join(',', map {'?'} @Phone_cols) . ')';

297:         unless ( $Connection->do($sql, undef, @phone{@Phone_cols}) ) {
```

Continued

Listing 14-3 *(continued)*

```
298:              $Main_win->messageBox(-icon => 'error', -type => 'OK',
299:                  -title => 'Error Adding Phone',
300:                  -message => "$DBI::errstr, please correct and retry.");
301:              return;
302:          }
303:      }

304:      else {  # assume we're updating
305:          $sql = 'UPDATE phone SET '
306:              . join(',', map {"$_ = ?"} @Phone_prompts)
307:              . ' WHERE id = ? AND phone_type = ?';

308:          unless ( $Connection->do($sql, undef, @phone{@Phone_prompts},
309:                  $phone{'id'}, $phone{'phone_type'}) ) {
310:              $Main_win->messageBox(-icon => 'error', -type => 'OK',
311:                  -title => 'Error Updating Phone',
312:                  -message => "$DBI::errstr, please correct and retry.");
313:              return;
314:          }
315:      }

316:      fill_pr_lst();
317:      fill_ph_lst($phone{'id'});
318:      $phone_form->withdraw();
319:      return;
320: }

321: sub chk_del_person {
322:      my $person = shift;
323:      my $person_id = get_person_id($person);

324:      my $button = $Main_win->messageBox(-icon => 'question',
325:          -type => 'YesNo', -title => 'Delete Person',
326:          -message => "Delete $person and related phone numbers?");

327:      if ($button eq 'Yes') {
328:          eval {
329:              my $sql = 'DELETE FROM phone where id = ?';
330:              $Connection->do($sql, undef, $person_id)
331:                  or die $DBI::errstr;
332:              $sql = 'DELETE FROM person where id = ?';
333:              $Connection->do($sql, undef, $person_id)
334:                  or die $DBI::errstr;
335:          };

336:          if ($@) {
337:              $Main_win->messageBox(-icon => 'error', -type => 'OK',
338:                  -title => 'Error Deleting Person',
339:                  -message => $DBI::errstr);
```

```
340:            }
341:        }
342:        return;
343: }

344: sub chk_del_phone {
345:     my $person = shift;
346:     my $phone = shift;
347:     my $person_id = get_person_id($person);

348:     $phone =~ /^(.*?):/;
349:     my $phone_type = $1;

350:     my $button = $Main_win->messageBox(-icon => 'question',
351:         -type => 'YesNo', -title => 'Delete Phone',
352:         -message => "Delete the number $phone for $person?");

353:     if ($button eq 'Yes') {
354:         eval {
355:             my $sql = 'DELETE FROM phone where id = ? AND phone_type = ?';
356:             $Connection->do($sql, undef, $person_id, $phone_type)
357:                 or die $DBI::errstr;
358:         };
359:         if ($@) {
360:             $Main_win->messageBox(-icon => 'error', -type => 'OK',
361:                 -title => 'Error Deleting Phone Number',
362:                 -message => $DBI::errstr);
363:         }
364:     }
365:     return;
366: }
```

✦   ✦   ✦

Creating a Web-Based Shopping Cart

Web shopping carts are common tools these days. With a shopping cart, you browse an online catalog, adding items to your cart as you shop. This is similar to grocery shopping.

The whole shopping cart idea does not have to be used only for e-commerce sites. A shopping cart program can be used to hold user preferences, vote tallies, scores, and just about anything else you can think of.

The shopping cart system we put together in this chapter is not a complete, ready-to-use e-commerce application. Instead, we use some of the tools we have already built and create a framework we can build upon. We can build this into an e-commerce application or use it simply to keep inventory of some items.

If you remember back in Chapter 12, we create a SOAP-based catalog. We use that catalog as our "product catalog" in this example. Also, if you can dig up the code from the tied-hash chapter, we use much of that as well. To implement a shopping cart, we need to support the concept of sessions. But HTTP has no support for sessions — servers know only about individual unrelated requests for URLs. But by using cookies, we can implement sessions. What's new in this chapter is that we store the contents of the shopping cart as part of the per-session data. The tied-hash method we've worked on is perfect for this.

The features our shopping cart application will have are:

✦ View catalog listing

✦ Add items to cart

✦ Remove items from cart

✦ Display specific items

✦ Show cart with totals

✦ Show invoice with totals

These features should be a great start to any sort of Web application needing a shopping cart.

We use templates again for our HTML output. Using templates really can make things easier by separating the Perl code from the HTML. You can find the code for these templates at the end of this chapter and on this book's companion Web site.

Building the Shopping Cart

This section contains a description of the code you can use to build the Web-based shopping cart.

BasicSession.pm

We base the whole shopping cart around the `BasicSession` module we create in the chapter on tied hashes. However, since we aren't keeping user preferences only, but are keeping a cart of items, we have to modify the code a bit.

The `@EXPORT = qw(Wrap_Page Get_Session);` needs to be changed to:

```
@EXPORT = qw(Wrap_Page Get_Session Print_Page);
```

We need to print some of the templates without wrapping them, so we need to export `Print_Page`. That is it for the changes to `BasicSession.pm`. Can you believe it? I love the smell of re-useable code in the morning!

The catalog program is used to display a listing of the items that can be added to the cart. This program uses the SOAP catalog to grab the whole listing. Figure 15-1 shows the catalog. Note that these fonts have been greatly enlarged for the book.

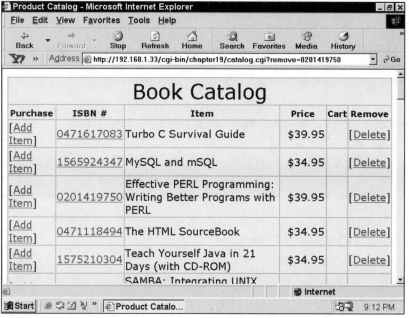

Figure 15-1: Catalog listing

When you click Add Item, the item is added to the cart. Take a look at the code we use for this.

catalog.cgi

```
01: #!/usr/bin/perl -wT

02: use strict;
03: use SOAP::Lite;
04: use CGI qw(:standard);

05: use lib qw(.);
06: use BasicSession;
```

Line 1 tells the system where to find Perl and turns on warnings and taint checking.

Line 2 loads the strict module.

Line 3 loads the `SOAP::Lite` module. We need this so that we can access the SOAP catalog.

Line 4 loads the `CGI` module and its `:standard` functions.

Line 5 tells Perl to look in the current directory for modules.

Line 6 loads the `BasicSession` module. This is the version we modify slightly so that we can use the `Print_Page` function as well.

```
07: our $sess;
08: my  %cart;
```

Line 7 declares the variable `$sess` as an `our` variable. This makes it accessible from the `BasicSession` module.

Line 8 declares a hash named `%cart`.

```
09: $sess = Get_Session();
10: tie %cart, 'BasicSession';
```

Line 9 uses the `Get_Session` function to get/set the session cookie for this user. This allows us to track the user between pages by storing a cookie that our session database table uses for its unique id.

Line 10 ties the `%cart` hash to the methods in the `BasicSession` module. By tying the hash to `BasicSession`, we are able to modify how the hash behaves and have it directly modify a database table just by doing the normal operations on the hash.

```
11: my $add_to_cart = param('add_to_cart');
12: ++$cart{$add_to_cart} if $add_to_cart;
```

Line 11 declares a variable named `$add_to_cart` and sets it to the value returned by the call to the `param` function `param('add_to_cart')`;

Line 12 adds 1 to the `$cart` with a key of `$add_to_cart` if `$add_to_cart` contains a value.

```
13: my $remove= param('remove');
14: delete $cart{$remove} if $remove;
```

Line 13 declares a variable named `$remove` and sets it to the value returned by the call to the `param` function `param('remove');`.

Line 14 deletes the item with the key of `$remove if $remove contains a value`. If there is no item in the `%item` hash with key `$remove`, nothing will happen.

```
15:  my $products = SOAP::Lite
16:    -> uri('http://goliath.perlguy.net/Catalog')
17:    -> proxy('http://goliath.perlguy.net/cgi-
              bin/soap_server19.cgi')
18:    -> Get_Product_List()
19:    -> result;
```

Line 15 declares a scalar variable named $products and assigns it to the value
returned by the call to the SOAP::Lite module. Since the Get_Products_List
SOAP method returns a reference to an array of references, a reference is stored in
$products.

Lines 15–19 are actually several methods from the SOAP::Lite module strung
together. These commands make up a SOAP client that gets data from the SOAP
server that we built in Chapter 12.

Line 16 tells the SOAP client the URI, or namespace, of the service we are calling.

Line 17 is the address of the SOAP server we are contacting. We actually have to modify one line in the soap_server.cgi, so this one is renamed soap_server19.cgi.
The modification simply adds the price field to the return results.

Line 18 is the remote function we are calling on the SOAP server.

Line 19 calls the result method, which returns the results of the function we have
called.

```
20:  Print_Page("./templates", "header.tmpl", \%cart);
21:  Print_Page("./templates", "catalog_header.tmpl", \%cart);
```

Line 20 calls the Print_Page function to print the page header HTML.

Line 21 calls the Print_Page function to print the catalog_header template
HTML. This prints the table header for the catalog page.

```
22:  for my $p (@$products){
23:      print qq(
24:        <tr><td>
25:    [<a href="catalog.cgi?add_to_cart=$p->[1]">Add Item</a>]
26:        </td><td>
27:     <a href="item_details.cgi?item_num=$p->[1]">$p->[1]</a>
28:        </td><td>$p->[0]
29:        </td><td> $p->[2]
30:        </td><td align="center"> $item{$p->[1]}
31:        </td><td>
            [<a href="catalog.cgi?remove=$p->[1]">Delete</a>]
32:        </td></tr>\n);
33:  }
```

Line 22 begins a loop that iterates through all of the values in the array that is referenced by $products.

Line 23 begins a qq block that prints the HTML for one table row of catalog data.

Lines 24–32 print one table row of catalog data. $products holds a reference to an array of arrays. So, each time through the loop, $p is actually a reference to an array. Notice that we access these items by using the arrow operator $p->[1] and so on.

Line 33 closes the for loop that begins on **line 22**.

```
34:  Print_Page("./templates", "catalog_footer.tmpl", \%cart);
```

Line 34 finishes off by printing the HTML in the catalog_footer.tmpl template.

That is it for the catalog program. Since we are reusing code and using the SOAP server to send us the catalog data, we are been able to save a lot of time.

Next, we cover the item_details.cgi program. This program is similar to the script we use when we create the book catalog in Chapter 12. This time, however, we add links to manipulate your cart. Figure 15-2 contains a view of what occurs when you view a specific item.

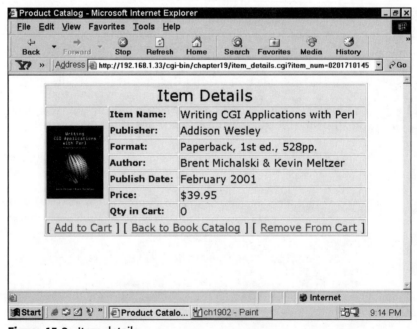

Figure 15-2: Item details

Notice the links at the bottom and the Qty in Cart item; these are added for the shopping cart.

item_details.cgi

```
01: #!/usr/bin/perl -wT

02: use strict;
03: use CGI qw(:standard);
04: use SOAP::Lite;
05: use XML::Simple;

06: use lib qw(.);
07: use BasicSession;
```

Line 1 tells the system where to find Perl and turns on warnings and taint checking.

Line 2 loads the strict module.

Line 3 loads the CGI module and its :standard functions.

Line 4 loads the SOAP::Lite module so that we can access the SOAP server.

Line 5 loads the XML::Simple module. We are accessing an alternative SOAP function; this time, the SOAP server returns XML data, so we need to be able to parse the catalog data.

Line 6 tells Perl to look in the current directory for modules.

Line 7 loads the BasicSession module.

```
08: our $sess;
09: my  %session;
```

Line 8 declares the variable $sess using the our function. By using the our function, we are able to access this data from the BasicSession module.

Line 9 declares the %session hash. We already have a hash named %cart in this program. To make code reuse easier, the hash we are adding to this program is renamed.

```
10: $sess = Get_Session();
11: tie %session, 'BasicSession';
```

Line 10 calls the `Get_Session` module to get/set the session cookie for this user.

Line 11 ties the `%session` hash to the `BasicSession` module.

```
12: my $input = param('item_num');
```

Line 12 declares a scalar variable named `$input` and sets it to the value returned by the call to the `param` function `param('item_num');`.

```
13: my $data = SOAP::Lite
14:    -> uri('http://goliath.perlguy.net/Catalog')
15:    -> proxy('http://goliath.perlguy.net/cgi-
               bin/soap_server.cgi')
16:    -> Get_Product_Data($input)
17:    -> result;
```

Line 13 declares a scalar variable named `$data` and assigns it to the value returned by the call to the `SOAP::Lite` module. The value returned by the `Get_Product_Data` is a string that makes up an XML document.

Lines 13–17 are actually several methods from the `SOAP::Lite` module strung together. These commands make up a SOAP client that gets data from the SOAP server.

Line 14 tells the SOAP client the URI, or namespace, of the service we are calling.

Line 15 is the address of the SOAP server we are contacting.

Line 16 is the remote function we are calling on the SOAP sever. We pass the value in `$input` to the `Get_Product_Data` function.

Line 17 calls the `result` method, which returns the results of the function we have called.

Note   Note that the `result` SOAP method does not have to be changed like the former method we've used. This module has returned all of the data we need.

```
18: $data =~ s/\&amp;|\&/\&amp;/g;
19: my $item = XMLin($data);
```

Line 18 replaces any ampersands HTML markups (`&amp;`) or lone ampersands (`&`) in the XML document that was returned, with their equivalent HTML markup (`&amp;`). A plain ampersand in an XML document causes an error when the document is parsed. We included `&amp;` in our search to ensure that we don't change an already marked-up ampersand from `&amp;` to `&amp;amp;`.

Line 19 declares a scalar variable named $item. This new scalar variable is set to the value returned by the call to the XMLin function. XMLin is part of the XML::Simple module; it returns a reference to a hash containing the parsed XML document.

```
20: ++$session{$item->{isbn}}  if(param('add_to_cart'));
```

Line 20 increments the number of this item in the cart by one if a value is passed in add_to_cart.

```
21: my $cart_qty = $session{$item->{isbn}};
22: $cart_qty    = 0 unless $cart_qty;
23: $item->{'cart_qty'} = $cart_qty;
```

Line 21 declares a scalar variable named $cart_qty and sets it to the value in %session at the key $item->{isbn}. This pulls the current cart quantity from the database; remember that %session is tied to the database.

Line 22 sets $cart_qty to 0 if nothing is in $cart_qty.

Line 23 sets the value in the %item hash to the current cart quantity. We set the %item hash because we are passing it to the templates for the output of the HTML.

```
24: Print_Page("./templates", "header.tmpl"      , $item);
25: Print_Page("./templates", "item_details.tmpl", $item);
```

Lines 24–25 use the Print_Page function to print the HTML contained in the templates header.tmpl and item_details.tmpl, respectively. Notice that we are passing $item instead of \%item. The function expects a reference to a hash, and $item holds a reference to a hash already.

This is a quick little program. By using a tied hash, we are able to remove much of the work we usually have to take care of in each program.

Now we take a look at the items in the cart (Figure 15-3). The cart.cgi program is designed to show the user what he or she has in the cart. It gives the user the option of adding more of an item or deleting an item altogether. This program is similar to catalog.cgi program, except we have to add a little more functionality to handle calculating the prices and printing the bottom line of the table.

If you click the Delete link next to an item, it will remove the item from the cart and redisplay the screen (Figure 15-4).

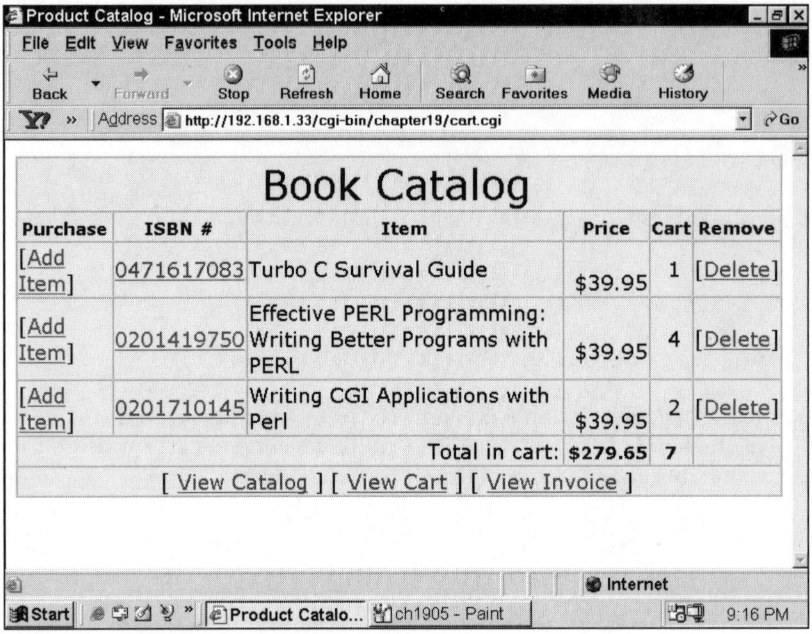

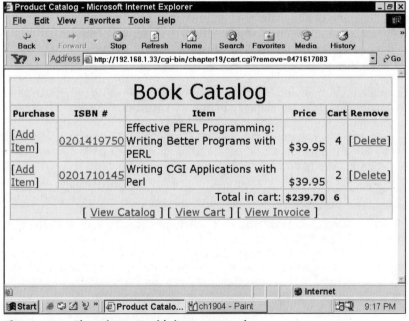

Figure 15-3: Items in the shopping cart

Figure 15-4: Shopping cart with item removed

cart.cgi

```
01: #!/usr/bin/perl -wT
02: # cart.cgi

03: use strict;
04: use SOAP::Lite;
05: use CGI qw(:standard);

06: use lib qw(.);
07: use BasicSession;
```

Line 1 tells the system where to find Perl and turns on warnings and taint checking.

Line 2 is simply a comment that contains this program's name.

Line 3 loads the `strict` module.

Line 4 loads the `SOAP::Lite` module so that we can access the SOAP catalog data.

Line 5 loads the `CGI` module and its `:standard` functions.

Line 6 tells Perl to look in the current directory for modules.

Line 7 loads the `BasicSession` module. This is the version we modify slightly so we can use the `Print_Page` function as well.

```
08: our $sess;
09: my  %session;
```

Line 8 declares the variable `$sess` as an `our` variable. This makes it accessible from the `BasicSession` module.

Line 9 declares a hash named `%session`.

```
10: $sess = Get_Session();
11: tie %session, 'BasicSession';
```

Line 10 uses the `Get_Session` function to get/set the session cookie for this user. This allows us to track the user between pages by storing a cookie that our session database table uses for its unique id.

Line 11 ties the `%session` hash to the methods in the `BasicSession` module. By tying the hash to `BasicSession`, we are able to modify how the hash behaves and have it directly modify a database table just by doing the normal operations on the hash.

```
12: my $add_to_cart = param('add_to_cart');
13: ++$session{$add_to_cart} if($add_to_cart);
```

Line 12 declares a variable named $add_to_cart and sets it to the value returned by the call to the param function – param('add_to_cart');

Line 13 adds 1 to the $session with a key of $add_to_cart if $add_to_cart contains a value.

```
14: my $remove= param('remove');
15: delete $session{$remove};
```

Line 14 declares a variable named $remove and sets it to the value returned by the call to the param function—param('remove');

Line 15 deletes the member of the %session hash with the key of $remove. If there is no item in the %session hash with key $remove, nothing will happen.

```
16: my $products = SOAP::Lite
17:    -> uri('http://goliath.perlguy.net/Catalog')
18:    -> proxy('http://goliath.perlguy.net/cgi-
              bin/soap_server19.cgi')
19:    -> Get_Product_List()
20:    -> result;
```

Line 16 declares a scalar variable named $products and assigns it to the value returned by the call to the SOAP::Lite module. Since the Get_Products_List SOAP method returns a reference to an array of references, a reference is stored in $products.

Lines 16–20 are actually several methods from the SOAP::Lite module strung together. These commands make up a SOAP client that gets data from the SOAP server.

Line 17 tells the SOAP client the URI, or namespace, of the service we are calling.

Line 18 is the address of the SOAP server we are contacting. We actually have to modify one line in the soap_server.cgi, so this one is renamed soap_server19.cgi. The modification simply adds the price field to the return results.

Line 19 is the remote function we are calling on the SOAP sever.

Line 20 calls the result method, which returns the results of the function we have called.

```
21: Print_Page("./templates", "header.tmpl", \%session);
22: Print_Page("./templates", "catalog_header.tmpl",
    \%session);
```

Line 21 calls the `Print_Page` function to print the page header HTML.

Line 22 calls the `Print_Page` function to print the `catalog_header` template HTML. This prints the table header for the catalog page.

Now we are finished with the code that is identical to the `catalog.cgi` program.

```
23: delete($session{'cart_qty_total'});
24: delete($session{'cart_price_total'});
```

Lines 23–24 delete whatever is stored at the `cart_qty_total` and `cart_price_total` hash indexes. We delete these values because any remaining old values are unnecessary. Remember, this is not a normal hash; it is tied to a database and can remember values between program calls.

We need to delete the old values to make sure that the calculations we are about to perform start fresh.

```
25: for my $prod (@$products){
26:     next unless ($session{$prod->[1]});
```

Line 25 is again like the `catalog.cgi` program. It loops through each of the items in the `@$products` array. Each time through the loop, the current value (a reference to another array) is set to `$prod`.

Line 26 checks to see if the current the hash `$session{$prod->[1]}` contains any data. If it does, this item is in the users shopping cart and we want to show it. If it does not contain any data, we want to cause the loop to move on to the next item, so we call the `next` function.

```
27:     $session{'cart_qty_total'}   += $session{$prod->[1]};
28:     $session{'cart_price_total'} +=
            Calc_Price($session{$prod->[1]} , $prod->[2]);
```

Line 27 reads the quantity of this item from `$session{$prod->[1]}` and adds that to the current value stored at `$session{'cart_qty_total'}`. This keeps a running total of the number of items in the cart.

Line 28 does basically the same thing as **line 27,** except this one is keeping a running total of the price. The `Calc_Price` function gets passed the *qty* (`$prod->[1]`) and the *price* (`$prod->[2]`) so that they can be multiplied and returned.

```
29:     print qq(
30:        <tr><td>
31:    [<a href="cart.cgi?add_to_cart=$prod->[1]">Add Item</a>]
32:        </td><td>
33:    <a href="item_details.cgi?item_num=$prod->[1]">$prod-
>[1]</a>
34:        </td><td>
```

```
35:              $prod->[0]
36:          </td><td align="right">
37:               $prod->[2]
38:          </td><td align="center">
39:               $session{$prod->[1]}
40:          </td><td>
41:              [<a href="cart.cgi?remove=$prod->[1]">Delete</a>]
42:          </td></tr>\n
43:      );
44: }
```

Lines 29–44 do the exact same thing as the **lines 22–33** in the catalog.cgi program; they print one table row of data corresponding to the current item.

```
45: $session{'cart_price_total'} =
          sprintf("%.2f", $session{'cart_price_total'});
```

Line 45 calls the sprintf function to format the cart price total value so that it contains two decimal points. We then overwrite $item{'cart_price_total'} with the newly formatted value.

```
46: Print_Page("./templates", "cart_total.tmpl"    , \%session);
47: Print_Page("./templates", "catalog_footer.tmpl", \%session);
```

Lines 46 and 47 use the Print_Page function to print the HTML from the cart_total.tmpl and catalog_footer.tmpl templates. This prints the bottom of the resulting HTML page.

```
48: sub Calc_Price {
49:     my($qty, $price) = @_;
```

Line 48 begins the Calc_Price subroutine.

Line 49 declares two variables and sets them to the values passed to this subroutine.

```
50:     $price =~ s/[ \$]//g;

51:     return($qty * $price);
52: }
```

Line 50 strips any spaces or dollar signs from the value in $price.

Line 51 returns the product of $qty and $price.

Line 52 ends the Calc_Price subroutine, as well as this program.

Finally, we write a script that generates a basic invoice. This program is very similar to cart.cgi program—so similar, in fact, that they can probably be merged into one program that determines which templates to use based upon a passed value. This is a great user exercise, enabling you to learn how to combine similar programs if you want to maximize shared code.

Figure 15-5 shows what a simple invoice looks like. The really nice thing about using templates is that you can create a much better looking invoice without changing anything in the invoice program at all.

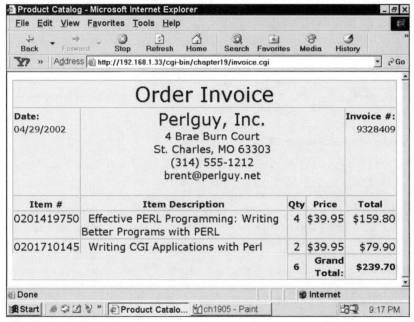

Figure 15-5: The invoice

invoice.cgi

```
01: #!/usr/bin/perl -wT

02: use strict;
03: use SOAP::Lite;
04: use CGI qw(:standard);

05: use lib qw(.);
06: use BasicSession;
```

Line 1 tells the system where to find Perl and turns on warnings and taint checking.

Line 2 loads the `strict` module.

Line 3 loads the `SOAP::Lite` module so that we can get the catalog data.

Line 4 loads the `CGI` module and its `:standard` functions.

Line 5 tells Perl to look in the current directory when looking for modules.

Line 6 loads the `BasicSession` module.

```
07: our $sess;
08: my  %session;
```

Line 7 declares the variable `$sess` as an `our` variable. This makes it accessible from the `BasicSession` module.

Line 8 declares a hash named `%session`.

```
09: $sess = Get_Session();
10: tie %session, 'BasicSession';
```

Line 9 uses the `Get_Session` function to get/set the session cookie for this user. This allows us to track the user between pages by storing a cookie that our session database table uses for its unique id.

Line 10 ties the `%session` hash to the methods in the `BasicSession` module. By tying the hash to `BasicSession`, we are able to modify how the hash behaves and have it directly modify a database table just by doing the normal operations on the hash.

```
11: my $products = SOAP::Lite
12:   -> uri('http://goliath.perlguy.net/Catalog')
13:   -> proxy('http://goliath.perlguy.net/cgi-
              bin/soap_server19.cgi')
14:   -> Get_Product_List()
15:   -> result;
```

Line 11 declares a scalar variable named `$products` and assigns it to the value returned by the call to the `SOAP::Lite` module. Since the `Get_Products_List` SOAP method returns a reference to an array of references, a reference is stored in `$products`.

Lines 11–15 are actually several methods from the `SOAP::Lite` module strung together. These commands make up a SOAP client that gets data from the SOAP server.

Line 12 tells the SOAP client the URI, or namespace, of the service we are calling.

Line 13 is the address of the SOAP server we are contacting.

Line 14 is the remote function we are calling on the SOAP sever.

Line 15 calls the `result` method, which returns the results of the function we have called.

```
16: Print_Page("./templates", "header.tmpl", \%session);
17: Print_Page("./templates", "invoice_header.tmpl", \%session);
```

Lines 16 and 17 use the `Print_Page` subroutine to print the `header.tmpl` and `invoice_header.tmpl` templates.

```
18: delete($session{'cart_qty_total'});
19: delete($session{'cart_price_total'});
```

Lines 18 and 19 clear any values that may be at the `cart_qty_total` and `cart_price_total` indexes.

```
20: for my $prod (@$products){
21:     next unless ($session{$prod->[1]});
```

Line 20 is like the `catalog.cgi` program. It loops through each of the items in the `@$products` array. Each time through the loop, the current value (which is a reference to another array) is set to `$prod`.

Line 21 checks to see if the current the hash `$session{$prod->[1]}` contains any data. If it does, this item is in the user's shopping cart, and we want to show it. If it does not contain any data, we want to cause the loop to move to the next item, so we call the `next` function.

```
22:     $session{'cart_qty_total'}   += $session{$prod->[1]};
23:     $session{'cart_price_total'} +=
            Calc_Price($session{$prod->[1]} , $prod->[2]);
```

Line 22 reads the quantity of this item from `$session{$prod->[1]}` and adds that to the current value stored at `$session{'cart_qty_total'}`. This keeps a running total of the number of items in the cart.

Line 23 does basically the same thing as **line 22**, except this one is keeping a running total of the price. The `Calc_Price` function gets passed the *qty* (`$prod->[1]`) and the *price* (`$prod->[2]`) so that they can be multiplied and returned.

```
24:     print qq(
25:       <tr>
26:         <td align="center" valign="top">
```

```
27:          $prod->[1]
28:          </td>
29:          <td align="left">
30:             $prod->[0]
31:          </td>
32:          <td align="center" valign="top">
33:           $session{$prod->[1]}
34:          </td>
35:          <td align="right" valign="top">
36:           $prod->[2]
37:          </td>
38:          <td align="right" valign="top">
39:      );
```

Lines 24–39 print *most* of the HTML for one row of data on the invoice. We need to format the price properly, so we stop short of a complete row of data.

```
40:    printf("\$%.2f", Calc_Price($session{$prod->[1]}, $prod-
>[2]) );
```

Line 40 uses the `printf` function to print the value returned by our call to `Calc_Price` and to format it so that it contains two decimal points. Notice here that we use `printf`, not `sprintf` as we did previously. `sprintf` is used when you are setting a variable or something to the result, whereas `printf` is used to print the item directly.

```
41:      print qq(
42:          </td>
43:         </tr>\n
44:      );
45: }
```

Lines 41–45 finish the HTML for the row of data. On **line 45,** we close the `for` loop that we began on **line 20.**

```
46: $session{'cart_price_total'} =
        sprintf("%.2f", $session{'cart_price_total'});
47: Print_Page("./templates", "invoice_footer.tmpl",
\%session);
```

Line 46 uses `sprintf` to set the current `cart_price_total` index so that it is formatted to two decimal places.

Line 47 prints the HTML in `invoice_footer.tmpl` to close this invoice page.

```
48: sub Calc_Price {
49:     my($qty, $price) = @_;
```

Line 48 begins the `Calc_Price` subroutine.

Line 49 declares two variables and sets them to the values passed to this subroutine.

```
50:      $price =~ s/[ \$]//g;

51:      return($qty * $price);
52: }
```

Line 50 strips any spaces or dollar signs from the value in `$price`.

Line 51 returns the product of `$qty` and `$price`.

Line 52 ends the `Calc_Price` subroutine, as well as this program.

And that wraps up the invoice program. This program is pretty much a re-do of the cart program but formatted to look like an invoice.

Summary

The shopping cart program that we create in this chapter has shown you that by reusing some of your existing code you can save a lot of time and energy. Keep in mind that the code you reuse needs to be a close fit to what you are looking for. In our case, the `BasicSession` module is almost exactly what we are looking for. And by using a general library for managing sessions (which happened to have a handy tied-hash interface), we were able to avoid any new direct database access.

Now that you have this as a good starting point, take any of the remaining common code, and merge it into a more versatile program. Add sales tax/VAT computations, shipping charges, or a gift wrapping option. You have the beginning; don't stop now!

Program Listings

Listings 15-1 to 15-12 contain the complete an uninterrupted code for the programs and templates used to create the Web-based shopping cart.

> ### Listing 15-1: **catalog.cgi**
>
> ```
> 01: #!/usr/bin/perl -wT
>
> 02: use strict;
> ```
>
> *Continued*

Listing 15-1 *(continued)*

```
03: use SOAP::Lite;
04: use CGI qw(:standard);

05: use lib qw(.);
06: use BasicSession;

07: our $sess;
08: my  %cart;

09: $sess = Get_Session();
10: tie %cart, 'BasicSession';

11: my $add_to_cart = param('add_to_cart');
12: ++$cart{$add_to_cart} if $add_to_cart;

13: my $remove= param('remove');
14: delete $cart{$remove} if $remove;

15: my $products = SOAP::Lite
16:   -> uri('http://goliath.perlguy.net/Catalog')
17:   -> proxy('http://goliath.perlguy.net/cgi-
                bin/soap_server19.cgi')
18:   -> Get_Product_List()
19:   -> result;

20: Print_Page("./templates", "header.tmpl", \%cart);
21: Print_Page("./templates", "catalog_header.tmpl", \%cart);

22: for my $p (@$products){
23:     print qq(
24:       <tr><td>
25:  [<a href="catalog.cgi?add_to_cart=$p->[1]">Add Item</a>]
26:       </td><td>
27:  <a href="item_details.cgi?item_num=$p->[1]">$p->[1]</a>
28:       </td><td>$p->[0]
29:       </td><td> $p->[2]
30:       </td><td align="center"> $item{$p->[1]}
31:       </td><td>[<a
             href="catalog.cgi?remove=$p->[1]">Delete</a>]
32:       </td></tr>\n);
33: }

34: Print_Page("./templates", "catalog_footer.tmpl", \%cart);
```

Listing 15-2: **item_details.cgi**

```
01: #!/usr/bin/perl -wT

02: use strict;
03: use CGI qw(:standard);
04: use SOAP::Lite;
05: use XML::Simple;

06: use lib qw(.);
07: use BasicSession;

08: our $sess;
09: my  %session;

10: $sess = Get_Session();
11: tie %session, 'BasicSession';

12: my $input = param('item_num');

13: my $data = SOAP::Lite
14:    -> uri('http://goliath.perlguy.net/Catalog')
15:    -> proxy('http://goliath.perlguy.net/cgi-
                bin/soap_server.cgi')
16:    -> Get_Product_Data($input)
17:    -> result;

18: $data =~ s/\&amp;|\&/\&amp;/g;
19: my $item = XMLin($data);

20: ++$session{$item->{isbn}} if(param('add_to_cart'));

21: my $cart_qty = $session{$item->{isbn}};
22: $cart_qty     = 0 unless $cart_qty;
23: $item->{'cart_qty'} = $cart_qty;

24: Print_Page("./templates", "header.tmpl"       , $item);
25: Print_Page("./templates", "item_details.tmpl", $item);
```

Listing 15-3: **cart.cgi**

```
01: #!/usr/bin/perl -wT
02: # cart.cgi

03: use strict;
```

Continued

Listing 15-3 *(continued)*

```perl
04: use SOAP::Lite;
05: use CGI qw(:standard);

06: use lib qw(.);
07: use BasicSession;

08: our $sess;
09: my  %session;

10: $sess = Get_Session();
11: tie %session, 'BasicSession';

12: my $add_to_cart = param('add_to_cart');
13: ++$session{$add_to_cart} if $add_to_cart;

14: my $remove= param('remove');
15: delete $session{$remove};

16: my $products = SOAP::Lite
17:    -> uri('http://goliath.perlguy.net/Catalog')
18:    -> proxy('http://goliath.perlguy.net/cgi-
                   bin/soap_server19.cgi')
19:    -> Get_Product_List()
20:    -> result;

21: Print_Page("./templates", "header.tmpl", \%session);
22: Print_Page("./templates", "catalog_header.tmpl",
\%session);

23: delete($session{'cart_qty_total'});
24: delete($session{'cart_price_total'});

25: for my $prod (@$products) {
26:     next unless ($session{$prod->[1]});

27:     $session{'cart_qty_total'}   += $session{$prod->[1]};
28:     $session{'cart_price_total'} +=
            Calc_Price($session{$prod->[1]} , $prod->[2]);

29:     print qq(
30:        <tr><td>
31:     [<a href="cart.cgi?add_to_cart=$prod->[1]">Add Item</a>]
32:        </td><td>
33:     <a href="item_details.cgi?item_num=$prod->[1]">$prod-
>[1]</a>
34:        </td><td>
35:          $prod->[0]
36:        </td><td align="right">
```

```
37:             $prod->[2]
38:         </td><td align="center">
39:             $session{$prod->[1]}
40:         </td><td>
41:            [<a href="cart.cgi?remove=$prod->[1]">Delete</a>]
42:         </td></tr>\n
43:      );
44: }

45: $session{'cart_price_total'} =
         sprintf("%.2f", $session{'cart_price_total'});

46: Print_Page("./templates", "cart_total.tmpl"    ,
\%session);
47: Print_Page("./templates", "catalog_footer.tmpl",
\%session);


48: sub Calc_Price {
49:    my($qty, $price) = @_;

50:    $price =~ s/[ \$]//g;

51:    return($qty * $price);
52: }
```

Listing 15-4: **invoice.cgi**

```
01: #!/usr/bin/perl -wT

02: use strict;
03: use SOAP::Lite;
04: use CGI qw(:standard);

05: use lib qw(.);
06: use BasicSession;
07: our $sess;
08: my %session;
09: $sess = Get_Session();
10: tie %session, 'BasicSession';

11: my $products = SOAP::Lite
12:    -> uri('http://goliath.perlguy.net/Catalog')
13:    -> proxy('http://goliath.perlguy.net/cgi-
               bin/soap_server19.cgi')
14:    -> Get_Product_List()
```

Continued

Listing 15-4 *(continued)*

```
15:   -> result;

16: Print_Page("./templates", "header.tmpl", \%session);
17: Print_Page("./templates", "invoice_header.tmpl",
\%session);

18: delete($session{'cart_qty_total'});
19: delete($session{'cart_price_total'});

20: for my $prod (@$products){
21:     next unless ($session{$prod->[1]});

22:     $session{'cart_qty_total'}   += $session{$prod->[1]};
23:     $session{'cart_price_total'} +=
            Calc_Price($item{$prod->[1]} , $prod->[2]);

24:     print qq(
25:       <tr>
26:        <td align="center" valign="top">
27:         $prod->[1]
28:        </td>
29:        <td align="left">
30:           $prod->[0]
31:        </td>
32:        <td align="center" valign="top">
33:         $session{$prod->[1]}
34:        </td>
35:        <td align="right" valign="top">
36:         $prod->[2]
37:        </td>
38:        <td align="right" valign="top">
39:     );

40:    printf("\$%.2f", Calc_Price($session{$prod->[1]}, $prod-
>[2]) );

41:     print qq(
42:        </td>
43:       </tr>\n
44:     );
45: }

46: $session{'cart_price_total'} =
        sprintf("%.2f", $session{'cart_price_total'});
47: Print_Page("./templates", "invoice_footer.tmpl",
\%session);
```

```
48: sub Calc_Price {
49:     my($qty, $price) = @_;

50:     $price =~ s/[ \$]//g;

51:     return($qty * $price);
52: }
```

Listing 15-5: **cart_total.tmpl**

```
01:    <tr>
02:     <td align="right" colspan="3">
03:      Total in cart:
04:     </td>
05:     <td align="right">
06:      <b>$%%cart_price_total%%</b>
07:     </td>
08:     <td align="center">
09:      <b>%%cart_qty_total%%</b>
10:     </td>
11:     <td align="center">
12:      
13:     </td>
14:    </tr>
```

Listing 15-6: **catalog_footer.tmpl**

```
01:    <tr>
02:     <td align="center" colspan="6">
03:      [ <a href="catalog.cgi">View Catalog</a> ]
04:      [ <a href="cart.cgi">View Cart</a> ]
05:      [ <a href="invoice.cgi">View Invoice</a> ]
06:     </td>
07:    </tr>
08:   </table>
09:  </body>
10: </html>
```

Listing 15-7: **catalog_header.tmpl**

```
01:   <body>
02:    <table border="1" cellspacing="0" align="center">
03:     <tr>
04:      <td colspan="6" align="center">
05:       <font class="big2">
06:        Book Catalog
07:       </font>
08:      </td>
09:     </tr>
10:     <tr>
11:      <td align="center">
12:       <b>Purchase</b>
13:      </td>
14:      <td align="center">
15:       <b>ISBN #</b>
16:      </td>
17:      <td align="center">
18:       <b>Item</b>
19:      </td>
20:      <td align="center">
21:       <b>Price</b>
22:      </td>
23:      <td align="center">
24:       <b>Cart</b>
25:      </td>
26:      <td align="center">
27:       <b>Remove</b>
28:      </td>
29:     </tr>
```

Listing 15-8: **header.tmpl**

```
01: <html><head><title>Product Catalog</title>
02: <style type="text/css">
03: <!--
04: td    { background:   #e0e0e0;
05:         color:        #000000;
06:         font-family: Lucida, Verdana, Helvetica, Arial;
07:         font-size:    12pt}

08: a:link    { color: #4444ff }
09: a:visited { color: #333377 }
10: a:active  { color: #0000dd }

11: b
```

```
12: { font-family: Lucida, Verdana, Helvetica, Arial;
13:    font-size:   10pt;
14:    color:       %%text_color%% }

15: .small
16: { font-family: Lucida, Verdana, Helvetica, Arial;
17:    font-size:   10pt;
18:    color:       %%text_color%% }

19: .medium
20: { font-family: Lucida, Verdana, Helvetica, Arial;
21:    font-size:   12pt;
22:    color:       %%text_color%% }

23: .big_error
24: { font-family: Lucida, Verdana, Helvetica, Arial;
25:    font-size:   14pt;
26:    font-weight: bold;
27:    color:       #ff0000 }

28: .big
29: { font-family: Lucida, Verdana, Helvetica, Arial;
30:    font-size:   14pt;
31:    color:       %%text_color%% }

32: .large
33: { font-family: Lucida, Verdana, Helvetica, Arial;
34:    font-size:   20pt;
35:    color:       %%text_color%% }

36: .big2
37: { font-family: Lucida, Verdana, Helvetica, Arial;
38:    font-size:   24pt;
39:    color:       %%text_color%% }

40: -->
41: </style>
42: </head>
43: <body>
```

Listing 15-9: **invoice_body.tmpl**

```
01:  <tr>
02:    <td align="center" valign="top">
03:     <b>Item #</b>
04:    </td>
```

Continued

Listing 15-9 *(continued)*

```
05:    <td align="center">
06:     <b>Item Description</b>
07:    </td>
08:    <td align="center" valign="top">
09:     <b>Qty</b>
10:    </td>
11:    <td align="center" valign="top">
12:     <b>Price</b>
13:    </td>
14:    <td align="center" valign="top">
15:     <b>Total</b>
16:    </td>
17:   </tr>
```

Listing 15-10: **invoice_footer.tmpl**

```
01:     <tr>
02:      <td align="center" colspan="2">
03:      </td>
04:      <td align="center"><b>
05:       %%cart_qty_total%%
06:      </b></td>
07:      <td align="right">
08:       <b>Grand Total:</b>
09:      </td>
10:      <td align="right"><b>
11:       $%%cart_price_total%%
12:      </b></td>
13:     </tr>
14:    </table>
15:   </body>
16: </html>
```

Listing 15-11: **invoice_header.tmpl**

```
01: <table border="1" width="100%" align="center"
cellspacing="0">
02:  <tr>
03:   <td colspan="5" align="center">
04:    <font class="big2">Order Invoice</font>
```

```
05:    </td>
06:    </tr>

07:    <tr>
08:    <td align="left" width="10%" valign="top">
09:     <b>Date:</b> <font class="small">04/29/2002</font>
10:    </td>
11:    <td align="center" width="80%" colspan="3">
12:    <font class="large">Perlguy, Inc.</font><br />
13:    4 Brae Burn Court<br />
14:    St. Charles, MO 63303<br />
15:    (314) 555-1212<br />
16:    brent@perlguy.net
17:    <br /><br />
18:    </td>
19:    <td align="right" width="10%" valign="top">
20:     <b>Invoice #:</b> <font
class="small">9328409</font>
21:    </td>
22:    </tr>

23:    <tr>
24:    <td align="center" valign="top">
25:     <b>Item #</b>
26:    </td>
27:    <td align="center">
28:     <b>Item Description</b>
29:    </td>
30:    <td align="center" valign="top">
31:     <b>Qty</b>
32:    </td>
33:    <td align="center" valign="top">
34:     <b>Price</b>
35:    </td>
36:    <td align="center" valign="top">
37:     <b>Total</b>
38:    </td>
39:    </tr>
```

Listing 15-12: **item_details.tmpl**

```
01: <table border="1" width="100%" align="center"
cellspacing="0">
02:    <tr>
03:    <td colspan="5" align="center">
04:     <font class="big2">Order Invoice</font>
```

Continued

Listing 15-12 *(continued)*

```
05:    </td>
06:    </tr>

07:    <tr>
08:    <td align="left" width="10%" valign="top">
09:     <b>Date:</b> <font class="small">04/29/2002</font>
10:    </td>
11:    <td align="center" width="80%" colspan="3">
12:    <font class="large">Perlguy, Inc.</font><br />
13:    4 Brae Burn Court<br />
14:    St. Charles, MO 63303<br />
15:    (314) 555-1212<br />
16:    brent@perlguy.net
17:    <br /><br />
18:    </td>
19:    <td align="right" width="10%" valign="top">
20:     <b>Invoice #:</b> <font
class="small">9328409</font>
21:    </td>
22:    </tr>

23:    <tr>
24:    <td align="center" valign="top">
25:     <b>Item #</b>
26:    </td>
27:    <td align="center">
28:     <b>Item Description</b>
29:    </td>
30:    <td align="center" valign="top">
31:     <b>Qty</b>
32:    </td>
33:    <td align="center" valign="top">
34:     <b>Price</b>
35:    </td>
36:    <td align="center" valign="top">
37:     <b>Total</b>
38:    </td>
39:    </tr>
```

✦   ✦   ✦

Creating a Web-Based Photo Album

Many different photo albums are on the Web, so why create another one? Well, first of all, many of the photo albums are clunky and difficult to customize. Second, creating a photo album is fun! The photo album in this chapter shows you that, in addition to creating your own photo album, you can modify your photo album to your own specifications.

The photo album in this chapter is really just a start, but it is a great start. The code to create this album is pretty short compared with many of the other Perl photo albums around. Plus, the photo album in this chapter is much faster than some of the current Web-based photo albums.

Again, this chapter builds from concepts we have already covered in this book. Also, we use the `BasicSession.pm` module we develop previously. This photo album weighs in at under 400 lines of code—if we don't count duplicate code and HTML templates. Considering that some photo albums consist of over 4,500 lines of code, fewer than 400 lines is very good.

Building the Photo Album Application

The photo album application is made up of several pieces. First, we have the `generate.pl` program. This is a command-line program that photo-album administrators use to generate the photo album from a directory of images. This program takes the images in the directory, converts them to the different sizes, moves them to where they need to be for the Web server, and adds the information to our database. This program takes a little while to run because of the image conversions it is doing.

The other pieces of the application are the `admin.cgi` script, used to add descriptions and comments for the photos, and the `index.cgi` script, which displays the images and albums.

The `index.cgi` and `admin.cgi` are 95 percent the same program, but they are made into two separate programs so that you can put the `admin.cgi` program in a safe place while `index.cgi` is available to the visitors of your album.

Let's take a look at the `generate.pl` program first, since it is what actually generates the photo album when passed a directory of images.

Something to be aware of with this program is that when you point it at a directory to add to your album, it traverses the subdirectories in the directory you point to. If you do not want this to happen, put your photos temporarily into a directory when you add them to the album. New copies of the images are added to the photo album directory, so you can remove the temporary files once the program has finished generating the files.

To run the program, just do this:

```
./generate.pl "album name" directory
```

The program handles the rest. As we'll see in a minute, however, there are several things to set in the program so that it knows where to put the files it generates.

This program uses a few new Perl modules we have not used before. `Imager.pm` handles our image manipulation; `Image::Info` is used to get the EXIF information (like the day it was taken, the shutter speed, etc.) embedded in JPEG files; `File::Basename` handles getting the filename for us from a complete path; and `File::Find` is used to get the files in the subdirectories. `Imager.pm` and `Image::Info` are available from CPAN or ActiveState if you are on Windows. `File::Find` and `File::Basename` should be part of your Perl installation.

generate.pl

```
01: #!/usr/bin/perl -w
02: # generate.pl

03: use strict;
04: use Image::Info qw(image_info dim);
05: use File::Basename;
06: use File::Find;
07: use File::Copy;
08: use Imager;
09: use DBI;
```

Line 1 tells the system where to find Perl and turns on warnings. Notice that we do not turn on taint checking with the -T flag here. We do this because this program should only be run manually by photo album administrators. Since this is not a program the users run, it is safe to leave off the taint checking.

Line 2 is a comment about the program.

Line 3 turns on strict mode. This helps ensure that all variables are declared before they are used. Also, it prevents many common programming errors.

Line 4 loads the Image::Info module and imports the image_info and dim functions.

Line 5 loads the File::Basename module so that we can easily split directory and filenames.

Line 6 loads the File::Find module so that we can easily get files and process them from directories.

Line 7 loads the File::Copy module so that we can easily copy files from one location to another on the file system.

Line 8 loads the Imager module. This module allows us to manipulate images.

Line 9 loads the DBI module so that we have database connectivity.

```
10: my $info;
11: my $album_name = shift(@ARGV) || die "Which album name?";
12: my $album_id   = time();
```

Line 10 declares a scalar variable we'll be using in this program.

Line 11 declares a scalar variable named $album_name and shifts in the first value from @ARGV. If nothing was passed the program will die and ask which album name.

Line 12 declares a scalar variable named $album_id and populates it with the current time value. This is the unique id that we use for this album. This is not a very clever trick, but since this program takes quite a bit of time to run, there is not a very good chance that more than one album will be generated per second.

```
13: ### Begin user modifications
14: my $relative_dir = "/photos";
15: my $album_dir    = "/var/www/html/photos";
16: my @SIZES        = qw(100 640 800);
17: ### End of user modifications
```

Line 13 is a comment telling the user that the area of the program he or she may need to modify is beginning.

Line 14 declares a scalar variable named $relative_dir and sets it to the value "/photos". This is the relative directory that goes in the URL when the browser is viewing the image. This is not the actual path to the directory; rather, it is the URL path.

Line 15 declares a scalar variable named $album_dir and sets it to the value "/var/www/html/photos". This is the absolute path to the directory that the files for the photo album are copied into.

Line 16 declares an array named @SIZES and loads it with the values 100, 640, and 800. These are the widths of the images this program generates. The width of 100 is the width of the thumbnail images displayed on the main album page.

Line 17 is simply a comment telling the program user that the manual-modifications section has ended.

```
18: $album_name      =~ s/ /\_/g;
19: $album_dir       .= "/$album_name";
20: my $rel_dir      = "$relative_dir/$album_name";
```

Line 18 replaces any spaces in the album name with the underscore character. The =~ on this line is called the *binding operator*. It binds the regular expression on the right to the variable on the left. This makes it so that the regular expression acts upon $album_name instead of the default variable of $_.

Line 19 adds /$album_name to the end of the album directory. This occurs so we can generate the directory we need.

Line 20 sets up the relative directory to the album and stores that value in $rel_dir.

```
21: mkdir($album_dir) || die "Can't mkdir: $!"   unless -e
$album_dir;

22: my $source_dir = shift(@ARGV) || ".";
```

Line 21 uses the mkdir function to create the new album directory. This line then checks to see if the directory was actually created with the -e (which means exists). If the directory does not exist, then the program will die and print out an error message.

Line 22 looks at the value passed on the command line to see what directory we want to get the photos from. @ARGV initially has the album name in it, but when we call the shift function on **line 10**, we remove that value from @ARGV. This line sets $source_dir to the current directory unless a directory name is passed on the command line.

```
23: my $dbh = DBI->connect("DBI:mysql:photoalbum",
       "bookuser","testpass")
24:      or die("Cannot connect: $DBI::errstr");
```

Lines 23 and 24 call the DBI->connect function to create a connection to the database. If there is a problem creating the database connection, the die on **line 24** will cause the program to exit and display an error message.

```
25: my @EXIF  = qw(width height resolution Flash Model
26:              Make MaxApertureValue FNumber DateTime
27:              ISOSpeedRatings ExposureTime FocalLength);
```

Lines 25–27 declare a new array named @EXIF and set it to the values we want to get from the image. EXIF information is image metadata that is written into JPEG files. Many digital cameras put EXIF information into the images when they write them. The preceding list of EXIF information is not complete; these are simply the fields that have been added to this program. The Image::Info module is how you get this data, and doing a *perldoc Image::Info* gets you a whole slew of information about what it can extract from a JPEG image.

```
28: Add_Album();
29: find({wanted => \&Wanted, follow => 1}, $source_dir);

30: print "\nDone generating new album...\n\n";
```

Line 28 calls the Add_Album subroutine. This subroutine adds the album information to the database.

Line 29 calls the find function. The values passed to find are a hash of parameters, and the directory to look at.

wanted => \&Wanted tells the program that we need to call the Wanted subroutine for each file we find.

follow => 1 mainly causes symbolic links to be followed, but also has a useful side effect: By saying `follow => 1`, the `File::Find` function also populates the `$File::Find::fulldir` variable — which we need so that we can get the complete path to the item. Without this, we do not get the full path information, only the relative path information.

`@ARGV` is the directory that we are getting photos from.

Line 30 prints a message telling the user that the program is done running. That is it! Well, the rest of the stuff this program does is stored in the following subroutines.

```
31: sub Add_Album {
32:     my $sql = qq{INSERT INTO album
33:              (album_id, name, comments)
34:              VALUES (?,?,?)};
```

Line 31 begins the `Add_Album` subroutine. This subroutine adds the album information to the database.

Lines 32–34 make up the SQL statement needed to add the album information to the database. On **line 33**, we use *placeholders* (that is, **?'s**) in the SQL statement so that we can pass the values when we call the `execute` the function.

```
35:     my $sth_album = $dbh->prepare($sql);

36:     $sth_album->execute($album_id, $album_name, '')
37:         or die("ERROR! $DBI::errstr\n");
38: }
```

Line 35 calls the `prepare` function to get this SQL statement ready for execution. The value returned from the `prepare` function is a handle to the statement, which we store in the `$sth_album` scalar variable.

Line 36 calls the `execute` function on the statement handle and passes in the *album id*, *name*, and an *empty string* for the comments. These values replace the placeholders that are in the SQL statement.

Line 37 is a continuation of **line 35**. This causes the program to exit and to print an error message if there is a problem executing the SQL statement.

Line 38 closes the `Add_Album` subroutine.

```
39: sub Update_Database {
40:     my $photo = shift;
41:     my $p_dir = "$rel_dir/$photo";
```

Line 39 begins the `Update_Database` subroutine. This subroutine updates the database with the photo information. It is called for each photo.

Line 40 uses the `shift` function to get the name of the photo we are dealing with.

Line 41 declares a variable named $p_dir (photo directory) and sets it to the relative directory name, with the name of the photo added to it.

```
42:         my $sql1  = qq{INSERT INTO photo
43:                 (img_id, width, height, resolution, flash,
44:                  model, make, aperture, fnumber, img_date,
45:                  iso_speed, exposure, focal_length,
46:                  img_title, img_location, album_id, comments)
47:                 VALUES
48:                 (?,?,?,?,?,?,?,?,?,?,?,?,?,?,?,?,?)};
```

Lines 42–48 make up the SQL statement to insert the photo information into the database. It is rather large, but there is nothing different about this SQL INSERT statement when we compare it with our smaller INSERT statements.

```
49:         my $sth_photo = $dbh->prepare($sql1);

50:         my $id = $info->{DateTime};
51:         $id     =~ s/[ \:]//g;
52:         $id    .= time();
```

Line 49 calls the prepare function and stores the result into the $sth_photo variable.

Line 50 declares a variable named $id and sets it to the value at $info->{DateTime}. This should contain the date and time this picture was taken.

Line 51 removes any spaces or colons that are in the $id variable. The DateTime value we get on **line 50** is in the form of 2002:05:13 15:32:54, so we want to remove the extra stuff.

Line 52 appends the current time onto the $id variable. This should pretty much ensure that the value in $id is unique. We need it to be unique because this is going to be the primary key of our table.

```
53:         $sth_photo->execute($id, @$info{@EXIF}, 'untitled',
54:                         $p_dir, $album_id, '')
55:             or die("ERROR! $DBI::errstr");
```

Line 53 calls the execute function and passes it the values to fill in all of the placeholders. The @$info{@EXIF} here is of importance. This is called a hash slice because it takes only a portion, or slice, of the hash. The %info hash contains all of the information we have gathered so far for this photo. At this point, we need to add the EXIF information to the database. We can $info{width}, $info{height}, and so on, but that requires too much typing. Instead, let's take advantage of what Perl can do for us. We already have the field names (hash keys) in an array named @EXIF. So, when we create the SQL statement on **lines 42–48**, we do so in the same order the @EXIF array is in. Then, by calling the %info hash with the @ in front of it, we create the hash slice that contains all of the values from the %info hash with the keys in the @EXIF array.

Line 54 continues the execute statement from **line 53**. It adds a few other values that replace the placeholders.

Line 55 calls the die function if there are any errors executing this SQL statement.

```
56:      print "Record inserted into database...\n";
57: }
```

Line 56 prints a message to the user so that he or she can see that an item has been inserted into the database.

Line 57 ends the Update_Database subroutine.

```
58: sub Massage_Data {
59:      my @RATIONAL = qw(FNumber FocalLength);
```

Line 58 begins the Massage_Data subroutine. This subroutine just takes the data passed to it and manipulates it how we need to, then sends it back.

Line 59 declares a new array named @RATIONAL and adds two values to it. These are the values that need to be rational numbers.

```
60:      for(@RATIONAL) {
61:          $info->{$_} = Rational($info->{$_},1);
62:      }
```

Line 60 begins a for loop that iterates over each of the values in the @RATIONAL array. If you have more values that need to be rational numbers, simply add them to the array on **line 58**.

Line 61 sets the current value of the %info hash to the value returned by the call to the Rational function on the right. The 1 in this function call is the number of digits we want after the decimal.

Line 62 closes this for loop.

```
63:      $info->{'MaxApertureValue'}
64:          = sprintf("%.1f", (1.4142 **
             $info->{'MaxApertureValue'} ));
65: }
```

Line 63 takes the value at $info->{MaxApertureValue} and performs a calculation on it. This converts the aperture value from a regular decimal to the form that is commonly seen and more widely recognized.

Line 64 is a continuation of **line 63**. This line formats the value to conform to common photographic terminology.

Line 65 closes the Massage_Data function.

```
66: sub Rational {
67:    my ($in, $dec)     = @_;
68:    my ($num, $denom) = split('/', $in);
69:    my  $fmt           = '%.' . $dec . 'f';
```

Line 66 begins the Rational subroutine. This subroutine is used to convert the numbers passed to it into rational numbers.

Line 67 reads in the value ($in) and the number of decimal places ($dec) to format this number to.

Line 68 uses the split function to split the value passed to the function into a numerator ($num) and denominator ($denom).

Line 69 creates the format string for the sprintf function. This creates the %.1f or %.2f , and so on, values that we use in the sprintf function call.

```
70:    return($denom == 0 ? "Err" : sprintf($fmt, $num/$denom));
71: }
```

Line 70 checks to see if the denominator is 0. If it is, we return "Err" because we cannot divide by 0. Otherwise, we return the value returned by the sprintf call to the right of the colon.

Line 71 ends the Rational subroutine.

```
72: sub Img_Copy {
73:     my $source_file = shift;
```

Line 72 begins the Img_Copy subroutine. This subroutine is simply used to copy the unmodified image file into the album directory.

Line 73 uses the shift function to read in the value passed to the subroutine and stores it in the variable named $source_file.

```
74:     $source_file =~ /^([\w\-\/]+)\.(\w{1,4})$/;
75:     my $dest_file = $1 . '.' . $2;
```

Line 74 filters the filename to remove any characters we don't want. This regular expression can be a bit confusing, so here is how it breaks down.

```
$file =~
```

Uses the *binding operator* (=~) to bind the variable $file to the regular expression.

```
/^
```

The / begins the regular expression, and the caret (^) means that the following pattern must occur at the beginning of the string.

```
([\w\-\/]+)
```

The parentheses () cause the regular expression engine to store the match into the variables $1, $2, $3, and so on. Each new pair of parentheses increments which variable it is stored in. Since this is the first set of parentheses, the result is stored in $1.

The square brackets here ([ ]) are a character class. This means that whatever is inside them matches — it is like matching anything from a group (for example, *all brunettes in a crowd*). The term *brunette* is the character class.

The \w matches any word character. A word character consists of all letters, numbers, and the underscore.

The \- matches the dash.

The \/ matches a forward slash.

And the + after the closing square bracket literally means *"match one or more of these characters."*

```
\.
```

Next, the \. matches the dot that separates the filename and extension.

```
(\w{1,4})
```

The next set in parentheses matches on the \w or word characters. The {1,4} means to match at least one, but no more than four, characters. The results of this match are stored in $2 since this is the second set of parentheses in this regular expression. We don't want to match more than four characters because we are really only looking for .jpg and .jpeg. So, if you want, you can change this to {3,4} and it should still work as needed — matching at least three, but no more than four, characters.

```
$/;
```

The $ anchors this last pattern to the end of the string. This means we are looking for the file extension at the very end of the string (where it should be).

The / closes the regular expression, and the ; ends this statement.

So, this line should basically get rid of any extra dots in the filename or illegal characters.

Line 75 creates a string containing the value in $1, a dot, and the value in $2 and stores the string in $dest_file. The $dest_file variable now holds the file name.

```
76:     copy($source_file, "$album_dir/" .
              basename($dest_file)) or die "Cannot copy: $!";
```

Line 76 uses the copy function from the File::Copy module to copy the file from the source to the destination. The basename($dest_file) ensures that we get just the base filename and not the complete path information.

```
77:         print "Done writing $dest_file...\n";
78: }
```

Line 77 prints a message to the user, telling him or her that the new file is done being written.

Line 78 closes the Img_Copy subroutine.

```
79: sub Resize {
80:     my ($file, $xfac) = @_;
81:     my $extn;
```

Line 79 begins the Resize subroutine.

Line 80 declares two new variables named $file and $xfac and copies the values passed to the subroutine into them. $file is the file name, and $xfac is the width of the new image.

Line 81 declares a new variable named $extn.

```
82:     my $img = Imager->new();
83:     $img->open(file => $file) or die $img->errstr();
```

Line 82 creates a new Imager object and stores a reference to it in the $img variable.

Line 83 opens the image file or aborts the program if there is a problem opening the file.

```
84:     $file =~ /^([\w\-\/]+)\.(\w{1,4})$/;
85:     $file = $1;
86:     $file = basename($file);
87:     $extn = $2;
88:     $xfac =~ /^([\d]+)$/ || die "Oops!";
89:     $xfac = $1;
```

Line 84 does the same thing as **line 74** of this program. It basically splits the filename into the name and extension.

Line 85 sets the $file variable to $1, which is the filename without the extension.

Line 86 calls the basename function to remove any path information from $file.

Line 87 sets the $extn variable to $2, which should contain the file extension at this point.

Line 88 passes the $xfac variable through the regular expression. This regular expression ensures that $xfac contains only digits (\d), and calls die if it finds anything other than digits in $xfac.

Line 89 sets $xfac to the value in $1. The parentheses in the regular expression on **line 91** capture any data that matches — this is the data we are looking for.

```
90:     my $newimg = $img->copy();
91:     $newimg    = $img->scale(xpixels => $xfac);
```

Line 90 creates a copy of the image we are working with and stores a handle to it in $newimg.

Line 91 scales the new image so that the X-axis is $xfac pixels wide. The Y-axis scales proportionally, so we don't have to worry about it in this application.

```
92:     $newimg->write(file => "$album_dir/$file.$xfac.$extn")
93:         or die $img->errstr();
```

Line 92 writes the new file to our album directory. The new file has the X axis value between the filename and the extension. This way, we can easily determine the width of this file. We'll also use this value later to grab the image of the correct size.

Line 93 calls die if there is a problem writing to the file.

```
94      print "Done writing $file.$xfac.$extn...\n";
95: }
```

Line 94 prints a message telling the user that the file is done being written.

Line 95 closes this subroutine.

```
96: sub Wanted {
97:     if( (/\.jpg|\.jpeg$/i) ) {
98:         my $file    = $_;
```

Line 96 begins the Wanted subroutine. This is the subroutine that gets called by File::Find to traverse the subdirectories and find the files.

Line 97 checks to see if the current file contains .jpg or .jpeg. If it does, this block of code is entered.

Line 98 sets the variable $file to the current value in $_, which is the filename.

```
99:         $info = undef;
100:        $info = image_info($File::Find::fullname);
```

Line 99 sets the $info variable to undef. We need to do this so that no data from a previous file remains referenced by $info.

Line 100 sets the $info variable to the values returned by a call to the image_info subroutine. The image_info subroutine is part of the Image::Info module.

```
101:            die "Can't parse image info: $info->{error}\n"
102:                if($info->{error});
```

Line 101 calls the die function to cause the program to abort if the program encounters an error getting the image information.

Line 102 is the condition for **line 103**. This line allows **line 103** to execute if there is a value in $info->{error}.

```
103:            for my $width (@SIZES) {
104:                Resize ($File::Find::fullname, $width);
105:            }
```

Line 103 begins a for loop that loops through each value in the @SIZES array. Each time through the array, the current value is stored into $width. This array contains the image sizes that we want to generate from the original images and to store in our album.

Line 104 calls the Resize function on the current photo in $File::Find::fullname and passes the width in pixels in the $width variable.

Line 105 closes the loop.

```
106:            Massage_Data    ();
107:            Img_Copy        ($File::Find::fullname);
108:            Update_Database ($file);
```

Line 106 calls the Massage_Data subroutine to get the data into the format we want.

Line 107 calls the Img_Copy subroutine so that we can make a copy of the original image and place it in the album directory. We don't want to move around or change the original photo, just in case something goes wrong.

Line 108 calls the Update_Database subroutine so that the photo information can be added to the database.

```
109:        print "\n";
110:        }
111: }
```

Line 109 prints a blank line.

Line 110 closes the if block of this subroutine.

Line 111 closes this subroutine.

And that is it for the `generate.pl` program. Once you have run this at least once to create an album, you can move to the next set of programs to view the photo or update the database data.

`index.cgi` is the CGI program that displays the photo to the user. It uses the `BasicSession` module we've used to store the user's image-size preferences. Once we are done looking at this program, we'll take a look at the `admin.cgi` program and cover the differences between the two.

Let's take a look at what this program can do. Figure 16-1 shows you what the `index.cgi` program displays if no values are passed to it.

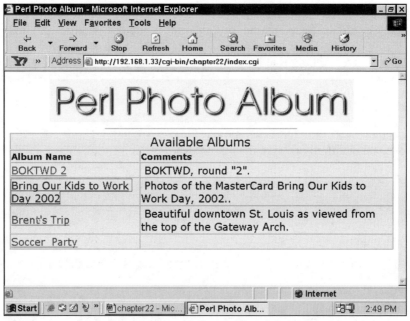

Figure 16-1: index.cgi main album screen

In Figure 16-2, you see the page that lists the thumbnail images for a specific album. Notice in the URL of this page that the album ID is passed (`album=1020740757`). This tells the program what album information to get from the database.

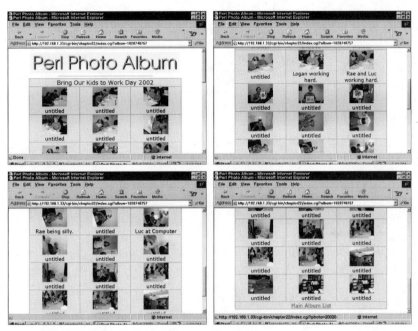

Figure 16-2: index.cgi album thumbnail listing

Notice the thumbnail images at the bottom of Figure 16-3. If we click the one to the left, we get the image in Figure 16-4.

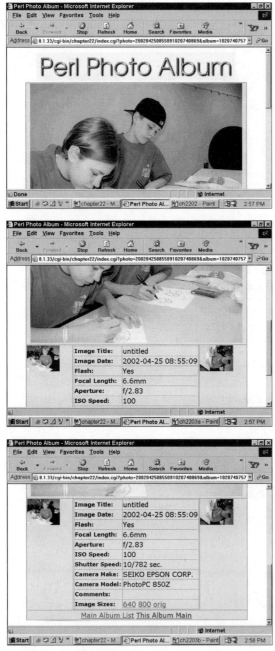

Figure 16-3: index.cgi photo display

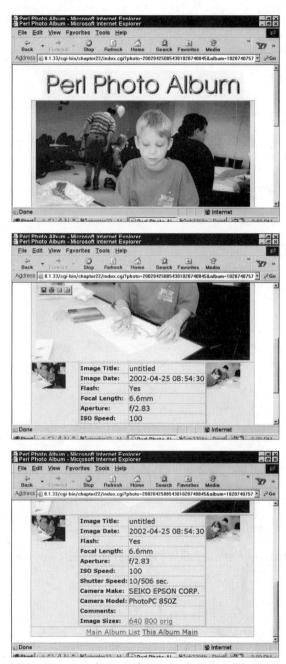

Figure 16-4: index.cgi photo display after the previous image has been clicked

So, now that we've seen what it can do, let's see *how* it does it all!

index.cgi

```
01: #!/usr/bin/perl -wT
02: # index.cgi  Photo Album Script
```

Line 1 tells the system where to find Perl and turns on warnings and taint checking. We are using taint checking for this program, since it will be available through the Web.

Line 2 is simply a comment about this program.

```
03: use strict;
04: use DBI;
05: use CGI qw(:standard);
```

Line 3 loads the strict module.

Line 4 loads the DBI module for our database access.

Line 5 loads the CGI module and its :standard functions.

```
06: use lib qw(.);
07: use BasicSession;
08: our $sess;
09: my  %item;
10: $sess = Get_Session();
11: tie %item, 'BasicSession';
```

Line 6 uses the lib module to push the directories passed to it into the @INC array. This line passes in the current directory so that Perl can find the BasicSession module when we load it in the next step.

Line 7 loads the BasicSession module.

Line 8 declares $sess as our variable. This allows it to be seen by all of the modules and functions in this application.

Line 9 declares the %item hash.

Line 10 calls the Get_Session function and stores the result of this call in the $sess variable. This creates a user session so that we can remember the user's preferences.

Line 11 ties he %item array to the BasicSession module. This allows us to maintain user-session data between program calls.

```
12: my $album = param('album');
13: my $photo = param('photo');
14: my $size  = param('size');
```

Lines 12–14 declare a scalar variable and read in some data from the calling HTML form, storing that data in the respective variables.

```
15: my $sizes = Make_Sizes(qw(640 800 orig));
```

```
16: $size ? ($item{'size'} = $size) : ($size = $item{'size'});
```

Line 15 calls the Make_Sizes subroutine on the values passed. This simply creates the HTML needed to generate the links that allow the user to change image size.

Line 16 checks to see if the $size variable contains any data. If it does, the first item after ? is executed. This sets the $item{'size'} hash element to the value in $size. If $size does not contain any data yet, the ternary operator sets the $size variable to the value that is currently in the $item{'size'} hash element.

So, this code either gets or sets the value in $item{'size'}. Since the %item hash is tied to the database, this also stores this data into the database. This allows us to remember what photo size our user prefers.

```
17: my $dbh = DBI->connect("DBI:mysql:photoalbum",
       "bookuser","testpass")
18:     or die("Cannot connect: $DBI::errstr");
```

Line 17 creates a connection to the database and stores a handle to that database connection in the $dbh variable.

Line 18 causes the program to abort and display an error message if there is a problem connecting to the database.

```
19: if($photo) {
20:     Show_Photo($photo, $album);
21:     exit;
22: }
```

Line 19 checks to see if the $photo variable contains any data. If it does, this block of code is entered.

Line 20 calls the Show_Photo subroutine, which displays the photo, as in Figures 16-3 and 16-4.

Line 21 exits the program. We have done what we need to do, and this ensures that the program goes no farther.

Line 22 ends this code block.

```
23: elsif($album) {
24:     Show_Album($album);
25:     exit;
26: }
```

Line 23 checks to see if the $album variable contains any data. If it does, this code block is entered.

Line 24 calls the Show_Album subroutine. This subroutine shows the albums thumbnail gallery.

Line 25 exits the program so that no further execution can take place.

Line 26 closes this block of code.

```
27: else {
28:     List_Albums();
29:     exit;
30: }
```

Line 27 is the default code for this if..elsif..else block. If nothing is in $photo or $album, we enter this block of code.

Line 28 calls the List_Albums subroutine. This subroutine is the main list of photo albums you get when this program is called without any arguments.

Line 29 exits the program. The rest of this program is all subroutines.

Line 30 closes this block of code.

```
31: sub Make_Sizes {
32:     my @sizes  = @_;
33:     my $string = '';
```

Line 31 begins the Make_Sizes subroutine. This is subroutine generates the HTML links for the images passed to it.

Line 32 declares a new array named @sizes and populates it with the values passed to this subroutine when it is called.

Line 33 declares a variable named $string and sets it to an empty string.

```
34:        for my $size (@sizes) {
35:            $string .=
36:            qq(<a
href="?photo=$photo&album=$album&size=$size">$size</a> );
37:        }
```

Line 34 loops through the values in @sizes and stores the current value in $size each time through the loop.

Line 35 uses the appendination operator .= to append the string on **line 36** to its current value.

Line 36 creates the HTML links for the different image sizes. This allows the user to choose a different image size.

Line 37 closes this loop.

```
38:        return($string);
39: }
```

Line 38 returns the value in $string.

Line 39 closes this subroutine.

```
40: sub List_Albums {
41:     my $sql = qq{SELECT * FROM album};
42:     my $sth = $dbh->prepare($sql);
43:     $sth->execute();
```

Line 40 begins the List_Albums subroutine. This subroutine lists all of the albums that are in the database.

Line 41 creates the SQL statement needed to grab all of the items in the album table.

Line 42 prepares the SQL statement created on the preceding line and stores the result into the $sth statement handle.

Line 43 executes the SQL statement.

```
44:        Print_Page("./templates", "header.tmpl");
45:        Print_Page("./templates", "list_top.tmpl");
```

Lines 44 and 45 call the Print_Page subroutine and pass it the appropriate directory and template file names to begin the HTML for this page.

```
46:        while(my $p = $sth->fetchrow_hashref){
47:            Print_Page("./templates", "list_row.tmpl", $p);
48:        }
```

Line 46 begins a `while` loop that continues looping as long as the call to `fetchrow_hashref` is returning data. Each time the data is fetched, the `$p` variable is loaded with a reference to a hash containing the returned data.

Line 47 calls the `Print_Page` subroutine to print a row of data.

Line 48 closes this loop.

```
49:        Print_Page("./templates", "list_end.tmpl");
50:        Print_Page("./templates", "footer.tmpl");
51: }
```

Lines 49 and 50 print the footer HTML with some help from the `Print_Page` subroutine again.

Line 51 closes this subroutine.

```
52: sub Show_Album {
53:        my $cols = 3;
```

Line 52 begins the `Show_Album` subroutine. This subroutine shows the thumbnails of all photos in the album.

Line 53 declares a variable named `$cols` and sets it to 3. This is the number of columns we display the thumbnails in.

```
54:    my $sql_p = qq{SELECT * FROM photo WHERE album_id = ?};
55:    my $sql_a = qq{SELECT * FROM album WHERE album_id = ?};
56:    my $sth_p = $dbh->prepare($sql_p);
57:    my $sth_a = $dbh->prepare($sql_a);
58:    $sth_p->execute($album);
59:    $sth_a->execute($album);
```

Lines 54–59 almost make you think you are seeing double. These lines create the SQL to grab the data from the `photo` table and the `album` table.

Lines 58 and 59 execute the SQL statements that we've just created. Notice that even for the SQL statement that gets data from the `photo` table, we pass the `$album` variable. We do this to limit our matches to the items in that album.

```
60:        Print_Page("./templates", "header.tmpl");
```

Line 60 prints the header for this page by calling the `Print_Page` subroutine and passing the appropriate template file.

```
61:        while(my $p = $sth_a->fetchrow_hashref){
62:            $p->{cols} = $cols;
63:            Print_Page("./templates", "album_top.tmpl", $p);
64:        }
```

Line 61 begins a while loop that continues looping as long as the calls to fetchrow_hashref keep returning data. Each time the data is retrieved, the $p variable stores a reference to a hash containing the data.

Line 62 sets the $p->{cols} hash element to the value in $cols.

Line 63 prints the page top.

Line 64 closes this loop.

```
65:        my $counter = 1;
66:        while(my $p = $sth_p->fetchrow_hashref){
67:    $p->{img_location} = get_image($p->{img_location}, 100);
```

Line 65 declares a new variable named $counter and sets it to 1.

Line 66 begins a while loop that loops as long as fetchrow_hashref is returning data.

Line 67 sets the $p->{image_location} to the value returned by the get_image function call.

```
68:            print "<tr>"  if($counter == 1);
69:            Print_Page("./templates", "album_row.tmpl", $p);
70:            print "</tr>" if($counter == $cols);
```

Line 68 prints the table-row tag if the value in $counter is equal to 1.

Line 69 prints an album row.

Line 70 prints the closing table-row tag if the value of $counter is equal to the value in $cols.

The print statements on **lines 68 and 70** are used to print the different table rows. These values need to get printed only once for each row, so we use a counter to keep track of how many columns we have printed. Then we print a new row only when needed.

```
71:            $counter++;
72:            $counter = 1  if($counter > $cols);
73:        }
74:    print "</tr>" unless($counter == 1);
```

Line 71 increments the value in $counter.

Line 72 sets $counter to 1 if the value of $counter is greater than that of $cols.

Line 73 closes this loop.

Line 74 prints a closing table tag unless the value in $counter is 1.

```
75:      Print_Page("./templates", "album_end.tmpl",
             {'cols' => $cols});
76:      Print_Page("./templates", "footer.tmpl");
77: }
```

Line 75 uses the Print_Page function to print some closing HTML. We again have to pass the number of columns to the Print_Page function so that we can generate valid HTML.

Line 76 also uses the Print_Page function to print some more HTML.

Line 77 closes this subroutine.

```
78: sub Get_Photo_List {
79:      my ($photo, $album) = @_;
80:      my ($index, @photos);
81:      my $count = 0;
```

Line 78 begins the Get_Photo_List subroutine. This subroutine is used to get all of the photos for a particular album.

Line 79 declares two scalar variables and loads them with the data passed to the subroutine.

Line 80 declares two more variables this subroutine uses.

Line 81 declares the $count variable and sets it to 0.

```
82:      my $sql  = qq{SELECT img_id FROM photo
                        WHERE album_id = ?};
83:      my $sth  = $dbh->prepare($sql);
84:      my @all;
85:      $sth->execute($album);
```

Line 82 creates the SQL statement to get all of the img_id's from the photo table for a particular album.

Line 83 uses the DBI's prepare method to get the SQL ready for execution. The result of the prepare call is stored in $sth as a statement handle.

Line 84 declares a new array variable named @all.

Line 85 executes the SQL statement and passes the value in $album to the SQL statement to take the place of the placeholder.

```
86:        while(my @tmp = $sth->fetchrow_array){push @all,
               $tmp[0];}
```

Line 86 is a while loop that loads up the @all array with the img_id values.

The condition for the while loop is the fetchrow_array call. As long as that is getting data, it is true, and the while loop continues. Each time fetchrow_array fetches a record from the database, the record is stored in @tmp.

Then, inside the (very small) code block, the push function is used to push the new value into the @all array. The value we are pushing into the @all array is in the $tmp[0] variable. Since we only fetch one record at a time with this SQL statement, the current value is always at element 0 of the array.

```
87:        for(@all) {
88:            $index = $count if(/$photo/); # Get index of photo
89:            $count++;
90:        }
```

Line 87 begins a for loop that traverses through the values in the @all array.

Line 88 stores the current value of $count into the $index variable if the current value matches the value in $photo. So, this line searches for the proper photo and sets the $index value appropriately.

Line 89 increments the $count variable.

Line 90 closes this for loop.

```
91:        unless($index) {
92:            @photos = @all[0, 1];
93:            unshift @photos, '';
94:        }
```

Line 91 checks to see if $index is 0, unless is the same as *if not*. If $index is 0, this is the first photo in the album. Since this is the first photo, we don't have a "previous" photo to display and need to handle this case appropriately—so we enter this block of code.

Line 92 populates the @photos array with the *array slice* @all[0, 1]. This simply copies the first two elements of the @all array into the @photos array.

Line 93 adds an empty item to the beginning of the array with the unshift function. The unshift function does the opposite of the shift function. Instead of removing the first value from an array, it plops a value onto the beginning of an array.

Line 94 closes this code block.

```
95:     else {
96:         @photos = @all[($indx-1)..($indx+1)];
97:     }
```

Line 95 is the else condition for this if..else block. We get here if the photo we are looking for is not the first photo.

Line 96 gets an *array slice* that includes the photo and the next and previous photos. The ($indx-1) is the previous photo, since $indx is the array index of the photo we want. Then ($indx+1) is the array index of the next photo.

What happens with ($indx+1) if $indx is the last photo? Well, simple: that element is not defined, so it contains no data. Perl simply instantiates the new array element and returns what it contains (nothing). If you had been programming in C or something similar, your program would have died right here; the array bounds would have been broken. But this doesn't happen in Perl!

Line 97 ends this if..else block.

```
98:     return (@photos);
99: }
```

Line 98 returns the @photos array.

Line 99 closes the Get_Photo_List subroutine.

```
100: sub Show_Photo {
101:     my ($photo, $album) = @_;
```

Line 100 begins the Show_Photo subroutine.

Line 101 declares the $photo and $album variables and loads them with the values passed to the subroutine.

```
102:     my @photos = Get_Photo_List($photo, $album);

103:     my $ptr = Get_Details(@photos);
```

Line 102 declares an array named @photos and calls the Get_Photo_List function. The result of this function call populates the @photos array.

Line 103 calls the Get_Details function and passes it the @photos array. The value returned by this function call is stored in the $ptr variable.

```
104:      $ptr->{img_location} =
              get_image($ptr->{img_location}, $size);
105:      $ptr->{image_sizes}  = $sizes;
```

Line 104 calls the get_image function and stores the result back into the value pointed to at $ptr->{img_location}. This handles getting the appropriate-sized image.

Line 105 sets the value at $ptr->{image_sizes} to the values in $sizes.

```
106:      Print_Page("./templates", "header.tmpl");
107:      Print_Page("./templates", "photo_main.tmpl", $ptr);
108:      Print_Page("./templates", "photo_footer.tmpl", $ptr);
109: }
```

Lines 106–108 call the Print_Page function with different template files. These simply print the HTML needed to generate the page we are displaying on the user's browser.

Line 109 closes this subroutine.

```
110: sub Get_Details {
111:      my @photos = @_;
112:      my ($p, %tmp);
113:      my %hsh = ('prev' => 0, 'curr' => 1, 'next' => 2);
```

Line 110 begins the Get_Details subroutine. This subroutine handles getting image details needed for the Web page.

Line 111 declares a hash named @photos and loads it with the values passed to the subroutine when it is called.

Line 112 declares a scalar variable and a hash that we'll need in this subroutine.

Line 113 declares a hash named %hsh and loads it with some data.

```
114:      my $sql1 = qq{SELECT img_id, img_location FROM photo
              WHERE img_id = ?};
115:      my $sql2 = qq{SELECT * FROM photo WHERE img_id = ?};
```

Line 114 creates our first SQL statement that gets the *image id* and *location* from the photo table.

Line 115 creates our second SQL statement. This one gets *all* of the data that matches the photo we are looking for.

We have two SQL statements because for the previous and next images, we need only their id and location. For the photo we are displaying, however, we need all of the data.

```
116:      my $sth1 = $dbh->prepare($sql1);
117:      my $sth2 = $dbh->prepare($sql2);
```

Lines 116–117 prepare the SQL statements and store them in their respective statement handles.

```
118:      for(keys %hsh){
119:          if(/curr/) {
120:              $sth2->execute($photos[$hsh{$_}]);
121:              $p = $sth2->fetchrow_hashref;
122:          }
```

Line 118 begins a for loop that iterates through all of the keys in the %hsh array. These keys we set previously and are *prev*, *curr*, and *next*.

Line 119 checks to see if the current key matches curr. If so, we enter this block of code.

Line 120 executes the statement pointed to by $sth2. Notice that we use the %hsh value as the index of the array for the placeholder value. That is why we set these values in the hash array. The current item in the array is index 1 — so $photos[1] is sent to the SQL statement.

Line 121 calls the fetchrow_hashref function to get the data returned by the database and stores it in $p.

Line 122 closes this part of the if..else block.

```
123:          else {
124:              $sth1->execute($photos[$hsh{$_}])
                      or die("Error!\n");
```

Line 123 begins the else part of this if..else block.

Line 124 executes the first SQL statement and passes the appropriate value to the *placeholder*.

```
125:              my $data = $sth1->fetch;
126:              $tmp{$_ . "_thumb_id"} = $data->[0];
127:              $tmp{$_ . "_thumb_location"} =
get_image($data->[1], 100);
128:          }
129:      }
```

Line 125 calls the `fetch` function and stores the result in `$data`.

Line 126 sets the value at `$tmp{$_ . "_thumb_id"}` to the value in `$data->[0]`.

Line 127 sets the value at `$tmp{$_ . "_thumb_location"}` to the value returned by the call to the `get_image` function with a witdh of 100 (our thumbnail).

Line 128 closes the `if..else` block.

Line 129 closes the `for` loop.

```
130:      while(my($key,$val) = each %tmp) { $p->{$key} = $val;
}

131:      return($p);
132: }
```

Line 130 begins a `while` loop that iterates through each item in the `%tmp` hash and stores it in the hash pointed to by `$p`.

Line 131 returns the pointer to the hash, `$p`.

Line 132 ends this subroutine.

```
133: sub get_image {
134:     my ($photo, $size) = @_;
```

Line 133 begins the `get_image` subroutine. This subroutine takes the photo name and size and returns the appropriate filename.

Line 134 declares two scalars and loads them with the values passed from the function call.

```
135:     if(($size ne "orig") and (!$size eq "")){
136:         $photo =~ s/\.jpg$/\.$size\.jpg/;
137:     }
```

Line 135 checks to see if `$size` is *not equal* to `orig` and that `$size` is also *not equal* to an empty string.

Line 136 is where we get if this is not the original photo size. This line replaces the `.jpg` extension with the `$size.jpg` extension.

Line 137 closes this `if` block.

```
138:      return($photo);
139: }
```

Line 138 returns $photo.

Line 139 closes this subroutine.

That is all there is to the index.cgi program. In these 139 lines of code, we handle the listing of all albums, the listing of each album's thumbnail gallery, and the display of the images. One of the reasons we can do so much with so little code is that we have removed most of the HTML from the code and placed it into template files.

There is one other piece to this whole Web-based, photo-album puzzle: the admin.cgi program, which handles adding titles and descriptions to the albums and photos.

We need some way to edit the titles and comments for the photos and the albums. This functionality could have been added to the index.cgi program — but you don't want just anyone editing these items. So, admin.cgi is a copy of the index.cgi program with a little extra added. That way, you can put admin.cgi in a safer location on your server so you don't have to worry about people changing your photo descriptions.

We'll cover the differences between these programs — but we won't cover the differences where just the template files have changed (only places where functionality is different).

The line numbers shown with this code correspond to the line numbers from this program, admin.cgi. The complete program listings are at the end of the chapter, so you can compare line numbers between index.cgi and admin.cgi if you desire.

Figure 16-5 is what the admin album display looks like. The only differences are the form fields at the top and bottom of the page and the button to submit the changes.

In Figure 16-6, an image is displayed along with the form fields to allow changes in the image title and comments. The code following the figure shows the changes needed to do this.

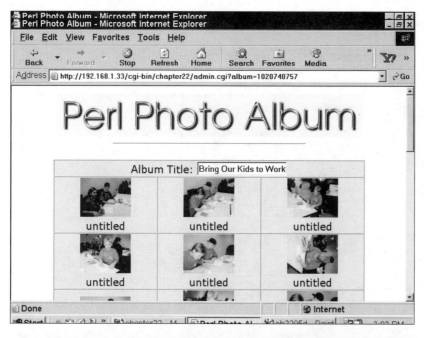

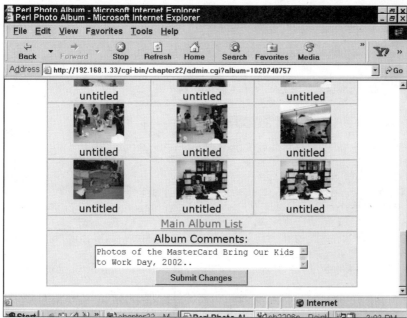

Figure 16-5: admin.cgi admin album display

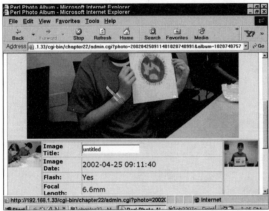

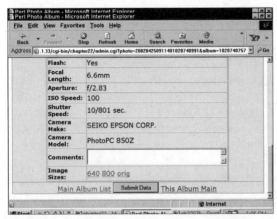

Figure 16-6: admin.cgi admin photo display

admin.cgi

```
52: sub Update_Data {
53:     my $type = shift;
54:     my ($title, $id, $sql);
```

Line 52 begins the Update_Data subroutine. This subroutine is the biggest change in this program. It is used to add the data to the database.

Line 53 declares a variable named $type and sets it to the value passed into the function call. This value determines whether this is a photo or an album table change.

Line 54 declares a few more variables that we'll use in this subroutine.

```
55:     if($type eq "photo") {
56:         $title = param('img_title');
57:         $id    = $photo;
58:         $sql = qq{UPDATE photo SET img_title=?, comments=?
                WHERE img_id = ?};
59:     }
```

Line 55 begins an if..elsif..else block. This section checks to see if the $type is *photo*. If so, this block is entered.

Line 56 sets the $title variable to the value passed in from the img_title form field.

Line 57 sets the $id variable to the value in $photo.

Line 58 creates the SQL statement to update the photo title and comments.

Line 59 closes this part of the if..elsif..else block.

```
60:     elsif($type eq "album") {
61:         $title = param('title');
62:         $id    = $album;
63:         $sql = qq{UPDATE album SET name=?, comments=?
                WHERE album_id = ?};
64:     }
```

Line 60 checks to see if $type is equal to *album*. If so, this block is entered.

Line 61 sets the $title variable to the value returned by the title field from the HTML form.

Line 62 sets the variable $id to the value in $album.

Line 63 creates the SQL statement to update the album-table data.

Line 64 closes this block.

```
65:      else {
66:          return 0;
67:      }
```

Line 65 begins the else block.

Line 66 returns 0. If $type doesn't match album or photo, something must be wrong, and we can trap the error if we need to.

Line 67 closes the if..elsif..else block.

```
68:      my $comments = param('comments');
69:      return unless($title or $comments);
```

Line 68 sets the $comments variable to the value passed from the comments section of the calling HTML page.

Line 69 returns unless $title or $comments contains data. We don't want to bother updating the database if there is nothing to update.

```
70:      my $sth = $dbh->prepare($sql);

71:      $sth->execute($title, $comments, $id);
72: }
```

Line 70 prepares the SQL statement for execution.

Line 71 executes the SQL statement and passes the $title, $comments, and $id variables to replace the placeholders in the SQL statements.

Line 72 ends this subroutine.

```
73: sub Show_Album {
74:      Update_Data("album");
```

Line 73 is actually no different from the index.cgi program, but it helps to see it because the next line is different.

Line 74 is a call to the Update_Data subroutine and is passed *album* because this is for an album update.

```
83:  my $alb = $sth_a->fetchrow_hashref;
84:  $alb->{cols} = $cols;
```

Line 83 declares a variable named $alb and sets it to the hash reference returned by the call to fetchrow_hashref.

Line 84 gets the number of columns from $cols and stores it in $alb->{cols}.

That is all that needs to be changed in the Show_Album subroutine to update the data.

```
121: sub Show_Photo {
122:     my ($photo, $album) = @_;

123:     Update_Data("photo");
```

Line 123 is the only that needs to be changed for the Show_Photo subroutine!

Summary

That is all there is to creating a Web-based photo album. You may want to add features. Some ideas for new features include:

✦ Better error handling

✦ Photo sorting

✦ Album folders

✦ Album themes

✦ Photo searching

Program Listings

Listings 16-1 to 16-19 contain the complete listings for the templates and the main programs.

Listing 16-1: **generate.pl**

```
01: #!/usr/bin/perl -w
02: # generate.pl

03: use strict;
```

Continued

Listing 16-1 *(continued)*

```
04: use Image::Info qw(image_info dim);
05: use File::Basename;
06: use File::Find;
07: use File::Copy;
08: use Imager;
09: use DBI;

10: my $info;
11: my $album_name = shift || die "What album name?";
12: my $album_id   = time();

13: ### Begin user modifications
14: my $relative_dir = "/photos";
15: my $album_dir    = "/var/www/html/photos";
16: my @SIZES        = qw(100 640 800);
17: ### End of user modifications

18: $album_name      =~ s/ /\_/g;
19: $album_dir      .= "/$album_name";
20: my $rel_dir      = "$relative_dir/$album_name";

21: mkdir ($album_dir) || die "Can't mkdir $!" unless -e $album_dir;

22: my $source_dir = shift(@ARGV)|| ('.');

23: my $dbh = DBI->connect("DBI:mysql:photoalbum","bookuser","testpass")
24:     or die("Cannot connect: $DBI::errstr");

25: my @EXIF     = qw(width height resolution Flash Model
26:                   Make MaxApertureValue FNumber DateTime
27:                   ISOSpeedRatings ExposureTime FocalLength);

28: Add_Album();
29: find({wanted => \&Wanted, follow => 1}, @ARGV);

30: print "\nDone generating new album...\n\n";


31: sub Add_Album {
32:     my $sql = qq{INSERT INTO album
33:                   (album_id, name, comments)
34:                   VALUES (?,?,?)};

35:     my $sth_album = $dbh->prepare($sql);

36:     $sth_album->execute($album_id, $album_name, '')
37:         or die("ERROR! $DBI::errstr");
38: }

39: sub Update_Database {
```

```
40:     my $photo = shift;
41:     my $p_dir = "$rel_dir/$photo";

42:     my $sql1  = qq{INSERT INTO photo
43:                 (img_id, width, height, resolution, flash,
44:              model, make, aperture, fnumber, img_date,
45:                   iso_speed, exposure, focal_length,
46:                   img_title, img_location, album_id, comments)
47:                 VALUES
48:            (?,?,?,?,?,?,?,?,?,?,?,?,?,?,?,?,?)};

49:     my $sth_photo = $dbh->prepare($sql1);

50:     my $id = $info->{DateTime};
51:     $id    =~ s/[ \:]//g;
52:     $id    .= time();

53:     $sth_photo->execute($id, @$info{@EXIF}, 'untitled',
54:                   $p_dir, $album_id, '')
55:             or die("ERROR! $DBI::errstr ");

56:     print "Record inserted into database...\n";
57: }

58: sub Massage_Data {
59:     my @RATIONAL = qw(FNumber FocalLength);

60:     for(@RATIONAL) {
61:         $info->{$_} = Rational($info->{$_},1);
62:     }

63:     $info->{'MaxApertureValue'}
64:       = sprintf("%.1f", (1.4142 ** $info->{'MaxApertureValue'}));
65: }

66: sub Rational {
67:   my ($in, $dec)     = @_;
68:   my ($num, $denom) = split('/', $in);
69:   my   $fmt          = '%.' . $dec . 'f';

70:   return($denom == 0 ? "Err" : sprintf($fmt, $num/$denom));
71: }

72: sub Img_Copy {
73:     my $source_file = shift;
74:     $source_file =~ /^([\w\-\/]+)\.(\w{1,4})$/;
75:     my $dest_file = $1 . '.' . $2;


76:     copy($source_file, "$album_dir/" . basename($dest_file)) or die "Cannot
copy $!";
```

Continued

Listing 16-1 *(continued)*

```
77:     print "Done writing $dest_file...\n";
78: }

79: sub Resize {
80:     my ($file, $xfac) = @_;
81:     my $extn;

82:     my $img = Imager->new();
83:     $img->open(file => $file) or die $img->errstr();

84:     $file =~ /^([\w\-\/]+)\.(\w{1,4})$/;
85:     $file = $1;
86:     $file = basename($file);
87:     $extn = $2;
88:     $xfac =~ /^([\w]+)$/ || die "Oops!";
89:     $xfac = $1;

90:     my $newimg = $img->copy();
91:     $newimg    = $img->scale(xpixels => $xfac);

92:     $newimg->write(file => "$album_dir/$file.$xfac.$extn")
93:         or die $img->errstr();

94:     print "Done writing $file.$xfac.$extn...\n";
95: }

96: sub Wanted {
97:     if( (/\.jpg|\.jpeg$/i) ) {
98:         my $file       = $_;

99:         $info = undef;
100:         $info = image_info($File::Find::fullname);

101:         die "Can't parse image info: $info->{error}\n"
102:             if($info->{error});

103:         for(@SIZES) {
104:             Resize ($File::Find::fullname, $_);
105:         }

106:         Massage_Data    ();
107:         Img_Copy         ($File::Find::fullname);
108: Update_Database ($file);

109: print "\n";
110:     }
111: }
```

Listing 16-2: **index.cgi**

```
01: #!/usr/bin/perl -wT
02: # index.cgi  Photo Album Script

03: use strict;
04: use DBI;
05: use CGI qw(:standard);

06: use lib qw(.);
07: use BasicSession;
08: our $sess;
09: my  %item;
10: $sess = Get_Session();
11: tie %item, 'BasicSession';

12: my $album = param('album');
13: my $photo = param('photo');
14: my $size  = param('size');

15: my $sizes = Make_Sizes(qw(640 800 orig));

16: $size ? ($item{'size'} = $size) : ($size = $item{'size'});

17: my $dbh = DBI->connect("DBI:mysql:photoalbum","bookuser","testpass")
18:     or die("Cannot connect: $DBI::errstr");

19: if($photo) {
20:     Show_Photo($photo, $album);
21:     exit;
22: }
23: elsif($album) {
24:     Show_Album($album);
25:     exit;
26: }
27: else {
28:     List_Albums();
29:     exit;
30: }

31: sub Make_Sizes {
32:     my @sizes  = @_;
33:     my $string = '';

34:     for my $size (@sizes) {
35:         $string .=
36:           qq(<a href="?photo=$photo&album=$album&size=$size">$size</a> );
37:     }

38:     return($string);
```

Continued

Listing 16-2 *(continued)*

```
39: }

40: sub List_Albums {
41:     my $sql = qq{SELECT * FROM album};
42:     my $sth = $dbh->prepare($sql);
43:     $sth->execute();

44:     Print_Page("./templates", "header.tmpl");
45:     Print_Page("./templates", "list_top.tmpl");

46:     while(my $p = $sth->fetchrow_hashref){
47:         Print_Page("./templates", "list_row.tmpl", $p);
48:     }

49:     Print_Page("./templates", "list_end.tmpl");
50:     Print_Page("./templates", "footer.tmpl");
51: }

52: sub Show_Album {
53:     my $cols = 3;

54:     my $sql_p = qq{SELECT * FROM photo WHERE album_id = ?};
55:     my $sql_a = qq{SELECT * FROM album WHERE album_id = ?};
56:     my $sth_p = $dbh->prepare($sql_p);
57:     my $sth_a = $dbh->prepare($sql_a);
58:     $sth_p->execute($album);
59:     $sth_a->execute($album);

60:     Print_Page("./templates", "header.tmpl");

61:     while(my $p = $sth_a->fetchrow_hashref){
62:         $p->{cols} = $cols;
63:         Print_Page("./templates", "album_top.tmpl", $p);
64:     }

65:     my $counter = 1;
66:     while(my $p = $sth_p->fetchrow_hashref){
67:         $p->{img_location} = get_image($p->{img_location}, 100);

68:         print "<tr>"  if($counter == 1);
69:         Print_Page("./templates", "album_row.tmpl", $p);
70:         print "</tr>" if($counter == $cols);

71:         $counter++;
72: $counter = 1  if($counter > $cols);
73:     }
74:     print "</tr>" unless($counter == 1);

75:     Print_Page("./templates", "album_end.tmpl",{'cols' => $cols});
```

```
76:      Print_Page("./templates", "footer.tmpl");
77: }

78: sub Get_Photo_List {
79:      my ($photo, $album) = @_;
80:      my ($index, @photos);
81:      my $count = 0;

82:      my $sql  = qq{SELECT img_id FROM photo WHERE album_id = ?};
83:      my $sth  = $dbh->prepare($sql);
84:      my @all;
85:      $sth->execute($album);

86:      while(my @tmp = $sth->fetchrow_array){push @all, $tmp[0];}

87:      for(@all) {
88:          $index = $count if(/$photo/); #Get index of photo we want
89:          $count++;
90:      }

91:      unless($index) {
92:          @photos = @all[0, 1];
93:          unshift @photos, '';
94:      }
95:      else {
96:          @photos = @all[($index-1)..($index+1)]; # Get photos next to it
97:      }

98:      return (@photos);
99: }

100: sub Show_Photo {
101:      my ($photo, $album) = @_;

102:      my @photos = Get_Photo_List($photo, $album);

103:      my $ptr = Get_Details(@photos);

104:      $ptr->{img_location} = get_image($ptr->{img_location}, $size);
105:      $ptr->{image_sizes}  = $sizes;

106:      Print_Page("./templates", "header.tmpl");
107:      Print_Page("./templates", "photo_main.tmpl", $ptr);
108:      Print_Page("./templates", "photo_footer.tmpl", $ptr);
109: }

110: sub Get_Details {
111:      my @photos = @_;
112:      my ($p, %tmp);
113:      my %hsh = ('prev' => 0, 'curr' => 1, 'next' => 2);
```

Continued

Listing 16-2 *(continued)*

```
114:     my $sql1 = qq{SELECT img_id, img_location FROM photo WHERE img_id = ?};
115:     my $sql2 = qq{SELECT * FROM photo WHERE img_id = ?};

116:     my $sth1 = $dbh->prepare($sql1);
117:     my $sth2 = $dbh->prepare($sql2);

118:     for(keys %hsh){
119:         if(/curr/) {
120:             $sth2->execute($photos[$hsh{$_}]);
121:             $p = $sth2->fetchrow_hashref;
122:         }
123:         else {
124:             $sth1->execute($photos[$hsh{$_}]) or die("Error!\n");

125:             my $data = $sth1->fetch;
126:             $tmp{$_ . "_thumb_id"} = $data->[0];
127:             $tmp{$_ . "_thumb_location"} = get_image($data->[1], 100);
128:         }
129:     }

130:     while(my($k,$v) = each %tmp) { $p->{$k} = $v; }

131:     return($p);
132: }

133: sub get_image {
134:     my ($photo, $size) = @_;
135:     if(($size ne "orig") and (!$size eq "")){
136:         $photo =~ s/\.jpg$/\.$size\.jpg/;
137:     }

138:     return($photo);
139: }
```

Listing 16-3: **admin.cgi**

```
01: #!/usr/bin/perl -wT
02: # admin.cgi  Photo Album Admin Script

03: use strict;
04: use DBI;
05: use CGI qw(:standard);

06: use lib qw(.);
```

```
07: use BasicSession;
08: our $sess;
09: my  %item;
10: $sess = Get_Session();
11: tie %item, 'BasicSession';

12: my $album = param('album');
13: my $photo = param('photo');
14: my $size  = param('size');

15: my $sizes = Make_Sizes(qw(640 800 orig));

16: $size ? ($item{'size'} = $size) : ($size = $item{'size'});

17: my $dbh = DBI->connect("DBI:mysql:photoalbum","bookuser","testpass")
18:     or die("Cannot connect: $DBI::errstr");

19: if($photo) {
20:     Show_Photo($photo, $album);
21:     exit;
22: }
23: elsif($album) {
24:     Show_Album($album);
25:     exit;
26: }
27: else {
28:     List_Albums();
29:     exit;
30: }

31: sub Make_Sizes {
32:     my @sizes  = @_;
33:     my $string = '';

34:     for my $size (@sizes) {
35:         $string .=
36:             qq(<a href="?photo=$photo&album=$album&size=$size">$size</a> );
37:     }

38:     return($string);
39: }

40: sub List_Albums {
41:     my $sql = qq{SELECT * FROM album};
42:     my $sth = $dbh->prepare($sql);
43:     $sth->execute();

44:     Print_Page("./templates", "header.tmpl");
45:     Print_Page("./templates", "list_top.tmpl");

46:     while(my $p = $sth->fetchrow_hashref){
```

Continued

Listing 16-3 *(continued)*

```perl
47:            Print_Page("./templates", "admin_list_row.tmpl", $p);
48:        }

49:        Print_Page("./templates", "list_end.tmpl");
50:        Print_Page("./templates", "footer.tmpl");
51: }

52: sub Update_Data {
53:        my $type = shift;
54:        my ($title, $id, $sql);

55:        if($type eq "photo") {
56:            $title = param('img_title');
57:    $id     = $photo;
58:            $sql = qq{UPDATE photo SET img_title=?, comments=? WHERE img_id = ?};
59:        }
60:        elsif($type eq "album") {
61:            $title = param('title');
62:    $id     = $album;
63:            $sql = qq{UPDATE album SET name=?, comments=? WHERE album_id = ?};
64:        }
65:        else {
66:            return 0;
67:        }

68:        my $comments = param('comments');
69:        return unless($title or $comments);

70:        my $sth = $dbh->prepare($sql);

71:        $sth->execute($title, $comments, $id);
72: }

73: sub Show_Album {
74:        Update_Data("album");
75:        my $cols = 3;

76:        my $sql_p = qq{SELECT * FROM photo WHERE album_id = ?};
77:        my $sql_a = qq{SELECT * FROM album WHERE album_id = ?};
78:        my $sth_p = $dbh->prepare($sql_p);
79:        my $sth_a = $dbh->prepare($sql_a);
80:        $sth_p->execute($album);
81:        $sth_a->execute($album);

82:        Print_Page("./templates", "header.tmpl");

83:        my $alb = $sth_a->fetchrow_hashref;
84:        $alb->{cols} = $cols;
85:        Print_Page("./templates", "admin_album_top.tmpl", $alb);
```

```
86:     my $counter = 1;
87:     while(my $p = $sth_p->fetchrow_hashref){
88:         $p->{img_location} = get_image($p->{img_location}, 100);

89:         print "<tr>"  if($counter == 1);
90:         Print_Page("./templates", "admin_album_row.tmpl", $p);
91:         print "</tr>" if($counter == $cols);

92:         $counter++;
93:  $counter = 1  if($counter > $cols);
94:     }
95:     print "</tr>" unless($counter == 1);

96:     Print_Page("./templates", "admin_album_end.tmpl", $alb);
97:     Print_Page("./templates", "footer.tmpl");
98: }

99: sub Get_Photo_List {
100:     my ($photo, $album) = @_;
101:     my ($index, @photos);
102:     my $count = 0;

103:     my $sql  = qq{SELECT img_id FROM photo WHERE album_id = ?};
104:     my $sth  = $dbh->prepare($sql);
105:     my @all;
106:     $sth->execute($album);

107:     while(my @tmp = $sth->fetchrow_array){push @all, $tmp[0];}

108:     for(@all) {
109:         $index = $count if(/$photo/); # Get index of photo we want
110: $count++;
111:     }

112:     unless($index) {
113:         @photos = @all[0, 1];
114: unshift @photos, '';
115:     }
116:     else {
117:         @photos = @all[($index-1)..($index+1)]; # Get photos next to it
118:     }

119:     return (@photos);
120: }

121: sub Show_Photo {
122:     my ($photo, $album) = @_;

123:     Update_Data("photo");

124:     my @photos = Get_Photo_List($photo, $album);
```

Continued

Listing 16-3 *(continued)*

```perl
125:     my $ptr = Get_Details(@photos);

126:     $ptr->{img_location} = get_image($ptr->{img_location}, $size);
127:     $ptr->{image_sizes}  = $sizes;

128:     Print_Page("./templates", "header.tmpl");
129:     Print_Page("./templates", "admin_main.tmpl", $ptr);
130:     Print_Page("./templates", "admin_footer.tmpl", $ptr);
131: }

132: sub Get_Details {
133:     my @photos = @_;
134:     my ($p, %tmp);
135:     my %hsh = ('prev' => 0, 'curr' => 1, 'next' => 2);

136:     my $sql1 = qq{SELECT img_id, img_location FROM photo WHERE img_id = ?};
137:     my $sql2 = qq{SELECT * FROM photo WHERE img_id = ?};

138:     my $sth1 = $dbh->prepare($sql1);
139:     my $sth2 = $dbh->prepare($sql2);

140:     for(keys %hsh){
141:         if(/curr/) {
142:             $sth2->execute($photos[$hsh{$_}]);
143:             $p = $sth2->fetchrow_hashref;
144:         }
145:         else {
146:             $sth1->execute($photos[$hsh{$_}]) or die("Error!");

147:             my $data = $sth1->fetch;
148:             $tmp{$_ . "_thumb_id"} = $data->[0];
149:             $tmp{$_ . "_thumb_location"} = get_image($data->[1], 100);
150:         }
151:     }

152:     while(my($key,$val) = each %tmp) { $p->{$key} = $val; }

153:     return($p);
154: }

155: sub get_image {
156:     my ($photo, $size) = @_;
157:     if($size ne "orig") {
158:         $photo =~ s/\.jpg$/\.$size\.jpg/;
159:     }

160:     return($photo);
161: }
```

Listing 16-4: **admin_album_end.tmpl**

```
01: <!-- Begin admin_album_end.tmpl -->

02: <tr>
03:   <td colspan="%%cols%%" align="center">
04:    <a href="?">Main Album List</a><br />
05:   </td>
06: </tr>
07: <tr>
08:   <td colspan="%%cols%%" align="center">
09:    Album Comments:<br />
10:    <textarea rows="2" cols="40" wrap="physical"
name="comments">%%comments%%</textarea><br />
11:    <input type="submit" value="Submit Changes">
12:   </td>
13: </tr>
14: </table>
15: </form>
16: <!-- End admin_album_end.tmpl -->
```

Listing 16-5: **admin_album_row.tmpl**

```
01:    <td align="center" width="200">
02:     <a href="/cgi-bin/admin.cgi?photo=%%img_id%%&album=%%album_id%%"><img
src="%%img_location%%" border="0"></a>
03:     <br>
04:     %%img_title%%
05:    </td>
```

Listing 16-6: **admin_album_top.tmpl**

```
01: <!-- Begin admin_album_top.tmpl -->
02: <hr width="50%">
03: <form>
04: <input type="hidden" name="album" value="%%album_id%%">
05: <table align="center" border="1" cellspacing="0">
06:  <tr>
07:   <td colspan="%%cols%%" align="center">
08:    Album Title: <input type="text" name="title" value="%%name%%">
09:   </td>
10:  </tr>
11: <!-- End admin_album_top.tmpl -->
```

Listing 16-7: admin_footer.tmpl

```
01:  <tr>
02:   <td colspan="3" align="center">
03:    <a href="?">Main Album List</a>
04:    <input type="submit" value="Submit Data">
05:    <a href="?album=%%album_id%%">This Album Main</a>
06:   </td>
07:  </tr>
08:  </table>
09:  </form>
10:  </body>
11:  </html>
```

Listing 16-8: admin_list_row.tmpl

```
01: <!-- Begin admin_list_row.tmpl -->

02:  <tr>
03:   <td>
04:    <a href="/cgi-bin/admin.cgi?album=%%album_id%%">%%name%%</a>
05:   </td>
06:   <td> %%comments%%</td>
07:  </tr>

08: <!-- End admin_list_row.tmpl -->
```

Listing 16-9: admin_main.tmpl

```
01: <form>
02: <input type="hidden" name="photo" value="%%img_id%%">
03: <input type="hidden" name="album" value="%%album_id%%">

04: <table border="1" cellspacing="0"  align="center">
05:  <tr>
06:   <td colspan="3" align="center">
07:    <img src="%%img_location%%">
08:   </td>
09:  </tr>
10:  <tr>
11:   <td width="100" valign="top">
12:    <a href="?photo=%%prev_thumb_id%%&album=%%album_id%%">
```

```
13:     <img src="%%prev_thumb_location%%" border="0">
14:    </a>
15:   </td>
16:   <td>

17:    <table border="1" cellspacing="0"  align="center" width="100%">
18:     <tr>
19:      <td><b>Image Title:</b></td>
20:      <td><input type="text" name="img_title" value="%%img_title%%"></td>
21:     </tr>
22:     <tr>
23:      <td><b>Image Date:</b></td>
24:      <td>%%img_date%%</td>
25:     </tr>
26:     <tr>
27:      <td><b>Flash:</b></td>
28:      <td>%%flash%%</td>
29:     </tr>
30:     <tr>
31:      <td><b>Focal Length:</b></td>
32:      <td>%%focal_length%%mm</td>
33:     </tr>
34:     <tr>
35:      <td><b>Aperture:</b></td>
36:      <td>f/%%aperture%%</td>
37:     </tr>
38:     <tr>
39:      <td><b>ISO Speed:</b></td>
40:      <td>%%iso_speed%%</td>
41:     </tr>
42:     <tr>
43:      <td><b>Shutter Speed:</b></td>
44:      <td>%%exposure%% sec.</td>
45:     </tr>
46:     <tr>
47:      <td><b>Camera Make:</b></td>
48:      <td>%%make%%</td>
49:     </tr>
50:     <tr>
51:      <td><b>Camera Model:</b></td>
52:      <td>%%model%%</td>
53:     </tr>
54:     <tr>
55:      <td><b>Comments:</b></td>
56:      <td>
57:      <textarea name="comments" rows="2" cols="40"
wrap="physical">%%comments%%</textarea>
58:      </td>
59:     </tr>
60:     <tr>
```

Continued

Listing 16-9 *(continued)*

```
61:    <td><b>Image Sizes:</b></td>
62:    <td>%%image_sizes%%</td>
63:   </tr>
64:  </table>

65:  </td>
66:  <td width="100" valign="top">
67:   <a href="?photo=%%next_thumb_id%%&album=%%album_id%%">
68:   <img src="%%next_thumb_location%%" border="0">
69:   </a>
70:  </td>
71: </tr>
```

Listing 16-10: **album_end.tmpl**

```
01: <!-- Begin album_end.tmpl -->

02: <tr>
03:  <td colspan="%%cols%%" align="center">
04:   <a href="?">Main Album List</a>
05:  </td>
06: </tr>
07: </table>

08: <!-- End album_end.tmpl -->
```

Listing 16-11: **album_row.tmpl**

```
01:    <td align="center" width="200">
02:     <a href="/cgi-bin/index.cgi?photo=%%img_id%%&album=%%album_id%%"><img
src="%%img_location%%" border="0"></a>
03:     <br>
04:     %%img_title%%
05:    </td>
```

Listing 16-12: **album_top.tmpl**

```
01: <!-- Begin album_top.tmpl -->
02: <hr width="50%">
03: <table align="center" border="1" cellspacing="0">
04:  <tr>
05:   <td colspan="%%cols%%" align="center">
06:    <font class="big">%%name%%</font>
07:   </td>
08:  </tr>

09: <!-- End album_top.tmpl -->
```

Listing 16-13: **footer.tmpl**

```
01:  </body>
02: </html>
```

Listing 16-14: **header.tmpl**

```
01: <html><head><title>Perl Photo Album</title>
02: <style type="text/css">
03: <!--
04: td    { background:  #e0e0e0;
05:         color:       #000000;
06:         font-family: Lucida, Verdana, Helvetica, Arial;
07:         font-size:   12pt}

08: a:link    { color: #4444ff }
09: a:visited { color: #333377 }
10: a:active  { color: #0000dd }

11: b
12: { font-family: Lucida, Verdana, Helvetica, Arial;
13:   font-size:   10pt;
14:   color:       #000000 }

15: .small
16: { font-family: Lucida, Verdana, Helvetica, Arial;
17:   font-size:   10pt;
```

Continued

Listing 16-14 *(continued)*

```
18:    color:      #000000 }

19: .medium
20: { font-family: Lucida, Verdana, Helvetica, Arial;
21:    font-size:   12pt;
22:    color:       #000000 }

23: .big_error
24: { font-family: Lucida, Verdana, Helvetica, Arial;
25:    font-size:   14pt;
26:    font-weight: bold;
27:    color:       #ff0000 }

28: .big
29: { font-family: Lucida, Verdana, Helvetica, Arial;
30:    font-size:   14pt;
31:    color:       #000000 }

32: .large
33: { font-family: Lucida, Verdana, Helvetica, Arial;
34:    font-size:   20pt;
35:    color:       #000000 }

36: .big2
37: { font-family: Lucida, Verdana, Helvetica, Arial;
38:    font-size:   24pt;
39:    color:       #000000 }

40: -->
41: </style>
42: </head>
43: <body>
44:   <div align="center">
45:     <img src="/images/album/perl_photo_album.jpg">
46:   <div>
```

Listing 16-15: **list_end.tmpl**

```
01: <!-- Begin albums_end.tmpl -->

02: </table>

03: <!-- End albums_end.tmpl -->
```

Listing 16-16: **list_row.tmpl**

```
01: <!-- Begin list_row.tmpl -->

02:  <tr>
03:   <td>
04:    <a href="/cgi-bin/index.cgi?album=%%album_id%%">%%name%%</a>
05:   </td>
06:   <td> %%comments%%</td>
07:  </tr>

08: <!-- End list_row.tmpl -->
```

Listing 16-17: **list_top.tmpl**

```
01: <!-- Begin list_top.tmpl -->
02: <hr width="50%">
03: <table align="center" border="1" cellspacing="0">
04:  <tr>
05:   <td colspan="2" align="center">
06:    <font class="big">Available Albums</font>
07:   </td>
08:  </tr>
09:  <tr>
10:   <td><b>Album Name</b></td>
11:   <td><b>Comments</b></td>
12:  </tr>

13: <!-- End list_top.tmpl -->
```

Listing 16-18: **photo_footer.tmpl**

```
01:  <tr>
02:   <td colspan="3" align="center">
03:    <a href="?">Main Album List</a>
04:    <a href="?album=%%album_id%%">This Album Main</a>
05:   </td>
06:  </tr>
07:  </table>
08:  </body>
09: </html>
```

Listing 16-19: **photo_main.tmpl**

```
01: <table border="1" cellspacing="0"  align="center">
02:  <tr>
03:   <td colspan="3" align="center">
04:    <img src="%%img_location%%">
05:   </td>
06:  </tr>
07:  <tr>
08:   <td width="100" valign="top">
09:    <a href="?photo=%%prev_thumb_id%%&album=%%album_id%%">
10:     <img src="%%prev_thumb_location%%" border="0">
11:    </a>
12:   </td>
13:   <td>

14:    <table border="1" cellspacing="0"  align="center" width="100%">
15:     <tr>
16:      <td><b>Image Title:</b></td>
17:      <td>%%img_title%%</td>
18:     </tr>
19:     <tr>
20:      <td><b>Image Date:</b></td>
21:      <td>%%img_date%%</td>
22:     </tr>
23:     <tr>
24:      <td><b>Flash:</b></td>
25:      <td>%%flash%%</td>
26:     </tr>
27:     <tr>
28:      <td><b>Focal Length:</b></td>
29:      <td>%%focal_length%%mm</td>
30:     </tr>
31:     <tr>
32:      <td><b>Aperture:</b></td>
33:      <td>f/%%aperture%%</td>
34:     </tr>
35:     <tr>
36:      <td><b>ISO Speed:</b></td>
37:      <td>%%iso_speed%%</td>
38:     </tr>
39:     <tr>
40:      <td><b>Shutter Speed:</b></td>
41:      <td>%%exposure%% sec.</td>
42:     </tr>
43:     <tr>
44:      <td><b>Camera Make:</b></td>
45:      <td>%%make%%</td>
46:     </tr>
47:     <tr>
```

```
48:      <td><b>Camera Model:</b></td>
49:      <td>%%model%%</td>
50:     </tr>
51:     <tr>
52:      <td><b>Comments:</b></td>
53:      <td>%%comments%% </td>
54:     </tr>
55:     <tr>
56:      <td><b>Image Sizes:</b></td>
57:      <td>%%image_sizes%%</td>
58:     </tr>
59:    </table>

60:   </td>
61:   <td width="100" valign="top">
62:    <a href="?photo=%%next_thumb_id%%&album=%%album_id%%">
63:    <img src="%%next_thumb_location%%" border="0">
64:    </a>
65:   </td>
66:  </tr>
```

✦   ✦   ✦

Configuring Your System

To use the examples in this book, it is very helpful to have a system set up with a Web server and database server that you can test the code on as you read. This book aims to be as cross-platform as possible so that we can reach the widest possible audience. This appendix covers how to configure Perl, the Apache Web server, and the MySQL database for Linux and Windows systems. The reason Apache and MySQL are used is that they are both free, easily attainable, and very good at what they do.

This appendix covers only basic installation and configuration. If you need to do some customizing or if you have an odd configuration, you may have to crack some of the manuals open and figure out how to configure the way you want to.

The installations for Windows systems have come a very long way since I started working with these tools. For the most part, the installations are as simple as installing any other Windows program.

> **Note** As I have learned while preparing this appendix, Apache for Windows32 systems *may not* run on Windows 98 or Windows 95. The documentation says that it "may" work, and one of my editors said it worked for him, but in my experience it did not. I have installed Apache on a Windows 2000 system. (Many thanks to **kane** from the **#perl** IRC channel for helping me get the tools I need for this section.)

Perl, Apache, and MySQL have great support available through the NNTP newsgroups and mailing lists. Community support for Open Source software is typically faster and more helpful than any sort of commercial-product support I've encountered.

Installing Perl on Windows

Installing Perl on Windows is basically like installing any other program on a computer running Windows.

1. Download the Perl software. ActiveState offers Perl for free at `http://www.activestate.com`.

2. Once you have Perl downloaded, double-click the file to begin installation. If you have downloaded the Microsoft Installer package, you may have to right-click the file and choose Install from the pop-up menu.

   Figure A-1 shows the first screen that comes up when you begin the installation.

Figure A-1: ActivePerl install screen

3. Click the Next button to continue the installation.

   Figure A-2 shows the license agreement. You must accept the terms of the license to continue with the installation.

4. Click the Next button to continue the installation.

   Figure A-3 shows the Custom Setup screen. Generally, you should leave these settings alone; the default installation is perfect for most situations.

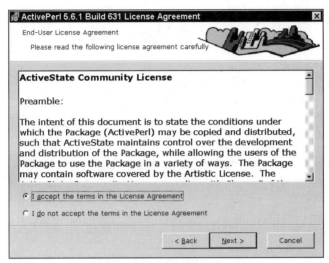

Figure A-2: ActivePerl License Agreement screen

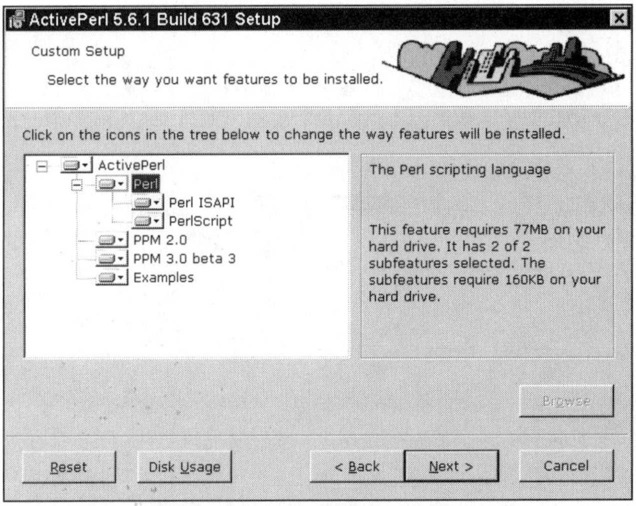

Figure A-3: ActivePerl Custom Setup screen

5. Click the Next button to continue the installation.

Figure A-4 shows the New PPM (Perl Package Manager) Features screen. The PPM is used to install precompiled modules onto Windows systems. If you want to enable ActiveState to see your system's Perl configuration, leave the box checked.

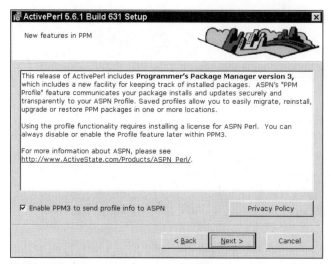

Figure A-4: New PPM Features screen

6. Click the Next button to continue the installation.

Figure A-5 shows the Choose Setup Options screen. Usually, these settings should also be left alone. The ActivePerl setup checks your system and attempts to choose the settings that are best for the system being installed on.

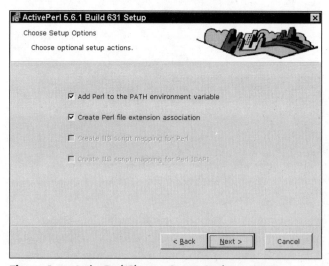

Figure A-5: ActivePerl Choose Setup Options screen

7. Click the Next button to continue the installation.

Figure A-6 shows the Ready to Install screen. This is the last screen you see before the installation begins.

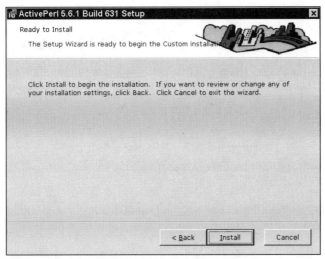

Figure A-6: ActivePerl Ready to Install screen

8. Click the Install button to begin the file installation.

Figure A-7 shows the final setup screen. This screen provides some promotional information as well as an HTML link to the ActiveState Perl site.

9. Click the Finish button to complete the installation.

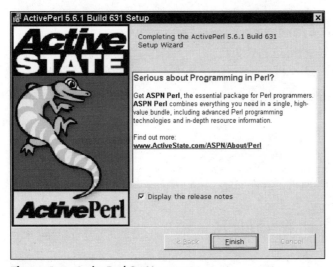

Figure A-7: ActivePerl SetUp screen

That is it for the Windows installation of ActivePerl. If you have any problems with the installation, check the ActiveState site's great support and troubleshooting information.

Installing Perl on Linux (and *nix) Systems

Installing Perl on a Linux box takes a little more work than installing it on a Windows system. The first step is to obtain Perl. There are several options that you can configure, but the installation program does a very good job at configuring your installation for you.

1. Go to http://www.perl.com and click on the "Downloads" link.

2. Click on the "Stable Production Release" link under the "Source Code Distribution" list item.

By compiling Perl from the source, you end up with a Perl that is configured best for your system. For *nix-based systems, I always install from the source.

This should then get you to a link that allows you to download the file named stable.tar.gz.

3. Download stable.tar.gz and place it somewhere that you want to untar it.

   For example:

   ```
   mkdir temp
   mv stable.tar.gz temp
   cd temp
   ```

4. Then unpack the distribution:

   ```
   tar -xzvf stable.tar.gz
   ```

   This creates a subdirectory named with the current Perl release.

5. Change to that directory:

   ```
   cd perl-5.x.x
   ```

6. Run the configuration script. The -d option will choose the defaults for all options; this is the easiest way to install Perl.

   ```
   sh Configure -d
   ```

7. Once the shell script is done configuring Perl, you get a prompt that says "Press return or use a shell escape to edit config.sh:." Press the Enter key. Once that is done, you must make Perl. Use the following command:

   ```
   make
   ```

   Wait—this part takes a few minutes.

When `make` is done, run the test suite to make sure everything is ok. If any tests fail, you must read the error message(s) and correct the problem(s) before continuing. The goal is for this to finish with a message that states "All tests successful."

```
make test
```

When `make test` is done, you must install Perl (this part must be done as `root`).

```
make install
```

Watch for any questions that may arise when you perform the install; the defaults are usually safe to choose.

Once this is finished, you can type `perl -v` to verify that Perl is installed and that the version number is what you expect it to be.

That is all there is to installing Perl on both Windows systems and Linux systems. The users of other Unixes should follow the Linux instructions, as these instructions are identical to what they would need to do.

Installing Apache on Windows

Installing Apache on Windows is as easy as installing any other program. As noted earlier in this appendix, the Apache Web server does not run on Windows 9*x* systems. There *are* instructions for installing Apache on Windows 95, but in my experience it does not run. However, there is no harm in trying—I have had reports from others who had no problems at all.

1. To download the latest version of Apache for Windows, go to `http://www.apache.org`.

2. From this page, click the "from here" link under the "Download!" section of the page. This brings you to a directory listing. You need to click the "binaries" folder, then the "win32" folder to get to the Windows software.

3. Download the latest *stable* version. There are at least two choices: one for the Microsoft installer and one that is a regular `.exe` file. Either works.

4. Once you have the file downloaded, execute it by double-clicking it if it is an `.exe` file or by right-clicking and choosing Install from the pop-up menu if it is a Microsoft Installer file.

   Figure A-8 shows the first screen for installing the Apache Web server. This screen is simply informational.

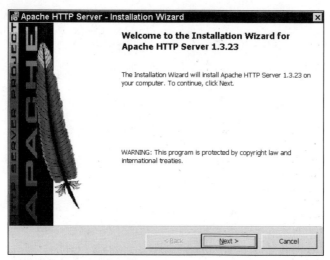

Figure A-8: Apache Installation Wizard

5. Click the Next button to continue the installation.

Figure A-9 shows the license agreement for the Apache Web server. You must accept the terms to continue the installation.

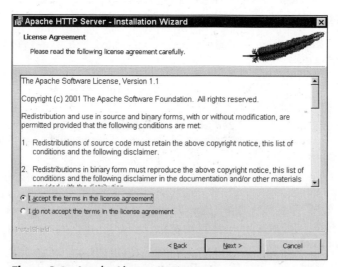

Figure A-9: Apache License Agreement

6. Click the Next button to continue the installation.

Figure A-10 shows the "Read This First" screen, which shows you the latest information about the Apache Web server you are installing.

Figure A-10: Apache Installation "Read This First"

7. Click the Next button to continue the installation.

Figure A-11 shows the Server Information screen. This screen gathers information about your system so that it can properly configure the Web server.

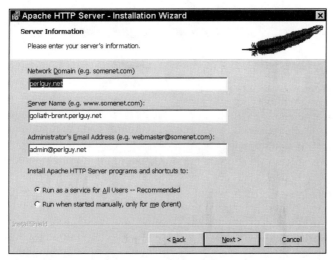

Figure A-11: Apache Server Information screen

8. Enter the information that pertains to the server you are installing Apache on, and click the Next button to continue the installation.

Figure A-12 shows the Setup Type screen. The default is best here, so leave the choice on "Complete."

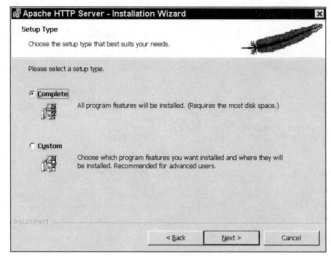

Figure A-12: Apache Setup Type screen

9. Click the Next button to continue the installation.

Figure A-13 shows the Installation Destination Folder screen, which shows you where the Apache software will be installed and gives you the option of changing this location.

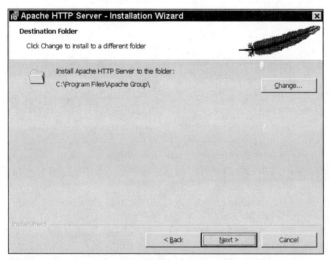

Figure A-13: Apache Installation Destination Folder screen

10. Click the Next button to continue the installation.

The installer copies the software to its destination folder and starts the Apache Web server service. If all goes well, you will get a screen telling you that the Installation Wizard completed.

Next, we have to edit one of the configuration files so that the Web server knows what to do with Perl CGI programs.

If you did a default install of Apache, the configuration files will be installed in the C:\Program Files\Apache Group\Apache\conf subdirectory. The file we want to edit is httpd.conf.

Make sure that the line that reads

```
ScriptAlias /cgi-bin/ "C:/Program Files/Apache
Group/Apache/cgi-bin/"
```

is not commented out. This line, unless commented out, causes the files in the listed directory to be executed as CGI scripts.

Also, look for, and add if needed, a line that reads:

```
AddHandler cgi-script .cgi .pl
```

This line causes files ending with .cgi or .pl to be treated as CGI scripts.

Next, you need to go into your "Administrative Tools" area, listed in the Control Panel, to stop and restart the Apache service.

You may need to make a change to your programs to get them to work. For example, the first line of a Perl program usually starts with #!/usr/bin/perl, but now you need to change it to the location on your system (something like #!C:/perl/bin/perl). This format works with Apache but might not work with other Web servers; make sure you check the documentation.

Installing Apache on Linux (and *nix) Systems

Installing the Apache Web server on a Linux box is much the same as installing Perl. But things can be a little trickier, and you don't have the nice GUI to work with. As far as I am concerned, this is just as well — GUIs just hide all of the details of what is really going on, and I prefer to see what is happening to my system rather than stare at a progress bar telling me to "Please wait."

The first step is to obtain the software.

1. To get the latest version of Apache, head over to `http://www.apache.org` and click the "from here" link under the "Download!" section of the page. This takes you to a directory listing; click the "httpd" directory to get a listing of the Web server downloads. Inside of this subdirectory, find the release you are looking for. The current stable release is version 1.3.23 — so I'll choose `apache_1.3.23.tar.gz` as the file to download.

2. Move the file to a directory where you can unpack it, like so:

```
mkdir temp
mv apache_1.3.23.tar.gz temp
cd temp
tar -xzvf apache_1.3.23.tar.gz
```

The following command creates a directory named apache_1.3.23:

```
cd apache_1.3.23
```

3. To configure Apache, enter the command `./configure` followed by the prefix where you want it to be installed. For example:

```
./configure --prefix=/usr/local/apache
```

Once that has completed, you need to build the source.

1. Build the distribution.

```
make
```

2. Then, as `root`, install the Apache Web server:

```
make install
```

You have now installed the Apache Web server, but you need to do a few more things to get it working properly.

Next, you must make sure that your configuration file, `httpd.conf`, contains the proper directives so that you can run CGI programs.

1. Look through the file; it will be at `/usr/local/apache/conf/httpd.conf` if you have installed using the preceding prefix.

Look for:

```
ScriptAlias /cgi-bin/ /usr/local/apache/cgi-bin/
```

And also for:

```
AddHandler cgi-script .cgi
```

If you want to have CGI programs outside of a `ScriptAlias` directory, this is optional.

2. Finally, you need to check the `<Directory>` directive. Look for:

```
<Directory /usr/local/apache/cgi-bin>
    AllowOverride None
    Options None
    Order allow,deny
    Allow from all
</Directory>
```

Make sure you change the directory to match where you have installed Apache.

3. To start the Web server, go to the `/usr/local/apache/bin` subdirectory and type:

```
./apachectl start
```

You should now be up and running!

Installing MySQL on Windows

MySQL is the database that we use most often throughout this book. This section of the appendix shows you how to install the MySQL database on a Windows system.

The first step is to download the software.

1. Head on over to `http://www.mysql.com`; click the "downloads" link, and choose the latest "stable" release.

2. Once you have the file, unzip it. Use whatever unzipping utility you normally use to unzip the file into a directory. Double-click the `setup.exe` file to begin installation of MySQL.

Figure A-14 shows the first screen for installing the MySQL database. This is simply a welcome screen.

3. Click the Next button to continue the installation.

Figure A-15 shows the second screen for installing the MySQL database. This screen tells where the default installation will take place and also gives some information about customization options.

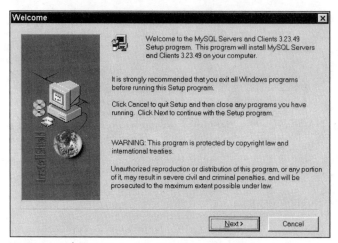

Figure A-14: MySQL Installation Welcome screen

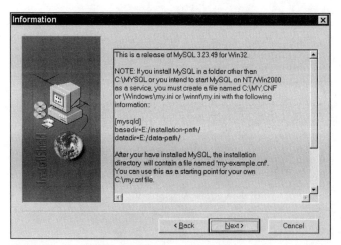

Figure A-15: MySQL Installation Information screen

4. Click the Next button to continue the installation. Figure A-16 shows the Setup Type screen for installing the MySQL database. You should be safe with the default.

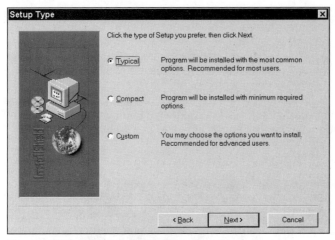

Figure A-16: MySQL Setup Type screen

5. Click the Next button to continue the installation.

Figure A-17 shows the Setup Complete screen for installing the MySQL database. You get here once all of the components are installed.

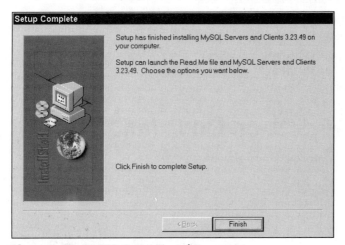

Figure A-17: MySQL Setup Complete screen

6. Click the Finish button to complete the installation.

Your system really doesn't look any different now; you don't even get anything installed into the system menu. To begin using MySQL, you need to open the Windows explorer and go to the \mysql directory. There you'll find a \bin directory with the binary files needed to perform tasks with MySQL. There is one binary called mysqlwinadmin.exe, which is the Windows administration tool.

If you want to just get in and play with MySQL, the command-line is how to do it. Double-click the mysql binary, and you get a screen like that in Figure A-18. This is the MySQL command-line tool and is how you can create tables, entries, etc. in MySQL.

```
Command Prompt - mysql -uadmin -padmin
    -> Atext VARCHAR(255) DEFAULT NULL,
    -> correct CHAR(1) DEFAULT "N",
    -> PRIMARY KEY(Aid)
    -> );
Query OK, 0 rows affected (0.33 sec)

mysql> CREATE TABLE test_config (
    -> TestID INT NOT NULL AUTO_INCREMENT,
    -> NumQs INT NOT NULL,
    -> Choices INT NOT NULL,
    -> PRIMARY KEY(TestID)
    -> );
Query OK, 0 rows affected (0.34 sec)

mysql> show tables;
+-------------------+
| Tables_in_quizzer |
+-------------------+
| answers           |
| questions         |
| test_config       |
+-------------------+
3 rows in set (0.00 sec)

mysql>
```

Figure A-18: MySQL command line

That is all there is to MySQL installation. It is a simple task, just like installing any other Windows application.

Installing MySQL on Linux (and *nix) Systems

First, you must download the software.

1. Head on over to http://www.mysql.com; click the "downloads" link, and choose the latest "stable" release.

 Note   I prefer to get the source packages rather than the binary packages. This way, I get to see more of what is going on with the installation and feel that I have a little more control. These instructions cover installing MySQL from a source package.

2. Download the source package, and put it into a directory where you can extract the .tar file.

3. Extract the source files.

```
tar -xzvf mysql-3.23.xx.tar.gz
```

4. As `root`, create the group and user for MySQL.

```
groupadd mysql
useradd -g mysql mysql
```

5. Switch to the directory where the source files are located; this directory is created when you extract the files.

```
cd mysql-3.23.49
```

6. Run the configuration script.

```
./configure --prefix=/usr/local/mysql
```

7. Compile the source.

```
make
```

8. Install the files.

```
make install
```

9. Install the initial databases.

```
scripts/mysql_install_db
```

10. Change the ownership of the MySQL files.

```
chown -R root /usr/local/mysql
chown -R mysql /usr/loca/mysql/var
chgrp -R mysql /usr/local/mysql
```

11. Copy the configuration file to the `/etc` directory.

```
cp support-files/my-medium.cnf /etc/my.cnf
```

12. Start the MySQL daemon.

```
/usr/local/mysql/bin/safe_mysqld --user=mysql &
```

MySQL should now be up and running for you!

Installing DBI on Windows Systems

The DBI is the DataBase Interface that Perl uses to interact with databases. The DBI is the main component; you also need to install a DataBase Driver (DBD) that corresponds to your database. DBI and DBD are actually supposed to mean DataBase Independent and DataBase Dependent because the DBI is used for all databases, whereas the DBD depends on the database that you are connecting to.

To install the DBI for Windows:

1. Go into the ActiveState ActivePerl menu and choose the "Perl Package Manager" menu item.

2. This brings up a DOS window with a prompt. All you need to do to install the DBI is type:

   ```
   install DBI
   ```

   This command downloads and installs the DBI module.

3. To install the DBD for Windows, we use the ODBC drivers, so type.

   ```
   install DBD-ODBC
   ```

   This downloads and installs the ODBC drivers for MySQL.

That is all there is to installing the proper Perl modules! When you are ready to leave the PPM tool, simply type **quit**.

Installing DBI on Linux (and *nix) Systems

Installing the DBI and DBD drivers for Linux is a bit more involved than the Windows installation procedures.

We'll use the CPAN module to install the DBI and DBD drivers.

1. To start the CPAN module, type:

   ```
   perl -MCPAN -e 'shell'
   ```

   This gets you to a prompt that looks like this:

   ```
   cpan>
   ```

2. To install the DBI, simply type:

   ```
   install DBI
   ```

3. To install the DBD drivers for MySQL, type:

   ```
   install DBD::mysql
   ```

These commands download and install the DBI and DBD drivers.

There may be permission problems when installing the DBD::mysql module; please refer to the MySQL documentation for instructions on setting up users and passwords. If you do get errors with the install, you can force the installation by using force install DBD::mysql instead of just using install DBD::mysql.

That should be all that you need to do to get the database modules installed onto your Linux system.

Installing MyODBC on Windows Systems

For Windows systems, you want to use an ODBC driver for connectivity to the MySQL database. Because of this, Windows users need to install one additional program—it is also by the MySQL people and is called MyODBC.

First, you must get the software.

1. Go to `http://www.mysql.com` and click "downloads." Then, under "Products," click MyODBC; then click the download link and the latest "stable" release link. Choose the download link that corresponds to your OS, and choose a download site.

2. Once download is done, unzip the file to a directory so that you can run the setup. Double-click the `setup.exe` file to begin the installation.

   Figure A-19 shows the first screen for installing the MyODBC drivers.

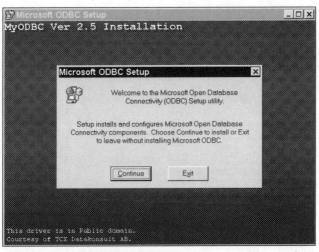

Figure A-19: MyODBC Installation screen

3. Click the Continue button to continue the installation.

   Figure A-20 shows the screen that asks which drivers you want to install; there should only be one—but if there are more choices, choose the MySQL option.

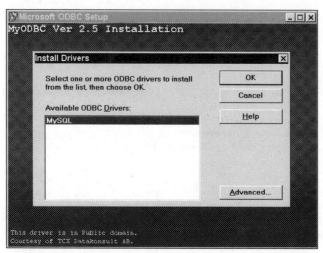

Figure A-20: MyODBC Installation screen

4. Click the "OK" button to continue the installation. Figure A-21 shows the screen for choosing a data source. A data source is used to create a name for the database that you are connecting to and a name for the connection to the database. Choose the sample MySQL option.

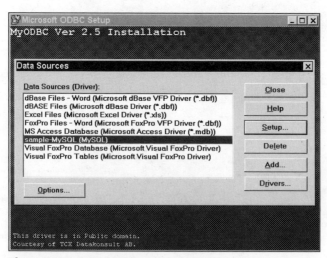

Figure A-21: MyODBC Data Sources screen

5. Click the Setup button to continue the installation.

Figure A-22 shows the screen for setting up a data source. For this example, stick with the defaults.

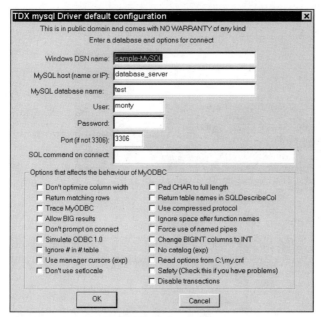

Figure A-22: MyODBC Data Source Setup screen

6. Click the OK button to continue the installation.

Figure A-23 shows the screen that you get when the setup is successful.

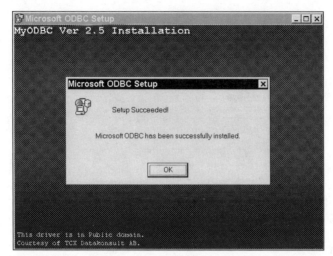

Figure A-23: MyODBC Successful Setup screen

7. Click the OK button to finish the installation.

You should now have a data source to connect to. When you are connecting to the database, use this name as the Data Source Name (DSN) name. For example:

```
my $dbh =
  DBI->connect("DBI::ODBC::datasourcename","user","passwd")
  or die...
```

✦   ✦   ✦

Common SQL Reference

This SQL reference is designed to help you with any questions you may have when going through this book. This is not meant to be a 100 percent total SQL reference; that requires an entire book on its own. Instead, this appendix contains the SQL keywords and the most common ways you may see them when working with MySQL.

For any of these statements, you need to be logged in to the database server and have the proper permissions to execute the commands. Contact your database administrator, or check out your databases documentation if you run into issues.

ALTER

ALTER is used to modify the structure in an existing table. It allows you to add, delete, or modify columns and to remove indexes from existing tables.

To add a new column to an existing table:

```
ALTER TABLE library ADD foo CHAR(50);
```

To remove a column from a table:

```
ALTER TABLE library DROP foo;
```

To change a column's type:

```
ALTER TABLE library MODIFY foo INT;
```

To remove the isbn index from a table:

```
ALTER TABLE library DROP INDEX isbn;
```

CREATE

CREATE is used to create databases or to add tables to a database.

To create a new database:

```
CREATE DATABASE foo;
```

To add a table to an existing database:

```
CREATE TABLE books (
  isbn   varchar(20)  default NULL,
  title  varchar(255) default NULL,
  author varchar(255) default NULL
);
```

DELETE

DELETE is used to remove data from a table. Be careful with this one; if you simply do a DELETE statement without a WHERE clause, *all* of the data in the database will be removed! See the "dangerous" example below to see how easy this can be.

To delete a row from a table named *library* with an ISBN of 9493812345:

```
DELETE FROM library WHERE isbn = '9493812345';
```

The following SQL statement will **remove ALL items** from the library table; do NOT do that unless you truly intend to!

```
DELETE FROM library;
```

DROP

DROP is typically used to delete a database or table from the DBMS.

To delete the foo table from the current database:

```
DROP TABLE foo;
```

INSERT

INSERT is used to add data to a database table.

There are several ways to insert data into a table by using the INSERT statement.

If you insert the data without specifying the field names, the data must be inserted in the same order in which it is stored in the database. To see how the database is storing the field names, you can type DESCRIBE *tablename* from a MySQL prompt, and MySQL shows you the layout of the table.

```
INSERT INTO library VALUES ('020163337X','Tcl and the Tk
Toolkit','John K. Ousterhout','$39.99','Paperback,
458pp.','Addison Wesley Longman, Inc.',' February 1994',NULL);
```

If you want to insert the data, but maybe not all of the data, or in a different order, you can do so like this (notice that the ISBN is now at the end, and we've omitted the notes field):

```
INSERT INTO library (title, author, price, format, publisher,
datepub, isbn) VALUES ('Tcl and the Tk Toolkit','John K.
Ousterhout','    $39.99',' Paperback, 458pp.',' Addison Wesley
Longman, Inc.',' February 1994', '020163337X');
```

If you want to explicitly name each field name along with the data, you can do so like this:

```
INSERT INTO library SET isbn='020163337X', title='Tcl and the
Tk Toolkit', author='John K. Ousterhout', price='$39.99',
format=' Paperback, 458pp.', publisher='Addison Wesley Longman,
Inc.', datepub=' February 1994');
```

SELECT

SELECT will probably be your most-used SQL statement. SELECT is used whenever you want to get data from the database tables. SELECT has many modifiers and options available. We'll show some simple SELECT statements here to get you started.

To get all books by the publisher "Wiley," do something like this:

```
SELECT * FROM library WHERE publisher = 'Wiley';
```

The * means to return all of the fields. If you want only the titles and the prices, do something like this:

```
SELECT title, price FROM library WHERE publisher = 'Wiley';
```

If you want the results to be sorted alphabetically, do this:

```
SELECT title, price FROM library WHERE publisher = 'Wiley'
ORDER BY(title);
```

SELECT can be a very powerful SQL statement. There are also mathematical arguments such as SUM and AVG, sorting arguments, and many more. Take a look at the MySQL documentation to get a complete understanding of the SELECT statement's capabilities.

For example:

```
SELECT AVG(price) FROM library;
```

Returns the average price of all of the books in the library table.

UPDATE

UPDATE is used to modify an existing record. If you have a record in your database, with a person's name, for instance, and that person's name changes, you can use an UPDATE statement to modify the name in the table.

```
UPDATE table_name SET lastname='Smith' WHERE
lastname='Michalski';
```

Note

Obviously, this appendix doesn't cover all the SQL statements and all their options, but we've covered the ones that make up the vast majority of actual SQL queries that you'd need to run. The statements discussed here are those you will come across most of the time when working with Perl on a MySQL database.

The documentation at http://www.mysql.com is an up-to-date, valuable resource for working with MySQL databases. The site contains exhaustive documentation on every aspect of MySQL, including a complete SQL reference.

✦　　✦　　✦

MySQL Command Reference

This appendix lists the MySQL commands you will use most often. These commands will not be used in Perl programs. Instead, these are the commands you will use to perform basic administration of a MySQL database.

The reason for this appendix is that MySQL will likely be the DBMS you use. If you are using another database, refer to its documentation for administration instructions. The latest MySQL documentation is at `http://www.mysql.com` if you need more complete documentation.

Connecting as a User

There will be many times when you will want to connect to MySQL directly from the command line. Connecting this way can be very helpful when creating queries because you can test them and make sure that they work before coding them in your program.

Connecting as an interactive user can also be very useful when debugging a problem. When debugging, it is usually best to log in as the user that the problem is occurring with. For example, if you have a user named *www* with a password of *supersecret* and you are having problems with a program using that account, log in as that user and try to run the same query. If the error has something to do with access permissions, you may be able to catch it and figure out a solution from here. If you log on as the admin user, you would never have seen the access-rights; the admin user has access rights to do anything, so the error does not happen when you are logged in as the admin user.

To connect as a non-admin user: (in this case, the `bookuser` user)

```
mysql -u bookuser -p testpass
```

This logs into mysql as the user *bookuser* with a password of *testpass*. The `-u` stands for *username*, and the `-p` stands for *password*. Specify a host if the MySQL server is on a different system.

```
mysql -u bookuser -p testpass -h hostname
```

If all goes well, you should get something that looks like this:

```
Welcome to the MySQL monitor.  Commands end with ; or \g.
Your MySQL connection id is 10 to server version: 3.23.47

Type 'help;' or '\h' for help. Type '\c' to clear the buffer.

mysql>
```

This means you are connected to MySQL and are at the MySQL prompt. From here, you can directly enter SQL statements and immediately see the results. All SQL statements entered at the `mysql>` prompt must be terminated with a semicolon.

For example:

```
mysql> use bookdatabase;
mysql> select * from library;
```

The above lines tell MySQL to use the database named `bookdatabase` and then perform a query to select and display all items from the table named `library`.

MySQL Prompt Commands

From the MySQL prompt, you can do more than just query data. In fact, to query data, you need to tell MySQL which database to use first. To see what databases are available, you can ask MySQL to show you the databases.

```
show databases;
```

This should yield something like:

```
mysql> show databases;
+-----------+
| Database  |
+-----------+
| PerlBook  |
| mysql     |
| test      |
+-----------+
3 rows in set (0.00 sec)
```

The database named *test* is what MySQL uses to run its tests when it is installed. The database named *mysql* is where MySQL stores all of its access information, such as user permissions.

The PerlBook database is the one we are using for this book. To use a database, just type use *databasename*; as in the following example:

```
use PerlBook;
```

MySQL should return a message telling you that the database has changed. At this point, you can have MySQL show you the available tables in the same manner that you ask it to show you the databases.

```
show tables;
```

One other command you may find useful at the mysql> prompt is describe. It displays a description of the table you ask for. For example,

```
describe library;
```

results in something like this being displayed:

```
mysql> describe library;
+-----------+--------------+------+-----+---------+-------+
| Field     | Type         | Null | Key | Default | Extra |
+-----------+--------------+------+-----+---------+-------+
| isbn      | varchar(20)  | YES  |     | NULL    |       |
| title     | varchar(255) | YES  |     | NULL    |       |
| author    | varchar(255) | YES  |     | NULL    |       |
| price     | varchar(20)  | YES  |     | NULL    |       |
| format    | varchar(50)  | YES  |     | NULL    |       |
| publisher | varchar(255) | YES  |     | NULL    |       |
| pubdate   | varchar(50)  | YES  |     | NULL    |       |
| notes     | text         | YES  |     | NULL    |       |
+-----------+--------------+------+-----+---------+-------+
8 rows in set (0.00 sec)
```

Other commands are available from the `mysql>` prompt, but they are not as widely used, so they aren't covered here. Make sure you take a look at the latest MySQL documentation to get an in-depth description of these commands as well as the ones we did not cover.

MySQL Administration Commands

MySQL has an administration program called `mysqladmin`, which is used to do things such as adding a database, dropping *(deleting)* a database (and all of its tables), or reloading the grant tables *(access control tables)*.

Unlike `mysql`, `mysqladmin` does not have an interactive interface. You pass `mysqladmin` the options on the command line, and it does the work requested; then you are back at your shell prompt.

To add a database, do something like this:

```
mysqladmin -uadmin -p create NewDatabaseName
```

The system asks you for a password, just as the `mysql` program does if you have not supplied one on the command-line. If you enter the correct password, you will be returned to the shell prompt and the database will be created, but there is no notification that a database has been created. An error, however, will result in some sort of error message.

If you get into the `mysql>` command-line interface and enter `show databases`, you will see the new database listed along with the others.

Also, you can drop databases. To drop a database means to delete it and all of its contents. To drop a database, just substitute `drop` in place of `create`. Since `drop` can *blow away an entire database* and all of its data, a prompt asking you if you really want to drop the database is displayed with a default of **N** (No) so that you can't accidentally hit Enter and lose your data.

Other administrative tasks can be done with the `mysqladmin` program. The MySQL documentation describes everything in great detail. If you need to do more than adding or deleting (dropping) databases, refer to the latest MySQL documentation.

The mysqldump Program

The program `mysqldump` will send to the screen a text representation (a "dump") of database and table structures, and optionally all of the data in those databases/tables. This dump can easily be redirected to a text file with a shell command like:

```
mysqldump ...parameters... > dump001.txt
```

The format of the dump will be commands that, when run, will recreate that database or table, as we'll see below.

Dumping just the table structure is handy for when you want to recreate the structure, say on another machine. By dumping the data too, you have a complete backup of your database, or of just the table(s) you specify.

This is handy either just for your own archival purposes, or for sending to others. For example, I used mysqldump to dump my 'library' database table's structure and all its data so that you can try out the examples in this book with it.

On the database we have been working with, which contains only a single table, we can do something like this:

```
mysqldump -u bookuser -p -d PerlBook
```

Once we ran the above command, we would get prompted for the password. Entering the password causes the following to be displayed on the screen.

```
# MySQL dump 8.16
#
# Host: localhost     Database: PerlBook
#--------------------------------------------------------
# Server version       3.23.47

#
# Table structure for table 'library'
#

CREATE TABLE library (
   isbn varchar(20) default NULL,
   title varchar(255) default NULL,
   author varchar(255) default NULL,
   price varchar(20) default NULL,
   format varchar(50) default NULL,
   publisher varchar(255) default NULL,
   pubdate varchar(50) default NULL,
   notes text
) TYPE=MyISAM;
```

This code can be cut-and-pasted into the mysql> command line, and it creates a copy of the table. Printing it directly to the screen is not usually the best idea, so typically you do something like this:

```
mysqldump -u bookuser -p -d PerlBook > table_structure.txt
```

The above command causes the preceding table information to be sent to a file called `table_structure.txt`. If you want the table structure plus *all* of the data in the table, simply remove the `-d` from the previous command. The `-d` means no data.

If someone sends you a file he or she has produced by using the `mysqldump` command and you want to add the file to a new database, you can simply pipe it into the database like this:

```
mysql -ubookuser -p DataBaseName < structure.txt
```

MySQL asks for the password; if it is entered correctly, all of the data in `structure.txt` is imported into the database that has been specified.

`mysqldump` is, in my opinion, under-appreciated. It can provide you with quick and simple backups, and it allows people to easily share database structures and data.

> **Note**
>
> MySQL has many commands and utilities beyond the basic ones that were covered here. The documentation provided at the MySQL Web site is excellent, however. Use it if you want to gain an even greater understanding of how MySQL works.

✦   ✦   ✦

DBI Reference

This is a reference to the most common DBI methods. Again, we'll cover them in enough detail to get you familiar with the basic concepts of each command. To get the latest documentation for the DBI module, please go to: http://dbi.perl.org.

available_drivers

This method, more of a convenience, would not necessarily be used in a program. A call to available_drivers returns an array of the DBD drivers installed on the system.

The following code:

```
@drivers = DBI->available_drivers;
print join("\n", @drivers), "\n";
```

 yields something like this.

```
ExampleP
CVS
Proxy
Mysql
```

This shows that we have four drivers installed. Using this method is a quick way to see what drivers are installed on a system.

bind_col

The bind_col method is used to create a *binding* (an association) between a variable and a column in a SELECT statement. This binding causes the variable to be automatically updated with the current value each time.

Example:

```
my ($title, $author);

my $sql = "SELECT title, price, author FROM library";
my $query_handle = $conn->prepare($sql);
$query_handle->execute();

$query_handle->bind_col(1, \$title, undef);
$query_handle->bind_col(3, \$author, undef);

while($query_handle->fetch) {
    print "Author: $author, Title: $title\n";
}
```

The preceding example prints a list of the authors and titles of all of the books in the library table. Notice that price is part of the SELECT statement but since we don't bind it to any variable, its value will just be ignored.

The first argument in the bind_col statement is the column number of the output, with 1 being the very first column. In the preceding example, title is column 1, price column 2, and author is column 3.

The second argument is a *reference* to the variable we want to bind this column to.

The third argument is not used with MySQL. Some database drivers (DBDs) may use it. In that case, it is a hash of attributes.

bind_columns

bind_columns is very similar to the bind_col method. With bind_columns however, all of the columns returned by the query are bound in one statement. This allows you to bind several columns with a single statement.

Example:

```
my ($title, $price, $author);

my $sql = "SELECT title, price, author FROM library";
my $query_handle = $conn->prepare($sql);
$query_handle->execute();

$query_handle->bind_columns(undef, \($title, $price, $author));

while($query_handle->fetch) {
    print "Author: $author, Title: $title, Price: $price\n";
}
```

In this example, we don't have to worry about binding each column, one at a time. Instead, we accomplish binding *all* the variables with one statement. One note about using this function is that you must have *exactly* the same number of variables to bind to as the SQL statement returns. If you are doing a SELECT * and there are eight fields, you must have eight variables in the bind_columns function call, even if you don't intend on using all of them.

The arguments to bind_columns are similar to the bind_col function. The first argument is not used by MySQL, but some DBDs may use it. If it is used, a hash of attributes is expected. The second argument is a reference to a list of scalar variables.

commit

commit is used to make the changes permanent for databases that support this function. On MySQL, transactions are currently not supported, so the commit function does nothing. Once MySQL gets transaction capability, this function will most likely be updated to work with the MySQL DBD.

Example:

```
$return_code = $query_handle->commit;
```

The above preceding example attempts to commit the most recent changes to the database. If there is a problem, an error code will be retuned and stored in $return_code.

Also, commit works only when Autocommit is turned off. Autocommit is a flag used in the connect statement on databases that support it. Autocommit will automatically commit changes as they occur if it is enabled.

connect

connect is used to create a connection to a data source. Here is an example of a simple connect statement:

```
$db_handle = DBI->connect($datasource, $user, $password)
    or die ("Error: $DBI::errstr\n");
```

A hash of attributes can also be passed:

```
$db_handle = DBI->connect($datasource, $user, $password,
\%attr)
    or die ("Error: $DBI::errstr\n");
```

If there is an error connecting, $DBI::errstr will be set, and the call will die with the message we include in the die call.

The $datasource string can be quite complex. For MySQL, it is commonly something like this:

```
DBI:mysql:PerlBook
```

where mysql is the DBD and PerlBook is the database name. If the data source happens to be on another server, then the data source needs to contain a bit more information.

```
DBI:mysql:PerlBook@database.perlguy.net:989
```

In this case, we specify the URL of the server where the database hosts. Also, we specify the port (989) that the database server listens on.

$DBI::errstr

$DBI::errstr contains the error message for the last DBI error that has occurred. $DBI::errstr retains the value until another error occurs, at which time it is replaced with the new error message. If no DBI errors have occurred, $DBI::errstr contains undef.

disconnect

Disconnects the database handle from the database it is connected to. With MySQL, a call to disconnect is not needed because transactions are not currently supported. However, if transactions do become supported, then you'll need to call $database->disconnect before you exit the program, to make sure ensure all the changes have been committed to the database.

A call to disconnect before ending a program is a good idea if you want to create portable code. If there is an error disconnecting from the database, the error message gets stored in $DBI::errstr.

Example:

```
$db_handle->disconnect or die ("Error: $DBI::errstr\n");
```

do

do is used to perform non-SELECT SQL statements. It does the same thing as a $handle->prepare and a $handle->execute, except it does it all in one function call. The return value for do is the number of rows affected.

Examples:

```
my $sql_statement = qq(INSERT INTO kids VALUES ?, ?, ?);
my @stuff =  qw(luc rae logan);
my $rows = $handle->do($sql_statement, {}, @stuff);
```

This example inserts the names of my kids into the database table *kids*.

The first argument is the actual SQL statement. This can be a variable containing the statement, or it can be the actual text of the SQL statement. The second argument is a reference to a hash of attributes and is unused in MySQL. The third argument is an array that contains the data that will replace the placeholders (the "?"s) in the SQL statement.

Only the first argument is required; the others are optional.

dump_results

You're not likely to use this method in a finished program, but it's very useful to call as you're developing (and/or debugging) a program.

A call to dump_results prints (via STDOUT) the data remaining in the statement handle. If none of the data has been accessed with a call to fetch (which is typically the case), all of the data from the SQL statement is printed.

Example:

```
$handle->dump_results;
```

execute

execute runs the SQL query and returns the number of rows affected.\execute is called after a prepare statement and can include data to replace any placeholders in the SQL statement.

Examples:

```
$sql1 = qq{SELECT * FROM library};
$sql2 = qq{INSERT INTO library (title, author, price)
    VALUES (?, ?, ?)};

$handle1 = $db_handle->prepare($sql1);
$handle2 = $db_handle->prepare($sql2);

my $rows1 = $handle1->execute;
my $rows2 = $handle2->execute("Evil Empires for Dummies", "Bill
Gates", 12.95);
```

These examples show how to call execute alone and also with placeholders. The values in $rows are the number of rows affected by the respective SQL statement.

fetch

fetch is used to grab a row of data and return an array reference. This returns a single row of data as an array reference, where each item in the array is an item in the row. The name "fetch" is short for "fetchrow_arrayref" — the two names mean the same thing, and call the same function.

Example:

```
while ($ref = $handle->fetch){
    print join(', ', @$ref), "\n";
}
```

This prints each row of data left in the $handle, with each field separated by a comma and a space.

fetchall_arrayref

fetchall_arrayref returns a reference to an array in which each item in the array is a reference to a row of data. This is very similar to the fetch function, except this one returns *all* of the data left in the $handle instead of just a single row.

Example:

```
my $ref = $handle->fetchall_arrayref;
foreach my $row (@$ref) {
    print "Row: ", join(', ', @$row), "\n";
}
```

This example also prints out each row of data, just as we do previously with the fetch method. However, this method can use up considerably more memory than fetch, since it holds *all* of the returned data instead of just *one* row at a time.

fetchrow_array

fetchrow_array returns an array rather than a reference to an array. This is another way it can be used to fetch data from a handle. Each method does basically the same thing, so you can choose the method you prefer.

Example:

```
while(my($author, $title, $price) = $handle->fetchrow_array){
    print "Title: $title, Author: $author, Price: $price\n";
}

while(my(@array) = $handle->fetchrow_array){
    print "Title: $array[1], Author: $array[0], Price:
$array[2]\n";
}
```

These examples simply loop through the data and print each record until there are no more.

fetchrow_hashref

fetchrow_hashref returns one record, a reference to a hash. The keys to the hash are the database field names, which help in remembering what data is being referenced.

Example:

```
while(my $hashref = $handle->fetchrow_hashref){
    print "Title: $hashref->{'title'},
        Author: $hashref->{'author'},
        Price: $hashref->{'price'}\n";
}
```

prepare

prepare takes an SQL statement as an argument and returns a statement handle. prepare takes the SQL statement and stores it in an internal, compiled form. It also gets the SQL statement ready for the execute function call.

Example:

```
$statement_handle = $db_handle->prepare("SELECT * FROM
library");
```

quote

quote is used to quote a string that is to be used in an SQL query statement. Some databases have different methods of quoting the data in SQL statements, so to maintain as much compatibility as possible, use the quote function instead of quoting the data manually.

Example:

```
my $oldstring = "Brent's kids are named: Luc, Rae, and Logan.";
my $newstring = $db_handle->quote($oldstring);
```

The string in $newstring is now ready to be used in an SQL statement and should have no problems with the handling of the apostrophe.

rollback

rollback is the opposite of the commit function. If you are using a database that supports transactions, rollback is used to revert to the previous data in case of a problem. So, if you begin a transaction and an error occurs in the program, you can set up a call to the rollback function so that any changes that have not yet been committed to the database will go back to their original values.

Example:

```
$return_code = $query_handle->rollback;
```

The preceding example reverts to the original data; any changes that have been made on the $query_handle handle will be thrown out. If there is a problem with the rollback, an error code will be returned and stored in $return_code.

✦   ✦   ✦

Index

Symbols and Numerics

Continued

Continued

Continued

Continued

Continued

Continued

Continued